SANITY, MADNESS, TRANSFORMATION:
THE PSYCHE IN ROMANTICISM

Sanity, Madness, Transformation
The Psyche in Romanticism

Ross Woodman

Edited and with an afterword by Joel Faflak

UNIVERSITY OF TORONTO PRESS
Toronto Buffalo London

© University of Toronto Press Incorporated 2005
Toronto Buffalo London
Printed in Canada

ISBN 0-8020-3841-7

Printed on acid-free paper

Library and Archives Canada Cataloguing in Publication

Woodman, Ross Greig
  Sanity, madness, transformation : the psyche in Romanticism / Ross
  Woodman ; edited and with an afterword by Joel Faflak.

  Includes bibliographical references and index.
  ISBN 0-8020-3841-7

  1. Blake, William, 1757–1827 – Criticism and interpretation.
  2. Shelly, Percy Bysshe, 1792–1822 – Criticism and interpretation.
  3. Romanticism – Great Britain.   4. Literature and mental illness.
  5. Psychoanalysis and literature.   6. English poetry – 19th century –
  History and criticism.   I. Faflak, Joel, 1959–   II. Title.

  PR468.R65W66 2005   821'.7093561   C2005-902403-8

University of Toronto Press acknowledges the financial assistance to
its publishing program of the Canada Council for the Arts and the
Ontario Arts Council.

This book has been published with the help of a grant from the Canadian
Federation for the Humanities and Social Sciences, through the Aid to
Scholarly Publications Programme, using funds provided by the Social
Sciences and Humanities Research Council of Canada.

University of Toronto Press acknowledges the financial support for
its publishing activities of the Government of Canada through the
Book Publishing Industry Development Program (BPIDP).

In memory of Bruce Boa
with whom now in death, after more than fifty years,
I still often stand alone 'a long half-hour together.'

'Whither is God?' he cried; 'I will tell you. *We have killed him* – you and I. All of us are his murderers. But how did we do this? How could we drink up the sea? Who gave us the sponge to wipe away the entire horizon? What were we doing when we unchained this earth from its sun? Whither is it moving now? Whither are we moving? Away from all suns? Are we not plunging continually? Backward, sideward, forward, in all directions? Is there still any up or down? Are we not straying as through an infinite nothing? Do we not feel the breath of empty space? Has it not become colder? Is not night continually closing in on us? Do we not need to light lanterns in the morning? Do we hear nothing as yet of the noise of the gravediggers who are burying God? Do we smell nothing as yet of the divine decomposition? Gods, too, decompose. God is dead. God remains dead. And we have killed him.'

... At last he threw his lantern on the ground, and it broke into pieces and went out. 'I have come too early,' he said then; 'my time is not yet. This tremendous event is still on its way, still wandering; it has not yet reached the ears of men. Lightning and thunder require time; the light of the stars requires time; deeds, though done, still require time to be seen and heard. This deed is still more distant from them than the most distant stars – *and yet they have done it themselves.'*

Friedrich Nietzsche, 'The Madman,' from *The Gay Science*

When Lao-tzu says: 'All are clear, I alone am clouded,' he is expressing what I now feel in advanced old age. Lao-tzu is the example of a man with superior insight who has seen and experienced worth and worthlessness, and who at the end of his life desires to return into his own being, into the eternal unknowable meaning. The archetype of the old man who has seen enough is eternally true. At every level of intelligence this type appears, and its lineaments are always the same, whether it be an old peasant or a great philosopher like Lao-tzu. This is old age, and a limitation. Yet there is so much that fills me: plants, animals, clouds, day and night, and the eternal in man. The more uncertain I have felt about myself, the more there has grown up in me a feeling of kinship with all things. In fact it seems to me as if that alienation which so long separated me from the world has become transferred into my own inner world, and has revealed to me an unexpected unfamiliarity with myself.

Carl Gustav Jung, *Memories, Dreams, Reflections*

Flying high the heavy wood grouse
Slash the forest sky with their wings
And a pigeon returns to its airy wilderness
And a raven gleams with airplane steel.

What is the earth for them? A lake of darkness.
It has been swallowed up by the night forever.
They, above the dark as above black waves,
Have their homes and islands, saved by the light.

If they groom their long feathers with their beaks
And drop one of them, it floats a long time
Before it reaches the bottom of the lake
And brushes someone's face, bringing news
From a world that is bright, beautiful, warm and free.

Czeslaw Milosz, 'The Bird Kingdom,' from *The World*

Contents

ACKNOWLEDGMENTS xi
SOURCES AND ABBREVIATIONS xiii

Introduction 3

1 Jung and Romanticism: The Fate of the Mythopoeic
  Imagination 23

2 Frye's Blake: The Site of Opposition 47

3 Blake's Fourfold Body 86

4 Wordsworth's Crazed Bedouin: *The Prelude* and the
  Fate of Madness 110

5 Shelley and the Romantic Labyrinth 148

6 The Sanity of Madness: Byron and Shelley 178

Conclusion 197

Afterword: Ross Woodman's Romanticism by JOEL FAFLAK 210

NOTES 237
BIBLIOGRAPHY 259
INDEX 267

Acknowledgments

At this last stage of my life my too few acknowledgments must stand for the too many that remain as alive as ever in my memory of them. Most immediately, I acknowledge the Romantic poets, who seem closer to me than my own life vein, and upon whose boldly encountered madness our sanity remains precariously perched; Joel Faflak, who launched this book and more than once rescued it from drowning, his afterword seeing to it that on its perilous sea it remain afloat; Marion Woodman, who outwatched with me during its composition many an envious night; Greg Mogenson, whose daily shared knowledge of Jung is still unsurpassed; David Clark, who never doubted where the sanity came from; Deanne Bogdan, who knew Frye in a way that I did not; Tilottama Rajan, an eminence eager and willing to share an otherwise 'intense inane'; Douglas Kneale, who took and continues to take the measure of my voice; David Kemp, who refined my excess; Philip Stratford, who even in death continues to turn up; René Weis, who walked with me the streets of London in search of William Blake; Richard Shroyer, who would come at the drop of a hat (among other things) to fix my computer; David Wagenknecht, who not only published my essays but inwardly kept track of where they were headed; Hugh McCallum, a witness to beginnings that have no end; Jack Chambers, who painted as I talked, making me see what I said; A.S.P. Woodhouse, who saw in my turning to Shelley that I had not abandoned Milton; Northrop Frye, who took into death far more than I yet understand; Malcolm Ross, who launched me in the first place; David McKee, whose 'Opposition' was 'true Friendship'; Josh Lambier, who made another kind of sense by preparing the index; Jill McConkey, who as editor made many an otherwise burden seem almost as light as air;

the readers for the University of Toronto Press, whose extraordinary generosity I needed time to digest; my graduate students, who at the end brought me to a new beginning; and, finally, the colleagues who freed up some needed time by ceasing to wonder what I was on about – and still am. Last but not least, knowing as a child of the Canadian prairies the blasts of the desert air, I acknowledge with gratitude the financial support of a grant from the Canadian Federation for the Humanities and Social Sciences, through the Aid to Scholarly Publications Programme, using funds provided by the Social Sciences and Humanities Research Council of Canada, without which this book, though it might well have been written, would never have been seen.

Sources and Abbreviations

References to the Bible are from the King James Version. References to Byron's poetry are from *Lord Byron: Major Works*, ed. Jerome J. McGann (New York: Oxford UP, 2000); cited by title, canto, and/or line number. References to Coleridge's poetry are from *Poetical Works*, ed. Ernest Hartley Coleridge (Oxford: Oxford UP, 1969); cited by title and line number. References to Keats's poetry are from *Poems of John Keats*, ed. Jack Stillinger (Cambridge, MA: The Belknap P of Harvard UP, 1978); cited by title, book, canto, and/or line number. References to Shelley's poetry not found in *Shelley's Poetry and Prose* (cited below) are from *The Complete Poetical Works of Percy Bysshe Shelley*, ed. Thomas Hutchinson. (London: Oxford UP, 1960); cited by title and line number. References to Shelley's prose not found in *Shelley's Poetry and Prose* are to *The Complete Works of Percy Bysshe Shelley*, ed. Roger Ingpen and Walter E. Peck, Julian Editions, 10 vols (New York: Charles Scribner's Sons, 1926-30), cited by volume and page number.

For the most frequently cited sources, the following abbreviations are used.

BL   Samuel Taylor Coleridge. *Biographia Literaria*. Ed. James Engell and W. Jackson Bate. Princeton: Princeton UP, 1983. Cited by volume and page number.

CW   Carl Gustav Jung. *Collected Works*. 20 vols. Ed. Herbert Read, Michael Fordham, Gerhard Adler, and William McGuire. Trans. R.F.C. Hull. Princeton: Princeton UP, 1957–79. Cited by volume and paragraph number.

DP   Percy Bysshe Shelley. *A Defence of Poetry. Shelley's Poetry and*

	Prose. Ed. Donald H. Reiman and Sharon B. Powers. New York: Norton, 1977. Cited by page number.
E	William Blake. *The Complete Poetry and Prose of William Blake*. Rev. ed. Ed. David V. Erdman. New York, Doubleday, 1988. Cited by page number either as 'E' or by title, plate number, and/or line number.
J	William Blake. *Jerusalem. The Complete Poetry and Prose of William Blake*. Cited by plate and line number.
KL	John Keats. *Letters of John Keats*. Ed. Robert Gittings. Oxford: Oxford UP, 1977. Cited by page number.
M	William Blake. *Milton. The Complete Poetry and Prose of William Blake*. Cited by plate and line number.
MDR	Carl Gustav Jung. *Memories, Dreams, Reflections*. Rev. ed. Ed. Aniela Jaffé. Trans. Richard and Clara Winston. New York: Vintage Books, 1965. Cited by page number.
MHH	William Blake. *The Marriage of Heaven and Hell. The Complete Poetry and Prose of William Blake*. Cited by plate number.
P	William Wordsworth. *The Prelude. The Prelude: 1799, 1805, 1850*. Ed. Jonathan Wordsworth, M.H. Abrams, and Stephen Gill. New York: Norton, 1979. Cited by book and line number from the 1850 version unless otherwise noted.
PL	John Milton. *Paradise Lost. Complete Poems and Major Prose*. Ed. Merritt Y. Hughes. New York: Macmillan, 1957. Cited by book and line number.
PU	Percy Bysshe Shelley. *Prometheus Unbound. Shelley's Poetry and Prose*. Ed. Donald H. Reiman and Sharon B. Powers. New York: Norton, 1977. Cited by act, scene, and line number.
PW	William Wordsworth. *The Prose Works of William Wordsworth*. Ed. W.J.B. Owen and Jane Worthington Smyser. 3 vols. Oxford: Clarendon P, 1974. Cited by volume and page number; by line number for the 'Prospectus' to *The Recluse*.
SPP	Percy Bysshe Shelley. *Shelley's Poetry and Prose*. Cited by page number for prose or line number for poetry, either as *SPP* or by individual title.
TL	Percy Bysshe Shelley. *The Triumph of Life. Shelley's Poetry and Prose*. Cited by line number.
WP	William Wordsworth. *Poetical Works*. Ed. Thomas Hutchinson. Rev. ed. Ed. Ernest de Selincourt. Oxford: Oxford UP, 1988. Cited by title and line number, either as *WP* or by individual title.

SANITY, MADNESS, TRANSFORMATION:
THE PSYCHE IN ROMANTICISM

Introduction

As an experience, madness is terrific I can assure you, and not to be sniffed at; and in its lava I still find most of the things I write about. It shoots out of one everything shaped, final, not in mere driblets, as sanity does. And the six months – not three – that I lay in bed taught me a good deal about what is called oneself.

Virginia Woolf, *Letters*

This book on Romanticism may be divided into two parts. The first part focuses upon Blake viewed within a critical frame largely provided by my contrary readings of Carl Jung and Northrop Frye. The second part focuses primarily upon Shelley viewed within a critical frame largely provided by my agonistic readings of Paul de Man and Jacques Derrida. The subject is madness understood in this study as the inability of man to inhabit himself.[1] The term 'man' is used in the generic rather than the gender sense to describe the logocentric drive towards self-knowledge and self-mastery, a drive that in Romanticism is ironically denied its object by virtue of the steadfast pursuit of it. The denial, negating from within the self-knowledge man pursues, is the madness that will not be denied. Jung, for example, binds madness (as Blake's Los binds the Spectre) to the dialectic, which in his psychology governs the process of an unfolding consciousness.

The critical frame within which I view Blake's vision is, from Frye's logocentric point of view, clearly counter-intuitive. The psychology of Jung has never been absorbed by the academic community to anything like the degree to which Freud has been absorbed. Jung remains on the lunatic fringe of the academic world.[2] Because my subject is madness, I have chosen Jung for his madness, since it informs the kind of sanity that, particularly in Blake, I intend to examine. The madness of Jung, I shall argue, far better serves the madness of Romanticism than does the more obvious sanity of Freud or, indeed, the even more logocentric sanity of Frye.

Deconstruction is found in Frye's 'metaphysics of presence' (his Christian notion of the Logos or Word), the pseudo-object of its linguistic disavowal. Making use of the systematic deconstruction of Frye's logocentric system, I am concerned in my treatment of Blake to release him from the kind of sanity Frye imposed upon him by exploring instead the kind of madness that, I believe, informs both the psychology of Jung and the kind of deconstruction I discuss. I approach deconstruction, particularly in Derrida's 'Cogito and the History of Madness,' his response to Michel Foucault's monumental *Madness & Civilization: A History of Insanity in the Age of Reason*, and in Paul de Man's 'Shelley Disfigured,' as essential supplements to Jung's approach to madness in his psychology, an approach that attends to the potentially creative role of madness in the release of consciousness from the symbolic orders in which it inevitably becomes fixed and dead.

My approach to Romanticism may therefore be loosely described as phenomenological; it examines the states of consciousness that a historical approach only partially, if at all, reveals in its prescribed moments of blinding constellation. Following in the footsteps of Jung, however, I view states of consciousness as arising out of an unconscious state. It is less with consciousness itself than with the process of rising to consciousness out of an unconscious state that I am concerned in the following pages. The rising to consciousness is the *praxis*, the making of the work. The unconscious is the *theoria* of it, not, however, as a conscious conception such as a critical theory may provide, but as what Blake calls a 'Moment: a Pulsation of the Artery' in which a work is unconsciously 'concievd' (*M* 29[31].2–3). The pulsations issue, for Blake, from the unconscious realm of the physical or 'Vegetable' body in which the senses sleep until they are awakened by consciousness to the presence of an external world, understood as that 'portion of Soul' (*MHH* 4) to which their discernment is bound. 'For Milton,' Shelley writes in his *Defence of Poetry*, 'conceived the Paradise Lost as a whole [in *theoria*] before he executed it [*praxis*] in portions' (504). In his *Biographia Literaria*, Coleridge calls this moment of conception or *theoria* the 'IMMEDIATE, which dwells in every man,' though 'it does not in every man rise into consciousness' (1:243). Keats, in *The Fall of Hyperion*, dramatically describes it as 'One minute before death' (1.132). For all of them, this 'Moment' is out of time rather than in time (or where the two intersect) – the point at which, for example, Blake in *Milton* 'fell outstretched upon the path / A moment' (42[49].25–6). Viewing this moment in the mythical perspective of the poet's Muse (Milton's Urania, for example), Shelley describes it as 'beyond and above consciousness' (*DP* 486). I, following Jung, call it the unconscious, more particularly the 'collective unconscious,' as being descriptive of its cultural role.

The realm of the unconscious, Jung argues, is in itself unknowable. The first thing to recognize about the unconscious is that it *is* unconscious. It comes to be known only to the degree that we rise out of it into consciousness. When, as what Shelley calls 'the mind in creation' (*DP* 503–4), this happens, the unconscious ceases to be what it is, becoming instead the fictions that consciousness attributes to it. If these attributions are acknowledged by the unconscious (in one way by matter in science; in another way by psyche in psychology) as its messengers bearing its authenticated tidings, then what otherwise exists as madness becomes sanity. Poetry in this sense is the sanity of madness. Shelley obviously struggles to articulate this position when he argues that poetry 'arrests the vanishing apparitions which haunt the interlunations of life [the blank darkness between the old and new moons], and veiling them or in language or in form sends them forth among mankind, bearing sweet news of kindred joy to those with whom their sisters abide – abide, because there is no portal of expression from the caverns of the spirit which they inhabit into the universe of things' (*DP* 505). Shelley here describes an interlunar connection between consciousness and the unconscious that serves as a frail bridge between them, so frail that he described himself as a poet carrying 'the shield of shadow and the lance of gossamere' (*Letters* 2:261). The interlunar connection, as 'apparitions,' would vanish if consciousness did not veil them 'in language or in form.' Veiled, they become apparelled messengers of consciousness to the unconscious; unveiled they remain 'vanishing apparitions' in which no real connection is made. Between them, that is, there is no direct portal of expression other than, perhaps, the gate of death, which all certainly enter, though without necessarily sending any messages back. One of the essential tasks of the Romantic poet explored in this book is to forge a metaphorical language that assured the poet, if not his readers, that he was in a two-way conversation with the dead. For Jung, as for the Romantics, the land of the dead became a highly workable metaphor of the unconscious.

Sanity resided for Jung in the attributions of consciousness to the unknown unconscious if and when they are received and acknowledged by the unconscious, whether as scientific evidence of the laws governing the motions of matter or as equally (though different) scientific evidence of the laws governing the motions of the psyche. For the Romantic poet, the acknowledgment of the unconscious lay in the vibrations (Julia Kristeva's semiotic 'pulsions') issuing from the metrical arrangement of language, which, as resonators, announced to consciousness the unconscious reception of them. 'Hence,' writes Shelley, 'the language of poets has ever affected a certain uniform and harmonious recurrence of sound, without which it were not poetry, and which is scarcely less indispensable to the communication of its influence, than the words themselves, without reference to their peculiar order' (DP 484). Even if words are devoid of 'their peculiar order,' as in some cases of madness (the figure of Tasso in Shelley's *Julian and Maddalo*, for example), Shelley argues that a 'certain uniform and harmonious recurrence of sound' will, at least to a degree, release words from the chaos they otherwise are. So long as the unknown unconscious announces itself to consciousness in the guise of 'harmonious recurrence,' the sound itself is an assurance of its primal sanity. When, therefore, Paul de Man reduces Shelley's final fragment to 'the madness of words' ('Shelley' 68), he disallows the sanity that Shelley, like all poets, attributes to the ritual dimension of language as 'harmonious recurrence.' Thus, Plato's notion of 'divine madness' in *Ion* (translated by Shelley) as the spell of harmonious sound constituted for Shelley a primal sanity upon which all higher levels are based. For the Romantic poet, the language of metaphor and myth, grounded in the ritual of recurrent sound, is the message of the unconscious, requiring and inviting an expansion of consciousness not only to receive it, but to enter a ceaseless dialogue with it. In 'Dejection: an Ode,' Coleridge is affirming the spirit of harmonious sound when he insists that we receive from it only what we give and that in this receiving and giving do all things live.

Poetry, then, as 'a dark / Inscrutable workmanship' (P 1.341–2) operating between the unconscious as madness and consciousness as sanity is the kind of 'workmanship' this book sets out to explore. As an engagement with madness, I join forces with Jungian psychology and deconstruction (unlikely bedfellows to be sure) to explore within the arena of Romantic poetry a madness that at present confronts us with its terrors of extinction, which is to say the terrors of our increasingly uninhabitable planet that, however unconsciously, we appear to be determined to reduce to a wasteland. The strategies by which we struggle to transform it – strategies that largely describe what culture is – have in the arts themselves become the victim of the madness culture is called upon to transform. This study of Romanticism is informed by what I take to be the present state of the arts as it mirrors the present state of the world. 'The sad truth is that we remain necessarily strangers to ourselves,' Nietzsche concludes his Preface to *On the Genealogy of Morals* in the fulsome style of Byron's fiction, which deeply disturbed Shelley: 'we don't understand our own substance, we *must* mistake ourselves; the axiom, "Each man is farthest from himself," will hold for us to all eternity. Of ourselves we are not "knowers"' (149).

Shelley's final fragment, *The Triumph of Life*, when set over against Blake's *Jerusalem*, enacts a struggle in Blake that in Shelley confronts its own ultimate defeat. Nietzsche's tightrope walker, analysed by Jung in his seminars on *Thus Spake Zarathustra* (1934–9), becomes, for the Jung presented in this study, an analysis of madness struggling, like *The Triumph of Life*, to remain conscious of itself by constructing a container for it, a container that, for Jung, was on the other side of the Swiss Alps about to collapse under the pressure of its own construction. National Socialism, like Shelley's final fragment, could not sustain itself in the folds of its own vision. It snapped under the pressure of its own excessive drive, overflowing its measured motion into a global catastrophe. In the added fourth act of *Prometheus Unbound*, Panthea describes the 'earth-convulsing behemoth,' devouring the 'weed-overgrown continents of Earth'; 'the blue globe / Wrapt Deluge round it like a cloak' as some passing God, its throne a comet, cried '"Be not!"' 'and like my words,' says Panthea, 'they were no more' (4.310–17).

Thus Spake Zarathustra remains for Jung the enactment of a body that could not absorb the psychic pressure imposed upon it and therefore snapped. 'The fiery band which held / Their natures, snaps' (*TL* 157–8), declares Shelley of the 'wild dance' (138) that, in *The Triumph of Life*, has become the action of his brain. The function of a poem, he insists, is to construct a body that can contain the psychic energy acting upon it. Following the alchemists, Jung calls this body the 'subtle body.' For the Nobel laureate quantum physicist, Wolfgang Pauli, who worked closely with Jung over a period of some twenty-six years, this 'subtle body' is the newly released (exploded) quantum body, the energy of which has yet to be absorbed. By absorption, both Jung and Pauli meant the rupturing (or interfering) role the unconscious psyche necessarily and inexplicably plays in whatever is observed. 'For, in the last analysis, '

Jung writes in *The Archetypes of the Collective Unconscious* (1954), 'psychic life is for the greater part an unconscious life that surrounds consciousness on all sides – a notion that is sufficiently obvious when one considers how much unconscious preparation is needed, for instance, to register a sense-impression' (*CW* 9i:57). In his psychoanalytical work with Jung, Pauli explored what was unconsciously at work in the inexplicable behaviour of particle and wave. For both Jung and Pauli, the failure to deal with the unconscious lay in the fiery extinction of matter itself, the erotic terrors of which are enacted in the madness of Shelley's 'one annihilation' (587) in his *Epipsychidion*.

Serving as an interchapter between the two parts, the essay on the crazed Bedouin in *The Prelude* records Wordsworth's longing for a lost madness ('Some called it madness' [*P* 3.149], he writes of his vision of childhood) that contained within its annihilating power the 'spousal' energy of its epic 'consummation' (Prospectus to *The Recluse* 57–8). Wordsworth, whose own poetic nature snapped under the pressure of the terror released by the French Revolution, finally brought it under the control (mastery) of the Word that ultimately governs Frye's logocentric reading of Blake. Frye's logocentric reading, I will suggest, largely ignores the history that Blake sought to absorb in much the same way as Jung sought to absorb it, its absorption in Jung's case remaining intimately bound to his own dealings with madness. Frye's conviction of what, with reference to Blake, he calls 'the sanity of genius and the madness of the commonplace mind' (*FS* 13) tends to ignore the fact that 'the sanity of [Blake's] genius' resides almost completely in his transformation of the 'madness of the commonplace mind.' His 'genius' resides in his steadfast concern with 'madness.' In this essential respect, Frye's dismissal of the 'commonplace' paradoxically amounts to a dismissal of Blake, or at least of the approach to Blake this book offers.

Perhaps crucial for a reader's active engagement with the argument of this book is the recognition of the nature of my own engagement. Reflecting after the fact upon one possible model for what I have written, I thought of Coleridge's *Biographia Literaria*. Coleridge described his work as a literary biography rather than an autobiography because, in some psychological sense (which in the larger framework of the *Biographia* he treated as metaphysical), the author was less himself than what Wordsworth calls 'some other Being.' Acknowledging a wide 'vacancy' between himself and what he is describing, Wordsworth tells us that he often seemed 'two consciousnesses, conscious of [him]self / And of some other Being' (*P* 2.32–3). Today we might distinguish between these 'two consciousnesses' by locating the 'some other Being' in the unconscious, in Wordsworth's case, both personal and collective. At the same time, however, because this 'other Being' had what Wordsworth calls 'such self-presence in [his] mind' (30), his notion of 'two consciousnesses' is probably a more accurate description. Elaborating on this 'other Being' as the real author of *The Prelude*, Wordsworth describes his 'workmanship' as 'dark' and 'inscrutable' (1.341–2), particularly in the mysterious way it reconciled the 'discordant elements' operative between the 'two consciousnesses' so that they could 'cling together / In one society' (1.342–4). The 'self-presence' of 'some other Being' in Wordsworth's mind helps to locate his dream of the crazed Bedouin in the ongoing narrative of *The Prelude* rather than in an excursion from it.

In my case, as, I think, is true for Coleridge, a Wordsworthian reconciliation has not taken place. Describing the kind of attention his *Biographia* imposed upon a reader ('more needful ... than acceptable'), Coleridge referred to it as an 'immethodical ... miscellany,' the 'obscurity' (1:88) of which may have had something to do with the fact that the work was dictated to a friend who was trying to help him to overcome his opium addiction, an addiction that aroused in Coleridge what Derrida refers to in himself when he speaks of 'writing in the passion for non-knowing [*'sans la passion du non-savoir'*] rather than of the secret' (*Cinders* 75). Though, like Wordsworth and Coleridge, I struggled towards a reconciliation of 'discordant elements,' the work of this book in the end proved rather more 'dark' and 'inscrutable' than the kind of Christian humanistic education I had received could existentially embrace. I am now all too aware of what Derrida calls the linguistic 'rupture' that renders 'one society' either in myself or in the world an impossibility as other than a metaphysical 'prospect in the mind' (*P* 2.352), which Wordsworth believed 'lies far hidden from the reach of words' (*P* 3.181).

In his dream of the crazed Bedouin, what lies 'far hidden from the reach of words' is, on the one hand, 'the waters of the deep / Gathering upon us' (5.130–1), the 'deluge' that is perpetually 'now at hand' (5.98) and, on the other, 'two books,' the one 'Euclid's Elements' that 'wedded soul to soul in purest bond / Of reason, undisturbed by space and time,' and the other 'a god, yea many gods' whose voices had 'power / To exhilarate the spirit, and to soothe / Through every clime, the heart of human kind' (5.102–8). Associating Coleridge with the crazed Bedouin, Wordsworth, in the composition of *The Prelude*, traced 'the waters of the deep' closing in upon his metaphysical mind, terror giving way to '[r]everence' as he realized that 'in the blind and awful lair / Of such a madness, reason did lie couched' (5.150–2). Far from rejecting Coleridge as his one consciousness was tempted to do, Wordsworth, momentarily overcome by the 'strong entrancement' of the other, believed that, given the 'deluge now at hand,' he could inhabit the 'maniac's fond anxiety, and go / Upon like errand' (5.160–2). This 'errand' lies in finding the 'power' of the gods less in an ascent to the realm of pure reason or divine revelation than in a descent into 'the blind and awful lair' of 'madness.'

In 'Cogito and the History of Madness,' Derrida identifies the Cogito with the instant of madness as the uninhabitable 'I Am' from which, as writing, the mind takes refuge in sanity. The Cogito is an identity that we escape by writing. The 'project of thinking this totality' (Wordsworth's 'one society'), Derrida explains, is 'mad, and acknowledges madness as its liberty and its very possibility. That is why it is not human ... but is rather metaphysical and demonic ... [It] opens and founds the world as such by exceeding it' (56–7). 'I philosophize only *in terror*,' Derrida concludes his essay, 'but in the *confessed* terror of going mad. The confession is simultaneously, at its *present* moment, oblivion and unveiling, protection and exposure: economy' (62). By economy he means, as Gayatri Spivak points out in her introduction to her translation of *Of Grammatology*, not a reconciliation of opposites (absence and presence) but rather a maintaining of disjunction (*Of Grammatology* xlii). The 'terror' that informs everything Derrida writes, I suggest, equally informs the Romanticism I discuss. Wordsworth's 'two consciousnesses' are 'madness' and the 'protection' against it by which he necessarily betrays the 'I Am' in the very pursuit of it. This peculiar dialectic, best articulated by Derrida, informs the argument of this book.

In my postgraduate work at the University of Toronto (1948–50), where I had gone with the intention of writing a thesis on the subject of nature and grace in Milton's poetry, I was richly instructed in three versions of Christian humanism in the graduate courses of A.S.P. Woodhouse (Milton), Northrop Frye (Blake), and Arthur Barker (Christian Humanism). These courses, for me, encapsulated the honours English program at the university. Although I was at home within this humanist tradition, I was surprised to discover in Frye's graduate class (in some ways the most challenging course I have ever taken) how thoroughly in Frye's reading Blake was assimilated to it. I had come to Blake from my reading of Milton under Malcolm Ross at the University of Manitoba, where I had written a relatively orthodox MA thesis on

Milton's portrayal of Satan. Malcolm Ross himself was a devout Anglo-Catholic, who was persuaded that there was something Satanic at work in the seventeenth-century collapse of the so-called medieval synthesis. In my reading of Blake at the time (1946–8), there was something genuinely Satanic about his vision. His reading of *Paradise Lost* in *The Marriage of Heaven and Hell* (Milton 'was a true Poet and of the Devils party without knowing it' [pl. 6]), which I had disposed of in my thesis, I now had to reconsider. So radical was the impact of Blake under the inspired instruction of Frye that I decided to shift my focus from Milton and the seventeenth century to Blake and the nineteenth, eventually writing my Ph.D. thesis on the apocalyptic vision in the poetry of Shelley under the supervision of Woodhouse and Frye, which was subsequently published by the University of Toronto Press in its Studies and Texts series.

Unknown to me at the time, inner trouble lay ahead, which had less to do with the shift from Milton to Blake than with the shift from Frye's notion of a literary archetype to Jung's very different notion of a psychological archetype. 'I mean by an archetype,' Frye explains in his *Anatomy of Criticism* (1957), 'a symbol which connects one poem with another and thereby helps to unify and integrate our literary experience.' 'And as an archetype is the communicable symbol,' he continues, 'archetypal criticism is primarily concerned with literature as a social fact and as a mode of communication. By the study of conventions and genres, it attempts to fit poems into the body of poetry as a whole' (99). This 'body of poetry as a whole,' Frye further suggests in *The Secular Scripture* (1976), is the secular analogue of the spiritual body of Christ of which all true believers are the limbs and members. From Jung's point of view, Frye's notion of the archetype as 'the communicable symbol' ignores the historical fact that the symbol is no longer communicable. The unified and integrated symbolic life embodied in the Catholic church, he argues, has been squandered by, among other things, the Protestantism that replaced it. Its once living body is now virtually lifeless. 'Only an unparalleled impoverishment of symbolism,' he then goes on to explain in *The Archetypes of the Collective Unconscious*, 'could enable us to rediscover the gods as psychic factors, that is, as archetypes of the unconscious' (*CW* 9i:50).

'"Did he who made the lamb make thee?" Some students of Blake, I regret to say, have tried to answer this question,' Frye writes in his 1967 Whidden Lectures delivered at McMaster University to honour the memory of its former Baptist chancellor. 'The world we are in is the world of the tiger,' Frye goes on to explain, 'and that world was never created or seen to be good. It is the subhuman world of nature, a world of law and of power but not of intelligence or design. Things "evolve" in it, whatever that means, but there is no creative power in it that we can see except that of man himself. And man is not very good at the creating business: he is much better at destroying, for most of him, like an iceberg, is submerged in a destructive element' (*Modern Century* 120). The 'most' of man, like 'most' of human history, is psychotic. Indeed, Frye concludes, 'the record of humanity from the beginning is so psychotic that is it difficult not to feel, with Joyce's Stephen Daedalus, that history is rather a nightmare from which we are trying to awake' (*Double Vision* 48). God, he insists, 'can only be connected with that tiny percentage of human activity that has not been hopelessly botched' (27). Jung disagreed. The 'human history' that has been 'hopelessly botched' is as 'connected' to God as the history that has not. 'Since the stars have fallen from heaven and our highest symbols have paled,' Jung argues, 'a secret life holds sway in the unconscious. That is why we have a psychology today, and why we speak of an unconscious' (*CW* 9i:50). This 'secret life' is the domain of Romanticism explored in this book.

The archetypal world the Romantics rediscovered in what Keats calls 'some untrodden region of my mind' ('Ode to Psyche' 51) is better suited to Jung's psychological account of the archetype than to Frye's more traditional account. 'I have used the term 'archetype' to describe these [persistent] building blocks, as I thought in the traditional sense,' Frye writes in *The Great Code* (1981), 'not realizing how completely Jung's more idiosyncratic use of the same word had monopolized the field' (48). Jung's 'more idiosyncratic view' lay in his identification of the archetype with his notion of the collective unconscious. This notion Frye dismissed as 'an unnecessary hypothesis in literary criticism, so far as I can judge' (*Anatomy* 112). Everything that Jung attributed to it, Frye argued, was consciously present in the communal myth inherited from the Bible, the Greeks, and the Romans. Agreeing with Jung, Julia Kristeva in 'The Importance of Frye' both acknowledges and contests what she describes as Frye's affirmation of a 'fundamental religious and metaphysical legacy.' 'I am,' she writes, 'among those who maintain that God can be analysed because he is the unconscious itself' (336).

Dismissing this 'idiosyncratic view' of God in favour of a more orthodox Christian notion of the Logos or Word, Frye largely abandoned the term archetype. The Jungian monopoly of the term, he feared, would needlessly mire his schematics in what he considered the occultism of Jung, an occultism that, unnecessarily for Frye, bound literature and the theory of it, even as it bound the Logos or Word, to the operations of the unconscious. Indeed, as John Ayre, Frye's biographer, suggests, Frye developed his own critical theory to 'ward off such bad or distorting influences' (217) as Jung's monopoly and use of the term archetype appeared to provide.

Jung, however, had his own problems with the term. The archetypal world described by Frye, he suggests (though not, of course, with reference to Frye's particular work, which he did not know), dealt with what Jung considered a medieval Christian cosmos that now, with its collapse, had been replaced with the mathematical cosmos of physics over which, as its Apollo, presides the 'archetypal numinosity of number' (Atom 131). '"In the Olympian host, Number eternally reigns" is a valuable acknowledgment from mathematicians as to the numinosity of number,' he writes to Pauli. 'Accordingly, there is sufficient justification for bestowing on number the characteristic of an archetype' (131). Because of the '"dynamis" of number,' it has, for Jung, 'the autonomy of the archetype' (131) and is therefore 'capable of making mythical statements' or what Pauli describes as 'inevitable' (132) statements answerable, not to their practical 'applicability,' but to their internal, logically self-sustaining numinosity or truth. In this respect, Jung regretfully concludes, 'psychology at the moment is lagging so far behind [quantum physics] that there is not much of value to be expected from it for quite a while yet' (133). By 'quite a while yet' Jung means in his own remaining lifetime now subject to his failing health.

Given his relative ignorance of the logical operations of the mathematical mind, Jung nevertheless recognized that in his work with Pauli, who was perhaps the finest mathematician among the quantum physicists, Pauli was 'tackling the problem of [Jung's] psychology' (133), particularly as Jung explored it with reference to the feminine in Answer to Job. In Pauli's dreams or 'fantasy images,' the 'archetypal numinosity of number' assumed the phenomenological form of a 'secret relationship' between a 'light anima' and the Devil. Haunted by these 'fantasy images' as his own response to the making and dropping of the atomic bomb (a haunting that brought him back from Princeton to Zurich to work with Jung), Pauli realized that the 'ethical foundations' of 'mathematical science, which has developed so rapidly since the seventeenth century,' had lost their 'credibility.' The loss lay not only in 'the material-chthonic, ostracized by Christianity,' but in the ego-pursuit of 'power' (140), which exploited the ostracization for its own ends. It appeared to Pauli as if the 'material-chthonic' had in the atomic bomb avenged itself on the Christian rejection of the chthonic nature of matter, which Jung considered the instinctual pole of the archetype. Only a 'chthonic, instinctive wisdom can [now] save mankind from the dangers of the atom bomb" (140), Pauli declares.

This 'ethical' understanding of what had happened to 'mathematical science' appeared, to both Pauli and Jung, to find support in the irrational or acausal behaviour of matter at the subatomic level as it manifested itself in quantum physics. In this acausal behaviour, assumed to be, though not yet measurably understood as, the presence of the unconscious observer interrupting what is observed, both Pauli and Jung were persuaded that not until the behaviour was psychologically understood could the 'ethical foundations ' of mathematical science be re-established on a new level of consciousness involving the coming together of Jung's psychology and quantum physics. Crucial to this achievement, for Jung, lay the recognition that the Logos as the masculine principle of spirit (*theoria*), left to its own powerful 'Hegelian' resources, is the *hybris* that, as madness, destroys the human. Psychologically understood as *praxis,* the human involves the feminine, phenomenological process of ceaseless becoming in which the madness of spirit, forever denied its purely rational end as the 'I Am that I Am,' nevertheless engages the process of becoming as a dialectical '*dynamis,*' Shelley's 'mind in creation.' While the instant of inspiration, described by Plato as 'divine insanity' (*Complete Works* 7.238) in Shelley's translation of *Ion,* may initiate and potentially contain the work, the actual working resides in what Derrida calls the tranquillization of madness. Shelley describes this tranquillization as a 'fading coal' in which, as composition begins, inspiration declines so that what finally emerges, as 'economy,' is 'a feeble shadow of the original conception of the poet' (*DP* 504).

Derrida, like Jung, calls this point of origin the 'zero point,' in which, Derrida argues, 'determined meaning and nonmeaning come together in their common origin' ('Cogito' 56). However, as Derrida explains, since the 'zero point' (or Cogito) 'exceeds all that is real, factual, and existent,' it is 'mad, and acknowledges madness as its liberty and its very possibility.' Without madness, the work of creation is impossible; madness, for Derrida, becomes the ceaseless possibility of the impossible. Here, he radically qualifies Jung's notion of '*hybris*' as a psychotic identification with the archetype. The 'demonic hyperbole,' Derrida writes, 'goes further than the passion of hybris, at least if this latter is seen only as the pathological modification of the being called man. Such a hybris keeps itself within the world. Assuming that it is deranged and excessive, it implies the fundamental derangement and excessiveness of the hyperbole which opens and founds the world as such by exceeding it. Hybris is excessive and exceeds only *within* the space opened by the demonic hyperbole' (57).

Describing this inner and outer space robbed of a Christian archetypal understanding of it, Jung writes: 'But "the heart glows" and a secret unrest gnaws at the roots of our being' (*CW* 9i:50). For Jung, as for Pauli, the 'secret unrest gnaw[ing] at the roots of our being' is 'the material-chthonic' into which the archetypal world has fallen, and where, as chaos, since the founding of physics by Kepler in the seventeenth century, it has been progressively tranquillized or economized (to use Derrida's metaphor) as 'mathematical science.' The act of perception, as what Coleridge describes as 'a repetition in the finite mind of the eternal act of creation in the infinite I AM' (*BL* 1:304), engages as its genesis, chaos or madness.

Not until my immersion in deconstruction during my final teaching years did I fully confront the depth of the 'secret unrest' that, beginning with Milton's presentation of Satan in *Paradise Lost*, gnaws at the roots of Romantic being, or recognize in Jung's psychological view of the archetype the way in which Frye's essentially Christian view aesthetically insulated him from the global psychosis that threatened to invade it, an insulation increasingly evident to me as I gradually, analytically against the grain, came to grips with his reading of Blake. This reading rejected the madness of Blake's poetry as the condition of its making, even as, as I slowly and painfully discovered, it rejected my madness as the essential ground of my knowing. The latter became the personal or individual ground of my postmodern, post-structural understanding of the reality that informs this book, an understanding that found its most immediate objective correlative in Derrida's confession, made in the context of Descartes's '*cogito ergo sum*': 'I philosophize only in *terror*, but in the *confessed* terror of going mad.'

The Blake I could not read under the tutelage of Frye lay in the madness that Frye denied in Blake. Struggling in vain to write a term paper on Blake's *Milton*, in the mirror of Blake's 'unreadable' epic I was finally driven to confront madness in myself. This confrontation released the poem from the kind of sanity I had attempted to impose upon it. It became an attempt to deconstruct *Milton* long before I knew what deconstruction was.

In retrospect, my situation in Frye's graduate class in 1948–9 was not unlike Derrida's situation in Foucault's class as he described it in a lecture delivered at the Collège Philosophique on 4 March 1963. In 'Cogito and the History of Madness,' Derrida, quoting Foucault, explains that in *Madness and Civilization* Foucault could present or understand the '"liberty of madness ... only from high in the fortress that holds madness prisoner"' (37). Aware of the fortress in which Foucault's project was held captive, Derrida, as (like Foucault) its silent prisoner, entered into what he describes as an 'interminable and silent dialogue' with Foucault on behalf of the madness that Foucault had necessarily interred. Describing his psychological position as the unhappy 'disciple' of his 'master' Foucault, who had been robbed of his freedom, Derrida, speaking in the third person, confesses:

> I retain the consciousness of an admiring and grateful disciple. Now, the disciple's consciousness, when it starts, I would not say to dispute, but to engage in dialogue with the master or, better, to articulate the interminable and silent dialogue which made him into a disciple – this disciple's consciousness is an unhappy consciousness. Starting to enter into dialogue in the world, that is, starting to answer back, he always feels 'caught in the act,' like the 'infant' who, by definition and as his name indicates, cannot speak and above all must not answer back. And when, as is the case here, the dialogue is in danger of being taken – incorrectly – as a challenge, the disciple knows that he alone finds himself already challenged by the master's voice within him that precedes his own. He feels himself indefinitely challenged, or rejected or accused; as a disciple, he is challenged by the master who speaks within him and before him, to reproach him for making this challenge and to reject it in advance, having elaborated it before him; and having interiorized the master, he is also challenged by the disciple that he himself is. This interminable unhappiness of the disciple perhaps stems from the fact that he does not yet know – or is still concealing from himself – that the master, like real life, may always be absent. The disciple must break the glass, or better the mirror, the reflection, his infinite speculation on the master. And start to speak. (31–2)

For Derrida, this 'instant' when he starts to speak is the 'instant' of madness that Derrida affirms as the 'proper and inaugural moment'

(56) of the Cogito. Quoting Joyce speaking of *Ulysses*, he describes it as '"terribly daring,"' only a '"transparent sheet separat[ing] it from madness"' (31). The 'proper and inaugural moment' of this volume is the moment in which I first confronted, in Blake's *Milton* as in myself, the madness that is its subject. Blake himself describes this subject as the action 'Within a Moment: a Pulsation of the Artery' in which 'the Poets Work is Done: and all the Great / Events of Time start forth & are concievd' (*M* 29[31].1–3).

Intimately connected to this 'Moment' was my 'Jungian' understanding of Nietzsche's confrontation with himself as the madman in *The Gay Science* announcing the death of God, his mind usurping the instant of creation, thereby rendering it a fiction. In Jung's psychology, this confrontation became the dark mirror in which Jung conducted a lifelong interrogation of madness, including his own. In a manner that, I believe, critically illuminates the work of Frye, Jung struggled less to imprison madness in an archetypal system than phenomenologically to transform it into an ever evolving consciousness evident in the poetry of Blake and the other Romantics. Tilottama Rajan invited me to contribute an essay on Nietzsche and the Romantics for an issue of *Studies in Romanticism* that she was editing (Spring 1990). In her introduction she argues that 'Nietzsche reconceived by theorists like de Man, Derrida, Deleuze and Foucault has coincided with a rereading of romantic texts which questions the organicist and idealist approach of Abrams and Wasserman, and sees the romantic assertion as jeopardized by the very language in which it is articulated' (3). Because there still was in Jung's notion of the self as the God image in man much that in my view aligned him 'with the organicist and idealist approach of Abrams and Wasserman' (Rajan, significantly, does not include Frye), my coming to grips with Nietzsche in this essay was my coming more consciously to grips with the death of God as the Logos or Word, a death present for de Man and Derrida in the very language in which the Logos is articulated. The break not only with Frye but with the entire humanist tradition that had constituted my formal education became a confrontation with madness far more severe than my confrontation with Blake's *Milton*. The result in the writing of the essay was another break in which finally a colleague had to persuade me that what I had written made sense; I, having read the proofs, had been convinced that it did not.

As a result of writing this essay, my own understanding of Jung became increasingly 'dark' and 'inscrutable,' a darkness and inscrutability that was more fearfully articulated by my immersion in deconstruction, particularly the work of de Man and Derrida. De Man's essay on Shelley's *Triumph of Life*, 'Shelley Disfigured,' was for me a darkness made visible on a scale I had never previously encountered. I saw in it some ultimate linguistic enactment of what Jung describes as 'an unparalleled impoverishment of symbolism,' an 'impoverishment' that conducted one not to a rediscovery of the gods 'as psychic factors' – there are no 'psychic factors' for de Man – but to nothingness. At my retirement dinner in 1988, I vowed to commit the rest of my writing life to answering de Man's challenge, which he described as 'the final test of reading,' fully aware of the Derridean notion that writing was a tranquillizing of madness. 'The final test of reading, in *The Triumph of Life*,' de Man writes, 'depends on ... how one disposes of Shelley's body' ('Shelley' 67). For de Man, I realized, the way one disposes of Shelley's corpse is the way one disposes of all literature.

This book is the fulfilment of the vow I made concerning de Man. Without my realizing it, it began with the paper, 'Figuring Disfiguration: Reading Shelley after De Man,' published in *Studies in Romanticism* (Summer 2001). After it appeared, I discussed with Joel Faflak, my former student and now my colleague, the possibility of publishing a volume of essays, most of them already in print, that might show the development leading up to this essay but, more important, some of the major critical approaches to Romanticism in the second half of the last century in terms of how they were related, at least in one individual mind. Faflak, who knew most of the essays well, having first read many of them at the time of their publication, was agreeable to the idea and generously accepted my invitation to assist me in the selecting and editing of them.

Once the selection was made and two new essays were added, Faflak set to work to write his foreword. Finding in this foreword an uncovering of a *Geist* that led me to think of the essays in a slightly different way, I decided that the original plan needed to be revised to include not only some editing, but a running commentary that would do some of the work a reader might be reluctant to perform. In short, I realized that something more than a volume of previously published essays, however much revised and bound together by a commentary, was demanded. There was a book in these essays and in Faflak's foreword that wanted out, however reluctant I might be to let it out. I knew I was standing in the way and that I had to get out of the way. I confronted head-on the feminine in myself, which demanded to be heard, if not with the assent of my will, then, if necessary, against it.

One result was that Faflak's completed foreword became the afterword. But after what? Over a period of time, like me, he became increasingly alarmed by the demands being made by the book that was taking shape. Both of us confronted a mind that would not stay still, that was continually seeking a way out of the traps it set for itself. What kind of afterword could deal with that without appearing to entrap or contain the very thing that energetically resisted it?

In some shared desperation to see the thing finally done, I remarked that I was haunted by all those unwritten poems of Shelley's Visionary in *Alastor*, which Silence had taken into her rugged cell because, too enamoured of them, she wanted them all to herself. I was haunted by the unheard melody of that great poem whose 'no tone' ('Ode on a Grecian Urn' 14), as Keats writes, is forever piped into the invisible chambers of Shelley's 'one mind' (*DP* 478). Faflak's afterword strikes me as responding to the same set of pipes.

In certain respects this book, as it now at last stands, is, as I have suggested, a Jungian analysis, filtered through de Man and Derrida, of that 'unrest' that draws into its orbit critical theory, literary analysis, psychoanalysis, and autobiography. It is in no formal sense a work of Romantic criticism, though many of its interpretive strategies were conceived and executed in that critical context. Like the *Biographia Literaria*, it is, as a kind of critical *roman à clef*, a discontinuous narrative, a critical hybrid that calls attention to the rupture in a metaphysics of Being that fragments into the 'economy' of sanity what Derrida calls the 'mad audacity' ('Cogito' 56) of the hyperbolic project. Coleridge's life-long project was the unwritten *Logosophia*, fragments of which appear in his *Biographia*. Assuming the guise of 'the transcendental philosopher' as its presumed author, in one of its fragments Coleridge writes: 'grant me a nature having two contrary forces, the one of which tends to expand infinitely, while the other strives to apprehend or *find* itself in this infinity, and I will cause the world of intelligences with the whole system of their representations to rise up before you' (*BL* 1:297). What rose before Coleridge as he strove to apprehend the infinity of impressions that overwhelmed his consciousness is, in part, what the work of free association provides. The 'whole system' that binds the associations together, his unwritten *Logosophia*, becomes a 'prospect' in his mind that, with reference to his own 'prospect,' Shelley called the 'void circumference' (*Adonais* 420) or 'intense inane' (*PU* 3.4.204), which is to say madness. To Coleridge's conjuration of a non-existent reader ('some other Being') of a hundred-page chapter on the imagination, which

Coleridge never wrote, the spectral reader hauntingly replies that what had never been written reminds him of 'the winding steps of an old ruined tower' (*BL* 1:303)

'Reading as disfiguration' receives here the kind of disfiguration that is, for de Man, what reading is. Reading de Man reading Shelley is myself reading *Bone: Dying into Life*, Marion Woodman's account of her own spectral habitation of a body dying into the strange cellular life of cancer. Shelley's spectral habitation of the 'triumph of life' is the proto- type of a cancer patient interrogating her own dying body. For de Man, the spectral reader, like the spectral author, is Death. The absence that is its presence haunts the following pages. So long as this presence re- mains an absence, the interpenetration of the realms of life and death so richly explored by the Romantics remains, for me, what writing is: the making present of what is otherwise not there, its thereness being what Jung calls the unconscious life of the psyche that 'surrounds conscious- ness on all sides.'

In agreeing to publish 'Cogito and the History of Madness' in the *Revue de métaphysique et de morale*, Derrida recommended that it 'should retain its first form, that of the spoken word, with all its requirements and, especially, its peculiar weaknesses.' 'If in general, according to the remark in the *Phaedrus*,' he explains, 'the written word is deprived of "the assistance of the father," if it is a fragile "idol" fallen from "living and animated discourse" unable to "help itself," then is it not more exposed and disarmed than ever when, miming the improvisation of the voice, it must give up even the resources and lies of style?' ('Cogito' 307n). Taking full advantage of 'the resources and lies of style,' this volume at the same time interrogates those resources and lies by de- fending the madness that, being voiceless, cannot defend itself. 'If the Abysm / Could vomit forth its secrets,' declares Demogorgon in an- swer to Asia's spell-casting and spell-binding metaphysical questions that only Demogorgon can abjure ('Thy words waken Oblivion' [4.543]), ' – but a voice / Is wanting, the deep truth is imageless' (*PU* 2.4.114–16).

Shelley's Demogorgon is the unconscious itself. As a 'mighty Dark- ness,' it is 'Ungazed upon and shapeless – neither limb / Nor form – nor outline' (*PU* 2.4.3–6). Its 'deep truth' is known only as the fictions the imagination constructs as the representations of it. Because the imagination lacks an objective correlative other than its own opera- tions, it 'to itself must be the oracle' (2.4.123). Once Asia recognizes the limitations of her oracular power, she is able to set in motion the psychic action of Shelley's lyrical drama as a fictional enactment of the 'deep truth' of the unconscious. Here Shelley contrasts her with Jupiter, who, granted the same oracular power by Prometheus, abused it by turning it into a 3,000-year-old religion in which he assumed the role of Jehovah. Now, he is determined to eternalize his tyrannical abuse of oracular power by begetting a son who will assume forever 'Demogorgon's vacant throne' (3.1.21). In his intercourse with Thetis, however, he experiences 'the desire which makes [her] one with [him]' (3.1.35) as the sting of the poisonous snake, a seps, which, in Lucan's *Parsalia*, dissolves the body of Sabellus as he crosses the Numidian desert.

Those who abuse the poet's oracular power, which is the imagination itself, by turning it into a religion, Shelley insists in his Preface to *Alastor*, are, like Wordsworth, doomed 'to a slow and poisonous decay' (*SPP* 69). Byron, who flourished as a poet on what he called in *Childe Harold's Pilgrimage* the 'vitality of poison' (3.299), became for a time an object of horror in Shelley's life. *The Triumph of Life* confronts the poisonous consequences of the abuse of oracular power arising from a delusory identification with the unconscious itself. If madness is the identification with the unconscious, sanity is the creative process arising from it as it separates itself out into those supreme fictions (what Shelley in 'Hymn to Intellectual Beauty' calls 'Frail spells' [29]) by which and in which the human soul, suspended between matter and spirit, fearfully confronts its threatened extinction.

Far more than Blake, who found in the biblical figure of Jesus the objective correlative for what, without it, Blake recognized as extinction, Shelley, in the absence of the archetypal figure, never ceased to confront the extinction that the subjectivity of his vision 'darkly, fearfully' (*Adonais* 492) constellated and, at the same time, as 'the soul of Adonais,' beaconed towards an archetypal 'abode where the Eternal are' (494–5). This archetypal 'abode,' with the numinosity of number in mind, he calls the 'One' (460). In the potentially creative tension between the imagination of eternity and the factuality of extinction in which, like Nietzsche's tightrope walker in *Thus Spake Zarathustra*, he remained dangerously suspended, Shelley located human freedom – the very freedom that Derrida identifies with madness – which 'opens and founds the world by exceeding it.' 'The spirit of that mighty singing / To its abyss was suddenly withdrawn' (271–2), he concludes his 'Ode to Liberty.' Comparing himself to a 'wild swan' (273) struck by a bolt of lightning that 'pierced its brain' (277), Shelley as the dying swan describes his dying moment. The 'great voice which did [his] flight sustain' hisses, like 'waves,' around his 'drown[ing] head' (283–5). Blake's Jesus, on the other hand, allowed Blake to walk on the waters. 'But when he saw the wind boisterous, [Peter] was afraid; and beginning to sink, he cried, saying, Lord save me. / And immediately Jesus stretched forth his hand, and caught him, and said unto him, O thou of little faith, wherefore didst thou doubt?' (Matthew 14.30–1). 'O Lord what can I do! my Selfhood cruel / Marches against thee deceitful from Sinai & from Edom,' Albion cries as Jesus suddenly appears standing before him 'as the Good Shepherd / By the lost Sheep that he hath found.' To which Jesus replies: 'Fear not Albion unless I die thou canst not live / But if I die I shall arise again & thou with me / This is Friendship & Brotherhood without it Man is Not' (J 96.3–16). By confronting what 'Man is Not' in his multiplicity of shifting perspectives, the 'mighty singing' of the Romantics guessed at what he yet might be. If madness is what 'Man is Not,' sanity, as an ever expanding consciousness bound to madness, is what he yet might be. Though, as polarized, madness and sanity are opposites, in the Romantic soul's dialectic they are bound together in what Blake calls 'true Friendship' (MHH 20).

1

Jung and Romanticism: The Fate of the Mythopoeic Imagination

It is of course ironical that I, a psychiatrist, should at almost every step of my experiment have run into the same psychic material which is the stuff of psychosis and is found in the insane. This is the fund of unconscious images which fatally confuse the mental patient. But it is also the matrix of a mythopoeic imagination which has vanished from our rational age.

Carl Gustav Jung, *Memories, Dreams, Reflections*

Like the Romantics before him, Jung viewed the human act of perception as a creative act bringing into play a whole range of psychic activity to which matter as physical sensations located in the brain is mentally bound. For Jung, the psyche is the creative process itself, which enacts both its binding to matter and the transformation of matter that the binding performs. The conversion of external sensations, which as sensations are no longer external ('felt in the blood,' writes Wordsworth), into mental images in the brain is the action Jung attributes to the psyche. The fact that an external sensation is perceived by the brain as a mental image that *is* the object tells us, Jung suggests, far more about the object than its sensible form as an object of sense will allow. 'For, in the last analysis,' as Jung notes in *The Archetypes of the Collective Unconscious*, 'psychic life is for the greater part an unconscious life that surrounds consciousness on all sides.'

The more this 'unconscious preparation' enters into consciousness, the greater the symbolic density and depth the object of perception assumes. Since for Jung, however, the unconscious can never be swallowed by consciousness, can never, that is, in its unknowability (Kant's *an sich*) cease to be unconscious, the symbol as object contains, as object, the numinous mystery of the unconscious, which can never be known as other than a symbol. Man inhabits a symbolic world that, to the degree that he remains unconscious of it as symbolic, he assumes to be literal. He inhabits a mystery – the unknowable realm of the unconscious – symbolically represented as the sensible world in the human act of perception. So long as he remains unconscious of human perception as an act of creation, the mystery of creation contained in the symbol is not recognized. '[A]ll objects (as objects),' Coleridge remarks, 'are essentially fixed and dead' (BL 1:304). Man, Jung argues, knows himself only to the degree that he understands the symbolic nature of the world he actually, as a psychic being, inhabits. To the degree that he does not inhabit it as a psychic being, he does not inhabit himself as the mystery that he is. Because the ultimate unveiling of the mystery would require that the unconscious become human consciousness itself, which it cannot become without ceasing to be unconscious, man as man must forever remain a mystery to himself.

As religion, Jung psychologically argues, the mystery is resolved as the unconscious conscious of itself ('I Am that I Am'). By identifying the unconscious with the religious notion of God, God's consciousness of himself becomes, for Jung, his human form. Within the limits of the Christian dispensation, to which he argues the west is still dangerously bound, God's human consciousness early reached an impasse that, within the dispensation, remains unresolved. The impasse resides in the crucifixion: the human form of God as the sacrifice of both God and the human. As a result, the crucifixion enacts the incompleteness of the incarnation as it is embodied in the dogma of the Trinity, the threefold as distinct from the fourfold as the symbol of the wholeness that constitutes the actualization of the God-man, Blake's 'human form divine' ('The Divine Image' 11, 15).

The incompleteness of the Trinity, arresting it as dogma into the final revelation of God in man, lies, for Jung, in the absence of the feminine archetypally imaged as Mary, the Mother of God, in whose virgin womb God is immaculately conceived. The dogma, that is, treats the patriarchal Trinity as a mystery embraced by faith, 'believing,' as Tennyson explains, 'where we cannot prove' (In Memoriam 4).[1] By psychologically exploring the meaning of the Trinity and treating it as he treated alchemy, Jung, in 'A Psychological Approach to the Dogma of the Trinity' (1948), hoped to unveil its more androgynous psychic meaning to include the feminine as a symbolic rather than a literal fact so as to restore it to the unfolding life of the psyche where, in his view, it properly belongs.² For Jung, this absorption of the Trinity into the psyche's unfolding life lay in the symbolic completion of the Trinity as the threefold in the fourfold as the symbol of wholeness. The fourfold, he argues, is the fully human form of consciousness in which it symbolically inhabits its own operations as the 'I Am that I Am.' This fourfold human state constitutes what Jung calls the soul, as distinct from the psyche, which is understood as the creative process by which soul becomes itself as its consciousness of itself. Wolfgang Giegerich describes this state as 'the soul's logical life,'³ which, prior to our conscious habitation of it, exists as the psychic process by which, as consciousness, it becomes known. Jung, he claims, largely failed to distinguish psyche and soul. As a result, it may be argued, Jung failed fully to recognize that soul is what Coleridge describes as 'the IMMEDIATE, which dwells in every man.' 'On the original intuition, or absolute affirmation of it (which is likewise in every man, but does not in every man rise into consciousness),' Coleridge explains, 'all the *certainty* of our knowledge depends' (BL 1:243). Describing the relation of soul to psyche as the relation of 'object and subject,' in which each involves and supposes the other, Coleridge writes: '[the I Am] is a subject which becomes a subject by the act of constructing itself objectively to itself; but which never is an object except for itself, and only so far as by the very same act it becomes a subject. It may be described therefore as a perpetual self-duplication of one and the same power into object and subject, which presuppose each other, and can exist only as antitheses' (BL 1:273).

For Coleridge, the subject's 'act of constructing itself objectively to itself' is the work of what he calls the 'primary IMAGINATION,' which he defines as 'the living Power and prime Agent of all human Perception, and as a repetition in the finite mind of the eternal act of creation in the infinite I AM' (BL 1:304). It is the act of perception itself viewed as a creative act, which repeats as a human (or 'finite') act God's divine act. The act of perception is, for Coleridge, the incarnation, the human form of God. In 1805 Coleridge coined the term 'psycho-analytical'⁴ to describe the psychology of this act by which it is raised to and inhabits its consciousness of itself, as distinct from its unconscious presence as matter, an object of sense devoid of the consciousness that makes it an object. In coining the term, he was describing his rejection of what he called the 'mechanical philosophy,' which argues that what we perceive as a mental image is an epiphenomenon of matter, an epiphenomenon that banishes the psyche 'to a land of shadows, surrounds us with apparitions, and distinguishes truth from illusion only by the majority of those who dream the same dream[.] "*I* asserted that the world was mad," explained poor Lee, "and the world said, that I was mad, and confound them, they outvoted me"' (*BL* 1:262).[5]

Opposing the 'mechanical philosophy' with his notion of the 'primary imagination,' Coleridge argues that 'it is the table itself, which the man of common sense believes himself to see, not the phantom of a table, from which he may argumentatively deduce the reality of a table, which he does not see. If to destroy the reality of all, that we actually behold, be [Platonic] idealism, what can be more egregiously so, than the system of modern metaphysics, which banishes us to a land of shadows' (*BL* 1:261–2). Coleridge is not a Platonist; he is an incarnationist in some larger Christian sense, a position he attempted psychologically to explore in a way that Jung vastly extended. Jung did so by rejecting Freud's materialism, repeating by expanding Coleridge's rejection of the 'mechanical philosophy.'

Coleridge's rejection lay ultimately in his Anglican conviction that God in Christ had achieved his full incarnation, an 'IMMEDIATE' conviction that, with the help of German philosophy, he sought 'psychoanalytically' to understand. Extending Coleridge's position, Jung dissociated Christ from institutional Christianity, releasing him as the symbol of an otherwise unknowable archetypal reality that, as human consciousness itself, continues to change as it psychically evolves. Like Blake's, Jung's Christ is the fourfold Christ of the New Jerusalem identified with the marriage feast of the Lamb as the marriage of heaven and earth, which he believed was symbolically affirmed in *Munificentissimus Deus* (1950), the papal bull of Pius XII promulgating the physical Assumption of the Virgin Mary to the heavenly bridal chamber of her Son. In what he describes as 'a state of unconsciousness' in which, hanging for twelve days 'on the edge of death,' he experienced 'deliriums and visions' (*MDR* 289), Jung found himself at the 'blissful wedding' (294). 'I myself was the "Marriage of the Lamb,"' he writes. He had, he explains in his memoirs, 'assumed his primal form' (293). 'There was no longer anything I wanted or desired,' he explains. 'I existed in an objective form; I was what I had been and lived. At first the sense of annihilation predominated, of having been stripped or pillaged; but suddenly that became of no consequence. Everything seemed to be past; what remained was a *fait accompli* [Nietzsche's *amor fati*], without any reference to what had been. There was no longer any regret that something had dropped away or been taken away. On the contrary: I had everything that I was, and that was everything' (291).

Jung relates this fourfold soul-sense of himself to his dream of a yogi sitting in the lotus position facing him in a chapel. Approaching him, he suddenly realizes that the yogi is wearing his face. Awakening in fright, he said to himself: 'Aha, so he is the one who is meditating me. He has a dream, and I am it.' 'I knew that when he awakened,' Jung explains, 'I would no longer be' (323). That is, he would be fully present as the symbol itself released from the psychic process of its becoming, the 'Self' free at last of the 'ego,' a freedom that in the mortal state constitutes madness and, according to Jung, is usually experienced only when one is about to die, and then not as madness, but as the unveiled reality of the soul.

'I experienced this objectivity once again later on,' Jung continues, describing a dream in which he saw his wife in her primal form wearing the dress that his cousin, the medium who became the subject of his medical thesis on occult phenomena, had made for her. 'I knew it was not she,' Jung explains, 'but a portrait she had made or commissioned for me. It contained the beginning of our relationship, the events of fifty-three years of marriage, and the end of her life also. Face to face with such wholeness one remains speechless, for it can scarcely be comprehended' (MDR 296).

'In God,' writes Jung in 'A Psychological Approach to the Dogma of the Trinity,' 'there is no advance from the potential to the actual, from the possible to the real, because God is pure reality, the "actus purus" itself' (CW 11:289). Viewed from a psychological standpoint,' he argues, 'the Trinity represents the progressive transformation of one and the same substance ['pure reality']' by which at the human level it becomes known. What becomes progressively known at the human level is always already known by the 'pure reality' that is God. In this radical sense psychology, as Jung understands it, is the progressive transformation conducted by the psyche in which man comes to know God. Thus, when John Freeman, asked him, in a BBC interview for its Face to Face program, if he believed in God, Jung replied: '"I don't believe, I know."' While 'this went down well with the orthodox Christians,' Frank McLynn remarks in his biography of Jung, he 'had to spend a lot of time explaining to his followers that when he said "God," he meant, of course, the "God-image" [which is the Self]' (526). As an unorthodox Swiss Protestant, Jung knew God from within his own 'occult' experience of him. His problem, as he describes it, lay in the inadmissibility of 'occult' experience as scientific, empirical evidence upon which his sanity (so far as his colleagues were concerned) depended. The scientific evidence that Jung could not provide for his 'occult' experience he found, or thought he found, in quantum physics, more particularly in his twenty-six-year relationship with the quantum physicist, Wolfgang Pauli. Working closely with Jung, Pauli embraced the unconscious operations of the psyche, as Jung described them, as the observer, excluded in the classical physics of Newton, this radically interfered with the operations of matter at the subatomic (i.e., unconscious) level to such a degree that the reality of its physical operations was subject to the unconscious operations of the psyche. Quantum physics, in short, provided the empirical evidence of the unconscious without which it was scientifically dismissed in much the same way that alchemy was dismissed. In the correspondence between Jung and Pauli, now published as *Atom and Archetype*, the unconscious processed by the psyche actively enters its scientific engagement with matter in a manner that has literally transformed the globe into a radically new perception of it,[6] which, far from new, is the perception of the Romantic poets that Coleridge, in the name of metaphysics, first consciously psychoanalysed.

The soul as the object of consciousness is not, for Jung, the product of consciousness. Though experienced only in the numinous symbols of it offered by the psyche, it remains in itself, like Adonai (as distinct from Adonis),[7] autonomously self-contained within its own consciousness of God as the archetypal form of consciousness itself. For Jung, the soul is the human form of God's consciousness of himself, the 'I Am that I Am.' However, unless God's consciousness of himself is progressively explored by the operations of the psyche, it consolidates into an impenetrable enigma in which, from a psychological point of view, God is essentially dead. As Coleridge describes it, the truth of the 'actus purus' is, like the 'most awful and mysterious, yet being at the same time of universal interest ... too often considered as *so* true, that [it loses] all the life and efficiency of truth, and lie[s] bed-ridden in the dormitory of the soul, side by side, with all the most despised and exploded errors' (*BL* 1:82). 'I have to ask myself also, in all seriousness,' Jung writes, 'whether it might not be far more dangerous if Christian symbols were made inaccessible to thoughtful understanding by being banished to a sphere of sacrosanct unintelligibility. They [like alchemical symbols] can easily become so remote from us that their irrationality turns into preposterous nonsense' (*CW* 11:170). Jung's psychological mission was to rescue the remote symbols of the irrational unconscious, such as those found in dreams and in the insane, from 'preposterous nonsense.'

A prefigurative Jungian understanding of the unconscious *as* unconscious symbolically made known to consciousness as a mystery is enacted by Shelley in his lyrical drama, *Prometheus Unbound*. As the unconscious, Demogorgon in its cave is described by Panthea as

> a mighty Darkness
> Filling the seat of power; and rays of gloom
> Dart round, as light from the meridian Sun,
> Ungazed upon and shapeless – neither limb
> Nor form – nor outline; yet we feel it is
> A living Spirit.   (2.4.2–7)

Oracularly sounding from its 'Abysm' ('I spoke but as ye speak' [2.4.112]), Demogorgon declares: '– If the Abysm[8] / Could vomit forth its secrets: – but a voice / Is wanting, the deep truth is imageless' (2.4.114–16). Descending to this semiotic 'Abysm,' which the post-Freudian analyst Julia Kristeva compares to the traces of the mother's body issuing as sounds from her infant's mouth before they become speech (described by Shelley as 'a Sea profound, of ever-spreading sound' [*PU* 2.5.84)]), Shelley prefiguratively enacts the creative process of perception upon which Jung's psychology is dialectically based. Partly with Shakespeare's *The Tempest* in mind, he enacts the creative process as the weaving of a spell, the added fourth act celebrating the weaving itself as a dance of the elements and planets (sun, moon, and earth) that the 'Abysm' dissolves ('We hear: thy words waken Oblivion' [4.543]). The words that 'waken Oblivion' suffer the inevitable dissolution of spells and incantations; 'Beams of brightest verse' are recognized by the 'happy dead' as 'clouds to hide, not colours to portray' (4.534–5). The 'happy dead,' as Shelley describes them, are united with their ghostly forms, which, he explains, are 'dreams and the light imaginings of men / And all that faith creates, or love desires' (1.200–1).

For Shelley, these 'ghostly forms' are the sensuous images of their archetypal reality, which Jung calls the 'Self.' Shelley's poetic vision is the ghostly form of an 'imageless,' archetypal realm that forever remains beyond the reach of the sensible. With death, the sensible falls away. The ghostly forms ('shadows of all forms that think and live' [1.198]) unite with (dissolve into) their archetypes 'and they part no more' (1.199). Shelley calls this 'imageless' realm 'the intense inane,' where Keats mythopoeically joins the 'happy dead' as Adonais, 'the loftiest star of unascended heaven' (*PU* 3.4.203–4). The 'mind in creation,' however, bound to the senses, struggles in vain to 'oversoar' the limits of the image; working with words in the act of composition, it is denied its 'imageless' object. In the end, the 'winged words on which [Shelley's] soul would pierce / Into the height of love's rare Universe' become 'chains of lead around its flight of fire' (*Epipsychidion* 588–90). Shelley's elegy becomes a funeral pyre, whose flaming words apparently defeat their alchemical purpose, reducing Keats's corpse to ash. Becoming increasingly conscious as he writes that the mind in creation is slowly consumed by its own operations, Shelley experiences the poet in himself becoming one with the corpse of Keats and then rising from its ashes (the poem itself) to join Keats in the imageless 'void circumference' that transcends the poem's reach, even as Adonai transcends Adonis. Urania, Shelley's Muse, becomes Keats's Moneta 'deathwards progressing / To no death ' (*Fall of Hyperion* 1.260–1).

Jung's seven-year intense engagement with Freud has its poetic analogue in Shelley's creative engagement with Keats's corpse in *Adonais*, an engagement in which, in a manner alien to the late Keats of the posthumously published *Fall of Hyperion*, he releases Keats from it. Jung's later understanding of Freud's psychology remains bound to the arrested form in which he early rejected it. This arrested binding, however, served to release him from it in something of the same way that Harold Bloom in *The Anxiety of Influence* describes the way in which a strong poet, in the name of the 'I Am that I Am,' misprisions himself from 'his Great Original' (31). 'Let us,' Bloom writes, 'pursue ... the quest of learning to read any poem as its poet's deliberate misinterpretation, *as a poet*, of a precursor's poem, or of poetry in general. Know each poem by its *clinamen* [swerve] and you will "know" that poem in the way that will not purchase knowledge by the loss of the poem's power' (43), which is to say its 'I Am.'

Viewing the creative process archetypally rather than biologically, Jung rejects Freud's sexual reading of the object of perception as an arresting of the psychic process that robs the symbol of its mystery by reducing it to matter and then, with the incest taboo in mind, making a dogma of it in the name of the ego. 'Above all,' Jung writes of his first meeting with Freud in Vienna (March 1907),

Freud's attitude toward the spirit seemed to me highly questionable. Wherever, in a person or in a work of art, an expression of spirituality (in the intellectual, not the supernatural sense) came to light, he suspected it, and insinuated that it was repressed sexuality. Anything that could not be directly interpreted as sexuality he referred to as 'psychosexuality.' I protested that this hypothesis, carried to its logical conclusion, would lead to an annihilating judgment upon culture. Culture would then appear as a mere farce, the morbid consequence of repressed sexuality. 'Yes,' he assented, 'so it is, and that is just a curse of fate against which we are powerless to contend.' I was by no means disposed to agree, or to let it go at that, but still I did not feel competent to argue it out with him. (*MDR* 149–50)

In his retrospective account of their meeting, Jung confesses that at the age of twenty-five he 'lacked the experience to appreciate Freud's theories' (*MDR* 147). He therefore laid *The Interpretation of Dreams* aside until 1903, when he realized that it provided an explanation for the repressions he encountered in his patients in his experiments with word association. However, while it explained the mechanism of repression in the building of an ego structure, it did not, for Jung, satisfactorily deal with the content of repression in relation to the larger concerns of the Self to which, in the Jungian process of individuation, the ego must surrender. The surrender of the ego in the service of the Self (the psychologically sublated God image) became the subject of the second part of Jung's *Symbols of Transformation*, which he knew would cost him his relationship with Freud. (*Totem and Taboo* was Freud's reply, written, in part, to get rid of Jung.) 'For I planned to set down in it my own conception of incest,' Jung explains,

the decisive transformation of the concept of libido [from sexual to spiritual], and various other ideas in which I differed from Freud. To me incest signified a personal complication only in the rarest cases. Usually incest has a highly religious aspect, for which reason the incest theme plays a decisive part in almost all cosmogonies and in numerous myths [the physical ascent of Mary to the marriage chamber of her Son, for example]. But Freud clung to the literal interpretation of it and could not grasp the spiritual significance of incest as a symbol. I knew that he would never be able to accept any of my ideas on this subject ... For two months I was unable to touch my pen, so tormented was I by the conflict ... At last I resolved to go ahead with the writing – and it did indeed cost me Freud's friendship. (*MDR* 167)

When Freud visited Jung in Zurich in 1908, Jung shared with him the work he was doing with some of his psychotic patients, all of which, while interesting, thoroughly bewildered Freud and, beyond that, haunted him with the fear that what Jung was attempting with them he was also attempting with himself. One of Jung's patients was a seventeen-year-old catatonic who heard voices, refused food, and no longer spoke. Jung gradually persuaded her to speak, partly because he had written his medical thesis 'On the Pathology and Psychology of So-Called Occult Phenomena,' which, among other things, dealt with the seances he had attended in which his fifteen-year-old cousin had acted as the medium and, in Jung's view, had later managed briefly to integrate the mythic realm she inhabited in trance into something like an adult consciousness before her death at the age of twenty-six. At the age of fifteen, Jung's patient had been seduced by her brother and abused by a schoolmate. From her sixteenth year on, she retreated into isolation from normal society and took up residence on the moon where the wives and children were kept in a sublunar dwelling. On the mountains of the moon dwelt a vampire who kidnapped and killed the wives and children. Jung's patient built a platform on a tower and waited with a sacrificial knife concealed in her gown for the vampire, wrapped in several pairs of wings, to appear. Approaching her, he spread his wings to reveal not a monster but a man of unearthly beauty. Raising her from the platform, he flew off with her.

While Jung had released her from her silence into speech, she could no longer escape from the earth and return to the moon. Jung had broken her spell. Relapsing again into her catatonia, after some two months she was restored to something like sanity in which again she could talk to Jung and even accept the apparent fact that life on earth was unavoidable. When an assistant doctor made a somewhat rash approach to her, however, she shot and wounded him. Had Jung done the same thing, she told him, she would also have shot him. During her last interview, at the end of her treatment with Jung, she gave him the revolver. According to Jung, she then married, had seven children, and survived two world wars in the east, without ever again suffering a relapse.

'Thereafter I regarded the sufferings of the mentally ill in a different light,' Jung writes. 'For I had gained insight into the richness and importance of their inner experience.' 'As a result of the incest to which she had been subjected as a girl,' Jung explains,' she felt humiliated in the eyes of the world, but elevated in the realm of fantasy. She had been transported into a mythic realm; for incest is traditionally a prerogative of royalty and divinities' (*MDR* 130). Shelley's *Laon and Cynthna*, withdrawn by the printer and revised without the brother and sister incest as *The Revolt of Islam*, enacts a similar scenario, though, in Shelley's case, there is no return to the world, which remains only as the ashes of the lover's alchemical fire.

After a major heart attack in 1944 conducted him for twelve days to the New Jerusalem of Revelation, in which he himself was the marriage of the Lamb, Jung's strongest fear was that his greatest wish not to return would be gratified. Instead, as he describes it in *Memories, Dreams, Reflections*, his doctor was sacrificed in his stead. 'From below, from the direction of Europe,' writes Jung, describing the 'mythic realm' to which he had been 'transported,'

> an image floated up. It was my doctor, Dr. H. – or, rather, his likeness – framed by a golden chain or a golden laurel wreath. I knew at once: 'Aha, this is my doctor, of course, the one who has been treating me. But now he is coming in his primal form, as a *basileus* of Kos. In life he was an avatar, of this *basileus*, the temporal embodiment of the primal form, which has existed from the beginning. Now he is appearing in that primal form.
>
> Presumably I too was in my primal form, though this was something I did not observe but simply took for granted. As he stood before me, a mute exchange of thought took place between us. Dr. H. had been delegated by the earth to deliver a message to me, to tell me that there was a protest against my going away. I had no right to leave the earth and must return. The moment I heard that, the vision ceased ... Disappointed, I thought, 'Now I must return to the "box system" again.' For it seemed to me as if behind the horizon of the cosmos a three-dimensional world had been artificially built up ['the Sexual is Threefold: the Human is Fourfold,' writes Blake in *Milton* (M 4.5)] in which each person sat by himself in a little box. And now I had to convince myself all over again that this was important! Life and the whole world struck me as a prison, and it bothered me beyond measure that I should again be finding that quite in order. (*MDR* 292)

Although Jung recognized Freud's account of the mechanism of repression as necessary to the building of a strong ego structure without which the ego is always in danger of being annihilated by the unconscious – Freud twice fainted in the presence of Jung; the second time Jung lifted him up and laid him on a couch, and Freud awakened with a sense of how rich it must be to die ('Now more than ever seems it rich to die' [55], writes Keats in his 'Ode to a Nightingale') – he rejected his interpretation of its content. The incest taboo dealt with by Freud in *Totem and Taboo* deals with the sexual dimension of taboo. The sexual taboo, Jung argues, compensates for the exaggerated focus upon the physical gratification of the instinctual by symbolically raising it to the wedding chamber where Mary is united with her Son, from the biological mother, that is, to the archetypal mother. 'Luckily for us,' Jung writes in 'The Philosophical Tree' (1954), 'symbols mean very much more than can be known at first glance. Their meaning resides in the fact that they compensate an unadapted attitude of consciousness, an attitude that does not fulfil its purpose, and that they [symbols] would enable it to do if they were understood. But it becomes impossible to interpret their meaning if they are [as in Freud's sexual theory] reduced to something else' (CW 13:397).

Illustrating his point with reference to some of the later alchemists who recognized that the literal practice was 'unadapted' to its symbolic object, Jung continues:

> That is why some of the later alchemists, particularly in the sixteenth century, abhorred all vulgar substances [as Jung abhorred Freud's sexual dogma] and replaced them by 'symbolic' ones which allowed the nature of the archetype [of the numinous mother as the renewing life source] to glimmer through. This does not mean that the adept ceased to work in the laboratory, only that he kept his eye on the symbolic aspect of his transmutations. This corresponds exactly to the situation in modern psychology of the unconscious: while personal problems are not overlooked (the patient himself takes very good care of that!), the analyst keeps an eye on their symbolic aspects, for healing comes only from what leads the patient beyond himself and beyond his entanglement in the ego. (CW 13:397)

When in 1913 Jung experienced his final, psychically violent break with Freud, he realized that he had, in its violence, murdered his ego rather than sacrificed it. The rupture with Freud released the madness that his conversion to Freud had kept under control. In Freud's view, he had succumbed to what, according to Jung, Freud described as '"the black tide of mud."' 'And here,' Jung continues, 'he hesitated for a moment, then added, "of occultism"' (MDR 150). Jung's ego drowned in the vast ocean of the unconscious and the rescue of it became on both the literal and symbolic levels (as an 'adept,' he 'never ceased to work in the laboratory') his lifetime's work, knowing in the performance of the work that the literal is always already symbolic insofar as it is perceived. Madness resides in the absolute zero point in which the intuitive recognition of the undifferentiated identity of matter and spirit is radically in excess of the consciousness of it. Consciousness depends upon the logic of their differentiation understood as a necessary deferral (Derrida's '*différance*') of truth. Truth, like the archetype, is always in excess of its metaphorical apperception. The madness that overcame Jung after his break with Freud was an undifferentiated state in which, knowing nothing, subject and object as the conscious occasion or condition of each other had ceased to exist. It was the madness of the zero point, which Derrida identifies with the moment of Descartes's Cogito devoid of any consciousness of itself, or Nietzsche's longing to live '*unhistorically*' and go, like the grazing herd, 'in[to] the present, like a number without any awkward fraction left over' ('On the Uses' 61), the latter being the unconsummated desire informing the mathematical work of the quantum physicist, Wolfgang Pauli. '*Just as physics seeks completeness, your analytical psychology seeks a home,*' Pauli wrote to Jung. 'For there is no denying the fact that psychology, like an illegitimate child of the spirit, leads an esoteric, special existence beyond the fringe of what is generally acknowledged to be the academic world.' Psychology's '*home*' is in the new quantum physics in which what is observed depends upon the psychic presence of the observer. 'Whether and when this *coniunctio* will be realized I do not know,' Pauli continues, 'but I am in no doubt at all that this would be the finest fate that could happen to both physics and psychology' (*Atom* 122).

The sexual nature of repression evident in the incest taboo as described by Freud in *Totem und Taboo* (1912), partly with the intention of getting rid of Jung, whom Freud now considered 'mad,' was, for Jung, the conscious action of the ego in its shaping of a defence structure based upon the repression of what Jung considered its profound religious meaning. While recognizing in certain cases the repressive influence of a sexual trauma, Jung, in dealing with his patients at the Burghölzli, recognized larger cultural and religious factors at work, which Freud reduced to the psychosexual. In his work on the dreams and fantasies of mental patients the unconscious was not simply a vast reservoir of repressed sexuality; it was, on the contrary, what he would later call the 'collective unconscious,' a vast reservoir of genetically inherited material that leaves its traces inscribed in the ceaseless operations of the brain. There, nightly in dream, with the withdrawal of the ego, this material takes the form of images that in the insane may assume complete control. After his break with Freud, Jung feared he might, like Nietzsche and Hölderlin, be destroyed by an 'incessant stream of fantasies' (*MDR* 176) that he could not control. At the same time, he recognized in these fantasies a break with, rather than an extension of, the 'animal soul' that is the very ground of human nature *as* human. The descent into madness contains within it, however precariously, the birth of the human.

In *The Triumph of Life*, his final fragment assembled and published posthumously, Shelley explores this realm as what he calls 'this valley of perpetual dream,' which is answerable to a 'realm without a name' (396–7). Mediating between them is an anima figure, whose dancing feet leave traces of the nameless realm on the brain. Shelley names her Iris, the goddess of the rainbow, suggesting that the nameless realm is the 'white radiance of Eternity,' which in *Adonais* is refracted through a 'dome of many-coloured glass' (462–3). Shelley's announced desire is to smash the dome of the phenomenal world and enter the imageless realm of the noumenal. In the tedious act of composition, he must witness the inevitable decline of his inspiration, so that what finally emerges on the white sheet is 'a feeble shadow' of his 'original conception.' '"And suddenly my brain became as sand,"' declares the Shade of Rousseau,

'Where the first wave had more than half erased
The track of deer on desert Labrador,
  Whilst the fierce wolf from which they fled amazed,

'Leaves his stamp visibly upon the shore
  Until the second bursts – so on my sight
Burst a new Vision never seen before.'   (405–11)[9]

The inspiration that Shelley in his *Defence of Poetry* embraces as the 'divine insanity' of Plato's *Ion* becomes in the 'new Vision never seen before' a demonic parody of it. Divine 'insanity' has descended to mere 'insanity.' Shelley in *The Triumph of Life* is exploring psychosis much as Jung explored it with his patients and, after his break with Freud, in himself.

Describing his slow, deeply disturbing (rather than sudden) awakening to the fact that he was a poet, Shelley, anticipating Jung's analysis of the psyche in his essay, 'On Life,' attributes it to what he calls 'the most refined abstractions of logic' that, in his case, 'conduct[ed him] to a view of life which, though startling to the apprehension, is in fact that which the habitual sense of its repeated combinations has extinguished in us.' The logic, he explains, stripped 'the painted curtain from this scene of things' (*SPP* 476). The 'painted curtain' is the habitual or passive mode of perception in which 'all objects, as objects,' are, as Coleridge describes them, 'essentially fixed and dead,' or, as Shelley describes it, 'blunted by reiteration' (*DP* 506). 'I confess,' Shelley concludes, 'that I am one of those who am unable to refuse my assent to the conclusions of those philosophers, who assert that nothing exists but as it is perceived' ('On Life' 476). Nothing exists, that is, but as metaphor, which is what language is.

Shelley goes on to explain that he was 'convicted' by the logic long before he was 'convinced' of it, his conviction that he was never a poet in his few years of poetical practice separating itself from the notion that the writing of poetry was a liberating crime in which he was as much a Christ as he was a Cain. Thus, when, in *Adonais*, Urania (Milton's Muse adopted by Shelley and abortively by Wordsworth) asks him who he is, Shelley, in the guise of Dionysus, 'with a sudden hand / Made bare his branded and ensanguined brow, / Which was like Cain's or Christ's.' 'Oh! that it should be so!' (304–6), the forever dying (and reviving) poet declares. 'It is,' Shelley confesses in 'On Life,' 'a decision against which all our persuasions struggle, and we must be long convicted, before we can be convinced that the solid universe of external things is "such stuff as dreams are made of [on]"' (*SPP* 476).

The 'decision against which all our persuasions struggle' is the decision against materialism understood as the omnipotence and omniscience of matter, Coleridge's 'mechanical philosophy' to a rejection of which he devotes five chapters of his *Biographia Literaria* (which Shelley clearly had read). 'The shocking absurdities of the popular philosophy of mind and matter, and its fatal consequences in morals, their violent dogmatism concerning the source of all things,' writes Shelley, 'had early conducted me to materialism. This materialism is a seducing system to young and superficial minds. It allows its disciples to talk and dispenses them from thinking.[10] But I was discontented with such a view of things as it afforded; man is a being of high aspirations "looking both before and after," whose "thoughts that wander through eternity," disclaim alliance with transience and decay, incapable of imagining to himself annihilation, existing but in the future and the past, being not what he is, but what he has been, and shall be' (*SPP* 476). Man is 'not what he is.' He cannot inhabit himself so long as he remains bound to the phenomenal realm of the senses understood as a 'valley of perpetual dream.' The function of the dream, as Shakespeare enacts it, is to awaken the dreamer to the realization that the dream 'defeats the curse which binds us to be subjected to the accident of surrounding impressions.' 'And whether it spreads its own figured curtain or withdraws life's dark veil from before the scene of things,' Shelley continues, 'it equally creates for us a being within our being. It makes us the inhabitants of a world to which the familiar world is a chaos' (*DP* 505). 'The fringed curtains of thine eye advance / And say what thou seest yond,' Prospero commands Miranda, awakening her from her sleep to the reality of her dream that, in the person of Ferdinand, stands before her. 'What is't? A spirit?' Miranda asks. 'No wench,' Prospero replies; 'it eats, and sleeps, and hath such senses /As we have, such' (*Tempest* 1.2.408–10, 413–14). Largely with Byron's poetry in mind, Shelley had come to see that composition itself embodies rather than defeats the curse.

Shelley's reaction against 'the violent dogmatism concerning the source of all things' that had 'early conducted [him] to materialism' prefigures Jung's violent rejection of what he considered Freud's dogmatism concerning sexuality (with its equally 'fatal consequences in morals'), a dogmatism that Jung also had for a brief period considered 'a seducing system' – indeed, so 'seducing' that he became for a time Freud's heir apparent, assuming the role of Joshua in relation to Freud's Moses. Shelley's major work as a poet issues from his rejection of materialism in something of the same way that Jung's major work issues from his rejection of Freud's materialism. In each case, the rejection of materialism was experienced as both a curse and a blessing because of the radical isolation that attended it. So severe was their sense of isolation from the 'habitual' world that they became infected with the madness with which the 'habitual' labelled their isolation, a madness they in turn identified with their 'daemon' or genius. In a very real sense, the resolution of the Christ/Cain dichotomy described by Shelley became the basis of a dialectic that acts as what Shelley in *Adonais* calls the work's 'plastic stress' (381). Composition can murder inspiration, the Christ of the Gospels becoming the Cain of institutional religion. 'Torturing th'unwilling dross that checks its flight / To its own likeness, as each mass may bear' (384–5), psychically, if ironically, enacts the tyranny that Shelley politically resisted. Byron, reading cantos of *Don Juan* aloud to Shelley before they went to the printer, confronted Shelley with what he called, with reference to *Cain: a Mystery*, an 'apocalyptic ... revelation not before communicated to man' (*Letters* 2:388).

The crisis of Romanticism lay in consciousness. The problem lay not in what Shelley calls 'the mind in creation,' which, he suggests, is 'beyond and above consciousness' (*DP* 486). ('Poetry is not like reasoning, a power to be exerted according to the determination of the will. A man cannot say, "I will compose poetry"' [503].) The problem lay in bringing a critical consciousness to bear upon it. It lay, as it would lie for Jung, in bringing the unconscious into consciousness, knowing that the unconscious cannot be brought to consciousness without ceasing to be the unconscious. Since 'the deep truth' of the unconscious is 'imageless,' the representation of the 'imageless' in an image of it, which is the condition of consciousness, is self-defeating.[11] Consciousness confronts the Romantic poet in the act of composition with the feigning of the 'deep truth.' 'But this rough magic / I here abjure,' declares Prospero, his 'airy charm' having served its purpose. He decides to break his staff, and 'bury it certain fathoms in the earth.' As for his 'book' (his plays, as his magic), 'deeper than did ever plummet sound / [He'll] drown [his] book' (5.1.50–7). In the final stanzas of *Adonais*, Shelley also decides to drown his book. Naming his sailboat *Ariel* (Shakespeare's 'airy charm'), Shelley, in the midst of composing *The Triumph of Life*, set sail in it, never to return. 'The breath whose might I have invoked in song / Descends on me,' he writes in the concluding stanza of *Adonais*,

> my spirit's bark is driven,
> Far from the shore, far from the trembling throng
> Whose sails were never to the tempest [*The Tempest*] given;
> The massy earth and sphered skies are riven!
> I am borne darkly, fearfully, afar.   (487–92)

Writing his medical dissertation 'On the Psychology and Pathology of So-Called Occult Phenomena,' which prepared him for his work on schizophrenia at the Burghölzli, Jung, it may be argued, achieved his revolutionary understanding of the psyche through the 'occult' rather than, as in Freud's case, through science. Strongly opposing the materialism of science, Jung nevertheless attempted, against the immaterial, non-quantifiable nature of the psyche, to employ science's quantifiable, experimental methods. Experiment, he regretted, was simply the psyche observing itself, bound to its own prejudices. The way out he hoped to find in quantum physics, a science that, as distinct from Newtonian physics, seemed to prove that the operations of matter engage the operations of the unconscious as Jung understood them. The immaterial, unquantifiable motions of the psyche were immutably connected to the material, quantifiable motions of matter in such a way that the psyche behaved, or could behave, like matter and matter behaved, or could behave, like psyche in an acausal rather than causal manner. The acausality, which Jung called 'synchronicity,' suggested that they were two different, interchangeable manifestations of one and the same thing, their differences, like Coleridge's subject and object, being the essential condition of their sameness. The causally grounded nature of mathematics, as Pauli discovered, itself would have to shift its logical foundations if an equation was ever to be found that could unite into one the motions of psyche and matter as they interpenetrated each other to become a new understanding of the archetypal unknown that informs them both. For Jung, this new understanding was the fourfold, the soul itself as the containing form of a new psychic perception of reality.

By the nineteenth century, Jung told the members of his seminars on Nietzsche's *Thus Spake Zarathustra*, in which between 1934 and 1939 he explored in depth the nature of Nietzsche's psychosis, 'our mind, our whole mental development, wound up with complete materialism. The celestial world entirely disappeared ["God is dead," cried Nietzsche's madman in *The Gay Science*. "*We have killed him you and I*"] and only a few idealists were left crying for help, for support for their shaking ideals; and with the war the whole thing tumbled down for good' (*Nietzsche's* Zarathustra 1:243–4). During the autumn of 1913, Jung experienced the 'tumbling down' of the 'celestial world' in a series of overwhelming visions in which he 'saw a monstrous flood covering all the northern and low-lying lands between the North Sea and the Alps. When it came to Switzerland [he] saw that the mountains grew higher and higher to protect [the] country. [He] realized that a frightful catastrophe was in progress.' Two weeks later the vision recurred, the conditions more vivid than before, the blood more emphasized. An inner voice spoke to him: "Look at it well; it is wholly real and it will be so. You cannot doubt it." Ruling out a revolution, not considering an outbreak of war, Jung decided he 'was menaced by a psychosis.' In the spring and early summer of 1914, he dreamt on three occasions that in mid-summer the whole land lay frozen, devoid of human life. As soon as the war broke out, his first task was 'to probe the depths of [his] own psyche' and explore the way in which his inner experience corresponded to outer events, a correspondence that led to his notion of the 'collective unconscious' and, in a more complex way, to his notion of 'synchronicity' as an acausal connection between inner and outer, between psyche and matter. Unless the unconscious was subjected to a 'psycho-analysis' of it as a way of bringing its operations into consciousness, the unconscious, he realized, could easily delude him into believing (as distinct from knowing) he was a prophet endowed with revelatory, healing powers. In one of the deep-frost dreams, the cold descended 'out of the cosmos' in the midst of which 'stood a leaf-bearing tree, but without fruit,' which Jung interpreted as his 'tree of life.' Its 'leaves,' he writes, 'had been transformed by the effects of the frost into sweet grapes full of healing juices.' Plucking them, he 'gave them to a large, waiting crowd' (*MDR* 175–6).

Jung then goes on to describe the inner process of transforming the grapes into wine. 'An incessant stream of fantasies had been released,' he writes, 'and I did my best not to lose my head but to find some way to understand these strange things. I stood helpless before an alien world ... When I endured these assaults of the unconscious I had an unswerving conviction that I was obeying a higher will, and that feeling continued to uphold me ['Others have been shattered by them – Nietzsche and Hölderlin'] until I mastered the task' (*MDR* 176–7). What saved him, he explained, was finding the hidden images in the emotions that attached the 'assaults of the unconscious' to mental images perceived by the operations of the brain. A 'higher will' was commanding him to find the images hidden in sensations pounding at his senses. He started to write what appeared to be dictated to him, analysing as best he could the psychic conditions under which the writing assumed the form of "high-flown language" so grating that he could only compare it to someone drawing his nails down a plaster wall or scraping his knife against a plate. 'Sometimes,' he explains, 'it was as if I were hearing it with my ears, sometimes feeling it with my mouth, as if my tongue were formulating words; now and then I heard myself whispering aloud. Below the threshold of consciousness everything was seething with life' (177–8).

Jung's psychotic introduction to the 'mind in creation,' which, Shelley writes, 'some invisible influence, like an inconstant wind, awakens to transitory brightness,' the 'conscious portions of our natures' remaining 'unprophetic either of its approach or its departure' (*DP* 504), led him to reject for himself the role of the artist in a way that Nietzsche failed to reject it. 'When I was writing down these fantasies,' Jung confesses, 'I once asked myself, "What am I really doing? Certainly this has nothing to do with science. But then what is it?" Whereupon a voice within me said, "It is art." I was astonished. It had never entered my head that what I was writing had any connection with art. Then I thought, "Perhaps my unconscious is forming a personality that is not me, but which is insisting on coming through to expression." I knew for a certainty that the voice had come from a woman, I recognized it as the voice of a patient, a talented psychopath who had a strong transference to me. She had become a living figure within my mind' (*MDR* 185). Fortunately, he did not think the 'talented psychopath' was the voice of the Holy Spirit.

Jung apparently went on writing, the anima, the feminine voice within him who gave him access to the unconscious, still insisting it was art. 'This time I caught her,' he declares, 'and said, "No, it is not art! On the contrary, it is nature."' Jung prepared to argue with her as he had with Freud. In his argument with Freud over occult phenomena, his diaphragm, he explains, became 'red hot – a glowing vault' (*MDR* 155), his anger resulting in two detonations in Freud's bookcase, which they feared was about to tumble down on both of them. No such violent encounter, however, took place in his resistance to his psychopathic anima. 'I reflected that the "woman within me" did not have the speech centers I had,' Jung explains. 'And so I suggested that she use mine. She did so and came through with a long statement' (186). Jung does not describe what she came through with. However, in writing down the fantasies he did, apparently against his will, treat them as art, transferring them from a Black Book embellished with mandala drawings to a Red Book, which he also embellished. In the Red Book he tried a further 'esthetic elaboration,' which, he says, he never finished because he knew he had to get away from the art that embarrassed him and 'translate it into something else.' 'I gave up this estheticizing tendency in good time, in favor of a rigorous process of *understanding*,' he writes reflectively, close to the end of his life. Had he not, he explains, the 'mythopoeic imagination,' which 'fatally confuse[s] the mental patient' (188), would have destroyed him. 'Thus the insinuations of the anima, the mouthpiece of the unconscious,' he concludes, 'can utterly destroy a man. In the final analysis the decisive factor is always consciousness, which can understand the manifestations of the unconscious and take up a position toward them' (187).

Associating 'the insinuations of the anima' with opium, Coleridge also knew they could utterly destroy him. Originally conceived as an introduction to a volume of his poetry, *Sibylline Leaves*, which he told Wordsworth he could finish 'in two or at farthest three days' (*Collected Letters* 4:576), he decided instead to extend the preface to what became *Biographia Literaria*. The decision eventually became a two-volume exploration of the 'mind in creation.' Fully aware of all the dangers involved (including the 'dramatic truth' of 'delusion' [*BL* 2:6]), Coleridge sought in his 100-page unwritten chapter on the imagination to establish on a sound metaphysical foundation what became, in certain respects, an original analysis of the operations of the psyche as the transformation of matter. For personal as well as collective reasons, Coleridge realized in the writing and dictating of *Biographia Literaria* that the reality of Romanticism lay in critical theory understood as the mind's analysis of its own operations, rather than in the poetry that provided the evidence for it. The *Biographia Literaria* became for Coleridge a 'psycho-analysis' of the poet, the object of which was to release the poet from an addiction to delusion which the writing of poetry tended in him unconsciously to induce.

The problem of addiction or possession, implicit if not explicit in Coleridge's *Biographia* and many Romantic poems, is explicitly treated by Jung in his analysis of Nietzsche's psychosis. When Jung explained to the members of the seminar that the 'celestial world' had 'entirely disappeared' into matter, leaving 'a few idealists ... crying for help,' he asked Blake's question:

When the stars threw down their spears
And water'd heaven with their tears:
Did he smile his work to see?
Did he who made the Lamb make thee?   ('The Tyger' 17–20)

'What has the mind done in the ground?' is Jung's more prosaic translation, which, in terms of understanding, protected him from the poetic dangers of Blake. A member of the seminar who knew Jung's answer to his rhetorical question replied: 'The new physics has turned the ground into spirit.' 'Yes,' answered Jung, settling more deeply into his own thoughts, 'the new physics has done the trick, exploded matter altogether, and the most recent development is reported in an article by a very modern physicist, in which he shows how modern physics becomes psychology; they climb in at the bottom of the collective unconscious.' The same seminar member then asked: 'how did they get into the collective unconscious?' To which, hearing the question as if he had just asked it himself, Jung replied: 'Through the fact that when you observe the phenomenon of the interior of the atom, you find that your observation disturbs the thing you observe; and if you go on observing, you observe the thing that disturbs, you discover the psyche. They are now dealing with the telepathic phenomenon, namely, the fact that the collective unconscious – what *I* call the collective unconscious – is a factor which is not properly in time and not properly in space. So the spirit that descended into the earth [as the triumph of materialism] has exploded matter, and come up again in the form of [analytical] psychology' (*Nietzsche's* Zarathustra 1:244).

Jung conducted this particular seminar on 14 November 1934, well before the splitting of the atom and the explosion of the first atomic bomb. The immediate context of the discussion is Zarathustra's noon-tide ('the sun stood at noon-tide') vision of an eagle in flight with a serpent coiled round its neck, though 'not like a prey, but like a friend.' '"These are mine animals," said Zarathustra, and rejoiced in his heart' (1:226). Zarathustra rejoicing in the union of the opposites (eagle as spirit, serpent as body) is Nietzsche's *Übermensch* (Superman) resolving in 'less than a pulsation of the artery' (*M* 28[30].62) the ancient opposition between psyche and matter, good and evil, night and day, as if the opposition never existed as other than a delusion of consciousness. Nietzsche in his madness has, Jung argues, released the unconscious psyche from the dialectical process of consciousness by which it becomes soul. 'You see,' Jung explained to the members of the seminar,

> the instincts always come up from the unconscious and give us a hint, perhaps in a dream. For, suppose I am identical with an archetype; I don't know it and the archetype of course won't tell me, because I am already possessed and inundated by the archetype. If it is the wise old man [Zarathustra], he will seek only to express himself, and the human instrument he is actually using [Nietzsche], say in the year 1883 [the first three parts of *Thus Spake Zarathustra* were published in 1883], doesn't count at all ... That is the way an archetype uses man, simply as an instrument, as a tool of a most transitory kind. We make a fuss about our lives, but nature makes no fuss whatever; if nature likes to wipe out several million people she quietly does so. In a war we wipe out the best of men by the million. Well, that is quite natural, that is war. We can do it because we are used by an archetype: people are all possessed and wiped out by each other. And that is what nature does. So the man Nietzsche counts precious little to the archetype. He just happens to be the tool. But the man is of course in an awful situation. He is possessed and he cannot defend himself, for he doesn't know he is possessed, and that is a wonderful opportunity for the unconscious. (*Nietzsche's* Zarathustra 1:231–2)

Jung's point about 'the phenomenon of the interior of the atom' being disturbed by the observer is that the disturber *is* the unconscious psyche using the quantum physicist as Zarathustra used Nietzsche. When men are in the grip of an archetype, they become its unconscious instruments, a 'tool of a most transitory kind.' From the point of view of the archetype, which is the point of view of nature, the splitting of the atom can, as the work of nature, 'wipe out several million people' without making any fuss about it. If possessed by the archetype, it all seems perfectly natural, though in human fact 'what nature does' as nature leaves the human beings 'in an awful situation' about which they can do nothing so long as they remain 'possessed,' unable to defend themselves. Wolfgang Pauli left Princeton and returned to Zurich and to Jung partly because he refused to participate in the Manhattan Project or to live in a country whose government was prepared to finance it in order to kill the enemy. For him, the splitting of the atom was not the work of nature, the collective unconscious. It was an *opus contra naturam.* Again with Jung in Zurich, he worked with his fantasies and dreams to bring the unconscious psyche to consciousness in order better to understand the disturbance caused by the observer in quantum physics. The 'spirit that had descended to earth as the triumph of [scientific] materialism' replacing the 'celestial world' had, indeed, 'exploded matter.' The issue was now 'in the form of psychology' to confront the splitting of the atom as the opening of the unconscious psyche to a consciousness of its operations.

The explosion of matter as the burial of spirit in earth is archetypally Zarathustra's ecstatic 'noon-tide' vison of the eagle and serpent embracing as friends. Jung calls it the 'psychoid archetype' in which psyche and matter, as 'two different aspects of one and the same thing,' meet 'in a point without extension – a real zero-point,' where they 'touch and do not touch' (CW 8:418).[12] Touching and yet not touching leaves a space, a gap, for consciousness to operate. That gap separates madness from sanity. The closure of the gap is madness.

If, that is, the gap is kept open, so that madness can be consciously interrogated rather than rejected, the dialectical engagement with madness becomes what Blake calls a ceaseless 'Mental Fight' (M 1.13). In Zarathustra's noon-tide vision ('The sun will not rise until noon' [PU 2.5.10]) of the eagle in flight wrapt in the embrace of the snake (friend rather than foe), Jung saw (or projected) Nietzsche's incipient psychosis as the mirror of a larger one shaping in Germany, which, he feared, might soon encompass the whole of Europe. Another version of this psychosis, its depressed rather than its manic pole, is to be found in Shelley's image of the Visionary in *Alastor* explored in my final chapter.

He compares his Visionary in his pursuit of the anima, which threatened to possess him as much as it threatened to possess Jung, to 'an eagle grasped / In the folds of the green serpent.' Instead of a loving embrace, however, the eagle 'feels her breast / Burn with the poison.' The visionary quest, now become a hallucination rather than a dialectic, 'precipitates' the eagle poet, 'frantic with dizzying anguish,' in a 'blind flight / O'er the wide aëry wilderness' (227–32).

Throughout his entire life, beginning in early childhood, Jung had reason to fear the archetypal world of the collective unconscious. His whole career, it may be argued, lay in analysing in the name of sanity the psychological process by which, as consciousness, the human being differentiates himself from it without losing creative contact with it. This process of differentiation is the *opus contra naturum* to which he remained committed, knowing all too well the ever present danger of madness as the unconscious realm of nature itself to which both biologically and psychically humanity must remain bound while at the same time struggling to release itself from it. In the tension between nature and culture, understood as the psychological tension between death and life, lay, for Jung, the playing field of psychology in which life itself becomes for the conscious human being the symbol that best embodies the ultimate mystery of death. 'If meaninglessness were absolutely predominant [as it is in nature itself], the meaningfulness of life would vanish to an increasing degree with each step in our development. But this is – or seems to me – not the case. Probably, as in all metaphysical questions, both are true: Life is – or has – meaning and meaninglessness. I cherish the anxious hope that meaning will predominate and win the battle' (*MDR* 359).

2

Frye's Blake: The Site of Opposition

A man who is born falls into a dream like a man who falls into the sea. If he tries to climb out into the air as inexperienced people endeavour to do, he drowns – *nicht wahr*? ... No! I tell you! The way is to the destructive element submit yourself, and with the exertion of your hands in the water make the deep sea keep you up.

Joseph Conrad, Lord Jim

Like the alchemical end product, which always betrays its essential duality, the united personality will never quite lose its painful sense of innate discord.

Carl Gustav Jung, 'The Psychology of Transference'

To exist historically means that knowledge of oneself can never be complete.

Hans-Georg Gadamer, Truth and Method

Jung and Frye

'Jung, in describing himself,' writes Donald Winnicott in his review of *Memories, Dreams, Reflections*, 'gives us a picture of childhood schizophrenia, and at the same time his personality displays a strength of a kind which enabled him to heal himself. At cost he recovered, and part of the cost to him is what he paid out to us, if we can listen and hear, in terms of his exceptional insight. Insight into what? Insight into the feelings of those who are mentally split' (*Psycho-Analytic Explorations* 483). As a compensation for his 'psychotic breakdown' at the age of three, Jung, Winnicott argues, developed a secret self, which allowed him to commune with his psychosis as a form of revelation (gnosis). In his memoirs (which Frye considered his greatest work), Jung healed the split by affirming his 'No. 2 personality' as his direct access to an archetypal reality within the collective unconscious, a higher reality to which his conservative 'No.1 personality' was necessarily subordinated. 'The daemon of creativity has ruthlessly[1] had its way with me,' Jung writes (*MDR* 358). 'The ordinary undertakings I planned usually had the worst of it – though not always and not everywhere. By way of compensation, I think, I am conservative to the bone.' Winnicott, I suggest, wrongly argues that Jung's 'No. 1 personality' was what Winnicott calls a 'False Self,' which nevertheless 'gave Jung a place in the world, and a rich family and professional life' (488). Identifying Jung's 'No. 2 personality' with 'infantile omnipotence,' Winnicott concludes that its psychological achievement as 'the centre of his self' was 'an obsessional flight from disintegration' (491). 'The centre of the self,' he argues, 'is a relatively useless concept.[2] What is more important is to reach to the basic forces of individual living, and to me it is certain that if the real basis is creativeness the very next thing is destruction' (491).

By focusing upon 'the basic forces of individual living,' Winnicott ignores the larger cultural issues with which Jung's archetypal psychology is directly concerned. He ignores the cultural fact that Jung's 'picture of childhood schizophrenia' was, in Jung's treatment of it, bound to the death of the Christian revelation as manifest in his father's religion and the psychotic rebirth of a long-repressed pagan religion that constituted what he called his mother's 'No. 2 personality.' Viewed in terms of her mental breakdown during Jung's childhood,[3] Jung had every reason to fear this compensatory rebirth in his mother as well as in himself. 'Like anyone who is capable of some introspection,' Jung explains, 'I had early taken it for granted that the split in my personality was my own purely personal affair and responsibility. Faust, to be sure, had made the problem somewhat easier for me by confessing, "Two souls, alas, are housed within my breast"; but he had thrown no light on the cause of this dichotomy. His insight seemed, in a sense, directed straight at me. In the days when I first read *Faust* [at the recommendation of his mother] I could not remotely guess the extent to which Goethe's strange heroic myth was a collective experience and that it prophetically anticipated the fate of the Germans' (*MDR* 234). While in his youth, Jung 'could not remotely guess' that his own personal problems were collective ones that, among other things, 'anticipated the fate of the Germans,' he gradually realized that a 'collective problem, if not recognized as such, always appears as a personal problem, and in individual cases may give the impression that something is out of order in the realm of the personal psyche. The personal sphere is indeed disturbed, but such disturbances need not be primary; they may well be secondary, the consequence of an insupportable change in the social atmosphere. The cause of disturbance is, therefore, not to be sought in the personal surroundings, but rather in the collective situation. Psychotherapy has hitherto taken this matter far too little into account' (233–4).

Jung rejected 'childhood schizophrenia' as a medical diagnosis in favour of a larger cultural diagnosis, which he was destined, if not to resolve, at least to endow with an archetypal understanding as a collective psychosis intimately bound to the light that Goethe, Wagner, Nietzsche, and National Socialism cast upon it. This light, Jung, via his mother, constellated in the archetypal figure of Wotan.[4] Creativity, for Jung, lay not in 'an obsessional flight from disintegration.' It lay, as it lay for Goethe, Wagner, and Nietzsche, in a descent into its psychotic core as an archetypal source of new life that had to be analytically channelled into a new understanding of it if it was not to annihilate western civilization in somewhat the same way that it annihilated Nietzsche. Jung explored this annihilation in his seminars on *Thus Spake Zarathustra,* which, against a backdrop of the rise of National Socialism in Germany, he conducted in Zurich between 1934 and 1939. For this reason, Jung, writing his medical thesis 'On Psychology and Pathology of So-Called Occult Phenomena,' accepted an appointment as an assistant at the Burghölzli Mental Hospital, where he spent the next ten years archetypally exploring the mythopoeic phenomena of his schizophrenic patients, less in the hope of healing them than as a laboratory in which to explore the unconscious operations of a collective psychosis.

Jung's cultural approach to schizophrenia as the unconscious enactment of 'an insupportable change in the social atmosphere' was partially shared by Frye. Although he considered Julian Jaynes's explanation of schizophrenia in *The Origin of Consciousness in the Breakdown of the Bicameral Mind* (1976) a valuable contribution to his own archetypal criticism, Frye complained about Jaynes's 'purely negative' treatment of 'hallucination' and 'schizophrenia.' Relating the terms to the prophetic imagination, Frye argues that Jaynes's book 'overlook[s] the constant tradition in poets to get *past* the tyranny of consciousness [Jung's 'No. 1 personality'] and reinforce it with a driving power that ... certainly isn't satisfied with the linear-discursive processes of the conscious mind' (*Notebooks* 5:161). Because 'in the Biblical myth there is no complementary creative force to set against the artificial creation of God, no earth-mother or sexual creator,' Frye argues, the 'cycle of nature' as the menstrual domain of the feminine took its place. As a result, though for Frye (as for Blake) 'Jesus is a redeemer,' 'Christian civilization [bound to nature] emphatically was not: it merely set up the old projection figures of gods, angels, priests and kings once again' ('Expanding' 112), binding Christ to Thanatos, the dead tree of inorganic matter described by Freud in *Beyond the Pleasure Principle*.[5] For Frye, the binding of Christ to the dead tree contains within it the binding of Christ to Mother Church and the binding of Adam to Eve. Far from releasing man from his imprisonment in what Frye describes as 'the demonic aspect of historical time,' the crucifixion interpreted as the moral law 'wholly imprisoned' (112–13) him within it. 'The Word, the male principle,' Frye writes with reference to Milton's 'left wing Protestant' Pauline position, 'should have "absolute rule"; the Church has only to murmur "unargued I obey." The autonomous Church, who claims the authority to teach the Word herself, is in the position of the unfaithful bride or harlot'[6] (*Stubborn Structure* 156). Setting the Christ of the gospels against 'Christian civilization' as the demonic parody of the Redeemer, Frye argues that 'Christ in the gospels, notably John, is portrayed as someone in which the "right [schizophrenic] lobe" of the brain has completely taken over: he can do nothing except what he sees the Father do. John in particular seems to be trying to force us to say: if this man wasn't what he said he was he was certainly the most deranged lunatic on record' (*Notebooks* 5:161–2).

In identifying the Christ of the gospels with the mythopoeic imagination, Frye avoids Jung's clinical exploration of it as psychosis by binding it to the Logos or Word, not as it is dogmatically interpreted by Christian theology or enacted in a sacramental order, but as he received it from Blake, who 'went much farther than anyone else in his day in identifying religion and human creativity' (*Great Code* xiv). 'In the study of literature,' Frye writes,

> the element of personal authority, surrendering one's own imagination to that of some master of it, cannot be eliminated, and the relation of master and disciple always remains at its centre, though the master is more commonly a writer of the past than an actual teacher. What gets the serious student really hooked into the study of literature is likely to be a feeling of a common element in life-style with some author whose interest for him is not exhausted by the scholarly work he does on him (he may of

course work on something quite different). I got hooked into Blake in this way very early, partly because I had been brought up in much the same evangelical sub-culture that Blake had developed from, and because he made an amount of imaginative sense out of that sub-culture that I had never dreamed was possible. Other people would find, and have found, very different points of contact with Blake: this happened to be mine. ('Expanding' 103)

Frye's Christ is essentially Blake's. Next to *Fearful Symmetry*, which Frye described as a deeply personal book, *The Great Code* best reveals the depth of Blake's influence. 'By the standards of conventional scholarship,' he writes, '*The Great Code* was a silly and sloppy book.' To which he adds: 'It was also a work of very great genius. The point is that genius is not enough' (*Notebooks* 5:160). Having abandoned, like Blake and Jung, the projection of a myth of Resurrection and recovered it for the human mind, Frye was determined to release the Christian Bible from the 'exploitation' of Christian civilization into the autonomous freedom of the human imagination. 'Once we have recovered our imaginative birthright,' he declares, 'we can look down on the world we have left behind and see that it forms a demonic parody of the world we are now in' ('Expanding' 111).

Far from looking down on an abandoned world, which Frye dismisses as psychotic, however, Blake and Jung actively engaged it as the necessary condition of its resurrection. For Blake, the resurrected body is the awakening of the 'Vegetable Body' to a fourfold consciousness of its powers, an awakening that Blake enacts in Milton's journey from the metatarsus of Blake's left foot to his brain, Ololon, Milton's Muse, journeying from out the portals of his brain down the nerves of his right arm into his writing hand. For Jung, the resurrected body is the consciousness of the operations of the unconscious psyche that, as the threefold, constitute the 'Sexual' ('The Sexual is Threefold: the Human is Fourfold') life of the senses in their active creation of what, as the fourfold, they eternally perceive. Winnicott's analysis of Jung's self-healing as 'an obsessional flight from disintegration' that left him in a resurrected world applies more accurately to Frye than to Jung. Frye describes it, not as 'renewal or rebirth in time, even when it uses such imagery, but rather [as] the opposite of rebirth, a movement upward into a different world' ('Expanding' 114). Frye describes this 'different world' as the 'Creator alone in nothing whom we meet on page one of all orthodox cosmogonies' (*Fearful* 431), a world that Winnicott, following Freud, psychologically describes as 'infantile omnipotence.' Returning more than once to Jaynes's notion of schizophrenia issuing as hallucination from the right lobe of the bicameral brain, Frye remarks that it is 'the kind of thing that makes us instinctively call the most mentally disturbed geniuses "prophetic."' Focusing briefly on 'the continuity between inner gods and the subconscious,' he argues that it is more rationally understood when this 'inner authority' is objectified in his 'authoritarian four-level structure' in which the 'ascending ladder is part of a "bicameral" recovery' (*Notebooks* 5:149).

An essential distinction between Jung and Frye lies in their very different treatment of what Blake calls the 'excrementitious' (*J* 88.39). Struggling in vain to absorb the many books on Christian theology available to him in his father's library, Jung describes his mounting anxiety in terms of a waking dream in which God, seated on his throne in heaven, drops a huge turd on the shining dome of Basel Cathedral and brings it down. Though the youthful Jung in his rite of puberty experienced a new sense of release, he knew at the same time that he was not thereby rid of God, whom he had now to find in the shit itself, which is to say in psychosis.[7] At the same age as Jung, Frye, as we shall see, on his way to high school suddenly cast off 'the shitty and smelly garment' of the fundamentalism in which he was raised, knowing that it was no longer a part of him. Describing the archetypes as the 'building blocks' (*Great Code* 48) of the eternal structure of the Logos or Word, Frye rejected Jung's more 'highly idiosyncratic sense' (*World* 203) of them as the chaotic energies of the collective unconscious that had to be pressed into the service of an ever evolving notion of the Logos, lest they imprison the mind in the autonomy of their otherwise psychotic operations. The 'excrementitious' as Blake describes it in *Jerusalem* is 'the dusky fires of Los's Forge' where Los's Spectre, 'eyeing / Enitharmon [Los's Emanation or Bride],' rejoices in her 'lulling cadences.' As she scatters '[Los's] love on the wind / Eastward into her own Center,' from her 'Female Womb' emerges Blake's hermaphroditic vision of the Antichrist 'stretchd over Europe & Asia' as a 'Human Dragon terrible' (*J* 88.44–52; 89.11–12).

Blake's apocalyptic vision is far more involved with the shaping of the Antichrist than it is with the Second Coming. Indeed, the Second Coming is concealed within the Antichrist, awaiting the release that depends upon the recognition of the Antichrist. Palamabron, who is Blake at Felpham, calls down in the 'Bards prophetic Song' (*M* 2.22), which serves as the Preludium to *Milton*, 'a Great Solemn Assembly /

That he who will not defend Truth, may be compelld to / Defend a Lie, that he may be snared & caught & taken' (8.46–8). 'And all Eden descended into Palamabrons tent,' Blake continues. There '[a]mong Albions Druids & Bards, in the caves beneath Albions / Death Couch, in the caverns of death,' Palamabron prays to God to 'protect [him] from [his] friends, that they have not power over [him]' (9.1–5). The site of Blake's vision is Albion's 'Death Couch,' where Albion gradually awakens from a 6,000-year nightmare, Newton's 'Trump' (*Europe* 13.5), sounding for Blake in Milton's *Paradise Lost*, serving as the alarum.

'The mythological universe of Christianity,' Frye explains, 'retained a close analogy with the human body: God was associated with the sky and the brain, the devils with the organs of excretion below. Any rising movement, attempting to leave the demonic world behind, would have to determine what and how much would have to be symbolically excreted. Because of the close anatomical connection of the genital and excretory systems, and even more because of society's constant fear of Eros, sexual love, even the physical body itself, was often included among the things that had to be left behind' ('Expanding' 115). Far from leaving the physical body behind, Blake descended into its psychotic state, as he saw it writ large both in Milton's *Paradise Lost* and in the demonically triangulated ('the Sexual is Threefold') relations at Felpham between his patron Hayley (Satan), himself, and his wife, Catherine, as all of it became constellated in his own diarroeic 'Vegetable Body' for which – he wrote to Thomas Butts – Bacon, Newton, and Pitt would prescribe a medicine, not realizing that 'Distress inflicted by Heaven is a Mercy' (E 716). The casting off of Blake's 'shitty and smelly garment' lay in his dialectical analysis of it.

Frye's Fourfold Word

Like Jung, Northrop Frye was born into and 'brought up' in what Frye called a 'converted' world. His mother educated him at home until the fourth grade, passing on to him what she had been taught by her evangelical father without, however, necessarily believing it. She had, Frye suggests, far too much common sense (which he identified with his notion of the archetype) to accept her evangelical father's literalist reading of scripture whose God Frye would later identify with Blake's Urizen. Frye therefore received as a child what she had to say, not as she said it, but as the way she said it. He knew that the meaning she consciously imparted was not the meaning she secretly kept to herself

as a secret from herself. Becoming increasingly deaf, she found it difficult to hear what she was saying or what others were saying. What she
heard, or may have heard, in the growing silence of her deafness was a
silence that, at the psychological level, found an archetypal voice in
Frye. Like the voice of Thel in Blake's early vision, *The Book of Thel*, it
was in his mother the voice of the unborn, fearful of its own sound
because of the end of innocence it would, if heard, enact. 'Thel,' Frye
explains, 'is an imaginative seed: she could be any form of embryonic
life, from a human body to an artist's inspiration, and her tragedy could
be anything from a miscarriage to a lost vision' (Frye's mother named
Northrop after her own dead son). 'Being an embryo in the world of the
unborn,' Frye continues, 'Thel longs to be of "use," that is, to develop
her potential life into an actual one and hence come into our world of
Generation. Like all seeds, she has to be buried in her 'grave-plot' in
order to spring to life' (*Fearful* 232–3).

Blake's Orc is the energy that springs out of Thel's 'grave-plot' from
which Thel flees in terror. It is the repressed energy in the tone of his
mother's voice in which Frye unconsciously experienced what she did
not say in what she said. It was what Blake, in *The Marriage of Heaven
and Hell*, calls the voice of the devil. In his reading of Blake as an
undergraduate at Victoria College in Toronto, Frye discovered the voice
of the devil in himself, which his mother had lodged within him as an
unconscious covenant that carried, as energy repressed, the prophesy,
however dark, of an apocalyptic fulfilment. That is, his mother, in her
literal interpretation of the Bible passively received from her father,
tonally transmitted a figurative meaning suspended in the relationship
between them. 'Beulah,' Frye goes on to explain,

> is a place of perilous equipoise, being as it is the region of the imagination
> which falls short of the disciplined unity of art. Eden is 'human'; Beulah is
> 'sexual,' the region of passive pleasure, a Freudian land of dreams in
> which all images are erotic. Like its prototype in Spenser, it is a world
> where forms dissolve and substance does not ... As such, Beulah provides
> only a temporary escape from the world, not a permanent creation out of
> it. Wonder that does not stimulate art becomes vacuity: gratifications of
> appetite that do not build up a creative life become destructive. Every-
> thing that enters Beulah must quickly emerge either by the south or the
> north door; up to Paradise, or back again to this world. (233–4)

Frye, however, appears not to have made his exit by either the south
or the north gate, either 'up to Paradise, or back again to this world.'

Nor did he remain in Beulah. 'I've said quite frequently and meant it very intensely that I don't run my writing operation, my writing operation runs me,' Frye pointed out in an interview. 'Whatever it wants is what I've got to produce. What it doesn't want is what a novelist or a poet can produce' (*World* 218–19). That is, Frye did not follow the *mythos* of a poet like Blake, which carried his life through the south gate 'up to Paradise' via his descent into the lower world, not only to the 'grave-plot' of his creative power, but into the grave itself in which, as Ulro, he anatomizes his corpse. Thus, when Blake describes his brief epic, *Milton,* as 'the Divine Revelation in the Litteral expression' (42[49].14), he is describing the Biblical vision as he has lived it in his 'Vegetable Body.' While in a 'Moment: a Pulsation of the Artery' the epic was 'concievd' (*M* 29[31].2–3), the actual writing, engraving, printing and illumination of it in his 'Printing house in Hell' (*MHH* 15) was the work performed in the 'mortal state' to which his 'Soul returnd ... / To Resurrection & Judgment in the Vegetable Body' (*M* 42[49].26–7). As an archetypal critic, Frye inhabited Blake's realm of 'Divine Revelation,' not in his 'Vegetable Body,' but in what he called a 'hypothetical' (*Great Code* 231) body, which, as the absolute freedom of the conceivable answerable only to itself, is 'the Creator alone in nothing whom we meet on page one of all orthodox cosmogonies.' That is, the 'hypothetical' is not bound to the imagination, which Blake calls 'Human Existence itself' (*M* 32[35].32). It reaches beyond 'Existence,' in which the human is the total Fourfold form of the Creation to the absolute disincarnate reality of the 'I Am that I Am,' as distinct from 'I will be what I will be.' The latter is the fallen form of God which, Frye argues, is the God we meet in the Bible in the language of myth and metaphor, a God whom he describes as 'a verb implying a process accomplishing itself' (*Great Code* 17). The former is 'the Creator alone in nothing,' a noun standing alone in no need of accomplishing anything. Frye identifies this God with 'the Eastern "yoga," which liberates man by uniting him with God,' a union 'in which both the human creature and the superhuman Creator disappear' (*Fearful* 431). As an archetypal critic, Frye stands outside the creation, whether of God or the poet, 'alone in nothing,' rather like Oedipus at Colonus, who simply disappears.

Not surprisingly, Frye rejects the notion of allegory that would bind the poet's text or, indeed, the schematic anatomy of it that binds it to all texts, to 'corporeal' or 'mortal' life. When asked in an interview what went through his mind when he realized, after he had rewritten *Fearful Symmetry* four times, that it still required another complete rewriting,

Frye replied: 'There's a strong sense of something with its form, trying to achieve the form. The best thing you can do is stay out of its way' (*World* 238). Staying out of the way meant to Frye allowing the archetypes as the 'building blocks' of an eternal structure to do their work by removing the ego. 'The will power that it takes to start writing,' he explained in the same interview, 'comes from what you might loosely call the ego.' Frye then went on to describe writing an article for *Canadian Forum* in which, with mounting excitement, the introduction grew to the point where the ego decided it would have to be the first of a two-section article. Frye having settled for what the ego demanded, 'a little voice in [his] ear' said he 'should keep only one sentence of it.' At considerable cost to his ego (like Othello, never clear about the distinction between sacrifice and murder until he had made a fatal error), Frye (in the name of the archetype) 'cut the project down to a single article and kept the one sentence' (*World* 238).

While in Frye's published 'single article' the ego, as in almost everything he published, has been removed through the rewriting of several drafts, in Blake's two epics, the struggle between the archetypal form of the work and the ego that stands in the way becomes the dialectic of the imagination (Los working with his Spectre at the forge) without which the work, whether as ego or as archetype, would be formless. 'I begin [to write] like a kitten with a ball of yarn,' Frye explained in the interview. 'Everything is fouled up. The thing is to get hold of one end, so that the sequence of B following A and C following B becomes clear. Once that starts, then you've got a lead. Then you're on the way to writing' (*World* 239). 'I give you the end of a golden string,' writes Blake, addressing the Christians in the final chapter of his Fourfold epic, *Jerusalem*, which he knew the Christians, imprisoned in the institutional realms of the Twofold Generation and the Onefold Ulro, would never understand as anything more than 'a ball of yarn' fouled up by a mindless kitten. 'Only wind it into a ball,' Blake pleads, hopefully enticing the Christians to 'wind it into a ball' by telling them it would lead them 'in at Heavens gate, / Built in Jerusalems wall' (*J* 77). The 'end of a golden string' he metaphorically hands to a metaphorical reader (he knew there were no 'corporeal' ones). By a monumental disentangling effort, Blake himself had wound it into a ball, which he confidently described to his patron Thomas Butts as a 'Sublime Allegory which is now perfectly completed into a Grand Poem' (E 730). By July 1803 (when he wrote the letter), having left *The Four Zoas* in its unengraved state, Blake may still have been in the process of turning his twelve-book epic on Milton into a two-book Preludium to *Jerusalem*, which he may or may not have begun. It is therefore difficult to know what Blake meant by 'perfectly complete' as other than 'concievd' by what he calls 'the Authors ... in Eternity' of which he was 'the Secretary' (E 730). The 'Secretary' working in space and time, as distinct from 'the Authors' in a spaceless and timeless 'Eternity,' produces, 'once composition begins,' what Shelley calls 'a feeble shadow of the original conception' (*DP* 504). For Blake, the 'feeble shadow' is the Spectre, who, against its will, works with Los at the forge under a constant threat of annihilation. Blake's 'perfectly completed' epic may therefore be the 'Grand Poem,' as it exists with its 'Authors' in 'Eternity' rather than with their 'Secretary' in time, who often seemed to be in 'Eternity.' 'I have written this Poem from immediate Dictation twelve or sometimes twenty or thirty lines at a time without Premeditation & even against my Will,' he told Butts. '[T]he Time it has taken in writing was thus renderd Non Existent. & an immense Poem Exists which seems to be the Labour of a long Life producd without Labour or Study' (E 728–9). In Frye's letters, notebooks, diaries, and interviews, all of which are now appearing in the monumental Works series published by the University of Toronto Press, we can at last catch glimpses in Frye of Los at the forge with his Spectre. In Frye's finished and published works the Spectre (the ego) has largely disappeared.

Without the Spectre as the 'Opposition' necessary to the 'true Friendship' (*MIII* 20), which is creative composition, Blake would find himself in 'Eternity,' where the 'Authors,' now lacking a 'Secretary' to receive their dictation, would be 'alone in nothing.' Caught up in 'the prodigious and unthinkable metamorphosis of the human mind' (*Fearful* 432), as Frye describes it in his note on Blake's mysticism, Blake in Frye's afterword takes the 'short and inevitable step,' not only 'beyond *Jerusalem*' (431), but beyond the entire created world (including his own) to its unimaginable source: the 'I Am that I Am.' For Blake as poet, however, this 'short and inevitable step' is a step in the opposite direction. It is a descent into the 'Void Outside of Existence' (*M* 41[48].37), the realm of Satan, which he entered at Felpham. Blake allegorically enacts his descent into the Satanic 'Void' in the 'Bards prophetic Song,' which serves as the Preludium to *Milton*. 'Mark well my words! they are of your eternal salvation' (*M* 2.25). Blake more than once addresses the reader, who is both the Milton of *Paradise Lost* and the Milton in Blake whom Blake met in reading aloud *Paradise Lost* to his wife in the garden at Felpham. Blake's Milton marks well the Bard's words! By the end of the song, 'the loud voic'd Bard terrify'd took refuge in Miltons bosom' (14[15].9). Milton rose up within his epic to cast it off as the work of Satan. 'He took off the robe of the promise, & ungirded himself from the oath of God' (*M* 14[15].13), writes Blake. 'I go to Eternal Death!' Milton declares. 'I in my Selfhood am that Satan: I am that Evil One! / He is my Spectre! in my obedience to loose him from my Hells / To claim the Hells, my Furnaces, I go to Eternal Death!' (14[15].29–32).

Addressing a psychotic world, which for the Old Testament prophets is what history largely is, a poet-prophet like Blake himself must enter it as the demonic form of himself in order to redeem it. The prophetic power of Romanticism resides in the poet's descent into the psychosis of history, not as the detached observer of it, but as the active participant in it.[8] What distinguishes the psychosis that Blake enacts in his poetry from 'the Elect' who remain imprisoned within psychosis resides in the treatment of it. The 'Elect' bind themselves to psychosis as if it were their redemption, rather than a demonic parody of it. The 'Elect,' writes Blake, 'cannot be Redeemd.' Instead they are 'Created continually / By Offering & Atonement in the crue[l]ties of Moral law' (*M* 5.11–12). For Blake as a poet-prophet, on the other hand, the 'Void Outside of Existence,' which is what psychosis is, becomes a 'Womb' (*M* 42[49].1) impregnated by the imagination. The Logos or Word of God lies buried in psychosis, into which the poet-prophet must descend in order to release it from 'Offering & Atonement in the crue[t]ies of Moral Law.' Blake identified this 'Offering & Atonement' in his own time with the Deism Milton founded in *Paradise Lost* by justifying the ways of Urizen as the 'eternal providence' of Satan.

Blake's apocalyptic vision, like Jung's archetypal psychology, is grounded in psychosis. Blake left *The Four Zoas* unengraved because he could not deal dialectically with Albion's 'Sleep of Ulro! and the passage through / Eternal Death' *as* his 'awaking to Eternal Life' (*J* 4.1–2). His imagination could not fully embrace Albion's 'torments of love and jealousy' lasting 'nine nights' as the spreading 'beams' of the Saviour's 'love.' The psychosis remained imaginatively (organically) unredeemed. Blake begins his account of the Last Judgment as the ninth night of the nightmare:

And Los & Enitharmon builded Jerusalem weeping
Over the Sepulcher & over the Crucified body
Which to their Phantom Eyes appear'd still in the Sepulcher
But Jesus stood beside them in the Spirit Separating

Their Spirit from their body. Terrified at Non Existence
For such they deemd the death of the body. Los his vegetable hands
Outstretchd his right hand branching out in fibrous Strength
Siezd the Sun. His left hand like dark roots coverd the Moon
And tore them down cracking the heavens across from immense to
    immense
Then fell the fires of Eternity with loud & shrill
Sound of Loud Trumpet thundering along from heaven to heaven
A mighty sound articulate Awake ye dead & come
To judgment from the four winds Awake & Come away.

                                    (*Four Zoas* 117.1–13)

The dialectical form of Blake's apocalyptic vision is the 'true Friend-ship' between building a Sepulchre of 'Phantom Eyes' for the 'Crucified body' and the spiritual eyes that preside over it. The resurrection nega-tively resides in the building of a sepulchre for a dead Jesus. Only as the poet-prophet building the sepulchre can the resurrection take place in and as the constellation of it. The psychosis constellates the release from it by becoming the 'Womb' within which it occurs. Psychosis is trans-formed into the divine insanity of the imagination. The result of this transformation is the higher Paradise of a fully regenerated sanity as the transformed energy of psychosis released from its frozen state. Blake's apocalyptic vision is the vision of a vast sepulchre in which, on a 'Couch of Death' (*M* 32[35].1, 8), Albion lies in 'the Sleep of Ulro,' a 6,000-year nightmare from the Creation to the Judgment from which in its concluding plates he finally awakens. The nightmare ('a female dream' [*Europe* 9.5]) sounds the awakening as its parodic form.

In Blake's reading of *Paradise Lost*, Urizen 'stoop'd down / And took up water from the river Jordan: pouring on / To Miltons brain the icy fluid from his broad cold palm' (*M* 19[21].7–9). In Milton's paralysed brain, his imagination has 'walked about in Eternity / One hundred years, pondring the intricate mazes of Providence / Unhappy tho in heav'n' (*M* 2.16–18). Now, in Blake's 'Vegetable Body,' which Milton enters at the metatarsus of his left foot,

    Milton took of the red clay of Succoth, moulding it with care
    Between his palms: and filling up the furrows of many years
    Beginning at the feet of Urizen, and on the bones
    Creating new flesh on the Demon cold, and building him,
    As with new clay a Human form in the Valley of Beth Peor.

                                    (*M* 19[21].10–14)

For Blake, Eden is the fourfold world in which as 'Mental Fight' this process of creating 'with new clay a Human form' of God is ceaseless. It is the eternal world of ceaseless becoming outside which, as the delusion of eternal being, resides the psychosis that must as a 'Womb' be entered again and again if one is to be released from it. 'I philosophize,' Derrida writes, 'only in *terror*, but in the *confessed* terror of going mad. The confession is simultaneously, at its *present* moment, oblivion and unveiling, protection and exposure: economy' ('Cogito' 62). Absent in 'the Creator alone in nothingness' is Frye's '*confessed* terror of going mad,' which is the 'terror' confronting Derrida as it confronted Blake in the figure of Satan. Its absence in the work of Frye lies in a metaphysics of presence (incarnation), which Derrida's philosophy deconstructs, as, in a sense, does Frye's notion of the Word become 'flesh' as his notion of the fall. 'What man naturally wants,' he writes, 'is to collapse back into a master-slave duality, of which the creature-creator duality is perhaps a projection' (*Great Code* 232).

'In any event,' Derrida explains, 'the Cogito is a work as soon as it is assured of what it says. But before it is a work, it is madness.' By madness, Derrida means 'a silence, the voluble silence of a thought that did not think its own words' ('Cogito' 59).[9] As soon as it thinks its own words, and 'is assured of what it says,' the Cogito is a 'work.' Several times in different contexts, Frye discusses the way in which Goethe's Faust 'deliberately alters "In the beginning was the Word" to "In the beginning was the Act"' (*Words* 34). The 'Act,' for Frye, takes the 'Creator alone in nothing' into something, which is the creation itself, understood by Frye as a fall from 'nothing' into something, which is necessarily less than 'nothing.' Faust, Frye writes in another context, 'rejects "das Wort," and traverses the whole cycle of language as outlined above [metaphor, metonymy, description], passing through the second-phase "der Sinn," and emerging finally with "die That," the event or existential reality that words describe at secondhand. At this point Faust begins to fall into the power of Mephistopheles' (*Great Code* 18). Further elaborating on the fall of language into existence (*langue* into *parole*), Frye argues that 'Faust was simply following the established Christian practice up to his time. In the beginning God did something, and words are the descriptive servomechanisms telling us what he did. This imports into Western religion what post-structural critics call the "transcendental signified," the view that what is true or real is something outside the words that the words are pointing to' (*Words* 34).

Frye's entire literary schematics are grounded in his determination to restore the 'outside' to the inside, by arguing that words point to themselves and to each other, that their reality is in themselves, not in what they may or may not point to outside themselves. 'It seems to me obvious,' Frye insists (Frye's argument avoids argument in the sense that it deals only with what seems to him obvious), 'that the opening of John's Gospel is expressly trying to block off that attitude, and to identify *logos* and *mythos*.' However, since the supreme sanity of what seems to Frye 'obvious' (the Word) is, as history, inevitably replaced by psychosis (the Act), Frye concludes that psychosis, as the fundamentalism that reduces the Word to historical fact, is 'deeply rooted in the human mind.' 'In the twentieth century,' he writes, citing an example of fundamentalist religion, 'Trotsky denounced certain Marxist deviants of his time for believing, like idealists, in the primacy of the word, whereas for him all genuine Marxists knew that in the beginning was the act' (*Words* 34).

The burden of anxiety that the psychosis of fundamentalism imposed upon Frye in his childhood and early youth was, because he was 'brought up' in it without actually going through a 'conversion process,' a burden of which he was not consciously aware, except as a tone of voice that indicated to him that his mother did not believe it any more than he did as other than a 'story.' Then one day, as he described it in several interviews, while hurrying along St George Street in Moncton on his unwilling way to Aberdeen High School, he had an epiphany, which John Ayre describes as 'a parody of the Methodist conversion experience his Howard and Demorest predecessors so earnestly demanded of themselves.' '"Just suddenly," he told Bob Sandler in an interview, "that whole shitty and smelly garment (of fundamentalist teaching I had all my life) just dropped off into the sewers and stayed there. It was like the Bunyan feeling, about the burden of sin falling off his back only with me it was a burden of anxiety. Anything might have touched it off, but I don't know what specifically did, or if anything did. I just remember that suddenly that was no longer a part of me and would never be again"' (cited in Ayre 44). The distinction between the 'burden of sin,' which, 'brought up converted,' he never experienced and the 'burden of anxiety,' which, 'brought up converted,' he did is that, for Frye, 'the burden of sin' is a cowardly failure of nerve. This failure produces inertia and a dependence on a god external to oneself whom Frye, like Blake, considered a false idol psychotically worshipped in the guise of an ideology in which myth is answerable to history. The 'burden of anxiety,' on the other hand, is the recognition that one is carrying a false idol, which usually cannot be cast off until one has analysed what it is

In Frye's more elaborate account of the epiphany to Roy Daniells, who had been brought up as one of the Plymouth Brethren, Frye clearly knew what had been cast off and how he had dealt with it. '"In early adolescence,"' he writes,

> 'I suddenly realized, with an utter and complete conviction of which I have never lost one iota since, that the whole apparatus of afterlife in heaven and hell, unpardonable sins, and the like was a lot of junk. There remained, of course, the influence of my mother, and the fact that I had already agreed to go to college as a church student. My mental processes were pretty confused, but restructuring them by hindsight I think they were something like this: if I go through the whole business of revolting against this, I shall be making a long and pointless detour back to where I shall probably come out anyway, and will probably have acquired a neurosis besides. I think I decided very early, without realizing it at the time, that I was going to accept out of religion only what made sense to me as a human being. I was not going to worship a god whose actions, judged by human standards, were contemptible. That was where Blake helped me so much: he taught me that the lugubrious old stinker in the sky that I had heard so much about existed all right, but that his name was Satan, that his function was to promote tyranny in society and repression in the mind. This meant that the Methodist church down at the corner was consecrated mainly to devil-worship, but, because it did not know that, it would tolerate something better without knowing what that was either.'
> (cited in Ayre 45)

In early adolescence, Frye cast off the psychosis of the religion in which he was raised as a false ideology that, without knowing it, reduced the realm of the spirit, not simply to the condition of the flesh, but to the spectral form of flesh as a 'Ratio of the five senses' (*MHH* 6). In this spectral form, the spirit became identified with the 'rotten rags of Memory' (*M* 41[48].4) (Frye's 'shitty and smelly garment'), which, as decaying sense, Blake describes as a 'false Body: an Incrustation over [the] Immortal / Spirit' (*M* 40[46].35–6). Blake's archetypal image of this state of 'Eternal Death' is the crucified Jesus nailed to the Tree of Satan as 'the crue[l]ties of the Moral Law.' In its 'Offering & Atonement,' the Methodist church in which Frye worshipped with his parents as a child was a 'Synagogue of Satan' consecrated to 'devil-worship.' Born already converted to Satan without knowing it, Frye on his way to high school instinctively cast him out as no part of himself. He was now prepared to engage in a liberal education free of the belief systems that in all forms of fundamentalism bound the imagination to a false ideology.

The demonic parody of death and resurrection as the worship of Satan became in Frye 'a prodigious and unthinkable metamorphosis of the human mind.' Frye concluded his added fourth chapter to the three lectures he delivered near the end of his life to the alumni of Emmanuel College, not by announcing the imminence of his coming death, but by declaring the death we are always already in. 'In the double vision of a spiritual and a physical world simultaneously present,' he concluded, 'every moment we have lived through we have also died out of into another order. Our life in the resurrection, then, is already here, and waiting to be recognized' (*Double* 85). To 'die out of' every 'moment we have lived through' is to experience 'every moment' (Blake's 'Moment: less than a Pulsation of the Artery') as the death and resurrection we are always already in. Every moment, that is, is an eternal now if we let it die into its resurrected life by not holding on to it as 'the rotten rags of Memory,' which, as 'Memory,' takes on the spectral life of a decaying corpse Frye calls history. The eternal now as a fully recognized resurrected life is the 'Word' itself released from the illusion of the 'Act' that binds it to its own death, a freedom Frye describes as 'the Creator alone in nothing.' This ultimate freedom is, for Frye, what the spirit always already is. The recognition of it announced in 'every Time less than a pulsation of the artery' (*M* 28[30].62) is the apocalypse itself rather than the image of it.

Frye's mind was anagogically engaged with the apocalypse itself as distinct from the vision of it that he found in the Bible and explored in literature. He turned from the mythical and metaphorical language of the Bible to a study of its 'secular' form as literature because in literature it was released from the 'conversion process' in which, as religious systems (ideologies), it became in his experience of it the worship of Satan. Frye distinguishes between the rhetoric of the Bible and the rhetoric of literature in terms of its designs upon the reader. The rhetoric of the Bible is a 'rhetoric coming the other way and coming from the other side of a mythical and metaphorical language' (*Double* 18), which, as '*kerygma*,' is divine revelation calling upon the reader to receive it by becoming actively engaged in its transforming power through his surrender to it. The ways in which *kerygma* inevitably settles into religious systems as demonic parodies of it drove Frye to explore in literature the same 'metaphorical and mythical language' released from the revelatory demands of *kerygma*.

In addressing the subject of *kerygma* in his three lectures at the Emmanuel College alumni reunion, partly as a tribute to Douglas Jay in his final year as principal of the College, Frye was thoroughly conscious of the fact that he himself was an alumnus honoured by the invitation to address a largely United Church audience as a member of it who, while also a minister in it, preferred to think of himself as part of the congregation. He did not, that is, think of the alumni as unknowingly 'consecrated mainly to devil-worship' and, because unknowingly, prepared to receive from Frye 'something better without knowing what that was either.' 'I am not trying to deny or belittle the validity of a credal, even a dogmatic, approach to Christianity,' he told his fellow alumni. 'I am saying that the literal basis of faith in Christianity is a mythical and metaphorical basis, not one founded on historical facts or logical propositions. Once we accept an imaginative literalism, everything else falls into place: without that, creeds and dogmas quickly turn malignant' (*Double* 17).

Whatever is believed in the absence of the imagination is 'malignant.' Whatever is present as the imagination of it is no longer present as religious belief or religious faith. It is present as what Coleridge calls 'poetic faith,' which he describes as 'a willing suspension of disbelief for the moment' (*BL* 2:6). But this 'suspension of disbelief' is not what Frye means by the 'imaginative literalism' of the biblical myth. 'The literary language of the New Testament,' he goes on to say in the next sentence, 'is not intended, like literature itself, simply to suspend judgment, but to convey a vision of spiritual life that continues to transform and expand our own. That is, its myths become, as purely literary myths cannot, myths to live by; its metaphors become, as purely literary metaphors cannot, metaphors to live in' (*Double* 17–18). What is malignant about a credal or dogmatic approach to Christianity, which Frye is doing his best not to 'deny or belittle,' is that, by being credal or dogmatic, it binds the Christian myth to historical fact or gets rid of myth entirely by declaring it literally (factually) true. Frye is not preaching a gospel of faith; nor is he preaching a gospel of the imagination. Recognizing the dangers of religion and the limitations of the imagination, he is coming 'the other way and from the other side of mythical and metaphorical language.' Here on 'the other side' resides his identity with the 'Word' as 'the Creator alone in nothing' free of the 'Act,' the highest form of which constitutes *kerygma*. Mythical and metaphorical language is the Word as 'Act,' not the apocalypse, but the metaphor of it. The 'Word' is the 'recognition' of the apocalypse, as distinct from the waiting for it, a waiting that, the longer it goes on, as in Beckett's *Waiting for Godot*, the more it inevitably becomes a nightmarish parody of it: Beckett's Pozzo cracking his whip, driving Lucky on, harnessed to a rope tied around his neck.

For Frye, the experience of Paul explains the kind of 'recognition' or 'enlightenment' that resides in an identity with the Word as the Word's identity with itself. 'Paul,' he writes,

> speaks of a moment of enlightenment (2 Corinthians 12) in which two things are remarkable. First, the sense of a solid ego dissolved so completely that he can hardly say whether the experience happened to him or to someone else – 'je est un autre,' as Rimbaud says. He even apologizes for 'boasting' in speaking about his experience as though it were his own. Second, he is not sure whether he was 'in' or 'out of' his body, or whether such distinctions really applied at all. He feels a certain reluctance in stressing the experience, mainly, no doubt, because of his strong revolutionary slant: he wants the world as a whole to wake up, and individual enlightenment is useful chiefly because it may be contagious, which it cannot be if it is incommunicable. He heard, according to the AV, 'unspeakable words' (*arreta rhemata*), 'not lawful for a man to utter.' The experience, however, seems to be of a new language, which he heard and to some extent understood, but cannot translate into the categories of ordinary language. The emphasis seems to fall on his inability to make it intelligible, rather than on his being forbidden to do so. (*Great Code* 231)

In a characteristic moment of insight in which everything simultaneously going on in Frye's mind seemed to coalesce into a single thought, Frye associates Paul's 'unspeakable words' – 'unspeakable' because he cannot make them 'intelligible' – with 'the superiority of what Kierkegaard calls "ethical freedom" to the contemplative values afforded by a synthesis of thought' (*Great Code* 26). Frye agreed with Kierkegaard.[10] He embraced an 'ethical freedom' beyond the good and evil binding the mind to 'the crue[l]ties of the Moral Law' and to the psychosis of an ideology. 'Ethical freedom,' he realized, allowed the mind to play with its own operations without the pressure to act upon them, as, in the name of *kerygma*, Paul displayed or, indeed, God displayed in his incarnation and death.

Frye rejects the existentialist appropriation of an absolute 'ethical freedom' to a revolutionary end that enslaves it to history. He locates it instead in Paul's notion of a fourth phase of language, which, if rendered 'intelligible' rather than 'forbidden,' would identify language with the Word itself as what Blake calls the 'human form divine.' What Frye has in mind, and what he continued to lay the ground for throughout his career, was a fourth phase of language in which metaphor, metonymy, and descriptive writing reassembled themselves in the mind as 'revelation' or *kerygma*, not as an inner transformation or conversion understood as an 'Act,' but as the polysemous nature of the Word.

It is this notion of the Word as the fourth stage of language that Frye has in mind in his final two sentences on death and resurrection in the added fourth chapter of *The Double Vision* published shortly after his death: 'every moment we have lived through we have also died out of into another order' (85). The other order is the Word as the 'fourth stage' of language in which, as mind revealed to itself *as* itself, Frye has Hegel's *Phenomenology* in mind. 'The hero of Hegel's philosophical quest,' Frye explains, 'is the concept (*Begriff*), which, like Ulysses in the *Odyssey*, appears first in an unrecognized and almost invisible guise as the intermediary between subject and object, and ends by taking over the whole show, undisputed master of the house of being.' 'But this "concept,"' he continues,

> can hardly exist apart from its own verbal formulation: that is, it is something verbal that expands in this way, so that the *Phenomenology* is, among other things, a general theory of how verbal meaning takes shape. Even the old metaphor of 'levels' is preserved in Hegel's term *Aufhebung*. What Hegel means by dialectic is not anything reducible to a patented formula, like the 'thesis-antithesis-synthesis' one so often attached to him, nor can it be anything predictive. It is a much more complex operation of a form of understanding combining with its own otherness or opposite, in a way that negates itself and yet passes through that negation into a new stage, preserving its essence in a broader context, and abandoning the one just completed like a chrysalis of a butterfly or a crustacean's outgrown shell. (*Great Code* 222)[11]

The Word preserves its 'essence' by 'abandoning' its narrower Biblical sense in which it becomes 'flesh' (that is to say, metaphor) and embraces its new fourfold stage as the 'undisputed master of the house of being.' For Frye, this is the final death understood as the awakening to the eternal now, the apocalypse or fourfold Word formally set forth in his post-Hegelian fourfold schematics, which he first presented in his *Anatomy of Criticism* as four 'essays' or attempts.

The Site of Opposition

When I registered in Frye's graduate course in Blake in 1948–9, I had just begun my first year of postgraduate studies at the University of Toronto, where I had gone, as already mentioned, with the intention of writing a PhD thesis on Milton under the supervision of A.S.P. Woodhouse. I had completed during the summer an MA thesis on Milton's Satan under the supervision of Malcolm Ross at the University of Manitoba and looked forward to continuing my work on Milton with one of the finest Milton scholars in North America and certainly the finest in Canada. Frye's magisterial book on Blake, *Fearful Symmetry*, which I had not yet read, was published in 1947, and the general excitement among English graduate students was one of the first things that struck me as soon as I arrived on the campus and was given an office, which I shared with three others. I decided to register in Frye's course, partly, if not largely, because I was familiar with Blake's Romantic notion that 'Milton wrote in fetters when he wrote of Angels & God, and at liberty when of Devils & Hell ... because he was a true Poet and of the Devils party without knowing it' (*MHH* 6). In my MA thesis I had, or thought I had, dealt with Blake's argument in terms of a view of Romanticism that identified Satan as the hero of *Paradise Lost*, a view that, I argued, found its psychological justification in the archetypal psychology of Jung. Jung had not yet written *Answer to Job*, which is in many respects the psychological text that best describes within an archetypal framework the Romantic view of Satan as the archetypal republican hero rebelling against the monarchy of Heaven. Jahweh in Jung's *Answer to Job*, not published until 1951, is challenged to absorb the feminine creation that he has cast off as that part of himself, which, as the *deus absconditus*, threatens his own masculine perfection, even as Milton's patriarchal God 'uncircumscribed' retires and 'put[s] not forth [his] goodness, which is free / To act or not' (*PL* 7.170–2). The Satan whom the 'high permission of all-ruling Heaven / Left ... at large to his own dark designs' (1.212–13) is Milton's God demonstrating his absolute freedom 'to act or not,' the absolute freedom becoming for the Romantic poet the divine right of the tyrant, which the republican Milton rejected in the archetypal guise of Satan.

Assigning papers for oral delivery in the second term, Frye granted my wish to write mine on Blake's *Milton*, which, though I had not yet read it, seemed at the time an obvious choice. One reason for choosing it was to enlarge my own understanding of Blake's unorthodox reading of *Paradise Lost*, which in my MA thesis I only superficially discussed within an already established argument. Though it was largely based on the archangel Michael's rational or masculine instruction of the wide-awake Adam, it also took into account Michael's irrational or feminine instruction of the sleeping Eve, the status of dreams in *Paradise Lost* bearing directly not only upon Milton's presentation of Satan but upon the 'great deliverance by her seed [the Woman's Seed] to come' (12.600–1), with which Milton was clearly uncomfortable. The relation of Satan to Eve became the subtext of my thesis, for which Jung's archetypal approach to dreams proved useful.

Frye's lectures in the first term, all of them delivered without notes and seldom dealing with the text except to illustrate a point (when he would quote the text as though quoting himself), I found both awesome and troubling, perhaps the more troubling for being awesome. The body of Blake's poetry became virtually indistinguishable from the body of English – and beyond that western – literature, so much so that I only gradually began to realize that, while I seemed to understand this larger body within the conceptual framework of Blake's own Fourfold vision of Beulah, Generation, Ulro, and Eden, I could not apply it to my attempted reading of the two epics and the unengraved *Four Zoas*. Obviously the test confronting me did not depend upon my reading the body of English and western literature to see how far Frye's stunning lectures worked in practice. The test in his graduate course on Blake resided in my reading of Blake's text, and this, when I got to *Milton*, I could not do. In the lectures, I was drawn into the encyclopaedic mind of Frye, and so long as I remained there, captured by his rhetoric and wit, I appeared to understand, even though many of the works he cited I had not read. That is, my understanding was in some measure a projection onto Frye as the container of it, which outside the lectures I could not claim as my own. Alone, I tended to retreat into my own understanding, though with the uneasy sense that what Frye was demonstrating in his lectures in the name of Blake was 'the sanity of genius and the madness of the commonplace mind'; 'and it is here,' Frye explains in the opening pages of *Fearful Symmetry* in building his case against Locke, 'that [Blake] has something very apposite to say to the twentieth century, with its interest in the arts of neurosis and the politics of paranoia' (13). Though I had not progressed far enough into Blake to be conscious of it, I nevertheless sensed that the unacknowledged relations unconsciously taking shape between Frye and me were mirrored in Los's dark, though ultimately creative, relations with his Spectre. The Spectre, Blake writes,

> saw now from the ou[t]side what before he saw & felt from within
> He saw that Los was the sole, uncontrolld Lord of the Furnaces
> Groaning he kneeld before Los's iron-shod feet on London Stone,
> Hungring & thirsting for Los's life yet pretending obedience.
> While Los pursud his speech in threatnings loud & fierce.   (J 8.25–9)

I spent the Christmas break struggling with Blake's brief epic, suspended as I was between Locke's empiricism, which Frye adamantly rejected, and the autonomy of the imagination, which I could not fully grasp. I was unable, that is, to take up residence in Blake's *Milton* as I later understood it: the making of a metaphorical body as the mythical form of Blake's physical body, which, as his 'Vegetable Body,' is already in his experience of it mythical.[12] The transformation of his 'Vegetable Body' into its resurrected form enacted as the journey of Milton through it, Milton having made his hermaphroditic entrance at the metatarsus of Blake's left foot, was a journey that engaged me in the psychotic realm of Blake's Ulro through which I could not find my way. In my struggle with *Milton* during the three-week Christmas break, I found myself in Blake's 'Void Outside of Existence' not knowing that that was what I was in. Had I known, it might have become a 'Womb,' the text becoming the embryonic shaping of a fully formed resurrected body the inner operations of which are the *mythos* of Milton's moving through it from the left foot to the brain. At the brain he confronts his twelve-year-old virgin Muse and unites with her, their union becoming the divine marriage that announces itself to Blake as the instant in which *Jerusalem* is conceived in its pre-existent state. To conceive this natural process of coming to birth as what Jung describes with reference to psychology as an *opus contra naturam* remained beyond the reach of the intelligence I brought to bear upon it.

Finally, not finding in *Fearful Symmetry* or in Frye's lectures the help I rather desperately needed, I fled the 'Void Outside of Existence' back into a familiar allegorical mode of consciousness that engaged my 'Corporeal Understanding' (E 730). My situation was rather like that of Blake's Thel, who fled her own 'grave plot' back to the false security of 'the vales of Har' (*Book of Thel* 6.9,22). Haunted by the spectre of what I was doing, as measured against the critical framework Frye had established in his lectures, I sensed that the allegorical approach into which I had retreated was a betrayal of the Logos or Word as Frye had interpreted it in a literary context. In my delusional state, which I compounded by working against it while knowing I was in it, I argued that Milton, as a 'true Poet,' *was* 'of the Devils party without knowing it' and that in Blake's epic he was coming to know it, the unconscious poet in *Paradise Lost* becoming the conscious poet in Blake's *Milton*. What I failed fully to realize was that the 'Devils party' as the party of the imagination in Blake's *Marriage of Heaven and Hell* was not the party of Satan in Blake's *Milton*. My failure lay in my 'Corporeal' binding of Blake's myth to historical fact rather than making it solely answerable to itself, which is to say to the 'Intellectual powers' of the imagination. Had I done this, I would have seen that the 'Devils party' in Blake's *Marriage* is the party of Orc, while Satan's party in *Milton* is the party of Urizen. Milton, in the body of Blake's epic, is releasing himself, as Blake released himself, from the Orc-Urizen cycle into the realm of Los. Why could I not see this when I was struggling to write my paper?

Exploring this question in a wide variety of literary, political, religious, psychological, and deconstructive contexts over a number of years became, now closer to the end of my life, the subject of this book, which, like Frye's *Fearful Symmetry*, has gone through at least five complete rewritings. In 1948 I was confronted in Frye's lectures less with a reading of Blake than with a reading of western literature as a secular scripture that was archetypally bound to the Bible as the '*analogia visionis*' of it. The archetypal, rather than the literal, binding of western literature to the Bible (Homer, Virgil, and Ovid had not read it) lay for Frye in his understanding of the Bible as a vast, ultimately unified *mythos* written by many authors, and edited by many editors, over a vastly extended period of time. All of them, in contributing their portions, appear to have had some living sense of the whole as a single complex metaphor the motions of which are contained within its own silent stillness. 'Why,' Frye asks, 'does this huge, sprawling, tactless book sit there inscrutably in the middle of our cultural heritage like the "great Boyg" or sphinx in *Peer Gynt*, frustrating all our efforts to walk around it?' (*Great Code* xvi). The question Frye asks of the Bible, which he set out to answer after he completed *Fearful Symmetry*, is the question that confronted me in my failed attempts to read Blake. Blake's canon, as I struggled in vain to find my way through it, became increasingly a 'huge, sprawling, tactless book' lying inscrutably on my desk demanding more of me than my intelligence appeared able to give, a '"great Boyg" or sphinx' whose riddle I could not solve. 'The teacher, as has been recognized at least since Plato's *Meno*,' Frye explained of himself, 'is not primarily someone who knows instructing someone who does not know. He is someone who attempts to re-create the subject in the student's mind, and his strategy in doing this is first of all to get the student to recognize what he already potentially knows, which includes breaking up the powers of repression in his mind that keep him from knowing what he knows. That is why it is the teacher, rather than the student, who asks most of the questions' (*Great Code* xiii).

Now that the University of Toronto Press is publishing Frye's notebooks, diaries, letters, and student essays, I am able better to grasp what was going on in Frye in relation to what was going on in me. Frye records in his diaries that he was having considerable trouble with his graduate course on Blake, primarily, though not entirely, because of the students in it, including myself. My paper on Blake's *Milton* was the first of the papers delivered throughout the second term, Frye having lectured for the first term. Frye in his diary records that he had been lecturing all morning on Milton's Satan and 'the paradox of evil as a metaphysical negation & a moral fact.' He had slept badly, dreaming of an 'unknown stranger,' and the dream became a nightmare. Thinking about it, he linked the stranger with 'the brother with my name who died in infancy.' He woke up 'feeling [he] was experiencing the first of the autonomous breakthroughs Jung talks about.'[13] Of my own paper in the afternoon, he wrote: 'The Blake was dull: Woodman read a paper on Blake & Milton.' Frye then goes on to summarize his own lecture on the female will that arose from it (I had talked about Blake's relations with his wife at Felpham and Milton's relations with his 'Sixfold Emanation,' his three wives and three daughters). 'In dealing with the female will,' Frye writes in his diary, 'I said the polarizing of regressive & progressive female was in Homer (Calypso-Penelope) & in a sense in Virgil too – Dido vs. the real bride, the city he built. The complete pattern in the Bible says that the bride (Jerusalem) *is* the forgiven harlot, & a dim perception of that made Samuel Butler write that curious essay about the whitewashing of Penelope' (*Diaries* 8:64–5).

There was, for Frye, perhaps a more immediate problem in my allegorical reading of Blake's *Milton*: the influence of Jung's archetypal psychology. As a prologue to his 1949 diary expressing his desire 'to tackle the diary scheme again on a bigger scale, as a means of systematizing [his] life' (8:51), Frye includes at the top of his list for his 'dozen-paper project' (8:53) a paper on Blake and Jung. Thinking about the paper in terms of what psychologically had gone into the agonized writing of *Fearful Symmetry*, Frye writes:

> It occurs to me that what I did in writing FS was perform the act described in much the same way by Freud & Jung. This is the act of swallowing the father, integrating oneself with the wise old man. Presumably [after Blake] I shall never find another father, not even in Shakespeare, & should realize that I am essentially *on my own*. I've really reached an individuated stage of thinking, if not of personal life. There's more to it than that – Blake is right in a way no one else is – but that's the psychological aspect of the book. What I should do now ... is explore mandalas. This is linked with the ideas I've had about the geometry of thinking ... Perhaps ... if every poem is necessarily a perfect unity, every thinker is necessarily perfectly right. (8:94)

Frye's interest in Jung's archetypal psychology lay less in the 'individu-ated stage' of his 'personal life' than in the 'individuated stage' of his 'thinking.' He had, in writing *Fearful Symmetry*, reached the stage of the 'wise old man' by swallowing all the fathers (including Blake) who had carried the projection for him. In 'swallowing' Blake's vision of the Fourfold man who is the incarnate God (the 'human form divine'), Frye had achieved 'a perfect unity' of thought in which he was, like Blake, 'right in a way that no one else is.' He had now fully to absorb being 'perfectly right' by exploring, as Jung explored, the 'mandala,' the squared circle as the symbol of 'perfect unity' in which, of necessity, everything the mind conceives in accordance with 'the geometry of thinking' is 'perfectly right.' His planned paper on Blake and Jung would, among other things, archetypally explore the fourfold unity of mind he had achieved in his book on Blake, Jung's notion of archetypes perhaps binding the 'perfect unity' of thought to the 'perfect unity' of one's 'personal life,' particularly as he realized that swallowing Blake as the last of his archetypal fathers was 'partly the reason [*Fearful Symmetry*] was so personal a book' (8:94).

But writing the paper on Blake and Jung proved more difficult than he had realized.[14] 'I think,' he writes in his diary, 'there's a jinx on my Blake & Jung paper, also on the damn course.' The student who was assigned to deliver a paper on Blake and Jung never showed up. Frye describes him as 'an emotional lame brain who got converted to God knows what by my Milton lectures & took the Blake course for inspiration.' 'Of course,' Frye continues (naming the student), 'the paper was too much for him, but why didn't he duck out of it in time. The last time I assigned a Blake & Jung paper ... [the student] not only didn't turn up, but had a complete nervous breakdown & became a violent homosexual' (8:146). By the end of April, Frye describes himself in his diary as staggering down to hold his Blake group. 'Nothing new,' he complains; 'only I wonder if Woodman is dropping out' (8:194).

Frye's main problem with Jung's view of the archetype lay in his 'idiosyncratic' notion that the archetype was bound to the 'Act' rather than, as in Frye' s more 'traditional' notion, to the 'Word.' 'Blake,' he argues, 'plays down his archetypal narratives ... partly because he's a painter' (*Diaries* 8:430) interested in the eternal structure for which the archetypes serve as 'building blocks.' The result is that his 'lack of interest in narrative ... makes him seem incommunicable to the general reader, or at least uncommunicative.' It was precisely my "Jungian" understanding of the archetype in relation to the 'Act' that had rendered Blake's *Milton* 'incommunicable ... or at least uncommunicative.' I had read it in search of an archetypal narrative, that is to say, a *mythos*, to which Blake's archetypal figures, conceived with a painterly imagination rather than a narrative one, refused to submit. I was reading *Milton* in terms of Keats's notion of 'Soul-making,' which Keats described as 'a grander system of salvation than the chrystain religion' (*KL* 250). It did not work, however, as Keats himself realized in his imitation of Milton's 'artful' or statuesque rhetoric in the composition of *Hyperion*. Keats's statuesque gods impeded the '*Soul-making*' process in their struggle rhetorically to arrest it. '*Soul-making*,' Keats realized, worked against the gods rather than with them ('No stir of life / Was in this shrouded vale' [*Fall of Hyperion* 1.310–11]).

'I think (with Keats),' writes Frye, 'that life may be purgatorial in shape, only I'd call it a vale of spirit (not soul) making' (*Notebooks* 5:148). For Frye, in the distinction between soul (*psychikos*) and spirit (*pneumatikos*) lay the distinction between his 'traditional' understanding of the archetype and Jung's 'idiosyncratic' one. Soul, Frye suggests, with Paul's distinction between *psychikos* and *pneumatikos* in mind, 'seems to have a general context of man as creature, as brought into being by a God thought of as external to man' (*Words* 121). Soul, that is, is identified with the fallen order of nature in which man, engaging the will, struggles towards consciousness as a way of controlling both his own human nature and the non-human nature around him, over both of which an omnipotent God presides as natural law in the non-human world and as the moral law in the human one. *Psychikos,* that is, is bound by Frye to psychosis. Spirit, on the other hand, is not created. It dwells eternally with God. 'The term "spirit,"' Frye writes, drawing heavily on Paul, 'seems to belong properly only to the Holy Spirit [no one would 'speak of the third person of the Trinity as the Holy Soul'] and, in a different context, to the angels: for man, and for discarnate beings like elemental "spirits," it seems to be a mere doublet of "soul"' (*Great Code* 20).

Referring again to the essay on Blake and Jung with which he was having so much difficulty, Frye in his diary (10 August 1950) explains that he has largely resolved his problem by essentially getting rid of Jung, because he did not fit into Blake's mature understanding of the imagination. 'The tactic of the Blake article is shaping up a little,' he writes.

> After I outline his archetypal imagery, which derives from the unfallen world [*pneumatikos*], I go on to [the] archetype of narrative [*psychikos*]. The archetypal narrative is the heroic quest, which is the Orc cycle. This is in Blake, but he's not primarily interested in it, as he sees the cyclic shape of it too clearly. That's the reason for the difficulty in trying to wedge Jungian archetypes, which are all narrative ones, into Blake. The shift over from the Orc cycle to the Los pattern of progressive & redemptive work is really the centre of the problem in L [Liberal] that converges on what I call the dialectic development of the conception of the hero. In Blake the cycle of narrative emanating from & returning to the unfallen world [*pneumatikos*] is seen so constantly as a simultaneous pattern of significance that the reader has to get this perspective before he can read: it isn't unfolded to him passively in a narrative sequence. (*Diaries* 8:431)

The archetypes, for Frye, belong to the realm of spirit, the *pneumatikos,* as distinct from the realm of the soul, the *psychikos.* There is no '*Soul-making*' going on in *Milton.* Unless the reader gets this spiritual perspective, he can't read Frye's Blake. To this I can testify, though it has taken me a long time to understand it, and without the help of Frye's note-books and diaries, I think I would still not fully understand it. If, I suppose, Frye is clearly a *pneumatikos,* then, I suppose, I am equally a *psychikos,* though both of us would reject an either/or mentality in favour of a both/and one. At the time, the tragedy for me, though not for Frye, was that we never forged the 'true Friendship' that resides in

'Opposition,' a true Friendship that I now think of as the subject of this book.

Frye describes the fallen realm of the *psychikos* as the external realm of the 'conscious soul-will,' which, as 'the center of all tyranny and hatred,' seeks 'to dominate one conscious soul-will externally by another.' The unfallen realm of the *pneumatikos*, on the other hand,

> seems to have some genuine independence of the single permanently anchored identity to which the *soma psychikon* is confined. The Jesus of history, according to most Christian views, was a soul-body unit like anyone else; the spiritual body of the risen Christ is everywhere and in everyone, and, as noted earlier, it may be a part of us or we may be a part of it. The *soma pneumatikon*, then, suggests a certain fluidity of personality, in which such metaphors as the 'one flesh' erotic metaphor, or metaphors of being influenced by another personality or the work of a creative artist, begin to take on more reality. (*Words* 125–6)

For Frye, archetypes are the 'building blocks' of the eternal realm of the spirit, which is the realm of the risen Christ or the resurrected body. As a 'secular scripture,' the archetypes of literature are received by the reader who is open to them as the communion wafer is received in the Mass, though as literature, not as *kerygma*, where, as a calling, myths are 'myths to live by' and metaphors are 'metaphors to live in.' The language of myth and metaphor in literature is a language of mental play ('Me to play,' declares Beckett's Ham in *Endgame*, setting out in centre stage to tell his story of creation, which he can no longer remember). The play of language in literature enacts the 'ethical freedom' of the spirit in which the human and divine are one, not as the process of the one becoming the other, but as the Word itself free at last of the 'Act.' In Frye's graduate class, it never occurred to me that in this world of the spirit I was invited to open my mind to the play of its divine operations as an end in itself. I experienced it as the *soma psychikon*, where a struggle towards a consciousness far exceeding my own was taking place in the indifferent presence of a God who abandoned me to the 'psychosis' he assumed I was in. Unknowingly at the time, however, I was bound to the *soma psychikon* into which, as a 'Jungian,' I had dragged the archetypal world. Though I had rather unknowingly demonstrated this unutterable attachment in my paper, I nevertheless did not drop out. 'Where God may belong in this duality [of the *soma psychikon* and the *soma pneumatikon*],' Frye told the alumni of Emmanuel

College, 'we have yet to try to see, but as he is not hidden in nature, he can only be connected with that tiny percentage of human activity that has not been hopelessly botched' (*Double* 27). In my paper for Frye, I knew I had 'botched' it, leaving Frye wondering until near the end of the second term when I would be dropping out. The truth is I had dropped not out, but down, and by the end of April was well on my still undiscovered heathen way. There were some inner signs that the 'Void Outside of Existence' into which I had fallen, leaving me for the rest of the year in Blake's state of 'Eternal Death,' had become a 'Womb.' My experience in Frye's class was a slow and painful waking from 'the Sleep of Ulro.'

Deconstruction

Not until I read in 'Cogito and the History of Madness' Jacques Derrida's account of being a student-disciple of Michel Foucault did I receive the kind of releasing confirmation that dialectically allowed me to engage with the Frye I could not confront in the classroom. I discovered in 1948–9 that I had no ground to stand on once the tenuous ground on which I attempted to stand had virtually swallowed me up. My experience was rather like the final scene in Mozart's *Don Giovanni*, in which the stone statue of the Commendatore clasps the hand of Don Giovanni and drags him into Hell. 'I retain[ed] the consciousness of an admiring and grateful disciple.' But the efficient, rather than formal or final, cause of this book lay in my decision to 'break the glass, or better the mirror, the reflection, [my] infinite speculation on [Frye]. And start to speak.'[15]

Starting to speak, however, may not ultimately resolve anything. What I have to say belongs to the 'existential' pole of the archetypal or Lacanian 'real,' as distinct from the literary pole as Frye describes it. 'I have even compared the literary universe to Blake's Beulah' (143), Frye writes in 'Reflections in a Mirror,' addressed, despite the title, to the members of the English Institute who in 1965 had gathered to evaluate and critique the literary 'schematics' of his work, a gathering at which I was present. Frye chose not to attend, lest his presence arouse him to defend his 'schematics,' in which case he would become, he feared, the whale swallowing Jonah ('Letter' 28). Though Frye argued that that was the way his critics viewed him, it is also the way he tended in the privacy of his notebooks to view himself. He knew, that is, that his schematics were 'perfectly right' and that 'the bulk of critical theory [with the exception of Jaynes's *The Origin of Consciousness in the Bicameral Mind*] is a chorus of koax [the babble made by the mystical frogs in Aristophanes] after the Anatomy' (*Notebooks* 5:147). Blake's Beulah, Frye explained, is, when perceived in his anagogical perspective, a realm 'where no dispute can come, where everything is equally an element of a liberal education, where Bunyan and Rochester are met together and Jane Austen and the Marquis de Sade have kissed each other.' 'This is not the way that works of literature enter history,' he continues, advancing upon the territory I had, despite Frye, continued as 'archetypal narratives' to explore, 'and it is quite possible that the wars of myth in time [Los as the Spectre of Urthona] are an aspect of criticism that I have not grasped' ('Reflections' 143).

I suggest that what Frye did not grasp, when he argues that myth is liberated by literature from the social myths that parody it, is that the liberation constructs the parody as the condition of it without which there is neither liberation nor parody. Blake's Jerusalem as the city and the bride of Albion is constellated in Blake's 100-plate epic, not as the celebration of their wondrous act of union, but in their 97-plate demonic betrayal of it. Jerusalem, in Blake's vision, exists in Ulro. The poet must descend to Ulro in order to find it. The quest that liberates myth resides in 'the gospel of getting on.' The liberation depends upon 'a reactionary force' in society, 'providing for prejudice and stock response.' The condition of the archetype in the human imagination is the cliché. In his reply to W.K Wimsatt, who reduced his archetypal theory to a defence of stereotypes, Frye rightly insists that 'all [his] educational views are based on [their] opposition, and have as their aim the attempt to win for literature the response generally given to social mythology' ('Reflections' 143). But the winning over depends upon the response that is bound to 'social mythology.' The creative energy required for the 'winning over' is congealed in the 'social mythology' as the storehouse of it. To 'win' it 'over' for 'literature' is an abuse of metaphor, the carrying over that *is* metaphor becoming in the winning over an ideological abuse of metaphor that binds it to the very world that Frye so strenuously, as an archetypal critic, rejects. 'Mr. Hartman also notes in me,' Frye writes, responding to Geoffrey Hartman's more generous paper, 'a combination of interests which are partly scientific (perhaps the wrong word, though mine) and partly evangelical (certainly the right word, though not mine), the same mixture of detachment and engagement which exists in most areas of scholarship in the humanities' ('Reflections' 133–4). Not surprisingly, therefore, Frye found it necessary to transcend the essential 'Opposition' that characterizes the dialectical operations of the imagination. When he writes that, on the existential level of the archetype, he had swallowed all the fathers and was now '*on* [*his*] *own*,' his archetypal position was that of the 'Creator alone in nothing whom we meet on page one of all orthodox cosmogonies.' Archetypally, this was my experience of Frye as he stood before the class delivering his brilliant noteless lectures, quoting from the texts he had swallowed. My awe had terror in it as the condition of it. I sensed in Frye the Christian evangelist whom I too had cast out, or at least I thought I had. Such was my projection onto Frye that, like Derrida in relation to Foucault, I became in his class the container of his unconscious. I became the Spectre of Frye's Los.

In writing *Madness and Civilization: A History of Insanity in the Age of Reason*, Derrida explains that Foucault

> wanted to write a history of madness *itself*, that is madness speaking on the basis of its own experience and under its own authority, and not a history of madness described from within the language of reason, the language of psychiatry *on* madness – the agonistic and rhetorical dimensions of the preposition *on* overlapping here – on madness already crushed beneath psychiatry, dominated, beaten to the ground, interned, that is to say, madness made into an object and exiled as the other of a language and a historical meaning which have been confused with logos itself. 'A history not of psychiatry,' Foucault says, 'but of madness itself, in its most vibrant state, before being captured by knowledge.' ('Cogito' 34)

In *Madness and Civilization*, Foucault enacted far more brutally as language the actual treatment of the insane in the Age of Reason, a treatment it considered humane and enlightened, the asylum in its constructed view sharing most of the conventions of the pastoral. In the treatment of insanity, it ironically enacted its literary vision of an ideal society as the other of an actual or historical one. The enlightened treatment of the insane was a vision of the enlightenment sufficiently removed from the actual not to be threatened by it. By taking every precaution to ensure its autonomy, the Age of Reason constructed in its treatment of madness a visionary world not unlike the autonomous one constructed by Frye in his *Anatomy of Criticism*.

Though I was unable to articulate it in his graduate course on Blake, I unconsciously sensed that Blake's madness was being 'dominated' by Frye, 'beaten to the ground, interned.' In reading *Milton*, I thought I encountered 'madness itself, in its most vibrant state,' which the 'sanity' of Blake protected from 'being captured by knowledge' by constructing a 'system,' not to contain it, but to support the ceaseless overthrow of it, a 'system' perpetually at war with system in a process of endless becoming that no notion of being could contain. One reason I could not read *Milton* was that, sensing in what was going on within Blake at Felpham as it is revealed in the writing of *Milton*, I unconsciously experienced the epic as 'madness speaking on the basis of its own experience and under its own authority.' To reduce this 'madness' to the language of reason, which Hayley as Satan was determined to do, was to impose upon *Milton* what Satan in the Preludium imposed upon Palamabron. What was required was a different understanding of insanity, closer to Plato's notion of divine insanity, though not, like Plato's notion, contained within the dialectic of the Logos that, in the name of the archetypes, rejects the divine energy upon which their life depends.

In his Seventh Letter, Plato insists that he has never written a work dealing with the object of knowledge because, he insists, 'there is no way of putting it in words like other studies.' The object of knowledge is the consciousness of itself not as object but as subject. Yet, he argues, 'acquaintance' with it, as distinct from a 'knowledge' of it, is possible 'after a long period of attendance on instruction in the subject itself.' At some point within the 'attendance' (comparable to a vigil), 'suddenly, like a blaze kindled by a leaping spark, it is generated in the soul and at once becomes self-sustaining' (1589). This 'blaze ... generated in the soul' that 'becomes self-sustaining' is what Plato means by divine insanity. The object of knowledge is the extinction of knowledge in the 'blaze' that kindles it.

The object of knowledge resides for Derrida in the 'madness' of the Cogito, which, like the Burning Bush, consumes the object of knowledge because it *is* the object, not of knowledge, but of itself, the 'I Am that I Am.' In submitting 'Cogito and the History of Madness' for publication in the *Revue de métaphysique et de morale*, Derrida insisted that it should retain 'its first form, that of the spoken word, with all its requirements and, especially, its particular weaknesses.' In this original form, the printed text, 'miming the improvisation of the voice' and giving up 'the resources and lies of style' (307n) available to written prose in the author's potentially endless revisions comes closer to 'madness speaking on the basis of its own experience and under its own authority,' which Foucault's PhD dissertation could not allow. Commenting on the printed reproduction of the spoken word, Alan Bass refers to the remark in Plato's *Phaedrus* that the written word is deprived of '"the assistance of its father"' (307n), whose metaphysical presence becomes, as writing, the form of his absence; writing, for Derrida, was a patricidal act, which in the Eucharist is both recognized and denied in the eating of the wafer (Frye swallowing the fathers, which left him *'on [his] own'*). By the father, Derrida means what Frye calls 'the Creator alone in nothing,' who, for Derrida, contains everything within himself as 'an anxiety about language' ('Force' 3) in us. This takes the form of 'the structuralist obsession,' a systematic containing of everything haunted by its own nothingness, 'particularly,' Derrida remarks, 'the structuralism of literary criticism, which [as what Jean-Pierre Richard describes as 'interrogative and totalitarian'] has eagerly joined the trend' (4).

Derrida compares the result of this 'structuralist obsession' to a 'city no longer inhabited, not simply left behind, but haunted by meaning and culture.' 'This state of being haunted,' he writes, 'which keeps the city from returning to nature, is perhaps the general mode of the presence or absence of the thing itself in pure language. The pure language that would be housed in pure literature, the object of pure literary criticism.' 'Thus it is in no way paradoxical,' he concludes,

> that the structuralist consciousness is a catastrophic consciousness ... Structure is perceived through the incidence of menace, at the moment when imminent danger concentrates our vision on the keystone of an institution, the stone [Frye's archetypes as 'building-blocks'] which encapsulates both the possibility and the fragility of its existence ... It is during the epochs of historical dislocation, when we are expelled from the *site* [patricide], that this structuralist passion, which is simultaneously a frenzy of experimentation and a proliferation of schematizations, develops for itself. The baroque would only be one example of it. Has not a 'structural poetics' 'founded on a rhetoric' been mentioned in relation to the baroque? But has not a 'burst structure' also been spoken of, a 'rent poem whose structure appears as it bursts apart'? ('Force' 5–6)

In his essay on Antonin Artaud, 'The Theater of Cruelty and the Closure of Representation,' Derrida examines more closely the catastrophe that has overtaken the sign, which is the fate of language once it is released from things. He begins his essay in the following manner:

> '... Dance / and consequently the theater / have not yet begun to exist.' This is what one reads in one of Antonin Artaud's last writings (Le théâtre

de la cruauté in *84*, 1948). And in the same text, a little earlier, the theater of cruelty is defined as 'the affirmation / of a terrible / and, moreover, implacable necessity.' Artaud, therefore, does not call for destruction, for a new manifestation of negativity. Despite everything that it must ravage in its wake, 'the theater of cruelty / is not the symbol of an absent void.' It *affirms*, it produces affirmation itself in its full and necessary rigor. But also in its most hidden sense, the sense most often buried, most often diverted from itself: 'implacable' as it is, this affirmation has 'not yet begun to exist.' (232)

Derrida goes on to describe Artaud's expulsion of the father (God) from the stage, which, he explains, 'is theological for as long as it is dominated by speech, by a will to speech, by the layout of a primary logos which does not belong to the theatrical site and governs it from a distance' (235) as a metaphysics of presence. Exploring at some length the 'structure' of the stage in 'the entirety of tradition,' Derrida treats it as analogous to the violence buried in the 'structuralist obsession' as it positively erupts in Artaud's theatre of cruelty to release the sign from the tyranny to which structuralism has reduced it. 'Released from the text and the author-god,' Derrida, as Artaud, explains, 'mise en scène [sign] would be returned to its creative and founding freedom' (237). Moving beyond Artaud, who, wrongly to Derrida, associates the founding freedom of speech with onomatopoeia, Derrida identifies it with glossopoeia. 'Glossopocia,' he explains,

> which is neither an imitative language nor a creation of names, takes us back to the borderline of the moment when the word has not yet been born [as in Kristeva's notion of the 'semiotic'], when articulation is no longer a shout but not yet discourse, when repetition is *almost* impossible, and along with it, language in general: the separation of concept and sound, of signified and signifier, of the pneumatical and the grammatical ... the difference between the soul and the body, the master and the slave, God and man, author and actor. This is the eve [Eve, Evoi] of the origin of languages, and of the dialogue between theology and humanism whose inextinguishable reoccurrence has never not been maintained by the metaphysics of Western theater. (240)

Insisting that the 'word is the cadaver of psychic speech,' Derrida quotes Artaud in support (even as Artaud is supporting Derrida in a way that Foucault could not): '"I am adding another language to the spoken language, and I am trying to restore to the language of speech its old magic, its essential spellbinding power, for its mysterious possibilities have been forgotten. When I say I will perform no written play, I mean that I will perform no play based on writing and speech, that in the spectacles I produce there will be a preponderant physical share which could not be captured and written down in the customary language of words, and that even the spoken and written portions will be spoken and written in a new sense"' (240).

Derrida and Artaud, speaking together as one, like Milton in the body of Blake, are talking about what Paul describes as '"unspeakable words" (*arreta rhemata*), not lawful for a man to utter.' Paul appears to have in mind the 'cloven tongues like as of fire' that descended upon the apostles on the day of Pentecost so that, 'filled with the Holy Ghost,' they 'began to speak with other tongues, as the Spirit gave them utterance' (Acts 2.3–4). Peter, who was present, assures those who witnessed it that they were not drunk, even as Paul is obliged to tell Festus that he is not mad. While not 'condemning' tongues of fire, Paul, as Frye points out, 'remarks caustically that he would rather speak five words that made sense than ten thousand that did not' (*Great Code* 219) (which is perhaps not quite what Paul meant by 'an *unknown* tongue' [1 Corinthians 14.19]). For Frye, as already noted, the '*unknown* tongue' is what he calls a fourth stage of language, in which all three forms (metaphor, metonymy, the descriptive) would be united and transformed by revelation. As a literary critic, he is free to speculate about a fourth stage because literary language is no longer answerable to the actual world, though, grounded as it is in Hegel, it is in no sense comparable to Derrida's account of glossopoeia.

In his essay on Artaud, Derrida goes on to examine the implications of what he calls Artaud's 'new language' as 'hieroglyphic writing, the writing in which phonetic elements are coordinated to visual, pictorial, and plastic elements.' As Derrida here describes it, 'hieroglypic writing' is essentially what Blake's writing is. The 'phonetic elements' are painted and arranged on the plate with their 'visual, pictorial and plastic elements' in mind. Blake writes as a painter paints, the painterly design of a plate interfering, as Frye noted, with the narrative flow, the *mythos* becoming visual or pictorial illumination in a way that becomes fully orchestrated in the full-plate pictorial representations of the *mythos*, which do not merely illustrate the text but become an integral part of it. '"The theater must organize [what is happening] into veritable hieroglyphs, with the help of characters and objects,"' Artaud explains in the *First Manifesto*, '"and make use of their symbolism and interconnections in relation to all organs and on all levels"' ('Theater' 240–1). Blake is doing the same thing in his poetry.

'On the stage of the dream, as described by Freud, speech has the same status,' Derrida continues, now quoting extensively from Freud:

> Present in dreams, speech can only behave as an element among others, sometimes like a 'thing' which the primary process manipulates according to its own economy. 'In this process thoughts are transformed into images, mainly of a visual sort; that is to say, word presentations are taken back to the thing–presentations which correspond to them ... It is very noteworthy how little the dream-work keeps to word-presentations; it is always ready to exchange one word for another till it finds the expression which is most handy for plastic representation' ... And when Freud, speaking of dreams, invokes ... the primitive painter who, in the fashion of authors of comic strips, hung 'small labels ... from the mouths of the persons represented, containing in written characters the speeches which the artist despaired of representing pictorially,' we understand what speech can become when it is but an element, a circumscribed site, a circumvented writing within both general writing and the space of representation ... 'If we reflect that the means of representation in dreams are principally visual images and not words, we shall see that it is even more appropriate to compare dreams with a system of writing than with a language. In fact the interpretation of dreams is completely analogous to the decipherment of an ancient pictographic script such as Egyptian hieroglyphs.' (241)

Blake's Albion, asleep for 6,000 years from the Creation to the Judgment upon a 'Couch of Death,' becomes in Blake's vision 'the stage of the dream' in which, as *mythos*, 'an ancient pictographic script such as Egyptian hieroglyphs' awaits 'the decipherment' of the reader, which includes Blake, not as its author, but as the secretary. 'I am not ashamed afraid or averse to tell You what Ought to be Told,' Blake wrote to Butts. 'That I am under the direction of Messengers from Heaven Daily & Nightly' (E 724). The result was a 'long Poem descriptive of ... the Spiritual Acts of [his] three years Slumber on the banks of the Ocean ... the Persons & Machinery intirely new to the Inhabitants of Earth' (728). With 'Divine Assistance,' Blake confidently concludes, it will 'be progressively Printed & Ornamented with Prints & given to the Public' (730).

What Blake gave to a 'Public' fully unprepared to receive it was indeed an epic, whose 'Persons & Machinery' were 'intirely new to the Inhabitants of the Earth.' So far as the 'Public' (the Deists, the Christians, and the Jews) were concerned, *Jerusalem* was no more decipherable than 'Egyptian hieroglyphs.' To absorb Blake's vision into Frye's interpretation of it is to sacrifice its 'divine insanity' to the tyranny of an eternal structure that is the secular enactment of the Logos whose spiritual form is Christ. The emerging sanity that resides in Blake's 'divine insanity' lay in a descent into Hell, which Frye rightly describes as psychosis. 'To claim the Hells, my Furnaces, I go to Eternal Death' (*M* 14[15].32), declares Blake's Milton as he is about to enter Blake's 'Vegetable Body.' At Felpham, seeing Blake at work in the service of Satan (Hayley), 'Los took off his left sandal placing it on his head, / Signal of solemn mourning' (*M* 8.11–12). This same sandal Los, standing in a 'fierce glowing fire' had 'stoop'd down' (22[24].9) and bound on Blake before hurling him into the whirlwind of his 'Vehicular'(17[19].31) body (a 'Pulsation of the Artery') from Lambeth to Felpham. Blake became 'One Man with him' (*M* 22[24].12) in what would appear to be in the full-page pictorial rendering (plate 47) the act of *fellatio* in which Blake receives from Los the divine afflatus or *spermatikos* by which *Milton* is 'concievd' (*M* 29[31].2). And when Milton enters his body at the metatarsus of the left foot, the entire 'Vegetable World' entered with him, Milton's hermaphroditic body being the 'Vegetable World' as the psychotic form of the divine one which Milton's arrested vision in *Paradise Lost* had imposed upon it. 'And all this Vegetable World appeard on my left Foot, / As a bright sandal formd immortal of precious stones & gold,' declares Blake; 'I stoopd down & bound it on to walk forward thro' Eternity' (*M* 21[23].12–14). The sandal belongs to Blake's 'pictographic script.' It appears on Los's left foot, on his head, then in its 'Vehicular' form taking him in a 'Pulsation of the Artery' from Lambeth to Felpham, and then again as the entire 'Vegetable World' in which he walks forward to the Judgment and Resurrection. Blake's apocalyptic vision is the imaginative struggle to transform the world's psychotic body, the struggle itself being the form of it.[16]

All of this dreamwork takes place in 'a Pulsation of the Artery' in which Blake lies unconscious ('outstretchd upon the path / A moment' [42[49].25–6]), not conscious of anything that is going on ('As when a man dreams, he reflects not that his body sleeps, / Else he would wake' [15[17].1–2]). Blake, like any reader, must decipher his dream as one might decipher 'Egyptian hieroglyphics.' The sanity that resides in the deciphering is the conscious recognition of an archetypal unconscious as a ceaseless process of becoming. The pictographic language of Blake's text lies, not in the Logos or Word, as Frye's archetypal criticism describes it, but in the representation of a 'divine insanity' into which Blake anatomically enters as the 'Secretary' of it. This anatomical entry, mirrored in the entry of the hermaphroditic Milton into Blake's 'Vegetable Body,' is a creative engagement with psychosis that the imagination transforms into a 'divine insanity.' The result of this transformation is 'the Divine Revelation in the Litteral expression' of the 'human form divine.' This 'human form divine' is a ceaseless process of becoming propelled by an infinite desire (spirit) that, as the condition of it, is forever psychically bound. Coming to grips with Blake's dreamwork as the figuration of desire rather than the logocentric rationalization of it became the issue that informed my reading of Frye's Blake.

3

Blake's Fourfold Body

The Sexual is Threefold; the Human is Fourfold.

Blake, Milton

When Blake asserts that 'the Human is Fourfold,' he is describing the way in which the fully 'Human' sphere, as distinct from its lower mineral, vegetable and animal spheres, relates to the world. The lower spheres together constitute a psycho-physical body that Paul, as Frye notes, calls the '*soma psychikon*,' understood as an unresolved temporal relationship between soul and body in which each struggles to bind the other to itself. In 'The Human Abstract' and 'A Poison Tree,' Blake describes this binding as a mutual entrapment in terms of the Miltonic myth in which Blake's Milton found himself and from which, in *Milton*, Blake sought to release him: 'Of man's first disobedience, and the fruit / Of that forbidden tree whose mortal taste / Brought death into the world, and all our woe, / With loss of Eden' (*PL* 1.1–4).

In *Milton*, Blake sets out to raise the Messiah of *Paradise Lost* from his fallen state as 'a Ratio of the five senses' in which, using Newton's compasses, he circumscribed chaos by binding it forever to natural law, the fallen human form of which is Deism or natural religion. The 'one man Jesus' who descends into Blake's garden in the final plates of *Milton* wrapped in Ololon's garment is Blake's redeemed Messiah. As Blake's illuminated text, Ololon's garment (Christ's 'linen clothes folded up' in the tomb guarded by an Angel [*MHH* 3]) is 'the Divine Revelation in the Litteral expression,' which is to say the literal work of Blake's hand. Referring to his own method of engraving, printing, and illuminating, Blake declares: 'Now is the dominion of Edom, & the return of

Adam into Paradise' (3). As the inspired poet, Blake is Milton's 'one greater Man' who 'regain[s] the blissful seat' (*PL* 1.5). This regaining takes place in Blake's 'Printing house in Hell,' where, Blake propheti- cally declares, 'at the end of six thousand years' the world 'will be consumed in fire' (*MHH* 14). The 'cherub with his flaming sword,' who in *Paradise Lost* stands guard 'at the tree of life,' will be commanded by Los, the prophetic imagination, to leave his post. His fire will then consume 'the whole creation,' so that as 'Energy' (4) the creation will 'appear infinite. and holy whereas it now appears finite of corrupt' (14). By 'printing in the infernal method, by corrosives, which in Hell are salutary and medicinal,' 'apparent surfaces' will be melted away to display 'the infinite which was hid' (14). *The Marriage of Heaven and Hell* is Blake's apocalyptic manifesto, in which he prophetically an- nounces himself as the Second Coming. The 'new heaven' that has begun is the New Jerusalem of Revelation 'coming down from God out of heaven, prepared as a bride adorned for her husband' (Revela- tion 21.2). In the final plates of *Milton*, this second 'coming' is Ololon descending into 'the Fires of [Blake's] Intellect that rejoic'd in Felphams Vale / Around the Starry Eight.' The 'Starry Eight' is the 'One Man Jesus the Saviour' (42[49].7 11) enfolded in Ololon's garment, Blake's illuminated text.

In *Songs of Experience*, Blake enacts the present state of the world circumscribed by Newton's compasses, the 'apparent surfaces' of which hide the 'infinite' it potentially contains. In 'The Human Abstract' and 'A Poison Tree,' 'the fruit / Of that forbidden tree' is the 'fruit of Deceit' ('The Human Abstract' 17), which ripens on the 'Poison Tree' growing 'in the Human Brain' (24). The 'mutual fear' (5), which binds soul and body in the 'Vegetable Body' (Paul's *soma psychikon*), is a perverse form of 'peace' (5) grounded in 'Cruelty' (7) rather than forgiveness. It is grounded, that is, not in the 'beams of love' which, in *Jerusalem*, 'ev'ry morn / Awakes [Blake] at sun-rise' (4.3–4), but in the anger of Milton's God, whom Blake calls Urizen, the Deist God who preaches a gospel of 'Deceit & False Forgiveness' (*M* 16[18]). 'Man, disobeying, / Disloyal breaks his fealty,' declares Milton's God,

> and sins
> Against the high supremacy of Heav'n,
> Affecting God-head, and so losing all,
> To expiate his Treason hath naught left,
> But to destruction sacred and devote,

He with his whole posterity must die,
Die hee or Justice must; unless for him
Some other able, and as willing, pay
The rigid satisfaction, death for death.   (*PL* 3.203–12)

In the perverse form of love, which Blake calls 'Cruelty,' pity lies in making 'somebody Poor' ('The Human Abstract' 2), mercy lies in making somebody unhappy. What appears to be love (divine forgiveness) is an increase of 'the selfish loves' (6) in which 'Cruelty knits a snare, / And spreads his baits with care' (7–8). The 'baits' are pity, mercy, and humility in which 'Cruelty' disguises itself. Watering the 'Poison Tree' night and morning with these vices which wear the appearance of virtue, sunning it 'with smiles, / And with soft deceitful wiles' (7–8), the 'Poison Tree' bears its poisoned fruit 'ruddy and sweet to eat' ('The Human Abstract' 18). Lured by the 'apple bright' ('A Poison Tree' 10), snared in a game of their mutual, unconscious devising, the two enemies, soul and body, confront each other in each other's death. 'And my foe beheld it shine,' writes Blake, enacting the diabolical dynamics of 'mutual fears' that seem to bring the 'peace' that keeps Milton a prisoner of his unholy epic. Stealing into the garden 'when the night had veild the pole,' the foe steals and eats the fruit. 'In the morning glad I see; / My foe outstretchd beneath the tree' (11–16), Blake concludes his lyric, both soul and body having paid 'the rigid satisfaction, death for death.'

Addressing the Newtonian state of the world bound by what Coleridge describes as the 'mechanical philosophy,' Blake, like all the Romantics, recognized that it had to be consumed by the 'Fire' of the dialectical imagination. Matter, whether at its limit of 'Contraction' as Adam, or at its limit of 'Opacity' (*M* 13[14].20) as Satan,[1] had to expand beyond the range of Newton's compasses in which Milton's God refused fully to put forth his goodness (*PL* 7.171) until it reached 'the bound or outward circumference of Energy' (*MHH* 4). Viewed in one of its many offered perspectives, English Romanticism is the struggle to release Milton from the fetters of *Paradise Lost*. In Blake's particular case, this release is enacted as the opening of the Eighth Eye of God. The Eighth Eye is the doubling of the Fourfold, which is the 'Human' becoming conscious of its own consciousness. The Eighth Eye is God's full recognition of himself as 'Human.'

Jung enacts the slow and painful opening of the Eighth Eye in his *Answer to Job* as Job's struggle with the *'deus absconditus,'* the dark unconsciousness of God as it rises towards consciousness in Job's afflictions, the consciousness to which it rises becoming for Jung 'the transformation of the *deus absconditus* (i.e., the *natura abscondita*) into the *medicina Catholica* of alchemical wisdom' (*CW* 11:358). God's unconsciousness is projected onto the figure of Satan, who is given the task of tempting Job to see if Job will reject God. In Jung's rendering of the figure of Satan, God is struggling in the projected agony of Job to bring himself to a consciousness of the negative operations of his Energy as his fearful way of transforming Energy rather than repressing it. In Jung's reading of his largely projected behaviour, God is confronting his own Shadow in a painful, unwilling attempt to integrate it. In this sense, the God of Jung's *Answer to Job* 'is a true Poet and of the Devils party without knowing it.' He is also Jung's model analysand undergoing a successful Jungian analysis as his ultimate recognition of himself as his own redeemer. Not satisfied with his own biblical behaviour in his treatment of his chosen seed, which necessitates the ruthless killing of all that does not issue from it according to his will, the Elohim unconsciously knows that he must change his ways. He is far too tribally oriented, far too concerned with his own immediate family to be worthy of his larger role as the Creator of everything that exists. Jung's *Answer to Job* is a psychological account of Blake's prophetic vision in *The Marriage of Heaven and Hell*. In the creative suffering of Job in which the 'Contaries' become 'necessary to Human existence' (*MHH* 3), 'the cherub with his flaming sword is ... commanded to leave his guard at the tree of life' (14) so that the contrary demands of the two trees may, in Job, become dialectically engaged.

In Jung's reading of the Book of Job, God still largely inhabits an unconscious realm in which everything is going on, but nothing is allowed to happen. In Blake's reading, he remains bound to the Twofold world of Generation, consciously determined to preserve it forever in this Urizenic arrested state as the immutable form of his own perfection. He is, in this sense, Milton's Messiah circumscribing chaos within a rational order from which God himself has partially withdrawn ('Though I uncircumscrib'd myself retire, / And put not forth my goodness' [*PL* 7.170–1]). Blake calls this arrested state 'the Seven Eyes of God' (*M* 24[26].7), which, as a history of the fallen world (humankind bound to the natural order), constitutes the 'Six Thousand Years' (28[30].63) from the Creation to the Judgment.

As a history of the fallen world initiated in *Paradise Lost* by Satan's rebellion, the Judgment becomes, for Blake, a Judgment against the Creation itself in which God effectively undoes all that he has as yet appeared to do. 'Whatever can be Created can be Annihilated,' Blake declares. To which he is quick to add, 'Forms cannot / The Oak is cut down by the Ax, the Lamb falls by the Knife / But their Forms Eternal Exist, For-ever. Amen Halle[l]ujah' (32[35].36–8). The 'Forms' transcend the God of Creation, who, in unconscious obedience to the 'Forms,' annihilates what he creates. In this radical sense, Blake embraces a notion of the archetype that Jung will later affirm, constructing his psychology upon it. Because the 'Forms' exist forever in the imagination, which 'is the Human Existence itself' (32[35].32), Blake, in obedience to them as the eternal Fourfold Human (the four Zoas), becomes the prophet of a fully awakened human consciousness, which he describes as the Eighth Eye. Embracing 'the Human Existence itself,' not just a 'portion' of it 'discernd by the five Senses. the chief inlets of Soul in [Blake's] age' (*MHH* 4). Blake's vision enacts its opening as the shaping of the eternal form of human consciousness prefigured in the death and resurrection of Jesus, prefigured because, as the Seventh Eye, it remains bound as natural religion to the natural cycle. It is not yet fully 'Human.'

Identifying Milton's God with the predetermined, circumscribed laws of motion enunciated by Newton's 'golden compasses' (*The [First] Book of Urizen* 20.39). Blake, in announcing the opening of the Eighth Eye,[2] is also announcing the end of Newtonian physics as the very embodiment of natural religion. The 'annihilation' of the universe constructed by Newton's compasses constitutes, for Blake, its gravitational collapse into its own matter as the negation of itself, its black hole or anti-matter. In *Milton*, this gravitational collapse is described as 'the Spectrous body of Milton,' which 'redounding from [Blake's] left foot into Los's Mundane space, / Brooded over his Body in Horeb against the Resurrection / Preparing it for the Great Consummation' (20[22].20–3). The 'Body' of *Paradise Lost* remains, for Blake, bound to 'the Body in Horeb,' which is the Ten Commandments of Urizen received by Moses 'on the secret top / Of Oreb' (*PL* 1.7–8). These same Ten Commandments are what Blake calls Milton's 'Mortal part' that 'sat frozen in the rock of Horeb' (*M* 20[22].10–11). His frozen 'Mortal part' is his 'Sixfold Emanation scatter'd thro' the deep / In torment' (2.19–20). 'In conflict with these Female forms' (Milton's three wives and three daughters), who, because of his blindness, were forced to serve as his amanuenses, Milton saw in them what Lear saw in his daughters: 'the Cruelties of Ulro' (17[19].7, 9). As his 'Wives & Daughters ... sat rangd round him as the rocks of Horeb round the land / Of Canan ... they wrote in thunder smoke and fire / His dictate' (10–14). 'And [Milton's] body,' writes Blake, 'was the Rock Sinai; that body, / Which was on earth born to corruption' (14–15). As for 'the six Females,' they are 'Hor & Peor & Bashan & Abarim & Lebanon & Hermon / Seven rocky masses terrible in the Desarts of Midian' (15–17).

Blake thus distinguishes between Milton's 'Sixfold Emanation' in Ulro and Urania in *Paradise Lost*, who dwells in Beulah. Playing with her sister, Sophia, before the throne of God, she nightly in dream sang to Milton, who received her song as his 'unpremeditated verse' (*PL* 9.24). What he received as music nightly in dream was in radical opposition to what consciously surrounded him when he awoke. His waking consciousness, 'in conflict with those Female forms,' surrounded him 'in blood & jealousy ... dividing & uniting without end or number' (*M* 17[19].7–8). Milton's consciousness was at war with his unconscious inspiration. His 'Selfhood,' which dwelt in 'Ulro' ('I in my Selfhood am that Satan' [14[15].30), was at war with the inspired poet. Unable to achieve the 'true Friendship' that resides in 'Opposition,' Milton, in a perpetual state of unresolved conflict, was excluded from the Fourfold world of Eden, which Blake celebrates in the final plates of *Jerusalem*. Trapped between Urania and his 'Sixfold Emanation,' he saw upon entering Blake's body at the metatarsus what Saul of Tarsus saw on the road to Damascus: he was crucifying his own inner Christ. This instant of recognition, 'less than a Pulsation of the Artery,' was as blinding to Saul as it was to Milton. In both cases, it opened their inward eyes. 'So much the rather thou Celestial Light / Shine inward,' writes Milton, invoking 'holy Light, offspring ... of th'Eternal Coeternal beam' (*PL* 3.1–2) which, as the 'Holy Ghost,' Blake describes in *Paradise Lost* as a 'Vacuum' [*MHH* 6]):

> and the mind through all her powers
> Irradiate, there plant eyes, all mist from thence
> Purge and disperse, that I may see and tell
> Of things invisible to mortal sight. (3.51–5)

Because, according to Blake, the 'Celestial Light' is a 'Vacuum' in *Paradise Lost*, Milton cannot enter the 'Fourfold' that is 'Human.' He remains bound to the 'Sexual' realm of Beulah, Urania becoming in relation to his 'Sixfold Emanation' a sublimated or idealized form of sexuality. In this respect, Blake's criticism of *Paradise Lost* mirrors Jung's criticism of Freud's dogma of sexuality; Jung enlarges the libido, even as Blake expands the 'Vegetable Body,' to include the 'Fourfold' world of spirituality and mythopoeia. As soon as Milton enters Blake's 'Vegetable Body,' Milton knows that the *Milton* Blake is writing – the Milton of Blake's *Milton* – is contained within a 'Fourfold' vision that has the power to transform his 'Threefold' vision in *Paradise Lost*. He can see with his inward eye that in the body of Blake he, like Jung and Pauli after him, is making 'the 2,000-year-old' journey 'from 'Three to Four' (*Atom* 129). 'Then Milton knew,' writes Blake,

> that the Three Heavens of Beulah were beheld
> By him on earth in his bright pilgrimage of sixty years
> In those three females whom his Wives, & those three whom his
>   Daughters
> Had represented and containd, that they might be resum'd
> By giving up of Selfhood: & they distant view'd his journey
> In their eternal spheres, now Human, tho' their Bodies remain clos'd
> In the dark Ulro till the Judgment: also Milton knew: they and
> Himself was Human.   (*M* 15[17].51–52; 17[19].1–6)

As 'Allegory addressed to the Intellectual Powers,' which 'is altogether hidden from the Corporeal Understanding' (E 730), Blake's *Milton* operates on both levels, the 'Corporeal' serving as a demonic parody, whose chief purpose is to hide the 'Intellectual.' Milton 'clos'd / In dark Ulro' with his 'Sixfold Emanation' is that 'portion of Soul discernd by the five Senses. the chief inlets of Soul in [Blake's] age.' Blake descended to this 'portion' in his reading aloud of *Paradise Lost* to his wife, Catherine, Milton in eternity listening to him read it. Suddenly, 'within a Moment: less than a Pulsation of the Artery,' Milton's text opened to Blake to reveal its apocalyptic form hidden within its 'Corporeal' body. 'My bones trembled,' writes Blake.

> I fell outstretchd upon the path
> A moment, & my Soul returnd into its mortal state
> To Resurrection & Judgment in the Vegetable Body
> And my sweet Shadow of Delight stood trembling by my side.
>   (*M* 42[49].25–8)

Milton records this 'Moment' in which his soul left 'its mortal state,' a state that cannot be described, however, except by relating it to the

'Vegetable Body.' The action of *Milton* takes place in 'less than a Pulsation of the Artery' within the 'Vegetable Body,' where, as in Jung's notion of the psychoid archetype, body and soul 'meeting in a point without extension – a real zero point – touch and do not touch.' Blake describes it in a passage as astonishing as anything he ever wrote, naming the lark as 'Los's messenger':

> When on the highest lift of his light pinions he arrives
> At that bright Gate [of Los], another Lark meets him & back to back
> They touch their pinions tip tip: and each descend
> To their respective Earths & there all night consult with Angels
> Of Providence & with the Eyes of God all night in slumbers
> Inspired: & at the dawn of day send out another Lark
> Into another Heaven to carry news upon his wings
> Thus are the Messengers dispatchd till they reach the Earth again
> In the East Gate of Golgonooza, & the Twenty-eighth bright
> Lark. met the Female Ololon descending into my Garden
> Thus it appears to Mortal eyes & those of the Ulro Heavens
> But not thus to Immortals, the Lark is a mighty Angel.   (36[40].1–12)

In the ceaseless process of metamorphosis in 'the Fires of [Blake's] Intellect,' which is metaphor's vital life, Blake's 'Twenty-eighth bright Lark' is the 'Seven Eyes' as the Threefold now become the Fourfold or 'Starry Eight.' This 'Starry Eight' is Ololon, the New Jerusalem, her wedding garment Blake's illuminated text 'written within & without in woven letters' (42[49].13. The writing itself is 'clouds of blood' and 'streams of gore' (8), that is to say, a 'Garment of War' (15), understood as ceaseless 'Mental Fight,' Blake's incisor serving as his 'sword,' not sleeping in his 'hand,' but engraving his text upon his copper plate in a method described to him in a dream by his dead brother. All of this in its eternal 'Form' is revealed to Blake in 'less than a Pulsation of the Artery.' 'Amen Halle[l]ujah.'

Conscious of the Fourfold body as the containing form of his vision, Blake can, as Milton, descend into the hidden depths of his 'Vegetable Body' to discover in 'every Time less than a Pulsation of the Artery' the eternal act of creation in its unfallen form, which Coleridge calls the 'primary imagination' as the 'living Power and prime Agent of all human perception.' In the 'Vegetable Body,' Blake locates this power in the brain, where

> by your [the Daughters of Beulah's] ministry
> The Eternal Great Humanity Divine. planted his Paradise,
> And in it caus'd the Spectres of the Dead to take sweet forms
> In likeness of himself.   (2.7–10)

The brain, that is, is the seat of sensations, where they are translated into mental images. So long as these sensations remain bound to the discernment of the five senses ('the chief inlets of Soul in this age'), they become as mental images 'the Spectres of the Dead.' As 'Spectres,' the mythopoeic imagination is reduced by the 'mechanical philosophy' to what Jung calls 'the stuff of psychosis' found 'in the insane' (*MDR* 188).

At Felpham, Blake experienced them in just this way. As a mental image, his patron William Hayley became Satan, and he himself became the radically compromised poet, Palamabron, who was beholden to him. 'Mark well my words! they are of your eternal salvation' (*M* 7.16), Blake addresses his reader as he describes his situation at Felpham:

> Palamabron. fear'd to be angry lest Satan [Hayley] should accuse him of
> Ingratitude, & Los believe the accusation thro Satans extreme
> Mildness. Satan [Blake working for Hayley] labourd all day. it was a
>   thousand years
> In the evening returning terrified overlabourd & astonish'd
> Embrac'd soft with a brothers tears Palamabron, who also wept
> ...
> Next morning Palamabron rose: the horses of the Harrow [Printing
>   Press]
> Were maddend with tormenting fury, & the servants of the Harrow
> The Gnomes, accus'd Satan, with indignation fury and fire.
> Then Palamabron reddening like the Moon in an eclipse,
> Spoke saying, You know Satans mildness and his self-imposition,
> Seeming a brother, being a tyrant, even thinking himself a brother
> While he is murdering the just; prophetic I behold
> His future course thro' darkness and despair to eternal death
> But we must not be tyrants also! he hath assum'd my place
> For one whole day, under pretence of pity and love to me.   (7.11–26)

Hayley, who had written a biography of Milton that reduced Milton's vision to the level of Hayley's 'Corporeal Understanding' (E 730), was equally determined, 'under pretence of pity and love,' to reduce Blake's vision to the same state. The psychic struggle between them repeats the deadly struggle enacted by Blake in 'The Human Abstract' and 'A Poison Tree.' Under these circumstances, Blake in the garden at Felpham read *Paradise Lost* aloud to his wife, sensing, among other things, that Hayley had designs upon her not much different from his designs upon Blake. Projecting this mental state onto Milton's text, Blake suddenly saw the apocalyptic form of his condition at Felpham as a twelve-book epic already 'Done' in 'Eternity' in 'less than a Pulsation of the Artery.' 'I may praise it,' he wrote to Thomas Butts (6 July 1803),

> since I dare not pretend to be any other than the Secretary the Authors are in Eternity I consider it as the Grandest Poem that This World Contains ... This Poem shall by Divine Assistance be progressively Printed & Ornamented with Prints & given to the Public – But of this work I take care to say little to Mr H[ayley] since he is as much averse to my poetry as he is to a Chapter in the Bible He knows that I have writ it for I have shewn it to him & he had read Part by his own desire & has lookd with sufficient contempt to enhance my opinion of it. But I do not wish to irritate by seeming too obstinate in Poetic pursuits. But if all the World should set their faces against This I have Orders to set my face like a flint. Ezekiel iii C 9 v.[3] against their faces & my forehead against their foreheads. (E 730)

Once Milton realizes that Blake's *mythos* is the vision of the Eighth Eye extending the 'Vegetable Body' to its 'bound or outward circumference,' thereby releasing it from the 'Ratio of the five senses' to which scientific materialism had reduced it, he can begin actively to cooperate with what is happening to him. He becomes conscious of his various embryonic states in the womb of Blake. The dialectical structure that is Blake's 'Allegory addressed to the Intellectual powers' comes together in the infinite array of its 'minute particulars' to enact the Jungian unconscious shaped by consciousness into the human form of God. 'Would to God that all the Lords people were Prophets,' Blake, quoting Moses (Numbers 11.29), writes in his preface to *Milton*. His goal is to bring Milton to an awareness of his prophetic power, which is the dialectic propelling the soul into a recognition of its Fourfold wholeness.

'I give you the end of a golden string,' Blake writes, addressing the Christians in the fourth chapter of *Jerusalem*, 'Only wind it into a ball: / It will lead you in at Heavens gate, / Built in Jerusalems wall.' For Blake, the 'golden string' of Ariadne is provided by the 'Daughters of Beulah,' the 'Muses who inspire the Poets Song' (*M* 2.1). These 'Daughters' are the readers' feminine portion, which quickens their Threefold Sexual to unite with the object of desire in Beulah, described by Blake as the 'Realms / Of terror & mild moony lustre, in soft sexual delusions / Of varied beauty, to delight the wanderer and repose / His burning thirst & freezing hunger' (2.1–5). In this sense, the 'Daughters of Beulah' are, like Jung's anima, not to be trusted because, as Jung argues, 'as the mouthpiece of the unconscious,' the anima 'can utterly destroy a man' (*MDR* 187). Blake's 'Daughters of Beulah' are 'Threefold.' They cannot ascend beyond the 'Sexual' to the 'Fourfold' realm of Eden. The 'golden thread' of Enitharmon is also Blake's 'Golden Net' (E 483), too easily entangled with 'the Spectres of the Dead' (E716), which, 'like echoes through long caverns, wind and roll' (*PU* 1.806). 'Beulah,' Blake explains, 'is evermore Created around Eternity; appearing / To the Inhabitants of Eden, around them on all sides' (*M* 30[33].8–9). The danger is that, surrounded 'on all sides' by Beulah, they may, like Blake's Wordsworth, be reduced to the condition of 'the beloved infant in his mothers bosom round incircled / With arms of love & pity & sweet compassion.' As a realm of 'a mild & pleasant Rest,' the 'Inhabitants of Eden,' like Shakespeare's Antony, may be lured away forever from the 'great Wars of Eternity, in fury of Poetic Inspiration, / To build the Universe stupendous' (11–20).

This, it may be argued, is what happened to Frye in his reading of Blake. He turned his back on history as the scene of psychosis to find in Blake's Beulah a source of endless pleasure that largely ignored Blake's warning against it. The verbal universe became for him an all-encompassing, self-contained encirclement answerable only to its own operations. In 'Reflections in a Mirror,' Frye explained that he urged the early study of biblical and classical myths because he considered them essential to 'building up the sense of a literary order and putting the student inside it' so as not to confuse it with life, or what he calls 'the attributing of poetic schematism to the objective world, which takes different forms in different historical epochs.' Driving his point home, Frye then compares his understanding of the autonomous 'literary universe to Blake's Beulah, where no dispute can come, where everything is equally an element of a liberal education, where Bunyan and Rochester are met together and Jane Austen and the Marquis de Sade have kissed each other.' 'This is not the way that works of literature enter history,' Frye continues, 'and it is quite possible that the wars of myth in time are an aspect of criticism that I have not grasped' ('Reflections' 142–3). What he has 'grasped,' however, is the fact that 'the wars of myth in time' (as distinct from eternity) are mainly a demonic parody of myth in which the archetypes become stereotypes, an accusation W.K. Wimsatt brought against Frye's scheme, Frye, in response, insisting that he had been misread.

In the opposition between Beulah and Eden – a source of considerable grievance for feminist readers – resides Blake's opposition to closure of any kind and of those logocentric structures that advance towards an end. Blake's vision inhabits a 'Moment: less than a Pulsation of the Artery,' which he describes in terms of the endless misencounters with it because the reason bound to sense is always a demonic parody of it which dismisses it as mad. In this sense, Frye's schematics in his *Anatomy of Criticism*, which grew out of his reading of Blake as described in *Fearful Symmetry*, attempts to contain Blake's poetry, indeed all poetry, in the kind of systematic enclosure Blake vehemently rejects. In some terribly ironic way, Frye as Blake's reader becomes Blake's Spectre, who labours against the grain of Blake's vision in a manner that strangely illuminates it by affirming what it is not.

Dismissing Jung's notion of the 'collective unconscious' in favour of the absolute consciousness of the Logos or Word, Frye insists that it 'is not necessary to invoke any more subtle entities, such as Jung's collective unconscious, to explain the fact that human creative expression all over the world has some degree of mutual intelligibility and communicating power.' There is, he argues, 'a common sense that can, up to a point, be translated' (*Great Code* 5). Precisely, however, in Frye's association of the archetypes with 'a common sense' resides, despite his protestations, the accusation of some of his critics that the 'degree of mutual intelligibility and communicating power' all over the world reduces Frye's archetypal criticism to stereotypes and clichés masquerading as profundity. 'Fictional stories, it is true,' writes W.K. Wimsatt in his critique of Frye,

> are all about what we wish to have or to be and what we wish not to have or not to be, what we like and what we don't like. Love and marriage and banquets and dances and springtime and wheat and fruit and wine are good. Hate and strife and downfall and death, disease, blight, and poison, are bad. A lamb is a good animal, a wolf or a tiger is a bad one, and frightening, especially in a pastoral society or tradition. 'Any symbolism founded on food,' says Frye, 'is universal.' We can live in a city or a garden, not in a stony or weedy wilderness. If we rummage out all the ideas of the desirable and undesirable we can think of, they fall inevitably

under the heads of the supernatural, the human, the animal, the vegetable, and mineral, as Frye himself comes close to explaining in his
allusion to the game of Twenty Questions. See the catalogues of apocalyptic and demonic imagery in the essay of 1951 and in the third essay of the
Anatomy. (93–4)

Blake's poetry is far more about 'hate and strife and downfall and
death, disease, blight, and poison' than it is about 'love and marriage
and banquets and dances and springtime and wheat and fruit and
wine,' because the former is the human condition that requires the
latter in order to be known, the knowing of it containing within it the
possibility of awakening from it. Blake enacts the building of Jerusalem
as Albion's opposition to it as he lies upon 'the Couch of Death,' endur-
ing the 6,000-year-old 'Sleep of Ulro.' The tree that would grow to
heaven, declares Nietzsche, must send its roots to hell.

The 'metaphyics of presence' informing, for example, Frye's enclosure of the Logos or Word within the English Bible is, Derrida suggests
(though not with reference to Frye), a closure that has to be linguisti-
cally deconstructed from within because there is nothing outside it
other than what Blake calls a 'Void Outside of Existence.' This 'Void,' I
suggest, is what, like Blake, deconstruction enters as what Blake calls a
'Womb.' What happens within this 'Womb' is a radical deconstruction
of the rational notion of Logos or Word as it becomes, for Blake, natural
religion, reason itself serving as its demonic form, which Blake calls 'the
Reasoning Negative' (*M* 5.14). 'There is no sense,' Derrida explains,

in doing without the concepts of metaphysics in order to shake metaphysics. We have no language – no syntax, and no lexicon – which is foreign to
this history [of metaphysics]; we can pronounce not a single destructive
proposition which has not already had to slip into the form, the logic, and
the implicit postulations of precisely what it seeks to contest. To take one
example from many: the metaphysics of presence is shaken with the help
of the concept of *sign*. But ... as soon as one seeks to demonstrate in this
way that there is no transcendental or privileged signified and that the
domain or play of signification henceforth has no limit, one must reject
even the concept and the word 'sign' itself – which is precisely what
cannot be done. For the signification 'sign' has always been understood
and determined, in its meaning, as sign-of, a signifier referring to a
signified, a signifier different from its signified. If one erases the radical
difference between signifier and signified, it is the word 'signifier' itself

which must be abandoned as a metaphysical concept ... But we cannot do without the concept of the sign, for we cannot give up this metaphysical complicity without also giving up the critique we are directing against this complicity, or without the risk of erasing difference in the self-identity of a signified reducing its signifier into itself or, amounting to the same thing, simply expelling its signifier outside itself. ('Structure' 280–1)

In Blake's vision of the Second Coming as the apocalyptic form of the Bible, its closure in the gospel figure of Christ as the Incarnation of the Logos or Word bringing revelation to an end is 'annihilated' by a new vision of resurrection as the Fourfold Human, the demonic form of which is Newtonian physics as the natural form of the Incarnation. Deconstruction explores the endless deferral of meaning that results from releasing the signifier from its bondage to the signified, leaving it to float in a condition of possibility, which the entire creation becomes when released from the frozen, Urizenic form of natural law into the limitless expanse of the imagination. 'Time flies faster, (as seems to me), here than in London,' Blake writes to Butts from Felpham, describing his struggle to bind himself to 'Duty & Reality' as defined by the 'natural piety' of his patron Hayley in its opposition to Blake's vision-ary world (E 716). The only way Blake could remain in a 'Moment' or 'Pulsation of the Artery' was to deconstruct the entire world of 'Duty & Reality' that separated him from it. He remained in it by enacting its absence as the negative form of its presence. This negative form is Blake's account of the realm of natural law (Newton's compasses) as the madness of the realm of the 'Mundane Shell'[4] in which 'the Spectres of the Dead wander' (716). Into this spectral realm of irreality all the Romantics descended in order to enter the void or madness as the initiatory rite of creation comparable to that of the shaman.

As an archetypal critic, Frye's commitment to 'the stability' of literature's 'structural units' lay in keeping the 'central myths of [Chris-tian] concern constantly in mind' in order to protect society from the 'psychosis' into which history descends when stripped of them. Blake's Los, as the 'Spectre of Urthona,' can either descend to the psychosis of the Selfhood ('Satans seat') or invest time with the redemptive power of the imagination ('Golgonooza'). Urthona's element, as Frye explains, is the earth. In eternity, where, as a Zoa, Urthona properly belongs, Urthona is 'an imaginative and unfallen underground of labyrinths and caves and fairy palaces' (Fearful 291), a description that accurately describes Jung's collective unconscious. Jung's point about the collective unconscious is that it *is* unconscious. Consciousness cannot enter it in order to know it without its ceasing to be what it is. What in itself it is, which cannot be known, is, as unknown, madness, 'a Void Outside of Exist ence,' which, if the sane world is to be deconstructed, must be entered as the annihilation of the commonsensical world of 'Duty & Reality.' When Frye argues that 'it is not necessary to invoke ... Jung's collective unconscious' to explain the art of Blake, he is rejecting the descent into the 'Void,' which constitutes the demonic form of the apocalyptic 'Moment,' a form that is essential to any enactment of it. The lark, who is Ololon who is the New Jerusalem who is Blake's text, 'mounts' where the limit of opacity finally 'finishes.'

Blake's brief epic, *Milton*, is an elaborate constellation of the infinitely complex eternal 'Moment' in which Blake in the garden at Felpham reading aloud *Paradise Lost* to his wife, Catherine (his 'sweet Shadow of Delight'), falls 'outstrechd upon the path' as his soul departs from his body. In this instant 'less than a Pulsation of the Artery,' Blake, as in the frontispiece to *Jerusalem*, is suspended between life and death, one foot across the threshold of death and the other raised to join it. This 'Moment,' Blake explains, 'is equal in its period & value to Six Thousand Years' from the fallen Creation of Genesis to the Judgment of Revelation, which is to say the total form of the Bible. The 'value' of this total form is the Second Coming: 'Surely I come quickly. Amen. Even so, come, Lord Jesus' (Revelation 22.20). By 'quickly' Blake means a 'Pulsation of the Artery.' In every 'Pulsation' Jesus unconsciously comes 'quickly' in the manner described in Revelation: 'as a bride adorned for her husband.' It is in this apocalyptic form that the 'One Man Jesus' descends into Blake's garden adorned in the wedding garment of Blake's text. Blake's text is, as Ololon, the bride of Blake's Jesus, who is the 'human form divine,' Blake's Fourfold Human.

In his own exploration of the psychic movement from Three to Four, Jung turned again and again to the papal bull of Pius XII, *Munificentissimus Deus*, promulgating the Assumption of the Blessed Virgin Mary. This new dogma affirmed that Mary as the Bride is united with the Son in the heavenly bridal chamber, and as Sophia (Wisdom) she is united with the Godhead. The significance of this papal bull, which Jung dealt with in part in his *Answer to Job*, lay, for Jung, in the absorption of the feminine into the patriarchal Godhead, thereby releasing into consciousness both a new understanding of the feminine, released from the mythological identification of Eve with Satan, and a new understanding of the masculine, released from the mythological identification with patriarchal power. The result, he suggests, is an androgynous understanding of God as what he calls 'a *kosmogonos*, a creator and father-mother of all higher consciousness' (*MDR* 353). He further elaborates this *kosmogonos* as the *hieros gamos*, the divine marriage understood as the inner marriage of the masculine and feminine principles. This marriage constitutes the whole soul released from its inner divisions, particularly as they are unconsciously projected outward into ceaseless conflicts between good and evil in which, by the very nature of the unconscious dynamics involved, there can be no victors. In other words, the *kosmogonos* as an inner marriage constitutes the notion of a peace that reaches beyond our present human understanding.

For Blake, as for Jung, this Fourfold peace has little or nothing to do with the mandala as a squared circle (the Fourfold Eden surrounded by the Threefold Beulah) described by Winnicott in his criticism of Jung's so-called escape to Nirvana tactics. The Fourfold, for both Blake and Jung, was a realm of ceaseless 'Mental Fight' understood as the dynamics of ceaseless becoming as the consciousness of being, rather than being itself. Blake describes it as 'living going forth & returning wearied / Into the Planetary lives of Years Months Days & Hours reposing / And then Awaking into his Bosom in the Life of Immortality' (*J* 99.2–4).

As Blake enacts it, the human soul engaged in ceaseless 'Mental Fight' productive of 'Visionary forms dramatic' (98.28) moves back and forth between Eden ('living, going forth') and Beulah ('returning wearied'). This ceaseless going forth and returning wearied as the action of the soul is not a gender struggle between the male and the female, as Shakespeare's *Antony and Cleopatra* enacts. The outward division of the soul into opposing sexes struggling in vain to reconcile their differences is, for Blake, yet another delusion of Generation and Ulro, which remains operative so long as the soul is reduced to a 'portion' of itself 'discernd by the five Senses.' In terms of the Fourfold, as distinct from the Twofold Generation and the Onefold Ulro, the soul is neither male nor female. Metaphorically, in terms of its creative dynamics, it is both masculine and feminine.

In the 'Void Outside of Existence' this Fourfold vision of the masculine and feminine ('And I heard the Name of their [Eden's] Emanations they are named Jerusalem' is the final line of Blake's *Jerusalem*) becomes in Satan a demonic parody of it. The androgyne as the symbol of a differentiated soul in which the masculine and feminine portions work creatively together becomes a hermaphrodite. Milton, going to 'Eternal Death' in order to bring Urania (who dictated to him while he slept) to a fully awakened consciousness of who she is, must first enter his Satanic form as the shadow side of his dreaming soul with which, in his wives and daughters, he became, upon awakening, increasingly identified.

> And Milton said. I go to Eternal Death! Eternity shudder'd
> ...
> A mournful form double; hermaphroditic: male & female
> In one wonderful body. and he enterd into it
> In direful pain for the dread shadow, twenty-seven-fold
> Reachd to the depths of direst Hell, & thence to Albions land.
>
> (*M* 14[15].33–40)

'Which is the earth of vegetation on which now I write,' Blake adds, as if to remind himself not only of where his 'Vegetable Body' is but of what is going on within it as the psychic form of its somatic state. Only when he has fully inhabited his psychosomatic state, which he found mirrored in *Paradise Lost*, will the 'twenty-seven-fold' shadow, which 'reachd to the depths of direst Hell' become 'the Twenty-eighth bright / Lark' descending as Ololon into his garden. All of this and, of course, far more Blake, writing on 'the earth of vegetation,' must bring to bear upon the 'Moment: less than a Pulsation of the Artery' in which *Milton* is 'concievd.'

Derrida's notion of the Cogito as the instant of madness in which a work can be said to exist 'as its liberty and very possibility' in the 'precomprehension of [its] infinite and undetermined totality' ('Cogito' 56) finds its analogue in Blake's notion of a 'Pulsation of the Artery.' Distinguishing this instant of madness as 'the project of exceeding the totality of the world' from 'the passion of hybris,' Derrida argues that the latter 'is [traditionally] seen only as the pathological modification of the being called man' (57). It is 'excessive and exceeds only *within* the space [of the pathological modification] opened by the demonic hyperbole.' The 'madness' of the Cogito, on the other hand, is, he argues with Descartes's Cogito in mind, 'excessive and exceeds' *outside* the space of a pathological modification. By certifying the madness of the Cogito through God, who guarantees it, Descartes, far from questioning the sanity of the Cogito by considering its madness, affirms it as the God who claims the madness as his own. 'The Cogito would escape madness,' Derrida insists, with reference to Descartes, 'only because at its own moment, under its own authority, it is valid *even if I am mad*, even if my thoughts are completely mad' (55).

Derrida concludes 'Cogito and the History of Madness' by summarizing what, with reference to Foucault's 'naive' reading of three pages of Descartes *Meditations*, Derrida has attempted: 'to-attempt-to-say-the demonic-hyperbole from whose heights thought is announced to itself, *frightens* itself, and *reassures* itself against being annihilated or wrecked in madness or in death' (61). Blake, I suggest, by entering a madness that, in his own radical way, he embraced as the madness of God, wrote from these 'heights,' as Derrida describes them. '*At its height*,' Derrida continues, 'hyperbole, the absolute opening [a 'Pulsation of the Artery'], the uneconomic expenditure, is always reembraced by an *economy* and is overcome by economy.' While Blake confronts this '*economy*' as the temptations of the 'Reasoning Negative' he is never 'overcome' by it. 'The relationship between reason, madness, and death,' Derrida goes on, 'is an economy, a structure of deferral whose irreducible originality must be respected' (62). In Blake's case, the 'structure of deferral,' in which the signifier must forever endure its ceaseless misencounters with the signified (the 'Pulsation of the Artery'), becomes less a 'structure of deferral' than a metaphorical structure. As metaphor, the 'Pulsation of the Artery,' which is the unconscious life of the 'Vegetable Body,' becomes, as consciousness, Ololon's garment 'written within & without in woven letters.' As Blake's illuminated text, each of these 'woven letters' is an expulsion of breath that Blake heard sounding in his ear, not as a pathology but as the divine madness of revelation. Thus, comparing 'the unfathomd caverns of [his] Ear' to 'mysterious Sinais awful cave,' Blake, addressing 'the Public,' declares that through him, as through Moses, God is again speaking 'in thunder and in fire! / Thunder of Thought, & flames of fierce desire.' 'Therefore,' he concludes, 'I print; nor vain my types shall be: / Heaven, Earth & Hell, henceforth shall live in harmony' (*J* 3.3–10). The 'harmony' of 'Heaven, Earth & Hell' resides, Blake argues, in his unfettering of poetry by, among other things, releasing it from 'the modern bondage of Rhyming,' and putting 'every word and every letter' into 'its fit place' (3).

'Nothing, further,' Derrida continues, 'would be more incapable of regrasping [the original profundity of will in general] than voluntarism, for, as finitude and as history, this attempt is also a first passion. It keeps within itself the trace of a violence. It is more written than said, it is *economized*. The economy of this writing is a regulated relationship between that which exceeds and the exceeded totality, the *différance* of the absolute excess' (62). Like Derrida, Blake rejects 'voluntarism' as being capable of 'regrasping' the 'original profundity' of the 'absolute excess,' which for Blake is the 'absolute excess' of divine revelation. 'We who dwell on Earth,' Blake tells his 'Public,' 'can do nothing of ourselves, every thing is conducted by Spirits, no less than Digestion or Sleep' (J 3). For this reason, the *mythos* or action of *Milton* takes place in Bowlahoola, 'the Stomach in every individual man,' where 'Los's Anvils stand & his Furnaces rage' (Blake suffered from severe stomach complaints in his 'Printing house in Hell'). 'Thundering the Hammers beat & the Bellows blow loud,' declares Blake, describing the violence of his own stomach disturbances (for which Newton, Locke, and Pitt would provide a medicinal cure),

> Living self moving mourning lamenting & howling incessantly
> Bowlahoola thro all its porches feels tho' too fast founded
> Its pillars & porticoes to tremble at the force
> Of mortal or immortal arm: and softly lilling flutes
> Accordant with the horrid labours make sweet melody
> The Bellows are the Animal Lungs: the Hammers the Animal Heart
> The Furnaces the Stomach for digestion. terrible their fury
> Thousands & thousands labour. thousands play on instruments
> Stringed or fluted to ameliorate the sorrows of slavery
> Loud sport the dancers in the dance of death, rejoicing in carnage
> The hard dentant Hammers are lulld by the flutes['] lula lula
> The Bellowing Furnaces['] blare by the long sounding clarion
> The double drum drowns howls & groans, the shrill fife. shrieks & cries:
> The crooked horn mellows the hoarse raving serpent, terrible, but
>   harmonious
>
> Bowlahoola is the Stomach in every individual man.   (24[26].51–67)

Treating the involuntary operations of the human body as a metaphor of the divine operations of the imagination, Blake's epics become a vision of the Fourfold Human, understood as the conscious habitation of the human body, which becomes human by virtue of the consciousness bestowed upon its involuntary operations. Derrida's notion of *différance* (as both the signifier's deferral of, and difference from, the signified) is thus annihilated, not by a 'metaphysics of presence,' but by raising the unconscious operations of the physical body to the imaginal perception of it. Herein lies the difference between Frye's notion of the archetype and Jung's: whereas Frye locates the archetype in a 'metaphysics of presence,' Jung locates it in the unconscious operations of the human body. The purpose of the 'Void Outside of Existence,' which is Satan's world, is to reduce the 'Vegetable Body' to a 'Spectre' haunting consciousness with its perpetual absence as a physical body. In this spectral form, a 'Pulsation of the Artery' becomes what Shelley's Prometheus, as he invokes the Phantasm of Jupiter, calls 'awful thoughts, rapid and thick,' sweeping 'obscurely through my brain like shadows dim' (*PU* 1.146–8). It is the 'Pulsation of the Artery' in the possession of Satan, as distinct from a 'Pulsation' that 'Satan cannot find / Nor can his Watch Fiends find it.' When (and if) the latter is found and entered, Blake explains, 'it renovates every Moment of the Day if rightly placed.' In this 'Pulsation' or 'Moment,' Ololon descends into Blake's imagination, which he describes as 'Los & Enitharmon [his inner feminine or Emanation] / Unseen beyond the Mundane Shell' (*M* 35[39].42–7). Gradually, that is, the entire externalized mythopoeia, which as allegory addressed to the 'Corporeal Understanding' spectrally corresponds to outer events, is restored to its source in the poetic imagination where, as the revelation of the soul's reality, the soul expands to the circumference of its 'Energy' to greet it. In this apocalyptic form, Los and Enitharmon become the 'One Man Jesus' wrapped in the garment of Blake's epic, the 'One Man Jesus' becoming the Fourfold man described in the final plates of *Jerusalem*.

Arming himself for 'Mental Fight,' Blake in his Preface to *Milton* calls upon Jesus as the 'Countenance Divine' to arm him for battle, his epic becoming his armour:

Bring me my Bow of burning gold:
Bring me my Arrows of desire:
Bring me my Spear: O clouds unfold!
Bring me my Chariot of fire!   (1.9–12)

In the concluding plates of *Jerusalem*, the 'Countenance Divine' appears to Albion in 'his Form / A Man. & they conversed as Man with Man, in Ages of Eternity,' / And the Divine Appearance was the likeness & similitude of Los'(*J* 96.5–7). When the cloud 'overshadowing' them divided, 'Albion,' writes Blake, 'stood in terror: not for himself but for his Friend / Divine, & Self was lost in the contemplation of faith / And wonder at the Divine Mercy & at Los's sublime honour' (29–32).

Throughout the epic, Albion's Selfhood, as 'the perturbed man,' has separated Albion from the Jesus whose earthly home is the imagination by reducing Albion's soul to a 'portion' of itself 'discernd by the five

Senses,' which is what the Selfhood is. 'But the perturbed Man away turns down the valleys dark,' writes Blake

> [*Saying. We are not One: we are Many, thou most simulative*]
> Phantom of the over heated brain! shadow of immortality!
> Seeking to keep my soul a victim to thy love! which binds
> Man the enemy of man into deceitful friendships:
> Jerusalem is not! her daughters are indefinite:
> By demonstration, man alone can live, and not by faith.
> My mountains are my own, and I will keep them to myself!
> The Malvern and the Cheviot, the Wolds Plinlimmon & Snowdon
> Are mine. here will I build my Laws of Moral Virtue!
> Humanity shall be no more: but war & princedom & victory!   (4.22–32)

For Blake the crucifixion becomes Albion's release from his Selfhood, a release that contains within it the resurrection, the cross becoming for Blake, as it was for Augustine, the marriage bed of the New Jerusalem. Enacting the crucifixion as the marriage bed (Jerusalem is his bride), Albion

> threw himself into the Furnaces of affliction
> All was a Vision, all a Dream: the Furnaces became
> Fountains of Living Waters flowing from the Humanity Divine
> And all the Cities of Albion rose from their Slumbers.   (96.35–8)

Albion's 'Four Senses' (eye, ear, nose, tongue) are now released from their spectral state as opaque matter in which they inhabit 'a Void Outside of Existence' to assume their eternal form as the Four Zoas (Urizen, Luvah, Tharmas, Urthona):

> Soon all around remote the Heavens burnt with flaming fires
> And Urizen & Luvah & Tharmas & Urthona arose into
> Albion's Bosom: Then Albion stood before Jesus in the Clouds
> Of Heaven Fourfold among the Visions of God in Eternity.   (96.40–3)

Now the arms brought to Blake in *Milton* for his 'Resurrection & Judgment in the Vegetable Body' are put on. 'Then Albion stretchd his hand into Infinitude. / And took his Bow,' writes Blake. This Bow is now held in the Fourfold hand, which stretches to 'Infinitude,' its arrows flying from its quiver in all four directions:

Fourfold the Vision for bright beaming Urizen
Layd his hand on the South & took a breathing Bow of carved Gold
Luvah his hand stretch'd to the East & bore a Silver Bow bright shining
Tharmas Westward a Bow of Brass pure flaming richly wrought
Urthona Northward in thick storms a Bow of Iron terrible thundering.
(97.6–11)

The 'Vegetable' world of the human body now fully expanded to the circumference of its 'Energy' becomes the internalization of the cosmos. Its opaque matter is now perceived as soul in the 'Moment' that 'Satan cannot find.' Blake's Bow and Arrow have replaced Newton's compasses.

'And the Bow is a Male & Female & the Quiver of the Arrows of Love, / Are the Children of this Bow,' Blake continues, addressing his allegory to the 'Intellectual Powers' of his readers, renovated by their engagement with his illuminated text:

a Bow of Mercy & Loving-kindness: laying
Open the hidden Heart in Wars of mutual Benevolence Wars of Love
And the Hand of Man grasps firm between the Male & Female Loves
And he Clothed himself in Bow & Arrows in awful state Fourfold
In the midst of his Twenty-eight Cities each with his Bow breathing
Then each an Arrow flaming from his Quiver fitted carefully
They drew fourfold the unreprovable String, bending thro the wide
    Heavens
The horned Bow Fourfold, loud sounding flew the flaming Arrow
    fourfold.   (97.12–17; 98.1–3)

At the circumference of its 'Energy,' the soul transforms its own madness as the 'Void Outside of Existence' by means of the dialectical operations of the imagination. Archetypally identifying these operations with the figure of Los, who is himself the likeness of Jesus fulfilling his promise to come again in the guise of the New Jerusalem, Blake's epic vision is the enactment of it. The actuality of this enactment, however, remains beyond the reach of his epic vision. Blake's 'flaming Arrow fourfold' flies 'loud sounding' into a silence beyond the reach of words. 'Within the dimension of historicity in general, which is to be confused neither with some ahistorical eternity, nor with an empirically determined moment of the history of facts,' Derrida concludes, silence plays the irreducible role of that which bears and haunts language, outside and *against* which alone language can emerge – 'against' here simultaneously designating the content from which form takes off by force, and the adversary against whom I assure and reassure myself by force. Although the silence of madness is the absence of a work, this silence is not simply the work's epigraph, nor is it, as concerns language and meaning, outside the work. Like nonmeaning, silence is the work's limit and profound resource. Of course, in essentializing madness this way one runs the risk of disintegrating the factual findings of psychiatric efforts. This is a permanent danger, but it should not discourage the demanding and patient psychiatrist. ('Cogito' 54)

Blake's 'essentializing madness' disintegrates the 'factual findings' to which the 'portion of Soul discernd by the five Senses' is bound. Though to 'the demanding and patient psychiatrist' this disintegration consti- tutes the 'nonmeaning' of the insane, it is, for Derrida (as for Blake), the 'meaning' of the 'Cogito' that dwells in 'silence.' Revelation, for Blake, is the breaking of the silence, which becomes in Blake's vision the breaking (opening) of the seven seals (the 'Seven Eyes of God'). 'And I saw in the right hand of him that sat on the throne a book written within and on the backside, sealed with seven seals' (Revelation 5.1) becomes, in *Milton*, Blake's illuminated text 'written within & without in woven letters,' which Blake further describes as 'the Divine Revelation in the Litteral expression.' By 'Litteral,' Blake means 'the Woof of Six Thou- sand Years' (*M* 42[49].13–15), that is to say, the history of the world from the Creation to the Judgment. 'And I saw a strong angel proclaiming with a loud voice,' Revelation continues, 'Who is worthy to open the book, and to loose the seals thereof?' The answer to this rhetorical question immediately follows: 'And no man in heaven, nor in earth, neither under the earth, was able to open the book, neither to look thereon.' Only the 'Lamb as it had been slain, having seven horns and seven eyes, which are the seven Spirits of God sent forth into all the earth' (5.2–6) is able to open it. Having opened it, the Lamb releases God's judgment upon his creation as his annihilation of it. After the Lamb releases the sevenfold Judgment, John as the author of Revelation sees 'another mighty angel come down from heaven, clothed with a cloud: and a rainbow was upon his head, and his face was as it were the sun, and his feet as pillars of fire.' As he is about to write what he has heard 'when the seven thunders had uttered their voices,' another voice from heaven commands him not to write it because 'there should be time no longer.' Instead, he is commanded to 'go and take the little book which is open in the hand of the angel.' John goes to the angel. 'Give me the little book,' he demands. 'Take it, and eat it up,' says the angel, 'and it shall make thy belly [Bowlahoola] bitter, but it shall be in thy mouth sweet as honey [Beulah].' John takes it and eats it. As soon as he had finished, the angel tells him that he 'must prophesy again before many peoples, and nations, and tongues, and kings' (10.1–11). What he must prophesy is the return of Jesus, the act of prophesying containing his coming in the 'Moment' of it. John in Revelation, falling 'at his feet as dead' (1.17) when he hears 'a great voice, as of a trumpet' (1.10) telling him to write, becomes Blake in *Milton* falling 'outstretchd upon the path / A moment' when he hears 'in Clouds of blood' and a 'Column of Fire' the 'immortal sound' of 'Four Trumpets' (42[49].20–6). Breaking the silence, opening himself to the madness of the hyperbolic project (the work's 'profound resource'), Blake inhabits a presence that, in the name of sanity ('economy'), Derrida deconstructs, not to deny the presence but to protect him from 'going mad,' his writing becoming his '*confessed* terror' of it. Blake writes, 'Terror struck the Vale ... / My bones trembled,' as he fell as if dead, 'outstretchd upon the path / A moment.' The path on which he fell is the *mythos* of Milton's epic within which Blake's brain in a 'Pulsation of the Artery' experienced the apocalyptic form of *Paradise Lost* as the 'wondrous' head-to-foot commingling of Milton and Ololon.

4

Wordsworth's Crazed Bedouin: *The Prelude* and the Fate of Madness

Full often, taking from the world of sleep
This Arab phantom, which I thus beheld,
This semi-Quixote, I to him have given
A substance, fancied him a living man,
A gentle dweller in the desert, crazed
By love and feeling, and internal thought
Protracted among endless solitudes;
Have shaped him wandering upon this quest!
Nor have I pitied him; but rather felt
Reverence was due to a being thus employed;
And thought that, in the blind and awful lair
Of such a madness, reason did lie couched.

Wordsworth, *The Prelude*

Blake and Wordsworth

A defining difference between Wordsworth's poetic vision and that of William Blake is the creative role that Wordsworth assigned to memory. Blake set out 'to cast off the rotten rags of Memory by Inspiration' (*M* 41[48].4) in a manner that Wordsworth identified with a 'madness,' which he both feared as psychotic and celebrated as divine. Having experienced both forms of it, Wordsworth settled for memory as a form of natural rather than divine inspiration. Wordsworth describes this natural inspiration as 'the gravitation and the filial bond / Of nature' (*P* 2.243–4). Rejecting Newton's law of gravity as 'the Sleep of Ulro,' Blake replaces Newton's interfusion along Wordsworth's 'infant veins' (2.242) with 'a Pulsation of the Artery' in which not only 'the Poets Work is Done,' but 'all the Great / Events of Time start forth & are concievd' (*M* 29[31].1–3).

Wordsworth initially experienced the French Revolution as the doing of 'the Poets Work' in this radically apocalyptic fashion. 'Bliss it was in that dawn to be alive, / But to be young was very Heaven!' (*P* 11.108), he exclaims. Wordsworth here identifies the outbreak of the Revolution with the 'Heaven' that would later become his childhood. It is as if the failure of the Revolution is restored to its original state by his recreation of it as his creation of himself. 'O times,' he continues, 'in which the meagre, stale, forbidding ways / Of custom, law, and statute, took at once / The attraction of a country in romance!' (11.109–12).

Wordsworth could be describing the childhood he constructed, the 'meagre, stale, forbidding ways / Of custom, law and statute' becoming the 'prison' of the opening lines of the 1805 *Prelude* 'where he hath been long immured' (1.8). Wordsworth, that is, imaginatively transformed his escape from prison into a vision of childhood as a return to Eden ('a country in romance') in which it was 'Heaven' to be alive. 'Yet should these hopes / Prove vain,' he concludes his first book,

> and thus should neither I be taught
> To understand myself, nor thou [Coleridge] to know
> With better knowledge how the heart was framed
> Of him thou lovest; need I dread from thee
> Harsh judgements, if the song be loth to quit
> Those recollected hours that have the charm
> Of visionary things, those lovely forms
> And sweet sensations that throw back our life,
> And almost make our infancy itself
> A visible scene on which the sun is shining?   (*P* 1.626–36)

By grounding his vision in memory, 'the gravitation and the filial bond / Of nature,' Blake saw 'in Wordsworth the Natural Man rising up against the Spiritual Man Continually.' '[And] then he is No Poet,' Blake concludes, 'but a Heathen Philosopher at Enmity against all true Poetry or Inspiration' (E 665). Ezekiel apparently agreed. Dining with Blake, Ezekiel told him, 'We of Israel taught that the Poetic Genius (as you now call it) was the first principle [of perception] and all others [nature and the senses] merely derivative, which was the cause of our despising the Priests & Philosophers of other countries, and prophecying that all

Gods would at last be proved. to originate in ours & to be the tributaries of the Poetic Genius' (*MHH* 12–13). As the poet of Nature and the 'Natural Man,' Blake insists, Wordsworth is 'at Enmity with God' (E 665), mocking inspiration 'with the aspersion of Madness,' and 'creep[ing] into State Government like a catterpiller to destroy' (*M* 41[48].8–11).

The 'madness' that Wordsworth feared as psychosis, having had a first-hand experience of it, he also defended as divine, the difference between them becoming difficult to distinguish, so that the latter appeared to contain the former as the spectral form of it. 'We Poets in our youth begin in gladness,' he writes in 'Resolution and Independence,' with Chatterton and Burns in mind, 'but thereof come in the end despondency and madness' (48–9). 'Some called it madness,' he writes of his first seventeen years in which he made a world that 'only lived to [him], / And to the God who sees into the heart';

> so indeed it was,
> If child-like fruitfulness in passing joy,
> If steady moods of thoughtfulness matured
> To inspiration, sort with such a name;
> If prophecy be madness; if things viewed
> By poets in old time, and higher up
> By the first men, earth's first inhabitants,
> May in these tutored days no more be seen
> With undisordered sight. But leaving this,
> It was no madness.   (*P* 3.149–58)

The fear of madness as it was bound to the memory of it prevented Wordsworth from embracing the 'divine madness' of the apocalyptic theme which Blake so richly enacted: the descent of the New Jerusalem 'prepared as a bride adorned for her husband' (Revelation 21.2). Even here, however, Wordsworth remained bound to nature; the marriage as he understood it was 'the discerning intellect of Man ... wedded to this goodly universe / In love and holy passion' (Prospectus to *The Recluse* 52–4). From Blake's point of view, Wordsworth had reduced Blake's Jerusalem to a 'mechanical bride.' Wordsworth described the wedded state of man and nature as the exquisite fitting of the 'individual Mind ... to the external World,' a fit so exquisite that it would allow him, in the name of the imaginative form of the 'mechanical philosophy' (if such a thing were possible as other than a parody), to penetrate the veil of the 'heaven of heavens' and pass Jehovah 'unalarmed' (Prospectus 30–5). 'You shall not bring me down to believe such fitting & fitted I know better & Please your Lordship,' declared Blake. As for passing Jehovah 'unalarmed,' Blake had this to say: 'Solomon when he Married Pharohs daughter & became a Convert to the Heathen Mythology Talked exactly in this way of Jehovah as a Very inferior object of Mans Contemplations he also passed him by unalarmed & was permitted. Jehovah dropped a tear & followd him by his Spirit into the Abstract Void it is called the Divine Mercy Satan dwells in it but Mercy does not dwell in him he knows not to Forgive' (E 666–7). Blake clearly sees that Wordsworth's vision of the apocalypse is a demonic parody of his own, which, in *Milton*, Blake set out to redeem by sending Ololon down into Satan's 'Abstract Void' in order to release Milton as an act of 'Divine Mercy.' In the same manner, it may be argued, had the Prospectus to *The Recluse* been available to him (it was written about 1800 but not published until 1814, along with *The Excursion*), Blake might have also set out to release Wordsworth, whose biblical type is Solomon married to Pharoh's daughter.

Wordsworth and Deconstruction

In the 1799 *Prelude*, Wordsworth, though tracing his life 'up to an eminence' (3.171) in the later versions ('Of genius, power, / Creation and divinity itself / I have been speaking' [3.173–5]), describes himself at the age of five as in the 'twilight' rather than at the dawn of 'rememberable life' (*1799* 1.298). In both the 1805 and the 1850 versions the phrase is dropped, though in his 'Immortality' ode another version is suggested when for 'twilight' Wordsworth substitutes 'shades of the prison-house' that, like the twilight, begin to descend 'upon the growing Boy' (67–8). Memory as darkness, twilight, imprisonment, forgetfulness finds for Wordsworth its oxymoronic equivalent in the Platonic myth of pre-existence in which birth itself becomes 'a forgetting' (58). As natural objects ('the earth, and every common sight' [2]) begin to register upon the senses, the soul's 'celestial light' (4) darkens into twilight, and 'fade[s] into the light of common day' (76). For Berkeley, Wordsworth substitutes Locke, 'celestial light' becoming a *tabula rasa*. Perhaps for this reason, the growing boy of 'Tintern Abbey,' 'bound[ing] o'er the mountains ... Wherever nature led,' is described as 'more like a man / Flying from something that he dreads than one / Who sought the thing he loved' (68–72). He dreads the descending darkness that is 'rememberable life.' In the 'Immortality' ode, he stands before that life as 'a guilty Thing surprised' (151). Wordsworth's guilt is his sudden realization of what had been abandoned or forgotten in the active surrender to nature and 'the language of the sense,' a surrender that had left him in 'Tintern Abbey' and the Preface to the *Lyrical Ballads* rather 'well pleased' (107–8) with himself. The nurse of his moral being in 'Tintern Abbey' becomes the 'homely Nurse' (81) in the 'Immortality' ode, who does all she can to make her foster child forget his heavenly origin. Rather than bind time to eternity, she binds day to day, imprisoning the poet for a crime he had not known he had committed until he was able to read the record of it in what he himself had written. His crime, as Coleridge recognized, was his defence of the 'language of the sense.' Wordsworth here had enacted, as if before the horrified eyes of Blake, the poet's descent into Ulro, Wordsworth becoming the sleeping Albion upon his 'Couch of Death.'

In his preface to the *Lyrical Ballads*, Wordsworth argued that he had chosen 'low and rustic life' because those living in daily communion with the 'beautiful and permanent forms of nature' – peasants, children, outlaws, and idiots – spoke 'a far more philosophical language than that which is frequently substituted for it by Poets, who think that they are conferring honour upon themselves and their art in proportion as they separate themselves from the sympathies of men, and indulge in arbitrary and capricious habits of expression in order to furnish food for fickle tastes and fickle appetites of their own creation' (*PW* 1:124). By 'philosophical' Wordsworth here has in mind Locke, who argued that, since all knowledge 'terminated in Things' (*Essay* 3:488), it must arise from the mind's direct encounter with things through the medium of the senses. ('Art thou not Newtons Pantocrator weaving the Woof of Locke?' Blake's Los asks Satan [*M* 4.11].) Ridding the mind of any innate ideas, reducing it to a *tabula rasa* (Blake's 'Void Outside of Existence'), Locke demonstrated how man can gain a real knowledge of the external world and, through that knowledge, properly fit himself to it. Not, however, until he was well into the third book did he suddenly realize that, in the composition of his *Essay Concerning Human Understanding*, it was not the senses with which he was directly dealing, but writing. The *tabula rasa* was the white sheet of paper on which, by dipping his pen into ink, he was making marks that were signs or traces of the action of his mind. What in writing, in the marks upon the page, he was in touch with was not the external world of things but mind itself. 'I must confess then,' he writes, 'that when I first began this

Discourse of the Understanding, and a good while after, I had not the least Thought, that any Consideration of Words was at all necessary to it.' Yet, since words rather than things were what directly confronted him in the act of composition, he had to conclude that, though knowledge 'terminated in Things, yet it was for the most part so much by the intervention of Words, that they seem'd scarce separable from our general Knowledge. At least they interpose themselves so much between our Understandings, and the Truth, which it would contemplate and apprehend, that like the *Medium* through which visible Objects pass, their Obscurity and Disorder does not seldom cast a mist before our Eyes, and impose upon our Understandings' (*Essay* 3:488).

Language, he realized, was 'like the medium through which visible objects pass.' It was, that is, like the senses. However, the senses were now as a medium far superior to language because, as a result of the mechanical equipment invented for experiment in the laboratories of the Royal Society, they were less obscure, less subject to disorder, less likely to distort the understanding. The lingering 'Obscurity and Disorder' of language casting 'a mist before our eyes' and imposing 'upon our understanding' are rhetoric, the poetic diction that Wordsworth was determined to eradicate, and Locke, by implication, identifies with the unassisted senses ill equipped to make accurate observations: 'But yet, if we would speak of Things as they are, we must allow, that all the Art of Rhetorick, besides Order and Clearness, all the artificial and figurative application of Words Eloquence hath invented, are for nothing else but to insinuate wrong *Ideas*, move the Passions, and thereby mislead the Judgment; and so indeed are perfect cheat;[1] ... they are certainly, in all Discourses that pretend to inform or instruct, wholly to be avoided; and where Truth and Knowledge are concerned, cannot but be thought a great fault, either of the Language or Person that makes use of them' (*Essay* 3:508).

Avoidance was not that easy, however, as Locke, reading what he just had written, must have realized that the 'great fault' was precisely what he was at that very instant indulging in and, as writing, enjoying. As if confessing his pleasure, Locke with considerable irony (itself a form of rhetoric) continues: '*Eloquence*, like the fair Sex, has too prevailing Beauties in it, to suffer it self ever to be spoken against. And 'tis in vain to find fault with those Arts of Deceiving, wherein Men find pleasure to be Deceived' (3:508). Locke, it may be argued, feared writing because, unless it terminated in things rather than states of mind, it could easily be carried away into unreal mental states. Struggling to bind himself to

'Duty & Reality,' Blake, as already noted, experienced this same fear ('my Abstract folly hurries me often away while I am at work [con struacting a likeness], carrying me over Mountains & Valleys which are not Real in a Land of Abstraction where Spectres of the Dead wander' [E 716]), though he quickly realized that the 'Duty & Reality' he was trying in vain to bind himself to was a delusion of Ulro.

Locke here could be Milton in a lighter vein writing about Adam and Eve after the fall, himself as Adam deceived by Eve, though finding pleasure in it, choosing her rather than truth. However, he could also be a Romantic writing about the psyche, which, because it lured the poet away from a 'termination in things,' he sought to exorcise by reducing it to a *tabula rasa*, even as Shelley in *Alastor* reduced the dream maiden embracing the Visionary to vacancy and as Keats, subjecting his Lamia to the cold stare of Apollonius, reduced her to nothing at all.

Wordsworth's poetical practice, as Coleridge demonstrated, was different from his poetical theory. Unlike Locke, his real interest was in the essential passions of the human heart as they manifested themselves more deeply or instinctively in the state of nature. Locke's interest was in the empirical methodology of the newly constituted Royal Society. Locke's nature was not Wordsworth's: Locke's object was to render the mind a true picture of nature, a clear mirror in which nature and its operations could behold itself; Wordsworth's object was to render nature a true picture of the mind, a clear mirror in which the mind could behold its own operations. As rhetoric, both poet and philosopher were deeply committed to metaphor as opposed to metonymy, an identification of mind and nature as the mirror images of each other. For both of them the language of metaphor became the problem, because in its exploration they were confronted by the nihilism that constitutes metaphor: the mind as nothing but nature, nature as nothing but mind; the one, that is, becoming the other, so that both disappear into Shelley's 'intense inane.' Thus, the problem of language becomes the problem of metaphor, understood as the power to fuse, to obliterate difference, a problem to which, as de Man has shown in *Blindness and Insight*, literature directly addresses itself. By locating language in fiction rather than empirical reality, he suggests that metaphor, like the other forms of rhetoric that originate in it, constitutes magic or spell understood as the reflexiveness of language – its identity with itself – as manifest most directly in incantation. Shakespeare's Macbeth, for example, rises as king out of the incantation of the witches, kingship becoming for him an evil spell. He is possessed by metaphor and the spell is not broken until his head is removed. What is revealed in his severed head held up as a warning is the danger of metaphor for the writer who is possessed by it. Shakespeare's *Macbeth*, like all his plays, is at once an enactment of metaphor and an exorcism of it, which culminates in *The Tempest*.

De Man, therefore, concludes that there can be no demystification of literature because literature is 'demystified from the start' (*Blindness* 18). As such, he further concludes, literature remains a primary source of our knowledge of nothingness as distinct from nothingness itself because, as a self-acknowledged fiction deconstructing its signifiers, it presents us with Blake's 'Void Outside of Existence' as an object of knowledge. Against the confrontation with the void, metaphor would initially arm us only in the end to bring us to an encounter with it that is not nothingness itself but the knowledge of it. It is, in Wordsworth's *Prelude*, the mind 'caught by the spectacle' of its own blindness unable to read the label 'of the utmost we can know' (7.643–5) or unable to read the 'monumental letters' made 'fresh and visible' from 'year to year, / By superstition of the neighbourhood' (12.241–5). It is the metaphor of nature as 'the speaking face of earth and heaven' (5.13) becoming suddenly the 'ghastly face' of a drowned man rising 'bolt upright' (5.449–50), which Cynthia Chase describes as 'an effaced figure unable to articulate any lesson' ('Accidents' 56).

In his 'Immortality' ode Wordsworth by metaphor would idealize, with Plato's and Milton's help, this nothingness by identifying it with an 'imperial palace' (84) that in early childhood survived, in however a ghostly fashion, as a 'celestial light' that appeared to apparel 'the earth, and every common sight.' Yet he knew in retrospect that, like Macbeth possessed by a spell, he was in some sense deluded. The delusion, as he describes it in his Fenwick note to the poem, lay in part in his conviction that, whatever might become of others, he himself would like 'Enoch & Elijah ... be translated ... to heaven' (*Fenwick Notes* 61). That is, he would not die. At the same time, however, his conviction of his own immortality was, as metaphor, a deliberate disguise against death. Several times while going to school, he confesses, he would grasp the nearest wall or tree to recall himself from what he calls the 'abyss of idealism to reality' (61) because, as he says, he was afraid of the process, a process that in the poem itself, in another, more sinister, metaphor, becomes identified with the grave where we in waiting lie, a metaphor so horrible that Coleridge persuaded him to remove it (*BL* 2:140–1). Metaphor in Wordsworth's ode is a fictional armour against the fact of death, which as fiction continually deconstructs itself. It is precisely this reading of his ode that Wordsworth explores in the Cartesian dream of the Arab. Wordsworth in a cave by the sea reading Cervantes's demystification of metaphor-making becomes in the dream a shell that he puts to his ear to hear 'an Ode, in passion uttered, which foretold / Destruction to the children of the earth / By deluge, now at hand' (*P* 5.96–8).

In *Of Grammatology* Derrida explores the tangible evidence of nothingness haunting Rousseau, as it haunted Wordsworth, driving him to constellate what is not there in and as rhetoric. Wordsworth in his 'Elegiac Stanzas' describes this constellated nothingness as his own extinction metaphorically idealized as pre-existence as the 'gleam' or trace of the 'light that never was, on sea or land, / The consecration, and the Poet's dream' (15–16). This dream, if pursued to the point where the figural becomes the actual, conducts not only to blindness ('when the light of sense / Goes out' [*P* 6.600–1]), but, as in 'Resolution and Independence,' to 'despondency and madness.' Wordsworth standing upon the pinnacle of self-deification at the age of seventeen, which is the controlling metaphor of the 1799 *Prelude*, is 'Chatterton, the marvellous Boy' (43), dead by his own hand at the same age. The attempt to constellate through language this 'gleam,' Derrida's 'fabulous scene' ('White Mythology' 213)[2] of metaphor-making, is an act of conjuration. Shelley, who understood this better than most Romantics, therefore images Wordsworth writing his 'Immortality' ode ('O joy! that in our embers / Is something that doth live' [133–4]) as

> the dream
> Of dark magician in his visioned cave,
> Raking the cinders of a crucible
> For life and power, even when his feeble hand
> Shakes in its last decay.   (*Alastor* 682–5)

Conjuring what is not there leaves as a kind of haunting its ghostly traces upon an otherwise empty page.

Still with Rousseau in mind, Derrida describes these marks or signs as the traces of a hypothetical 'full speech that was fully *present* (present to itself, to its signified, to the other, the very condition of the theme of presence in general)' (*Of Grammatology* 8). Like Wordsworth, who follows here in Rousseau's footsteps to leave traces of his own, Rousseau in *Emile* affirms the 'Poet's dream' a '"*natural language* common to all"' as the '"*language of children before they begin* [*have learned*] *to speak*,"' a language that '"*is inarticulate*,"' though it has '"*tone, stress, and mean-*

ing"' (247). Such a language 'fully present,' Wordsworth suggests in *The Prelude*, was 'most audible ... when the fleshly ear ... Forgot her functions, and slept undisturbed' (*P* 2.416–18). Less audible than the dreaming sleep that is man's initial post-natal condition, though still prelinguistically present, it can be heard again in the 'mock apparel' with which Hartley Coleridge semiotically at the age of six 'fittest to unutterable thought / The breeze-like motion and the self-born carol' ('To H.C., Six Years Old' 2–4). In much the same form this prelinguistic language as the 'mock apparel' of the unutterable can be heard and understood by Betty Foy in the 'burrs' ('The Idiot Boy' 377) of her idiot son.

In 'The Idiot Boy,' Wordsworth, in a manner that taxed Coleridge's 'willing suspension of disbelief,' boldly implies that Johnny is a pre-Homeric, prelinguistic poet who, like the Boy of Winander, speaks the language of the crowing cocks ('to-whoo, to-whoo' [450]). Such a poet is a magican, a shaman who, like Johnny, through actions that serve as body-speech, unconsciously commands the sick to rise and walk. Thus, old Susan Gale lying on her sick bed suddenly declares, 'I'll to the wood.' 'The word scarce said,' the poem continues, 'Did Susan rise up from her bed, / As if by magic cured' (424–6).

Defending in a manner that belied his own more rational judgment Wordsworth's conviction that his idiot boy spoke a more philosophical language than most poets, Coleridge acknowledged that Wordsworth's genius has tapped a 'freshness of sensation which is the constant accompaniment of mental, no less than bodily convalescence.' He had, Coleridge was persuaded, 'rescue[d] the most admitted truths from the impotence caused by the very circumstance of their universal admission' (*BL* 1:81–2). He had tapped a prelinguistic world of sensation as immediate and direct as 'the eternal act of creation in the infinite I AM.' Out of Coleridge's own need to come to grips with that achievement, a need directly related to his own bodily and mental convalescence, emerged his metaphysical understanding of the imagination in both its primary and its secondary senses, though particularly in the primary sense as the act of perception itself, a metaphysics that both poets would partially deconstruct in their own poetry. Wordsworth's poetry, he announced, was as fresh as if all that it contained 'had then sprang forth at the first creative fiat' (1:80). Wordsworth as a poet had felt as metaphor the riddle of the world, and in his poetry he had helped to unravel it.

For Wordsworth, however, it was one thing to feel the riddle of the world – that is, to be directly in touch with the 'fabulous scene' of metaphor-making; it was another thing entirely to unravel it, a task far more suited to Coleridge than to himself, though even Coleridge would admit that it had stolen from his own nature 'all the natural man' ('Dejection' 90). To unravel became for Wordsworth in some sense a crime against nature; it meant to pull apart, to dismember, to permit the 'meddling intellect' to mis-shape 'the beauteous forms of things' ('Tables Turned' 26–7). It also meant to read ('Close up those barren leaves' [30]). Derrida casts considerable light on Wordsworth's dilemma, particularly as it took shape under the direct influence of Coleridge's 'abstruser musings' ('Frost at Midnight' 6).

In 'Cogito and the History of Madness,' Derrida describes writing as a 'structure of deferral' in which what he calls the 'absolute excess' that constitutes the 'fabulous scene' from which writing emerges to leave its trace is tranquillized into a rational structure in order to exclude madness. In that exclusion of madness, Derrida argues, philosophy 'betrays itself (or betrays itself as thought)' to enter what he calls 'a crisis and a forgetting of itself' like Wordsworth's account of birth as 'a sleep and a forgetting.' 'I philosophize,' Derrida writes (as earlier noted), 'only in *terror*, but in the *confessed* terror of going mad. The confession is simultaneously, at its *present* moment, oblivion and unveiling, protection and exposure: economy.'

In the writing of *The Prelude*, Wordsworth became increasingly aware of this disjunction between himself as the first-person narrator who is present to himself as a forming and hardening ego (Keats's 'egotistical sublime' [*KL* 157]) and what he calls 'some other Being' (*P* 2.33) who is always in some sense absent, and perhaps most absent when almost present as in those conjured hours 'that have the charm / Of visionary things' (1.632–3). 'Even now,' writes Shelley, 'I call the phantoms of a thousand hours / Each from his voiceless grave: they have in visioned bowers / Of studious zeal or love's delight / Outwatched with me the envious night' ('Hymn to Intellectual Beauty' 63–7). The 'some other Being' is metaphor or 'charm' rendered almost 'visible' by incantation or 'song.' It is essentially a voice, usually identified with wind or water, a 'gentle breeze' (*P* 1.1) that can become a 'tempest, a redundant energy, / Vexing its own creation' (1.37–8), or a gentle river with 'alder shades and rocky falls ... fords and shallows' (1.272–3) that can become 'the mighty flood of Nile / Pour[ing] from his fount of Abyssinian clouds / To fertilise the whole Egyptian plain' (6.614–16). It is, above all, the unacknowledged hero of the first two books, more particularly of the

1799 *Prelude*. Beyond that, it is the unacknowledged legislator of the thirteen-book 1805 and fourteen-book 1850 versions.

The struggle in *The Prelude* between these 'two consciousnesses' (2.32) is rhetorically the conflict between metaphor as voice and allegory as the en-graving or in-scribing of the voice as epitaph. Metaphor operates in a world of Heraclitean flux, where the law of perpetual change is the law of life, a world of radical instability, of continuous metamorphosis presided over by a magician: Hermes in Greece, Mercurius in Rome, Merlin in Britain. Allegory, on the other hand, struggles to arrest and stabilize metaphor by taking it out of the timeless, undifferentiated world associated with the imaginal life of a child and grounding or burying it in time.[3] The relationship between them, therefore, may perhaps be best summed up in Wordsworth's standing 'a long half hour together ... Mute, looking at the grave in which [the Boy of Winander] lies' (5.396–7). Not only is the muteness Wordsworth's silence; it is as epitaph the 'lengthened pause / Of silence' (379–80) when the owls no longer answer the boy's 'mimic hootings' (373). That silence, however, perhaps like Wordsworth's 'long half hour together' (together with the boy?), is not as death-like as it might at first appear; for sometimes in that silence the boy 'hung / Listening' and was rewarded with 'a gentle shock of mild surprise' (381–2). Instead of mere mimicry (copies of natural sound, the voice as the literal or actual voice of nature), it becomes figurative. The 'voice / Of mountain torrents' is 'carried far into his heart,' or 'the visible scene ... enter[s] unawares into his mind' as a kind of haunting by 'solemn imagery, its rocks, / Its woods' (383–7). This haunting ('the ghostly language of the ancient earth' [2.309]) is an 'uncertain heaven, received / Into the bosom of the steady lake' (5.387–8). As 'a prospect in the mind' (2.352), it is a living epitaph to a dead child.

Metaphor continues to live in the allegory, as indeed metaphor must; for it is, by definition, the resurrected form of the literal or the copy. Rhetoric with its tropes enacts its own life in ways the author cannot fully control, language as language writing itself. Thus, in constructing a figurative life out of a literal or historical one, Wordsworth in *The Prelude* gradually confronts in what de Man calls 'the rhetoric of temporality' the making of a shrine where metaphor becomes epitaph and *The Prelude* itself an elegy to an unwritten epic. The process of memory becomes a memorial, a burial, which, subject to the rhetoric of elegy, contains the possibility of some 'future restoration' (12.286). The 'spots of time' (208) that are 'scattered everywhere' throughout *The Prelude*, 'taking their date / From our first childhood' (224–5), are metaphors that feed and propel the allegory to the limited degree it can absorb them. As metaphors, these 'moments' are signs of renovation, which, because of the temporality that allegory reimposes in a different, rhetorical form, can never become what they aspire to be: a 'metaphysics of presence.' For this reason, de Man concludes, 'the secularized allegory of the early romantics ... necessarily contains the negative moment which ... in Wordsworth [is] that of the loss of self in death or in error' ('Rhetoric' 207). Finally, in its most ghostly form, this 'negative moment' awakens in de Man – and with particular reference to Shelley's final fragment, *The Triumph of Life* – 'the suspicion that the negation is a *Verneinung*, an intended exorcism' ('Shelley' 68). In the context of this 'suspicion' that haunts and propels deconstruction in its exorcism of the text, *The Prelude* becomes Wordsworth's attempt to understand himself 'that always again demands to be read.' 'And to read,' de Man explains, 'is to understand, to question, to know, to forget, to erase, to deface, to repeat – that is to say the endless prosopopoeia by which the dead [*The Prelude* was published posthumously] are made to have a face and a voice which tells the allegory of their demise and allows us to apostrophize them in our turn' (68).

In the opening lines of the 1805 *Prelude* (1.1–115), the narrator as captive (the defining allegorical stance) comes 'from a house / Of bondage' (1.6–7) to greet the 'welcome messenger' (1.5) (equally the metaphorical stance). In terms of the allegory that Wordsworth is already shaping through a release from the literal into the figural, the narrator is encountering the essential energy of an otherwise imprisoned imagination, which immediately begins its metaphoric work by transforming the narrator's habitual or historical self (Wordsworth coming from London, Bristol, or even Gosler) into the figurative dimension of an allegorical life. The messenger is the releasing metaphor that sets the allegory in motion. As such, it is the poem's unconscious or unknown author whom the narrator must now come to know.

Not surprisingly, the meeting between a newly released captive and a spirit not unlike Shakespeare's Ariel is at once a greeting and a collision. On the one hand, the captive as 'renovated spirit' (in the 1850 version) is clothed in the 'priestly robe' of 'poetic numbers' and singled out, by virtue of that apparel, 'for holy services' (1.51–4). On the other hand, however, he cannot cope with this sudden transformation that metaphor imposes. The messenger who anoints him with his priestly vocation is also, like all metaphors, a rather sinister figure: 'a tempest, a redundant energy, / Vexing its own creation.' Unable finally to deal with the 'trances of thought and mountings of the mind' (1.19), which come fast upon him under the messenger's spell, the narrator seeks a 'respite to this passion' (1.60) in what he calls in the 1850 version 'the sheltered and the sheltering grove' (1.69), adding 'the sheltering' to the 1805 text's 'the sheltered.' In this place of burial, Wordsworth in true elegiac fashion rises as the sun sets, the acorns dropping from their cups to the bare earth prefiguring an oak grove that, as a metaphor of his natural cathedral, *The Recluse* (as subtle and as varied as the one he is actually in), would never be accomplished.

Having buried the metaphor in the sheltered grove, the figurative life of Wordsworth descends again to the literal. Making a new trial of strength, he falls back upon a mechanical image entirely alien to the figurative world he will eventually inhabit and hopefully be able to read. What will become the blended murmur of a nurse's song and a flowing river sending a voice along his dreams becomes, in the absence of his messenger, a harp defrauded of its 'Æolian visitations,' leaving 'the banded host / Of harmony dispersed in straggling sounds' (1.96–8). Settling down in his chosen vale to prepare himself 'for such an arduous work' (147) as the opening lines imposed, he finds himself reviewing the literature of the past in search of a subject until at last, confronted by his own emptiness ('much wanting, so much wanting' [264]), he 'recoil[s] and droop[s], and seek[s] repose / In listlessness from vain perplexity' (265–6). Precisely at this point the messenger intervenes again (269), this time as a 'babe in arms' (276) rocked to sleep by its nurse's song, which blended its murmurs with 'the fairest of all rivers' (270), a song that echoes, however distantly, the 'gentle breeze' of the first line, which brings with it a blessing. More significant, however, is the fact that the 1799 *Prelude*, complete in itself (and as a prelude the most complete of the various versions), begins with the welcoming of the babe as messenger, further to develop as metaphor as the nurse becomes nature itself, the relationship of mind to nature becoming as metaphor the madonna and child, Wordsworth's closest evocation of what Derrida calls 'full speech that was fully *present*,' '*the language of children before they begin to speak*' (*Of Grammatology* 247).

Wordsworth, it would appear, has unveiled in his first book the 'fabulous scene' of metaphor-making by moving back to what he calls 'days / Disowned by memory' (1.614–15). Not surprisingly in what constitutes the most powerful evocation of presence after Rousseau, Wordsworth as narrator can declare: 'my mind / Hath been revived'

(637–8). That 'mind' is the figurative mind, whose life is the life of metaphor and whose history is a continuous allegory,[4] an allegory that as writer Wordsworth must learn to read by recognizing in it the 'other Being' for whom he acts as scribe. That recognition, as perhaps is by now apparent, involves accepting metaphor as also a 'dark magician' full of dark disguises that only an equally dark interpreter can read and understand. The 'babe in arms' is also the Devil's child, who can, and in France almost does, drive the poet to madness.

The captive 'coming from a house / Of bondage' to greet the 'welcome messenger' in the opening lines of the 1805 *Prelude* is, in its larger epic context, the poet invoking his muse. As metaphor, the muse is initially 'this gentle breeze / That blows from the green fields and from the clouds / And from the sky' (1.1–3) to beat against the poet's cheek. The breeze as metaphor or muse is not, therefore, what Wordsworth calls in his 1815 preface 'merely a faithful copy, existing in the mind, of absent external things.' It is, rather, the 'operations of the mind upon those objects, and processes of creation or of composition, governed by certain fixed laws' (*PW* 3:31). Those operations are metaphorically present as invoked in the breeze as the half-conscious messenger conferring its blessing upon all that it touches. Its initial gentleness is the mind's pleasure in its own inward action, described by Wordsworth as a slight 'exertion' (32) of the imagination. Wordsworth invoking the breeze as muse is at the very outset of his epic calling attention to his subject: the mind itself as his 'haunt, and the main region of [his] song' (Prospectus to *The Recluse* 40). More than that: he is enacting the marriage of the mind to 'this goodly universe / In love and holy passion' as that marriage is present not in 'Paradise, and groves / Elysian,' which are a 'history only of departed things, / Or a mere fiction of what never was,' but in the 'simple produce of the common day' (47-55). It is present in the breeze caressing the poet's cheek.

A problem, however, immediately arises. Every exertion of the imagination, no matter how slight, that moves the mind away from a 'faithful copy' in the direction of the figurative is, in some sense, an act of deception, which, as Wordsworth points out in his note on 'The Thorn,' can lead to superstition unless one remains conscious of the actual workings of the mind. The breeze is made to 'seem' (*P* 1.3) other than it is, even as, for example, the mountain in the boat-stealing episode is made to seem as if it were striding after the boy 'as if with voluntary power' (379) or 'with purpose of its own' or a 'measured motion like a living thing' (383–4). Metaphor in this respect constitutes a 'vain belief' ('Tintern Abbey' 50) or what Shelley in his preface to *Alastor* calls an 'illustrious superstition' (*SPP* 69).

Locke's rejection of rhetoric or 'eloquence' as the mind's irresponsible pleasure in its own delusory activity, a pleasure that required the imposition of various instruments to correct distortion and ensure accurate observations in the future, is based, of course, upon the assumption that reality resides in 'things' and that all knowledge must therefore terminate in them. It assumes that mind, as distinct from nature, in itself has no reality like that of nature. Left to its own pleasurable activity (the imagination as pleasure principle), the mind, far from producing a faithful copy of a horse and rider, will produce a centaur. 'He that thinks the Name *Centaur* stands for some real Being, imposes on himself, and mistakes Words for Things' (*Essay* 3:507), Locke writes. Wordsworth, however, in creating a half-conscious breeze is not mistaking words for things. He does not confuse the figurative and the literal. Rather, at this point he is affirming the pleasure of writing, a pleasure that Locke affirms only to reject it as a form of seduction, Wordsworth's messenger being for him a temptress with whom "tis in vain to find fault' so long as 'Men find pleasure to be Deceived.' Locke's attack on rhetoric is a Puritan attack (in the new guise of empiricism) on pleasure. It also anticipates Freud's *Beyond the Pleasure Principle*.

The figurative as opposed to the literal has, for Wordsworth, its source in what he calls in his 1800 preface, 'the grand elementary principle of pleasure, by which [man] knows, and feels, and lives, and moves' (*PW* 1:140). Wordsworth's defence of poetry is, above all, a defence of the pleasure principle as the most immediate and direct affirmation that the mind, as the observer of its own creative power, grants to its own activity. Pleasure, that is, is the mind's affirmation of itself, the blessing it confers upon itself in the presence of its own activity. That pleasure it expresses directly in and as metaphor, the mind's pleasure in itself becoming a captive greeting a messenger, a breeze beating against a cheek. For Wordsworth, these tropes are not mistaken for things; they are the direct evidence of an inward state described by Shelley as 'the mind in creation.' Unlike Locke, who wrote under the illusion that in the immediate and sensual presence of the words upon the page he was also in the presence of 'things,' Wordsworth, as a poet confronting writing as writing, had no illusions about what writing is. He was, that is, in the presence of figuration, of metaphorical language, experiencing it as the blessing that the mind in creation confers upon itself. Wordsworth's joy is in words, not in things.

Yet the problem remains: the pleasure affirms a fiction. Quarrelling with Wordsworth's failure to distinguish between the language of poetry and prose, Coleridge writes:

> A difference of object and contents supplies an additional ground of distinction. The immediate purpose may be the communication of truths; either of truth absolute and demonstrable, as in works of science; or of facts experienced and recorded, as in history. Pleasure, and that of the highest and most permanent kind, may *result* from the *attainment* of the end; but it is not itself the immediate end. In other works the communication of pleasure may be the immediate purpose; and though truth, either moral or intellectual, ought to be the *ultimate* end, yet this will distinguish the character of the author, not the class to which the work belongs. (*BL* 2:12)

As metaphor, a half-conscious gentle breeze conferring a blessing by striking a cheek, *The Prelude* in its opening lines locates itself in 'the class to which,' as poetry, it 'belongs.' Pleasure is the immediate end and it is, therefore, immediately achieved. The initial utterance, 'Oh,' not yet a word, but a prelinguistic sound (an emission of breath or 'gentle breeze') like Johnny's 'burrs,' constitutes for the poet the release of utterance itself that takes him immediately into a figuration of himself that only later, as figuration, becomes allegory in the service of the ego, becomes character. At that point, metaphor absorbed into allegory, 'truth, either moral or intellectual,' becomes the immediate rather than the ultimate end, thereby displacing metaphor and relocating poetry in a class to which as poetry it does not properly belong. Poetry placed in the service of truth, 'either moral or intellectual,' is poetry subjected to 'the character of the author' rather than to itself. Keats immediately recognized Wordsworth's subjugation of poetry to truth when he attacked the presence in his poetry of the 'egotistical sublime,' contrasting it to 'Negative Capability' (*KL* 43), which, as in Shakespeare, resulted in a purer form of poetry because the author, as author, had no character at all. Coleridge makes the same point when, in his remarks to Barbauld, he condemns the moral stanzas of his *Rime*, which he may have included in response to Wordsworth's complaint that his ancient mariner lacked a character. He also makes it when he rejects allegory in favour of symbol.

What distinguishes the 1799 version of *The Prelude* from its 1805 and 1850 extensions is the relative absence of allegory. The hero, like Coleridge's mariner, has no ego, remaining as yet blessedly unconscious of his own creative power. As *The Prelude* develops into a continuous allegory, however, Wordsworth as its narrator will have to provide the hero with an ego structure that at once judges and, with reservations, affirms the egoless child of the first two books. Unlike the extensions of *The Prelude*, the unconscious in the 1799 version is not yet answerable to consciousness; metaphor has not yet been relocated in the more limited confines of allegory. The poetry, that is, remains answerable largely to itself rather than to the character of the author.

Metaphor, as Derrida suggests, has what Wordsworth calls its 'hiding-places' (*P* 12.279) of power in the 'fabulous scene' of writing itself, which allegory largely suppresses or buries. This 'fabulous scene,' Derrida's 'white mythology' entombed in allegory, like Shelley's 'white radiance' (*Adonais* 463) entombed beneath his 'dome of many-coloured glass' (462), protects the ego from the terrors of the deep. The apocalyptic scene of Wordsworth's *Prelude* is 'disowned by memory.' If it were not, it would be a scene of divine madness, which, Wordsworth recognizes, is 'far hidden from the reach of words' (3.187). This scene, metaphorically identified with 'remotest infancy,' Wordsworth would like to render as 'a visible scene on which the sun is shining.' He would like to endow it with what Derrida calls the 'full speech' that does not exist except as the absence of it articulated as a 'best conjecture' (*P* 2.233). Wordsworth's 'best conjecture' is the undifferentiated infant at the breast of the mother (Lacan's 'mirror stage'), perceiving with the eye of the mother the world as himself. Inflating this primary narcissistic perception into a metaphysics of presence ('celestial light'), Wordsworth in his 'Intimations' ode is careful not to recommend it as a matter of faith or belief, which would reduce it to mere superstition. In *The Prelude*, therefore, Wordsworth is conscious of shaping a creation myth as what Blake calls a poetic tale, which is always in danger of becoming, as in Milton's epic, a form of worship. Milton, Keats argues, 'appears to have been content' with the regenerated 'Dogmas and superstitions' of a Protestantism that 'was considered under the immediate eye of heaven' (*KL* 96).

Blake's quarrel with Wordsworth lies in his binding of his creation myth to the biological binding of the infant to the mother, the mother's eye, as Tirzah, becoming a far more tyrannical eye than all 'Seven Eyes of God.' 'Thou Mother of my Mortal part,' writes Blake, addressing Tirzah,

With cruelty didst mould my Heart.
And with false self-decieving tears,
Didst bind my Nostrils Eyes & Ears.

Didst close my Tongue in senseless clay
And me to Mortal Life betray:
The Death of Jesus set me free,
Then what have I to do with thee?   ('To Tirzah' 10–16)

For Blake, by shaping a natural creation myth, Wordsworth bound himself to the Orc-Urizen cycle, which carries within it its own destruction. 'Whate'er is Born of Mortal Birth,' Blake explains, 'Must be consumed with the Earth / To rise from Generation free; / Then what have I to do with thee?' ('To Tirzah' 1–4). Shelley, after reading *The Excursion*, composed in *Alastor* an elegy on the death of Wordsworth, remarkable for its refusal to mourn. Echoing 'The Boy of Winander,' in which Wordsworth stands silently at the boy's grave, he writes,

There was a Poet whose untimely tomb
No human hands with pious reverence reared,
But the charmed eddies of autumnal winds
Built o'er his mouldering bones a pyramid
Of mouldering leaves in the waste wilderness.   (*Alastor* 50–4)

The passage ends: 'And Silence, too enamoured of that voice, / Locks its mute music in her rugged cell' (65–6).

The Recluse, as Wordsworth originally conceived it with the help of Coleridge, was intended as a hymn to the creation, a hymn to man's creative power as that power works through the medium of the senses to produce not nature itself ('a termination in things') but a rhetorical world. This world, like the presence of the Convent of Chartreuse, 'bodie[s] forth the ghostliness of things' (*P* 6.428) by granting to that 'ghostliness' ('things' as separate from the action of the mind) 'a speaking face of earth and heaven': nature as figure, rhetoric, figuration. '[Wordsworth] was,' as Coleridge later describes the original plan for *The Recluse* in a 21 July 1832 entry in *Table Talk*, 'to treat man as man, – a subject of eye, ear, touch, and taste, in contact with external nature, and informing the senses from the mind, and not compounding a mind out of the senses' (*Collected Works* 14ii:177).

What went wrong? Blake's answer is writ large in Blake's own poetry: 'the Natural Man' rose up against 'the Spiritual Man' to place him 'at Enmity against all true Poetry or Inspiration.'

Described in another way, allegory oppressively intervened. Truths 'either moral or intellectual' became, particularly in *The Excursion*, Wordsworth's immediate rather than ultimate end. The 'character of the author' assumed control of the 'some other Being.' Described in terms of Jung's typology, Wordsworth's 'No. 1' ego personality assumed control of his 'No. 2' personality, which Jung calls the Self, and Coleridge calls the 'I AM' as the 'IMMEDIATE, which dwells in every man ... the original intuition, or absolute affirmation of it, (which is likewise in every man, but does not in every man rise into consciousness)' (*BL* 1:243). Described in terms of Foucault's account of Descartes's 'great internment' in the first *Meditation*, Wordsworth philosophically interned his madness, thereby setting the tone for all that was to follow. Viewed in terms of Derrida's further exploring what Foucault had to say about Descartes's madness, Wordsworth, 'who must [as in the case of the crazed Bedouin] evoke madness from the *interior* of thought (and not only from within the body or some other extrinsic agency), can do so only in the realm of the *possible* and in the language of fiction or the fiction of language. Thereby, through his own language, he reassures himself against any actual madness ... and can keep his distance, the distance indispensable for continuing to speak and to live' ('Cogito' 54). The failure of Wordsworth's hyperbolic project (the descent of the New Jerusalem) is, as Coleridge recognized in his *Biographia Literaria*, the failure of his natural language as it remains answerable to 'things.' The 'IMMEDIATE,' Coleridge insists,

> becomes intelligible to no man by the ministry of mere words from without. The medium, by which spirits understand each other, is not the surrounding air; but the *freedom* which they possess in common, as the common ethereal element of their being, the tremulous reciprocations of which propagate themselves even to the inmost of the soul. Where the spirit of a man is not *filled* with the consciousness of freedom (were it only from its restlessness, as one still struggling in bondage) all spiritual intercourse is interrupted, not only with others, but even with himself. No wonder then, that he remains incomprehensible to himself as well as to others. No wonder, that in the fearful desert of his consciousness, he wearies himself out with empty words, to which no friendly echo answers, either from his own heart, or the heart of a fellow being; or bewilders himself in the pursuit of *notional* phantoms, the mere refractions from

unseen and distant truths through the distorting medium of his own
unenlivened and stagnant understanding! (*BL* 1:243–4)

None of this could Coleridge directly address to Wordsworth himself,
though in the same way that *The Prelude* was addressed to Coleridge,
the *Biographia Literaria* was addressed to Wordsworth.

Wordsworth philosophically interned madness as his experience of
the 'IMMEDIATE.' The result was something closer to prose, or a poetry virtually indistinguishable from it, for which Coleridge must assume considerable responsibility. His conviction that Wordsworth could
and should write the 'FIRST GENUINE PHILOSOPHIC POEM' (*BL*
2:156) was grounded in his theological conception of the imagination,
which, in theory if not in practice, bound the imagination to truth.
Coleridge's view of the primary imagination, which rendered the act of
perception a 'repetition in the finite mind of the eternal act of creation in
the infinite I AM,' imposed upon Wordsworth the very 'priestly robe'
he incongruously put on in the opening lines of *The Prelude*. As theological rather than imaginal apparel, associated with truth rather than
fiction, with the 'infinite I AM' rather than a wind god or an oracular
voice, the 'priestly robe' became, in the primal context of immediate
pleasure, 'those poisoned vestments.' In his third essay on epitaphs,
Wordsworth describes these vestments as having the 'power to consume and to alienate from his right mind the victim who put them on'
(*PW* 2:84–5). The 'welcome messenger' of the opening lines is not a
bishop but a wind god, a conjurer, who, like the voice issuing from the
shell (itself the sea-cave in which the dreamer sits as in Shelley's 'still
cave of the witch Poesy' ['Mont Blanc' 44]), is 'many gods' with 'voices
more than all the winds' (*P* 5.106–7). For the narrator coming from
the bondage of the habitual self, it is obviously overpowering; the
'trances of thought and mountings of the mind' that 'come fast upon
[him]' (*P* 1.19–20) become a 'tempest, a redundant energy / Vexing its
own creation' (37–9). Wordsworth, I suggest, settled too deeply into
what Derrida calls 'economy' in order to avoid the madness of the
inaccessible 'Moment' of the 'Cogito' (62).

In the dream of the Arab, which assembles into itself the entire action
of *The Prelude* around the figure of the 'Cogito,' the 'tempest' becomes a
'loud prophetic blast of harmony' (P 5.95) issuing from a shell that, as
commanded by the Bedouin, Wordsworth in his dream brought to his
ear. As a cave of winds, Wordsworth heard issuing from it in 'an
unknown tongue,' the 'articulate sounds' of which he understood as

A loud prophetic blast of harmony;
An Ode, in passion uttered, which foretold
Destruction to the children of the earth
By deluge, now at hand.   (5.95–8)

The 'Ode' he hears is the 'Intimations' ode he never wrote, though its possibility was buried within. To have written it, however, would have been to destroy it in the same way that Shelley in the final stanzas destroyed *Adonais*. To have written it would have required Wordsworth to remain the six-year-old Hartley Coleridge whom Wordsworth addresses in the Intimations ode as a 'Mighty Prophet! Seer Blest!' (114). He would have to abandon language altogether by returning to what Kristeva calls the 'semiotic,' prelinguistic 'articulate sounds,' which carry, as sounds that are not yet language, traces of the mother's absent body. Such 'sounds,' he intuitively realized, being himself subject to them, 'foretold / Destruction.' Yet, as Wordsworth also knew, without those 'articulate sounds' below the reach of language sounding in his ear no real poetry can be written. The crazed Bedouin was the archetypal poet within himself haunting Wordsworth with the 'articulate sounds' of his absence that constituted his presence.

Wordsworth's Crazed Bedouin

In his response to Foucault's insistence that Descartes interns madness, Derrida argues that Descartes incorporated it rather than interned it:

> Descartes not only ceases to reject madness during the phase of radical doubt, he not only installs its possible menace at the very heart of the intelligible, he also in principle refuses to let any determined knowledge escape from madness. A menace to all knowledge, insanity – the hypothesis of insanity – is not an internal modification of knowledge. At no point will knowledge alone be able to dominate madness, to master it in order to objectify it [as the other of sanity] ... The certainty [of '*I think, therefore I am*'] thus attained need not be sheltered from an emprisoned madness, for it is attained and ascertained within madness itself. It is valid *even if I am mad* – a supreme self-confidence that seems to require neither the exclusion nor the circumventing of madness. Descartes never interns madness, neither at the stage of natural doubt nor at the stage of metaphysical doubt. *He only claims to exclude it during ... the nonhyperbolical moment of natural doubt.* ('Cogito' 55–6)

So long as Wordsworth allowed his *'natural doubt'* to exclude from his imagination its *'nonhyperbolic moment'* (the descent of the New Jerusalem), understood as the divine madness that is proper to it ('some called it madness'), madness becomes the other of his own divided consciousness (himself and 'some other being'), which must be 'interned' as Foucault's 'Birth of the Asylum' in the Age of Reason as a way of handling the fear of what would later be called schizophrenia. In the cause of sanity and reason, the 'some other being' is declared insane. As 'some other being,' Derrida argues, Descartes did not treat his dreams in this way. He incorporated them into his consciousness as the 'Cogito' that informs it. Madness is the 'I am' that becomes conscious of itself ('I Am that I Am') in the absorption of it. While this absorption tranquillizes madness so that it is certified sanity, the sanity partakes of its madness so as to affirm itself with 'supreme self-confidence.' This role of madness as the sanity of the 'Poetic Genius' is performed in *The Prelude* by Wordsworth's dream of the crazed Bedouin, which, as Jane Worthington Smyser has pointed out, is loosely based on three dreams that Descartes had during the night of 10 November 1619.[5] In the three dreams, which he interpreted both awake and as he slept, Descartes was persuaded that the Spirit of Truth had descended upon him and guided him into all truth. In the first dream the Holy Spirit descended in the form of a whirlwind, which initially filled him with terror. In the second dream it descended as a thunderbolt, which, when he awakened, seemed to fill the room with sparks of fire. In the third and confirming dream, in which his terror was appeased, it descended in the guise of two books: a dictionary showing the unity of the sciences and a volume of poetry that, transcending the reason of the philosophers, itself was a direct revelation of the spark of divinity in man. Believing the dreams and the revelation they contained to be 'the most important thing in his life,' Descartes vowed to make a pilgrimage on foot from Venice to Lorette, a vow he fulfilled some five years later.[6]

Like Wordsworth in *The Prelude*, Descartes, as a result of what he considered a mystical experience, believed he was 'a renovated spirit singled out ... for holy services.' Descartes's pilgrimage to the shrine of the Madonna in Lorette finds its analogue in Wordsworth's three-day pilgrimage to join his sister in the 'chosen Vale' (*P* 1.93). The difference between Wordsworth's three-day journey to the 'Vale' and Blake's journey to Felpham fully indicates the wide gap between the two poets, a gap that Wordsworth, by his own admission, had every reason to regret as what he called 'a subjugation of an opposite nature' (*Fenwick*

Notes 61). 'For when Los joind with me,' writes Blake,

> he took me in his firy whirlwind
> My Vegetated portion was hurried from Lambeths shades
> He set me down in Felphams Vale & prepard a beautiful
> Cottage for me that in three years I might write all these Visions.
>
> (*M* 36[40].21–4)

Wordsworth's slow-paced three-day journey to his 'chosen Vale' in which he remains 'keen as a Truant or a Fugitive' but also 'as a Pilgrim resolute' (*P* 1.90–1) contains within it a vast circuitous meditation in which all three – the 'Truant,' the 'Fugitive,' and the 'Pilgrim resolute' – combine, separate, and contend towards a resolution impossible to achieve. In something of the same way, Blake's *Milton* circumambulates as the 'Pulsation of the Artery.'

In her account of the dream text, Smyser suggests that the 'studious friend' who told Wordsworth the dream (Wordsworth did not claim it as his own until 1839) was Michael Beaupuy rather than Coleridge, because Wordsworth would never have used the third person in speaking of Coleridge, 'since throughout the poem Coleridge is intimately addressed in the second person' (272). Coleridge rather than Beaupuy is the more likely candidate, however, though for quite obvious reasons Wordsworth took care in the poem not to equate with Coleridge the crazed Bedouin, whose reason was couched 'in the blind and awful lair / Of such a madness' (5.151–2). Yet precisely as the Spirit of Truth descended upon Descartes, Coleridge in a letter to Godwin (25 March 1801) describes Wordsworth descending upon him: 'If I die, and the Booksellers will give you anything for my Life, be sure to say – "Wordsworth descended on him, like the Γνῶθι σεαυτόν from Heaven."' More than that: comparing himself to Wordsworth (who made him know that he himself 'was no poet'), he describes himself as 'once a Volume of Gold Leaf, rising & riding on every breath of Fancy – but I have beaten myself back into weight & density, & now I sink in quicksilver, yea, remain squat and square on the earth amid the hurricane, that makes Oaks and Straws join in one Dance, fifty yards high in the Element' (*Collected Letters* 2:714).

The dream text of the Arab, I suggest, enacts in the most profound and startling manner the controlling metaphor of *The Prelude*: the symbiosis of Coleridge and Wordsworth as joint authors of the apocalyptic poem describing the descent of the New Jerusalem as an action within the mind itself. Not even chaos itself, writes Wordsworth, 'can breed such fear and awe / As falls upon us often when we look / Into our Minds, into the Mind of Man, / My haunt and the main region of my song' (Prospectus to *The Recluse* 38–41). Wordsworth's *Recluse*, doomed to die before it was barely begun, everything becoming either a prelude to it or an excursion from it, found its proper burial, memorial, or epitaph in and as *The Prelude*. In the dream text, enchanter and Holy Spirit (the 'sweet breath of heaven' [1.33]) meet in that permanent disjunction, which, as allegory, is the necessary Derridean betrayal to protect the narrator from madness by means of 'some philosophic song / Of Truth that cherishes our daily life' (1.229–30). Though tempted like Milton (and like Descartes) to bind himself to the 'I Am that I Am' who met Moses 'on the secret top / Of *Oreb*' (*PL* 1.6-7) (and almost meets Wordsworth on the top of Snowdon), Wordsworth in the end absorbs the metaphor into a fitting epitaph.[7]

Metaphor as metaphor belongs to 'days / Disowned by memory,' which from a moral point of view can lead men astray by an 'infirmity of love' (*P* 1.614). It belongs to the polymorphously perverse babe at its mother's breast and to the incestuous union that is its strongest metaphor. Thus, when Wordsworth announces the theme of *The Recluse* in the metaphor of the descent of the New Jerusalem adorned as a bride to meet the bridegroom, Wordsworth's apocalyptic theme has all the strength of a metaphoric usurpation that rejects the moral taboos, including union with Mother Nature as well as his union with Coleridge. He is voicing at once John's vision in Revelation and 'the language of children before they begin to speak.' He is proclaiming what Geoffrey Hartman calls a 'silenced ur-fiat' ('Words' 199) understood as Derrida's 'full speech' or 'original language,' which is present only as absence, a 'fiat' described by Hartman as calling not for an object of desire, but in Wordsworth's words 'something evermore about to be' (*P* 6.608). The mood of the phrase, Hartman persuasively suggests, 'at once goads and restrains the reality-hunger of an infinite will desiring omnipotent and manifest fulfilments' (199). In Coleridge's words, he is contemplating in his announcement of his apocalyptic theme 'the ANCIENT of days and all his works with feelings as fresh, as if all had then sprang forth at the first creative fiat' (*BL* 1:80). Precisely here in Coleridge's ultimately paralysing identification of the first creative fiat of 'the ANCIENT of days' with the act of perception itself resides the blindness that Wordsworth rightly feared, though it was far more a blindness arising from insight than from any failure of the physical organ. The 'first creative fiat' brought into play everything that Derrida identifies with '*différance.*'[8]

Hartman explores what he calls 'a silenced ur-fiat' in Wordsworth's poetry, the substitution of *akedah* (or binding) for apocalypse (*Wordsworth's Poetry* 225), which as rhetoric is the substitution of allegory, a moral and intellectual convenant represented as a descent from a 'celestial' realm of pure light into the 'light [darkness] of common day.' What distinguished the one from the other in Derrida's reading of Rousseau's uncovenanted man in the state of nature is the prohibition against incest, the prohibition against the apocalyptic marriage that Wordsworth announced as the theme of his unwritten *Recluse.* That prohibition, properly understood, is the prohibition against the union of mind and nature as a single undifferentiated body, which would as union constitute oblivion or nothingness. Mind and nature face to face as one face (the 'workings of one mind, the features / Of the same face' [*P* 6.636–7]) is God alone in 'the Void Outside of Existence' described by Wordsworth as 'the Uncreated' (2.412).

Prefiguring his own madness, Nietzsche attempts an invocation of it in his account of a grazing herd in 'On the Uses and Disadvantages of History for Life':

> This is a hard sight for man to see; for, though he thinks himself better than the animals because he is human, he cannot help envying them their happiness ... A human being may well ask an animal: 'Why do you not speak to me of your happiness but only stand and gaze at me?' The animal would like to answer, and say: 'The reason is I always forget what I was going to say' – but then he forgot this answer too, and stayed silent: so that the human being was left wondering.
>
> But he also wonders at himself, that he cannot learn to forget but clings relentlessly to the past: however far and fast he may run, this chain runs with him ['More like a man / Flying from something that he dreads, than one / Who sought the thing he loved' ('Tintern Abbey' 71–3)] ... A leaf flutters from the scroll of time, floats away – and suddenly floats back again and falls into the man's lap. Then the man says 'I remember' and envies the animal, who at once forgets and for whom every moment really dies, sinks back into night and fog and is extinguished for ever. Thus the animal lives *unhistorically*: for it is contained in the present, like a number without any awkward fraction left over. (60–1)

Metaphor is the attempt to live '*unhistorically,*' to go perpetually into the present, 'like a number without any awkward fraction left over.' It is an attempt, in Derrida's words (whose source is Nietzsche) to recover a 'full speech.' It is a presence that Wordsworth will approximate in a babe at the mother's breast or his idiot, Johnny, or even himself as a five-year-old making 'one long bathing of a summer's day' (*P* 1.290). It is a presence that Nietzsche, bursting through the bounds of 'the human, all too human,' entered as madness. Wordsworth, on the other hand, 'could wish [his] days to be / Bound each to each by natural piety' ('Rainbow' 8–9). That binding is the allegory *The Prelude* becomes, and, in the book on 'Books,' he attempts for the first time to read. The 'welcome messenger' of the opening lines becomes in the dream of the Arab the 'tempest' or 'redundant energy' of the crazed Bedouin. Rather than put on his 'priestly robe' as a deliberate disguise in order to exorcise him, Wordsworth in the dream confronts the Arab as his struggle to confront the lost apocalyptic core of his own text. The dream becomes what de Man calls 'a scene of reading' (*Allegories* 162).

Essential to any understanding of Wordsworth's rhetorical figuration of his life (at once figured and disfigured) is the permanent and necessary disjunction between the 'two consciousnesses' that only nothingness can repair. Metaphor, so long as it continues to function as a creative agent, must continue to unbind what 'natural piety' would join together. 'What allegory would join together let metaphor put asunder' constitutes a law of poetic composition. Allegory is *akedah*, the binding of the covenant, the taboo against incest, the moral centre as ultimate end rendered immediate. The child as metaphor, as *puer aeternus*, in fathering the poet unfathers the man because he is, as metaphor, as *puer*, wedded to the Great Mother conjured in infancy in what for the allegorical or moral man is an 'infirmity of love,' an unholy passion. The *puer* as poet is the criminal, the outcast, the revolutionary who, far from being apparelled in 'priestly robe,' decked out for 'holy services,' is in the village church the 'uninvited guest / Whom no one owned,' standing like Satan in silence 'fed on the day of vengeance yet to come' (*P* 10.297–9). The world that the unconscious child constructs in the 1799 *Prelude* constitutes an unconscious process of self-deification ('Of genius, power, / Creation and divinity itself / I have been speaking'), which leaves him at seventeen enthroned upon a pinnacle beyond the throne of Jehovah to view the unconscious creation of the child (Lacan's mirror stage) as his own creation.

This God-like metaphor ('some called it madness') contains as allegory the seeds of a horrendous crime. This crime, Wordsworth's 'independent intellect' (*P* 11.244) that passes 'unalarmed' 'Jehovah – with his thunder' (Prospectus to *The Recluse* 35, 33), repeats the action of Satan in *Paradise Lost* turning the paradise of childhood into Milton's hell. Precisely this fate is recounted by the narrator in the books on the revolution as he moves uneasily back and forth between the literal and the figurative, unable to locate himself in either because he cannot decide where as a revolutionary in a failed and foreign revolution he either in fact or in figure belongs. Though metaphor would conduct him one way, subverting the ego's demands, allegory as an ego defence (as 'far as angels are from guilt' [*P* 10.145]) demanded another. His 'egotistical sublime,' seemingly secure within the barricades that allegory erects, struggled with the help of the conscious will (Coleridge's 'secondary imagination') to maintain his stationing of himself as 'Adam, yet in Paradise / Though fallen from bliss' (8.659–60). The result, a radical conflict between the 'two consciousnesses' that dialectically shape *The Prelude*, was a nightmare bringing the poem close to collapse in Book 10, a collapse that Wordsworth examines more as metaphor than as allegory in the dream of the Arab, the metaphor of the crazed Bedouin releasing him from the allegorical frame *The Prelude* has established. The dream of the crazed Bedouin, that is, momentarily releases Wordsworth from the false 'I AM,' which has usurped the role of 'some other being.' Interpreting the dream, the 'two consciousnesses' negotiate with one another. What Wordsworth awake appears to affirm contains within it its own defeat. The ego structure so painfully shaped by its psychotic defeat in the failure of the French Revolution binds Wordsworth's soul to a history he is powerless to change. The hard-won victory of his ego as the spectral form of his apocalyptic vision is a form for which, Blake recognized, Wordsworth finally settled.

Annotating Spurzheim's *Observations on Insanity* (London 1817), in which Spurzheim argues that 'religion is another fertile cause of insanity,' citing 'Methodism for its supply of numerous cases,' Blake wrote: 'Cowper came to me & said. O that I were insane always I will never rest. Can you not make me truly insane. I will never rest till I am so. O that in the bosom of God I was hid. You retain health & yet are as mad as any of us all – over us all – mad as a refuge from unbelief [natural religion] – from Bacon Newton & Locke' (E 663). For the sake of his dialectic, Blake put on the 'shitty garments' that Frye cast off never to put on again, Blake's entire vision entering Frye's moment of casting off in order to embrace what this moment apocalyptically contained. Because Wordsworth made his apocalyptic vision answerable to history ('the light of common day'), however, he suffered the necessary consequences of it. What 'we are toiling all our lives to find,' he writes in his 'Intimations' ode, is 'in darkness lost, the darkness of the grave' (116–17). In its original form, Wordsworth identifies the six-year-old son of Coleridge with the apocalyptic light and goes on to describe him lying awake in the grave awaiting the resurrection. Wordsworth, however, found himself in the grave awaiting a resurrection that he no longer believed would come, as the French Revolution descended first into a Reign of Terror and then to the crowning of Napoleon: 'this last opprobrium, when we see a people, / That once looked up in faith, as if to Heaven / For manna, take a lesson from the dog / Returning to his vomit' (*P* 11.360–3). Because of this experience, Wordsworth had 'ghastly visions ... of despair' and 'unbroken dreams entangled [him]' in which he

> strove to plead
> Before unjust tribunals, – with a voice
> Labouring, a brain confounded, and a sense,
> Death-like, of treacherous desertion, felt
> In the last place of refuge – [his] own soul.   (10.402–15)

In the dream of the Arab, Wordsworth struggles to resolve the nightmare of opposition by finding a *modus vivendi* between the moral demands of allegory and what, in terms of those demands, have become the terrors of metaphor, terrors inherent in the experience of hyperbolic desire as fear. Metaphor, too much suppressed or too long buried as the self-deifying vision of his first seventeen years recedes, now turns around to reveal its dark face. This face would reduce allegory as a scene of reading to 'a label on a blind man's chest,' which in Wordsworth's original description of his encounter with the blind beggar signifies for him 'the very most of what we know / Both of ourselves and of the universe, / The whole of what is written to our view' (*P 1805* 7.620n). If the scene of reading is to become again anything more than this, if *The Prelude* itself is not to find its fitting emblem in a *mise en abyme*[9] (an 'abyss structure' in which the poet confronts directly the nothingness that the 'Immortality' ode rhetoric disguises as 'celestial light'), then Wordsworth must affirm Blake's dialectic of imagination in which opposition remains 'true Friendship.'

In his account of the drowned man (yet another of his disfigurations in Book 5), Wordsworth suggests that he could accept 'a spectre shape /

Of terror' with 'no soul-debasing fear' because even by the age of nine his inner eye had already seen such sights 'among the shining streams / Of faëry land, the forests of romance' (P 5.450–5). Yet, in the reversal of the revolution in a reign of terror and an imperial conquest that made him for a time traitor to his country, Wordsworth could not hallow 'the sad spectacle / With decoration of ideal grace.' He could not, that is, preserve his 'dignity,' his 'smoothness, like the works / Of Grecian art, and purest poesy' (5.456–9). Faery lands, now forlorn, had opened onto perilous waters, described as 'the devouring sea' in his 1805 introduction to his 'Residence in France' and changed to 'the ravenous sea' (9.4) in the final 1850 version. He could not, that is, transform the literal into a work of Grecian art any more than he could comfortably wear 'priestly robes.' Wordsworth's world of metaphor was Gothic, unruly, expansive, accommodating, aspiring, and retreating, gargoyles about its portals and devils in sacred places. It lacked, as metaphor, the grace of 'purest poetry' to become instead a 'loud prophetic blast of harmony.' Wordsworth in the dream of the Arab is struggling, as The Prelude continues to grow even against his will, to accommodate himself to the pressure of metaphor that continued to assert itself as the work of 'single and of determined bounds' (the 1799 Prelude) became a 'work / Of ampler or more varied argument / Where [he] might be discomfited and lost' (1.642–5), as now indeed he was. Like Keats, though perhaps less consciously, Wordsworth in Book 5 realized that the emergence of the psyche, rather than the ego, as the hero of the action necessarily brought with it the destruction of Grecian form. A temple to the psyche, to 'Soul-making,' was inherently Gothic rather than Greek. Wordsworth in the dream of the Arab is finding in a scene of reading, which is simultaneously a scene of writing, a new centre, neither a madman nor a sublime egotist but a soul in the process of making itself. He is confronting what Keats in The Fall of Hyperion calls 'this warm scribe my hand' (1.18). The scene of writing becomes a scene of reading; fiction as fiction demystifies its illusory claims to truth, while at the same time opening up the 'deluge' that in writing is always 'now at hand' (P 5.98).

In the scene of reading-writing that is the Bedouin's dream dwells the dawning realization that not Wordsworth but the imagination is authoring itself by bringing itself to consciousness. The dynamics of a continuous allegory always threatened by its own extinction (the extinction of The Recluse as the presence of The Prelude) is not governed by a moral consciousness harnessed to the will; nor is it harnessed to the 'secondary imagination' struggling 'to idealize and to unify' (BL 1:304) the texts as an incarnation of the Logos or Word. The admonishments from another world are less the admonishments of the 'I Am that I Am' addressing Moses on Mount Horeb ('genius, power / Creation and divinity itself') than the admonishments of rhetoric understood as a secret collusion between allegory and metaphor in the interests of 'Soul-making.' Above all, and again as rhetoric, it is a reminder that poetry has its immediate source and its immediate end not in moral or intellectual truth, but in the pleasure the mind receives from its own creative activity and the contemplation of it. Only in the recognition of this activity, which is the scene of reading superimposed upon the scene of writing, can writing survive its oblivion as mark or sign; only in this way can the face of the page become a 'speaking face' issuing from the 'parent tongue' of the inspired poet who, as one of the four Zoas, Blake names Tharmas. The '"waters of the deep"' which the crazed Bedouin tells Wordsworth are '"gathering upon us"' (*P* 5.130–1) are indeed the 'mind turned round / As with the might of waters' (7.643–4). Wordsworth in this instant sees again the 'gentle breeze' of the opening line of *The Prelude* become 'a redundant energy.' This time, however, he does not seek respite in 'the sheltered and the sheltering grove.' The very 'tempest' propels him on as it propels the crazed Bedouin whom, in a metaphorical sense, he now becomes. The 'monumental letters' from which he once fled, the 'written paper' attached to the breast of a blind beggar become in the dream the moving pen interpreting its own marks. The pen as metaphor is consciousness reading itself.

'Monumental letters' as 'a written paper' telling a blind man's story is the dark side of an apocalyptic event, the imagination's 'strength / Of usurpation' (6.599–600), which, in putting out the 'light of sense,' 'with a flash ... reveal[s] / The invisible world' (6.601–2). The counterpart of this 'written paper' attached to the breast of a blind beggar is Wordsworth and his companion following a 'conspicuous invitation to ascend / A lofty mountain,' where they meet a peasant from whose mouth (not unlike the 'written sheet') they learn that, far from climbing higher, they must, in fact, descend, that their 'future course, all plain to sight, / Was downwards, with the current of [the] stream.' Loth to believe what they so grieved to hear ('for still [they] had hopes that pointed to the clouds'), they questioned the peasant 'again, and yet again.' 'But every word,' Wordsworth concludes, 'that from the peasant's lips / Came in reply, translated by our feelings, / Ended in this, – *that we had crossed the Alps*' (6.572–91). Precisely in recording this encounter with 'low and rustic life,' which spoke a more philosophic language than did poets artificially aiming at the sublime, Wordsworth experienced the imagination's 'strength / Of usurpation.' By pointing in the opposite direction of his mounting mind, the peasant, with his barely understood peasant speech, released as rhetoric (rather than as fact) a presence beyond the reach of sense, even as a happy shepherd or idiot boy, wearing speech as a 'mock apparel,' can awaken some vanishing gleam of a celestial world. Wordsworth's 'imperial palace,' the apocalyptic imagination, is a peasant whose 'speaking face' directs him in what appears to be the opposite direction. Wordsworth's encounter with a peasant pointing in a literal direction becomes in the act of composition an encounter with metaphor itself. 'Imagination,' Wordsworth exclaims,

> Through sad incompetence of human speech,
> That awful Power rose from the mind's abyss
> Like an unfathered vapour that enwraps,
> At once, some lonely traveller. I was lost;
> Halted without an effort to break through;
> But to my conscious soul I now can say –
> 'I recognise thy glory': in such strength
> Of usurpation, when the light of sense
> Goes out, but with a flash that has revealed
> The invisible world, doth greatness make abode.   (6.592–602)

Wordsworth's 'flash' is Blake's 'Pulsation of the Artery' (M 29[31].3) apocalyptically awakened to a consciousness of itself. Blake, however, was sufficiently 'mad' to enter this 'Pulsation' and people it with the figures inhabiting its eternal life as the discovery of what, as the 'Six Thousand Years' from the Creation to the Judgment, it archetypally contained as even 'less than a Pulsation of the Artery' (M 28[30].62–3).

Wordsworth comes closest to entering this 'Moment,' which is to say this 'divine madness,' when, following the instructions of the peasant, he and his companion 'journey[ing] several hours / At a slow place,' enter a 'gloomy strait' (P 6.622–4). Suddenly, upon their entry, the literal account of their descent into the 'gloomy strait' explodes into an account of what, as their mounting disappointment, the slow-paced journey of several hours psychically constellated: a 'tempest, a redundant energy / Vexing its own creation.' 'The immeasurable height / Of woods decaying, never to be decayed,' Wordsworth writes,

The stationary blasts of waterfalls,
And in the narrow rent at every turn
Winds thwarting winds, bewildered and forlorn,
The torrents shooting from the clear blue sky,
The rocks that muttered close upon our ears,
Black drizzling crags that spake by the way-side
As if a voice were in them, the sick sight
And giddy prospect of the raving stream,
The unfettered clouds and region of the Heavens,
Tumult and peace, the darkness and the light –
Were all like workings of one mind, the features
Of the same face, blossoms upon one tree;
Characters of the great Apocalypse,
The types and symbols of Eternity,
Of first, and last, and midst, and without end.   (6.624–40)

Still clothed in the garment of nature, though torn like Blake's 'rotten rags of Memory' by the sheer force of 'Inspiration,' imagination with the 'strength / Of usurpation' struggled to break free of its imprisonment in sense and reveal itself as 'the workings of one mind,' the 'types and symbols of Eternity,' the 'great Apocalypse' itself seen face to face as the face of God, rather than merely as the backside of God (nature) as God passes by, which was all that Moses was allowed to see. Like that of Milton before him, Wordsworth's imagination is here struggling to surpass the imagination of Moses, which was bound to the law, and unveil the 'Heaven of Heavens' before which Jehovah stood as its covering veil, not unlike Blake's 'Covering Cherub.' 'I tell you, no virtue can exist without breaking these ten commandments,' Blake's 'Devil in a flame of fire' tells his opposing Angel. 'Jesus was all virtue, and acted from impulse [a 'Pulsation of the Artery']: not from rules.' 'When [the Devil] had so spoken,' Blake continues, 'I beheld the Angel who stretched out his arms embracing the flame of fire & he was consumed and arose as Elijah' (*MHH* 23–4).

'But it was not so much from [excess] of animal vivacity that *my* difficulty came, as from a sense of the indomitableness of the spirit within me,' Wordsworth writes in his *Fenwick Notes*, describing his struggle to accept death in (or as?) the slow process of composing his 'Intimations' ode over a period of two years:

I used to brood over the stories of Enoch & Elijah & almost to persuade myself that whatever might become of others I s^d [should] be translated in

something of the same way to heaven. With a feeling congenial to this I
was often unable to think of external things as having external existence &
I communed with all that I saw as something not apart from but inherent
in my own immaterial nature. Many times while going to school have I
grasped at a wall or tree to recall myself from this abyss of idealism to the
reality. At that time I was afraid of such processes. In later periods of life I
have deplored, as we have all reason to do, a subjugation of an opposite
character & have rejoiced over the remembrances, as expressed in the
lines 'obstinate questionings' & c. ['obstinate questionings / Of sense and
outward things, / Fallings from us, vanishings' ('Intimations' 145–7)]
(*Fenwick Notes* 61)

In both the Simplon Pass and the Mount Snowdon episodes, Wordsworth
is subjecting 'sense and outward things' to 'obstinate questionings' as,
with fear and awe, he feels them falling away to settle again into the
workings of his own mind as 'the haunt, and the main region of [his]
song.' ('I had a world about me – 'twas my own; / I made it' [*P* 3.144–
5]). 'In years that bring the philosophic mind' ('Intimations Ode' 190),
Wordsworth subdued the 'madness' of his childhood vision. Unlike
Wordsworth 'brooding over' the stories of Enoch and Elijah, Blake
dined with them. In Bowlahoola, his 'Stomach for Digestion,' they
nourished his 'Vegetable Body,' allowing it to expand to the 'outward
circumference of [its] Energy' (*MHH* 4).

Wordsworth's apocalyptic vision in the Simplon Pass episode still
wears the torn garment of nature as if it were Hercules' shirt of Nessus
burning his flesh to become his funeral pyre releasing his soul into its
immortal state. Wordsworth's nature as the world of sense hides within
it 'a majestic intellect' (*P* 14.67). To bind this 'intellect' to the five senses
is to reduce the soul to a 'portion' of itself. In his ascent of Mount
Snowdon in the final book, he returns again to his visionary experience
in the 'gloomy strait.' This time the very Atlantic seen by moonlight
through 'solid vapours' appeared 'to dwindle, and give up his majesty,'
as if 'usurped upon far as the sight could reach' by a 'fixed, abysmal,
gloomy breathing place,' 'roaring with one voice / Heard over earth
and sea, and, in that hour, / For so it seems, felt by the starry heavens'
(*P* 14.45–62).

In the metaphorical world of the Bedouin's dream, which is the literal
world of the imagination as it is of the soul, the 'fleet waters of a
drowning world' (*P* 5.137) are at the same time a 'bed of glittering light'
diffused 'over half the wilderness' (5.128–9). ('The water, like a witch's
oils / Burnt green, and blue and white' [129–30], writes Coleridge in

The Rime of the Ancient Mariner.) The 'mind in creation' inhabiting a metaphorical world of perpetual metamorphosis, works upon chaos, courting, de Man argues, annihilation as the rhetorical form of nothingness, which is not nothingness itself but the aesthetic knowledge of it. Wordsworth's 'celestial light' is, for de Man, the rhetorical apparel in which Wordsworth clothed nothingness so as, in the endless prosopopoeia that poetry is, nothingness assumed, as a delusional metaphysics of presence, the aesthetic form of immortality. Wordsworth appeared to admit as much when, in his 'Elegiac Stanzas,' he describes this 'celestial light' as 'housed in a dream, at distance from the Kind' (54) which, as earlier noted, is 'surely blind' (56). This 'blindness,' de Man insists, is what any 'insight' necessarily contains. This apparent contradiction, when suspended in consciousness and held there without any irritable itch to resolve it, constitutes, as the aesthetic sense, the knowledge of nothingness. The 'celestial light' with which Wordsworth arms himself against the terrors of the deep leaves on the page the traces of his fear, language itself becoming, in his imagination of it, the traces of 'something evermore about to be' buried in a 'poor earthly casket of immortal verse' (*P* 5.164). For Derrida this burial is the madness of the Cogito as the '*present* moment' etherized in language as 'oblivion and unveiling, protection, and exposure: economy.'

Following the crazed Bedouin 'o'er the illimitable waste' (5.136) (a rather more frenzied vision of Adam and Eve leaving Paradise 'waved over by that flaming brand, the gate / With dreadful faces thronged fiery arms' [*PL* 11.644–5]), Wordsworth is, like Milton's couple, in search of 'economy,' a place to settle, a place to engrave or inscribe metaphor in however frail a shrine. He is searching for a way of going on with writing by learning how to live with the abysm that is always waiting, the 'abyss of idealism' that metaphor throws up to remind us that it is there, even as Coleridge's chasm in 'Kubla Khan' flings up momently the sacred river. Allegory as the ego's defence against metaphor is not the only way. Metaphor, properly understood as a scene of reading, is soul. What metaphor reveals, Keats realized, is what allegory attempts to understand. Soul, that is, is the human identity of 'sparks of divinity' (*KL* 250),[10] Wordsworth's 1799 *Prelude* granted a personal identity: the narrator at last in the full psychic sense not a god or a devil but a person.

Wordsworth's fear, like that of all poets, is that the 'hiding-places' of creative power may as 'Old Ocean' dry up, leaving the poet 'singed and bare' (*P* 5.34), as man, not extinguished, but surviving, 'abject, de-

pressed, forlorn, disconsolate' (5.28). In Wordsworth's case, this spectacle of abjection became increasingly present to him as, in the actual
absence of Coleridge, he continued to imagine the ruin that was already
in progress when Coleridge left for Malta, taking with him the 1805
version of *The Prelude*. For Wordsworth, in the ruin of Coleridge lay the
ruin of their planned *Recluse*, a ruin that became in the imagining of it
his further extensions of *The Prelude* up to the years of its actual composition, years that haunt *The Prelude* as the spectral form of its writing.
Wordsworth is not alone as a poet in his discovery that the 'still cave of
the witch Poesy,' in which he allegorically sits perusing the quixotic
nature of metaphor, is, as Shelley writes in *Hellas*, 'pavilioned upon
chaos' (772). He consciously numbers himself, however, among the
greatest, Milton and Shakespeare included, in his decision to follow the
Bedouin to the end, whatever that end may be. The vows originally
made for him on a summer day during the long vacation (*P* 4.334–5),
Wordsworth now affirms for himself as he awakens from the dream,
having managed to read his poem, with all its necessary disfigure-
ments, up to a point, in a new light that yet remains as 'Soul-making'
one more refraction of its prismatic shape.

Thus, 'full often' during the continuing course of writing-reading
(inscribing) *The Prelude* as a continuous allegory that has finally no end
other than writing itself, Wordsworth takes 'from the world of sleep /
This Arab phantom' as his wind god or inspiration, giving him a 'substance' through the inscription of a voice to become thereby, as in the
dream, his scribe. He fancies him 'a living man,' a recluse whose 'internal thought' is 'protracted among endless solitudes' (5.141–8). He imag-
ines himself, that is, as writing *The Recluse*. He projects him, as he
projects the infant rocked to sleep by the blended music of singing
nurse and murmuring river, which launches the 1799 *Prelude*: a 'fore-
taste, a dim earnest' (1.280), though of 'tempest' rather than 'calm.' He
is not, therefore, the recluse that Coleridge images as the hero of their
joint-labours: 'a man in mental repose, one whose principles were made
up, and so prepared to deliver upon authority a system of philosophy'
(*Collected Works* 14ii:177). As Keats recognized, 'Coleridge ... would let
go by a fine isolated verisimilitude caught from the Penetralium of
mystery, from being incapable of remaining content with half knowledge' (*KL* 43). This incapability Wordsworth sought to resist by turning,
as Coleridge himself turned, to the phantom world of dream where
metaphors, like fish swimming in a stream, might be 'caught from the
Penetralium of mystery.'

Far from pitying him, as indeed Coleridge as an addicted dreamer pitied himself (while mining the dreams for a knowledge of them that, inventing the term in 1805, he called the 'psycho-analytical'), Wordsworth, having read the dream, now feels 'reverence ... to a being thus employed' (*P* 5.150). Dealing with the dream in a fully awakened state (the dream as his awakening), Wordsworth is able to embrace what lies couched within its madness. Consciousness becomes for Wordsworth the saving grace of allegory, rescuing the poet from madness. Blake's allegory, as already noted, is 'addressed to the Intellectual powers, while it is altogether hidden from the Corporeal Understanding.' Wordsworth's allegory, on the other hand, becomes increasingly addressed to 'the Corporeal Understanding,' that is to say to the moral law governing his increasingly conservative view of human society. 'In honoured poverty,' writes Shelley in his sonnet, 'To Wordsworth,' 'thy voice did weave / Songs consecrate to truth and liberty, – / Deserting these, thou leavest me to grieve, / Thus having been, that thou shouldst cease to be' (11–14).

Aroused by the dream of the crazed Bedouin proclaiming both the destruction and preservation of his verse, Wordsworth accepts the hero of Cervantes's novel, which he had been reading when he fell asleep, as himself. When 'overcome' by the 'strong entrancement' (*P* 5.162) of the *mise en abyme* at the core of his psyche ('an event so dire, by signs in earth / Or heaven made manifest' [5.158–9]), he will think not of the leech-gatherer, but of the 'Arab phantom' (5.142) buried in himself, even as the Boy of Winander resides and does not reside in the grave by which 'a long half hour together' Wordsworth sometimes stood listening 'to notes that are / The ghostly language of the ancient earth' (2.308–9). This 'ghostly language' is the 'notes' to which Blake's Albion listens upon his 'Couch of Death.' Blake contrapuntally reshapes them into the sound of the 'Four Trumpets' entering 'Albion's Bosom, the bosom of death.' '[And] the Four surrounded him,' Blake continues, 'In a Column of Fire in Felphams Vale; then to their mouths the Four / Applied their Four Trumpets & them sounded to the Four winds' (*M* 42[49].21–3). In Wordsworth's 'chosen Vale' awaiting him at the end of his three-day journey whose interior is *The Prelude*, few trumpets sounded, though he heard their echoes dying away. 'I see by glimpses now' (12.280), he writes of the 'spots of time' (12.207) whose 'renovating virtue' (12.209) is 'scattered everywhere, taking their date / From our first childhood' (12.223–4), 'when age comes on, / May scarcely see at all' (12.281–2). *The Prelude* is a shrine to his childhood and youth as it died into 'the light of common day.' 'Yet another / Of these memorials' (12.286–7), he writes of returning home at Christmas to witness the death of his father and with his three brothers to follow his body to the grave. Recalling 'the business of the elements' (12.318) associated with his father's death, Wordsworth records that 'down to this very time,' he still feels in 'a strong wind ... / Some inward agitations,' which may 'beguile / Thoughts over busy in the course they took, / Or animate an hour of vacant ease' (12.327–35).

5

Shelley and the Romantic Labyrinth

Madness has become man's possibility of abolishing both man and the world – and even those images that challenge the world and deform man. It is, far beyond dreams, beyond the nightmare of bestiality, the last recourse: the end and the beginning of everything. Not because it is a promise, as in German lyricism, but because it is the ambiguity of chaos and apocalypse: Goya's *Idiot* who shrieks and twists his shoulder to escape from the nothingness that imprisons him – is this the birth of the first man and his first movement toward liberty, or the last convulsion of the last dying man?

Michel Foucault, *Madness & Civilization*

Shelley and Wordsworth

In the late spring of 1822, approximately nine weeks before he drowned, Shelley and Mary Shelley moved with Jane and Edward Williams into Casa Magni, which faced the gulf of Spezia. One night, shortly before the drowning, Shelley dreamt that Edward and Jane, their bodies lacerated and covered with blood, came into his bedroom shouting '"Get up Shelley, the sea is flooding the house & it is all coming down."' Still asleep, Shelley rushed into Mary's bedroom, where she was slowly recovering from a miscarriage, only to confront his own figure bending over the bed strangling her. Walking along the portico of his villa, which so closely faced the sea that its inhabitants felt as if they were living on board ship, Shelley met his own image walking towards him. '"How long do you mean to be content?"' (cited in Holmes 727) it asked him, much as Adonais called to Shelley, asking him how long he meant to 'let Life divide what Death can join together' (*Adonais* 477). This call comes to Shelley in his elegy on the death of Keats in the whispering of the 'low wind' (475).

Like the 'gentle breeze' that in the opening lines of *The Prelude* fans the cheek of Wordsworth as if 'half-conscious of the joy it brings' (*P* 1.3), the 'low wind' whispering to Shelley quickly becomes in the final stanzas of *Adonais* a 'tempest' (490). For Wordsworth, the 'tempest' is a 'redundant energy, / Vexing its own creation.' For Shelley, the purpose of the 'tempest' overtaking the composition of the final stanzas of *Adonais* is precisely to vex and overcome their creation. Having in a 'Pulsation of the Artery' conceived itself 'beyond and above [Shelley's] consciousness,' Shelley's elegy had, in descending into his consciousness, achieved its earthly purpose. The poem should now destroy itself by surrendering to the source from which it emerged, leaving the 'spacious might' of Shelley's spirit free to inhabit its 'void circumference' (*Adonais* 419–20). Commenting upon the 'rhythm' of Plato's language as it propels the 'superhuman wisdom of his philosophy,' Shelley describes it as 'a strain which distends, and then bursts the circumference of the hearer's mind, and pours itself forth together with it into the universal element with which it has perpetual sympathy' (*DP* 485).

Wordsworth, as previously noted, describes this process as an 'awful Power' arising from 'the mind's abyss' with the 'strength / Of usurpation,' which puts out 'the light of sense' and 'with a flash' reveals the 'invisible world.' The particular 'flash' to which he refers occurred as he was describing his unconscious crossing of the Alps, his physical senses having put out the light of his imagination, which had prefigured a crossing the senses belied. Later in *The Prelude*, Wordsworth explores at some length the inner war between the imagination and the faculties of sense, particularly sight. Describing 'a twofold frame of body and mind' that 'almost seems inherent in the creature,' Wordsworth refers to a time 'when the bodily eye, in every stage of life / The most despotic of our senses, gained / Such strength in *me* as often held my mind / In absolute dominion' (*P* 12.125–31). He then goes on to

> endeavour to unfold the means
> Which Nature studiously employs to thwart
> This tyranny, summons all the senses each
> To counteract the other, and themselves,
> And makes them all, and the objects with which all
> Are conversant, subservient in their turn
> To the great ends of Liberty and Power.   (12.134–40)

It is precisely the thwarting of the tyranny of the senses that Wordsworth describes with reference to the imaginations's 'strength / Of usurpation' confounding a usurpation of an opposite kind: 'stationary blasts of waterfalls', 'winds thwarting winds, bewildered and forlorn' (6.626–8). The imagination, it would appear, is crushing the tyranny of the senses by forcing them to counteract each other in order to release the imagination from their dictates.

Having read *The Excursion* with its preface, Shelley, like many of his contemporaries, was aware of Wordsworth's unpublished poem, passages from which had been separately printed. The fact that in his preface Wordsworth locates *The Excursion* as the middle portion of 'a long and laborious Work,' the first part of which was complete, clearly led Shelley seriously to question what Wordsworth had to say about it: 'The preparatory poem is biographical, and conducts the history of the Author's mind to the point when he was emboldened to hope that his faculties were sufficiently matured for entering upon the arduous labour which he had proposed to himself' (*PW* 589). The proposed 'arduous labour' is an epithalamion, a vast 'spousal verse' celebrating the coming marriage of 'the Mind of Man' to 'this goodly universe / In love and holy passion.' While the fact that this marriage was to take place in a 'gothic church' (*PW* 589), which Wordsworth was constructing for the occasion, may well have given Shelley pause, his conviction after reading *The Excursion*, that the proposed church was already a ruin, resulting in *Alastor*. Wordsworth's account of the unwritten *Recluse* 'as having for its principal subject the sensations and opinions of a poet living in retirement' (589) becomes in *Alastor* Shelley's Visionary, who had 'lived,' 'died,' 'sung, in solitude' (60). Far from there being a vast gothic church newly constructed to receive his remains, 'no human hands with pious reverence reared' for him an 'untimely tomb.' On the contrary, 'the charmed eddies of autumnal winds / Built o'er his mouldering bones a pyramid / Of mouldering leaves in the waste wilderness' (50–4).

However, Shelley did write *Alastor*. His 'human hands,' in this sense, did rear for him an 'untimely tomb.' But what sort of 'untimely tomb' is *Alastor*? In what ways, if any, does it resemble the 'untimely tomb' he would rear some six years later for Keats in *Adonais*? And, it may be asked, in what ways, if any, did it resemble the 'untimely tomb' he finally reared for himself in *The Triumph of Life*? Both in *Alastor* and in *Adonais*, Shelley 'in another's fate now wept his own' (*Adonais* 300), as if in both poems he was rehearsing his own. 'In the Spring of 1815,' Mary

Shelley writes in her note on *Alastor*, 'an eminent physician pronounced that [Shelley] was dying rapidly of a consumption; abscesses were formed on his lungs, and he suffered acute spasms.' Though she goes on to describe Shelley's sudden recovery, the poem itself has nothing to say about it. On the contrary, she writes, 'The death which he had often contemplated during the last months as certain and near he here represented in such colours as had, in his lonely musings, soothed his soul to peace' (*Complete Poetical Works* 30–1).

If Wordsworth in *The Excursion* had, for Shelley, simply 'cease[d] to be' ('To Wordsworth' 14), the account of his ceasing in *Alastor* contained within it Shelley's projected account of his own dying. Launching his brief career as a poet with an account of his dying as it was fully enacted by Wordsworth in *The Excursion*, Shelley managed to construct a dialectical struggle with Death as the creative process within which his apocalyptic vision took shape. Shelley's identification with Wordsworth becomes in *Alastor* a failed struggle dialectically to separate himself from Wordsworth. This failed struggle is present in the relations between the Visionary and the Narrator, who, distancing himself from the Visionary ('There was a Poet'), as Wordsworth distances himself from the Boy of Winander, gradually becomes increasingly identified with him as his 'simple strain' increasingly entangles him in the 'divinest lineaments' of the Visionary as they are 'worn by the senseless wind.' The Narrator's 'simple strain' *is* 'the senseless wind' in the 'frail pauses' of which, the Narrator remarks, the dead Visionary 'shall live alone' (704–6). The Narrator's entanglement in his 'simple strain' becomes his entanglement in the Visionary's decaying body. The process is ultimately 'senseless'; it has no more meaning than 'mouldering leaves in the waste wilderness' destined to become, in the very different context of his 'Ode to the West Wind,' 'pestilence stricken multitudes' driven 'like ghosts from an enchanter fleeing' to 'their dark wintry bed' (3–6). As for the dead Visionary living alone in the 'frail pauses' (*Alastor* 706) of the Narrator's 'strain,' he becomes in Shelley's ode a 'winged seed[ ]' lying 'cold and low / ... like a corpse within its grave' until 'the dreaming earth' is awakened by the west wind's 'azure sister of the Spring' (7–9). The imagistic pattern that repeats itself in a shifting context is further reassembled in *Adonais* until, finally, in *The Triumph of Life*, it becomes, as the Chariot of Life, the mindless destruction of all earthly existence.

Invoking the 'Mother of this unfathomable world' (18) as his muse in *Alastor*, the Narrator describes the making of his bed

In charnels and on coffins, where black death
Keeps record of the trophies won from thee,
Hoping to still these obstinate questionings
Of thee and thine, by forcing some lone ghost,
Thy messenger, to render up the tale
Of what we are.   (24–9)

Shelley here has in mind Wordsworth's 'Intimations' ode, in the first published version of which the 'lone ghost' as 'messenger' is the child awake in the grave 'on whom,' Wordsworth writes, 'those truths do rest, / Which we are toiling all our lives to find, / In darkness lost, the darkness of the grave' (115–17). Invoking Wordsworth's child awake in the grave (which, as already noted, Coleridge persuaded him to remove), in 'Hymn to Intellectual Beauty,' as in *Alastor*, Shelley describes himself as a boy searching for ghosts, speeding 'through many a listening chamber, cave and ruin ... pursuing / Hopes of high talk with the departed dead' (50–2). Now as an adult, the process of composition repeats his childhood experience. Writing depends upon calling up 'the phantoms of a thousand hours / Each from his voiceless grave: they have in visioned bowers / Of studious zeal or love's delight / Outwatched with me the envious night' (64–7).

Shelley, it would appear, survived the death of the Visionary in *Alastor*, as he survived the death of Wordsworth in *The Excursion*, because, unlike the Visionary and unlike Wordsworth, he was able partially to resurrect the dead by releasing them, though only as phantoms or ghosts, into the mythical life of his poetry. Invoking the Great Mother, Shelley's Narrator in *Alastor* compares his skull to the 'solitary dome / Of some mysterious and deserted fane' in which a 'long-forgotten lyre' remains 'moveless' (42–4) awaiting her breath. At the end of the poem, the 'lyre,' now a 'fragile lute, on whose harmonious strings / The breath of heaven did wander,' is 'quenched for ever, / Still, dark, and dry, and unremembered now' (667–71). Between his invocation of the Great Mother and the quenching of her breath, the Narrator describes what is essentially a haunting in which, as the Visionary (the dead poet in himself), he tells his ghostly tale. The Narrator's tale is neither the first nor the last of Shelley's many ghost stories, all of them culminating in *The Triumph of Life* and raising, as already noted, what de Man calls the suspicion of 'an intended exorcism.'

In *Alastor*, the Narrator slowly fuses with the Visionary to enact in the

Visionary his own extinction as a poet, even as Shelley in the Narrator enacts, as the Visionary, who is Wordsworth, *his* own extinction. 'For what we have done with the dead Shelley,' de Man explains,

> and with all the other dead bodies that appear in romantic literature – one thinks, among many others, of the 'dead man' that ' 'mid that beauteous scene / Of trees and hills and water, bolt upright / Rose, with his ghastly face ...' in Wordsworth's *Prelude* (5.448–50) – is simply to bury them, to bury them in their own texts made into epitaphs and monumental graves ... Such monumentalization is by no means necessarily a naive or evasive gesture, and it certainly is not a gesture that anyone can pretend to avoid making. It does not have to be naive, since it does not have to be the repression of a self-threatening knowledge. Like *The Triumph of Life*, it can state the full power of this threat in all its negativity; the poem demonstrates that this rigor does not prevent Shelley from allegorizing his own negative assurance. ('Shelley' 67–8)

Haunting Shelley in the ghostly body of his poetry is 'his own negative assurance' about poetry as, at best, nothing more than 'a feeble shadow' of what he calls 'the original conception of the poet' (*DP* 504).

Far from repressing this 'self-threatening knowledge,' Shelley engages it in a powerful dialectic of creation, which is radically undermined by his recognition that the mind cannot create. 'Mind,' he writes in 'On Life,' 'as far as we have any experience of its properties, and beyond that experience how vain is argument, cannot create, it can only perceive' (*SPP* 178). But what does it perceive? Shelley's answer is: its own operations. 'I confess,' he writes, 'that I am one of those who am unable to refuse my ascent to the conclusions of those philosophers, who assert that nothing exists but as it is perceived' (476). While the mind does not create what it perceives, nevertheless, without perception 'nothing exists.' Rejecting nothingness because he is 'incapable of imagining to himself annihilation,' Shelley is forced to conclude that the 'nothing' that exists in the absence of perception is something other than 'nothing,' which is not dependent upon perception. While this something other than perception is not mind ('It is infinitely improbable that the cause of mind, that is, of existence, is similar to mind' [478]), it must nevertheless hypothetically be said to be (rather than exist) independent of perception because it is not nothing (for nothing to be, it cannot be nothing).

On the basis of his reading of *The Excursion*, Shelley concluded that the death of Wordsworth as a poet lay in the failure of his imagination mythically to affirm an uncreated reality inaccessible to the senses, which nevertheless *is*, though not as the creator, there being for it no creation, but as the causeless source of what does exist. In his 'Intimations' ode, Wordsworth's mind could still tolerate the mysterious presence of this causeless source, which he describes as 'those obstinate questionings / Of sense and outward things, / Fallings from us, vanishings; / Blank misgivings of a Creature / Moving about in worlds not realised' (145–9). Not only could he still tolerate them as the gift of childhood, he could and did affirm them as 'the fountain-light of all our day' and 'a master-light of all our seeing' (155, 156). 'Thou wert as a lone star, whose light did shine / On some frail bark in winter's midnight roar' (7–8), Shelley writes in 'To Wordsworth,' remembering Wordsworth as the 'master-light of all [his] seeing,' when he himself, along with many others, was 'some frail bark.'

Wordsworth's 'Songs consecrate to truth and liberty' (12) were grounded, Shelley insists, not in the 'frail bark' of the 'mechanical philosophy,' but in the 'obstinate questionings / Of sense and outward things.' In *The Excursion*, however, his 'obstinate questionings' became, to Shelley's horror, the despair of the Solitary arising from his disillusionment with the French Revolution. Wordsworth, he realized, had reduced the 'obstinate questionings' of his 'Intimations' ode to the mechanical despair of the Solitary. As the Wanderer, he had become a parody of himself, a paltry Wanderer who, as a retired pedlar of trivial wares now 'prepared / For sabbath duties' (*Excursion* 1.421–2), had, as 'the prized memorial of relinquished toils' (1.436), substituted a shepherd's staff for his once consecrated pen. His sole task, mad Margaret being dead, was quietly though insistently to chastise the Solitary for his needless despondency. His 'obstinate questionings' of the New Jerusalem now confronting him in the demonic guise of a failed revolution were satisfactorily answered by the natural religion, which for Wordsworth (as for Blake) Christianity had become, a natural religion that Shelley (like Blake) considered a demonic parody of the vision of freedom originally proclaimed by Jesus. Wordsworth's 'Songs consecrate to truth and liberty,' that is (and as Blake also realized), had been reduced to the moral law. Reading *The Excursion* aloud with Mary Shelley, who concluded that Wordsworth had become a slave, Shelley could not fail to be struck by Wordsworth's moral abuse of the very language he had earlier used:

vows, renewed
On the first motion of a holy thought;
Vigils of contemplation; praise; and prayer –
A stream, which, from the fountain of the heart
Issuing, however feebly, nowhere flows
Without access of unexpected strength.
But, above all, the victory is most sure
For him, who, seeking faith by virtue, strives
To yield entire submission to the law
Of conscience – conscience reverenced and obeyed,
As God's most intimate presence in the soul,
And his most perfect image in the world.   (4.216–27)

'A Poet,' Shelley explains, 'therefore would do ill to embody his own conceptions of right and wrong, which are usually those of his place and time, in his poetical creations, which participate in neither' (DP 488). By embodying them, Wordsworth had not only assumed 'the inferior office of interpreting the effect [of poetry],' but radically distorted it. In The Excursion, he had abandoned poetry altogether, as Shelley (and Blake before him) understood it. While 'those in whom the poetical faculty, though great, is less intense, as Euripides, Lucan, Tasso, Spenser,' Shelley continues, 'have frequently affected a moral aim,' in Wordsworth's case the 'moral aim' had completely taken over. Wordsworth in the figure of the Wanderer had withdrawn from his profession as a poet. Replacing his pen with a shepherd's staff as his 'prized memorial,' Wordsworth had reduced to a parody the pastoral elegy he thought he was writing. 'Let not high verse, mourning the memory / Of that which is no more,' Shelley concludes his non-elegy on the death of Wordsworth in The Excursion, 'or painting's woe / Or sculpture, speak in feeble imagery / Their own cold powers' (Alastor 707–10).

As a non-elegy, the formless form of nothingness, which would continue to haunt every form he would henceforth employ, Shelley continues to describe what he has wrought in a manner that anticipates his final fragment, The Triumph of Life:

Art and eloquence,
And all the shews o' the world are frail and vain
To weep a loss that turns their lights to shade.
It is a woe too 'deep for tears,' when all

Is reft at once, when some surpassing Spirit,
Whose light adorned the world around it, leaves
Those who remain behind, not sobs or groans,
The passionate tumult of a clinging hope;
But pale despair and cold tranquillity,
Nature's vast frame, the web of human things,
Birth and the grave, that are not as they were.   (710–20)

The 'One Mind'

The unrelieved despair articulated in *Alastor* is the spectral life haunting Shelley's vision as a 'pestilence stricken multitude' driven by Shelley
as 'enchanter' to a 'dark wintry bed' it refuses to inhabit. Calling upon
the Phantasm of Jupiter to repeat the curse that he will no longer
remember, Shelley's Prometheus commands him: 'Speak the words
which I would hear, / Although no thought inform thy empty voice'
(*PU* 1.248–9). The burial Shelley attempted was a burial that, in the end,
he was driven in *The Triumph of Life* to enact upon himself as he folded
himself back into his fragment as into his winding sheet. 'Happy those
for whom the fold / Of' on the last manuscript page has, as de Man
points out, its objective correlative in 'the actual death and subsequent
disfigurement of Shelley's body, burned after his boat capsized and he
drowned off the coast of Lerici.' 'This defaced body,' he continues, 'is
present in the margin of the last manuscript page and has become an
inseparable part of the poem,' though, he adds, it is 'not present in its
represented or articulated meaning' ('Shelley' 66–7). As I have suggested in this book, the 'represented or articulated meaning' of a Romantic text not only belies what lies hidden within it, but recognizes the
process of hiding as a necessary protection against the madness it
otherwise is. This madness, beyond the reach of poetry, is an 'empty
voice' informed by 'no thought,' that is to say, not nothingness, but the
acausal assumption of it as the presence of what is not perceived. This
same acausal assumption continues to haunt quantum physics, even as
it haunted Jung's notion of synchronicity.

'But cause,' Shelley explains as he continues in 'On Life' to interrogate the operations of his own mind, 'is only a word expressing a
certain state of the human mind with regard to the manner in which
two thoughts are apprehended to be related to each other.' Pausing to
consider this manner, Shelley then adds: 'If any one desires to know
how unsatisfactorily the popular philosophy employs itself upon this

great question, they need only impartially reflect upon the manner in which thoughts develope themselves in their minds' (*SPP* 478). Shelley then goes on to describe this manner in terms of what Coleridge in his *Biographia Literaria* calls the 'mechanical philosophy': 'As men grow up, this power [to fuse into one, which characterizes the undifferentiated sensations of a child] commonly decays, and they become mechanical and habitual agents. Their feelings and their reasonings are the combined result of a multitude of entangled thoughts, of a series of what are called impressions, planted by reiteration' (*SPP* 477).

In his *Defence of Poetry,* Shelley, viewing this 'multitude of entangled thoughts ... planted by reiteration' within an imaginative perspective, describes it as 'chaos.' 'But poetry,' he writes, 'defeats the curse which binds us to be subjected to the accident of surrounding impressions,' by making us 'the inhabitants of a world to which the familiar world is a chaos.' By annihilating the world of recurrent impressions 'blunted by reiteration,' it 'creates anew the universe' (*DP* 505–6). This new creation, however, becomes with time, like Milton's *Paradise Lost,* equally 'blunted by reiteration' so that, if no new poets arise ceaselessly to create poetry anew (in the way the Romantics sought to create *Paradise Lost* anew), poetry itself dies, as Wordsworth's poetry died, the victim of its own liberating purpose. The issue of ceaseless creation within the mind that 'cannot create' is the issue boldly confronted by Shelley in perhaps the most puzzling of all his poems, 'Mont Blanc.'

Distinguishing between the 'one mind' and separate individual minds, Shelley argues in 'On Life' that 'the existence of distinct individual minds similar to that which is employed in now questioning its own nature is ... a delusion. The words, *I, you, they,* are not signs of any actual difference subsisting between the assemblage of thoughts thus indicated, but are merely marks employed to denote the different modifications of the one mind' (*SPP* 477–8). However, it is only by these 'different modifications' (in themselves a 'delusion') that the undifferentiated 'one mind' is intuited and, as in the cases of Wordsworth and Rousseau, identified with the unconscious state of infancy as what Derrida calls 'full speech,' which is the 'speech' of infants before they begin to speak. This 'full speech' may be indicated in the opening lines of 'Mont Blanc' as 'theeverlastinguniverseofthingsflowsthroughthemind,' which the individual mind, employing its 'marks' of differentiation, modifies into 'The everlasting universe of things / Flows through the mind,' which Shelley describes as a 'delusion,' though a necessary one if '*I, you, they*' are to exist for their moment in time and space. If they are not allowed a temporal/spatial existence, then the 'full speech' of the 'one mind,' like the 'full speech' of the infant, is nothing, in the sense that it does not indicate anything external to itself, nor does it even indicate itself, because, like the poet as Keats describes him ('it is not itself – it has no self' [*KL* 157]), the infant has no self. In this radical sense, 'Mont Blanc' is the 'delusion' of a separate self, which ceases to be a 'delusion' only because Shelley recognizes it as a 'delusion,' though a necessary one. 'And what wert thou' Shelley asks of Mont Blanc as it is perceived in his poem, 'and earth, and stars, and sea, / If to the human mind's imaginings / Silence and solitude were vacancy?' (142–4).

If, that is, the imagination of the poet did not have some fleeting glimpse of the 'one mind' in a state of 'divine madness,' as Plato describes it in Shelley's translation of *Ion*, Mont Blanc would be a white sheet of paper on which nothing (no thing) is written. Derrida describes this as the 'fabulous scene' of white writing, the palimpsest that erases its marks even in the making of them, Shelley's Iris in *The Triumph of Life* trampling into dust beneath her dancing feet every word Shelley inscribes upon his scattered sheets, which Mary Shelley did her best to assemble after his death. The nightmare that constitutes the madness of writing (de Man's 'madness of words') is released from its madness by the poet's recognition of it, a recognition that need not stop him writing, though it will detach him from it sufficiently to grasp what it is. Ironically, perhaps, by virtue of this grasp, which releases him from 'delusion' into a recognition of it, the poet, Shelley suggests, is released into an awareness of what the white sheet with its marks signifies: the 'white radiance of Eternity' stained by 'a dome of many-coloured glass.' That this may be the poet's ultimate delusion, his direct encounter with madness, is enclosed, Shelley argues, within the folded sheets like a child awake in the grave waiting to be released. 'Whether the dream now purposed to rehearse,' writes Keats of *The Fall of Hyperion*, 'Be poet's or fanatic's will be known / When this warm scribe my hand is in the grave' (1.16–18).

Copied on the outside of a folded sheet on which, after turning it over and around, he drafted stanzas 45–51 of *The Jealousies*, Keats wrote these words, which appear upside down on the page containing stanza 51:

This living hand, now warm and capable
Of earnest grasping, would, if it were cold
And in the icy silence of the tomb,

So haunt thy days and chill thy dreaming nights
That thou would wish thine own heart dry of blood,
So in my veins red life might stream again,
And thou be conscience-calm'd. See, here it is –
I hold it towards you.

What Keats holds towards the reader of these lines is his account of what they have cost him to write. For the reader to recognize this cost – Keats's life blood – is for the reader to experience Keats's life blood as his own. Only then, he suggests, is it possible to know what poetry is: a moment by moment dying into the life of the poem. Only after his actual death will it be known whether or not the poem lives. Poetry is, in this radical sense, a covenant with Death in which the stakes are life itself. This covenant, Shelley argues, Faust made with Mephistopheles even as, without knowing it, Milton made it with his Devil. Inherent in this convenant, the stakes of which are life and death, resides what Shelley in 'On Life' calls 'the great miracle.' 'It is well,' he writes, 'that we are thus shielded by the familiarity of what is at once so certain and so unfathomable ['Life, the great miracle'] from an astonishment which would otherwise absorb and overawe the functions of that which is [its] object' (*SPP* 475).

Derrida calls this 'astonishment' that overawes all the functions – whether sensual, emotional, rational, or spiritual – the 'moment' of the 'Cogito,' which, in terms of 'the functions,' is madness. The purpose of 'the functions,' which desire the 'unfathomable,' is to shield us from it by negotiating a relationship to it as if it existed, when, in fact, it does not exist, in the sense that it is dependent upon our perception of it. Dialectically negotiating a relationship to it is to construct a 'metaphysics of presence' that recognizes its absence by virtue of our construction (creation) of it. Wordsworth's failure as poet lay in his growing inability to inhabit himself as a fiction. Only in 'poetic tales,' as distinct from 'forms of worship,' are human beings, Shelley insists, capable of participating in the 'great miracle' that is life. Only as a fiction of themselves can human beings enter and celebrate the 'great miracle' that life is. To the construction of a supreme fiction Shelley would devote the rest of his brief life. In his preface to *Alastor*, created after he had written it as an attempt to understand it, Shelley identifies the poet with those who are 'deluded' by a 'generous error,' who are 'instigated' by a 'sacred thirst of doubtful knowledge,' and who are 'duped' by an 'illustrious superstition,' assigning all those who are not to 'a slow and poisonous

decay' (*SPP* 69) under the influence of the 'popular [mechanical] philosophy' of mind as the mere epiphenomenon of matter.

Shelley, that is, approached poetry in the same spirit that Jung in the
1930s approached alchemy: to discover in it the projected life of the soul
that scientific materialism had reduced to a delusion. Shelley, like Jung
after him, went within himself to discover the psychic reality of delusion as it manifested itself in the realm of metaphor and myth. As Jung
well knew, this realm was also the realm of schizophrenia which for ten
years he explored in depth at the Burghölzli. Having listened to the
ranting of an asylumed patient, Shelley, as Julian in *Julian and Maddalo*,
is persuaded that, if he had the time and the patience, he could find the
entrance into the madman's mind and reclaim him from his dark estate.
'The colours of his mind seemed yet unworn,' Julian declares, and 'the
wild language of his grief was high, / Such as in measure were called
poetry' (540–2).

Jung devoted some ten years to investigating the acausal realm of
synchronicity that drew the inner and outer worlds together in a 'Pulsation of the Artery' in a way that strongly suggested to him that the inner
and outer worlds acausally merge to become one at what he called 'a
real zero point,' which is 'without extension.' Derrida called this 'zero
point' the 'zero point at which determined meaning and nonmeaning
come together in their common origin' ('Cogito' 56), which as 'madness' is no-thing, not yet every-thing, in a fully undifferentiated or
unconscious state. Blake, as already noted, identifies it with 'every Time
less than a Pulsation of the Artery' in which 'the Poets Work is Done:
and all the Great / Events of Time start forth & are concievd' (*M*
29[31].1–2). It is the state in which, for Shelley, Milton momentarily had
access to the 'one mind.' 'Milton,' he writes, 'conceived the Paradise
Lost as a whole before he executed it in portions' (*DP* 504) as the work
of his individual mind. In *Paradise Lost*, Milton identifies Shelley's notion of the 'one mind' with his 'Celestial Patroness, who deigns / Her
nightly visitation unimplor'd, / And dictates to me slumb'ring, or
inspires / Easy my unpremeditated Verse' (9.21–4).

For Shelley, the inspired poet has access to the 'one mind' through the
medium of a 'Celestial Patroness' who dictates to the modification of it,
which, if not recognized as a 'modification,' leads to the 'delusion' of an
individual mind. In this sense, madness resides not in the undifferentiated action of the 'one mind' in which the 'many' that 'change and pass'
are still the 'One' that 'remains' (*Adonais* 460). It resides, rather, in the
delusion that the individual mind is the 'one mind,' that the '*esemplastic*

power' (*BL* 1:295), as Coleridge calls it, resides in the conscious mind under the control of the conscious will. The latter (Blake's 'rotten rags of Memory') is mere madness; the former (Blake's 'grandeur of Inspiration') is divine madness. In any hallucinatory state, the two are falsely identified. All visionaries, as Coleridge describes them in his *Biographia Literaria*, are subject at times to this false identification of mere madness with divine madness. Blake had to labour to keep them apart, accusing himself under the pressure of what he calls 'Duty & Reality' of mere madness, when he knew that the pressure working upon him was divine madness, understood as the highest form of sanity. Only by constantly distinguishing between them, he realized, could he cooperate with the mythological figures who belonged to his 'celestial' world.

Shelley confronted the same struggle to differentiate divine madness from mere madness, the realm of mere madness increasingly towards the end of his life appearing to crowd out divine madness, so that he felt he had to devote most of his time to keeping them separate lest divine madness, upon which he depended as a poet, was devoured completely by mere madness, his Spectral form assuming control of his faculties. 'I write nothing but by fits,' he wrote to John Gisborne in January 1822. 'I have done some of Charles I; but although the poetry succeeds very well I cannot seize the conception of the subject as a whole yet, & seldom now touch the *canvas'* (*Letters* 2:388). In a later letter he tells Gisborne that he has been reading Goethe's *Faust* 'over and over again' and that it increasingly seemed to him with each rereading that it was 'an unfit study for any person who is a prey to the reproaches of memory, & the delusions of an imagination not to be restrained.' Looking at some 'astonishing etchings' illustrating Goethe's drama, he dared to look at the etching of Margaret in the summer house with Faust only once, because it made his brain 'swim round only to touch the leaf on the opposite side of which I knew that it was figured' ('Happy those for whom the fold / Of') (*Letters* 2:406–7).

In Blake, this struggle is fully integrated. It is the essential 'Opposition' between Los and his Spectre that, as 'true Friendship,' propels his vision as Los struggles to keep control by forcing his Spectre to obey him. Because this struggle is the conscious dynamic that shapes his poetry to a degree that it does not shape Shelley's, it would appear that Blake as poet was more sane than Shelley. By more sane I mean that his poetry was able to operate at a more sustained level of creative tension than Shelley's was. The ability to sustain this level over a lifetime I would explain in terms of Blake's 'Great Code of Art' (E 274), a 'Code' that was not available to Shelley in the way it was to Blake. Unlike Blake, who found in his apocalyptic reading of the Bible the sanity essential to his vision, in certain radical ways Shelley had to invent his own 'Code' from his more problematic access to the undifferentiated 'one mind,' which is, for Shelley, the author of 'that great poem, which all poets, like the cooperating thoughts of one great mind, have built up since the beginning of the world' (*DP* 493). 'In a sense,' writes Milton Wilson in *Shelley's Later Poetry*, 'Shelley is trying singlehanded to re-make the history of thought since the Incarnation' (281). Unlike the Bible (Shelley is 'almost the only English poet who had no desire to profess Christianity' [Wilson 281]), this 'one great poem' only hypo-thetically exists. As the undifferentiated work of the 'one mind' it can-not actually exist as other than the 'full speech' of infants before they begin to talk. Shelley's 'one great poem,' that is, is 'pinnacled dim in the intense inane.'

'Mont Blanc'

In Shelley's 'Mont Blanc,' the site of revelation is not the Bible; it is the act of perception in the poet's mind perceiving what is there before him: 'Mont Blanc appears' (61); 'Mont Blanc yet gleams on high' (127). For Mont Blanc to 'appear,' to 'gleam on high,' is, Shelley argues, a 'miracle.' Why should it appear? Why does it exist at all? Why is there everything rather than nothing? To ask such a question is, Shelley realized in 'On Life,' no longer to be 'shielded by the familiarity of what is at once so certain and so unfathomable from an astonishment which would other-wise absorb and overawe the functions of that which is [its] object.' Shelley in 'Mont Blanc' is confronting in his own mind 'an astonish-ment' that could 'overawe' its 'functions' by plunging them into a realm which is 'so unfathomable' as to constitute a drowning of them in what, in *Prometheus Unbound*, he describes as a 'Sea profound, of ever-spreading sound' (2.5.84).

However, because in *Prometheus Unbound* this sea of 'ever-spreading sound' is the domain of the Oceanides (Asia and her two sisters, who are Prometheus's threefold Muse), Prometheus need have no fear of drowning. Though Milton writes *Lycidas* as an elegy lamenting the drowning of his Cambridge friend, he, in the context of Shelley's 'one mind' (who is, for Milton, Christ), need also have no fear of drowning:

Weep no more, woeful Shepherds weep no more,
For *Lycidas* your sorrow is not dead,
Sunk though he be beneath the wat'ry floor.
...
So *Lycidas*, sunk low, but mounted high,
Through the dear might of him that walk'd the waves.

(*Complete Poems* 165–73)

In 'Mont Blanc,' there is for Shelley no such 'dear might' to keep him afloat, nor does he have Prometheus's Oceanides to inspire and protect him. He has instead the absent presence of the 'one mind' that, as 'Power dwells apart in its tranquillity [on the secret throne that is the glacier peak of Mont Blanc] / Remote, serene, and inaccessible' (96–7). Unlike the 'dear might' of Christ available to Milton as it was to Blake, the Power Shelley invokes remains serenely remote from the world it apparently propels without actually engendering it. It does not differentiate between life and death, inhabiting as it does its own undifferentiated state. As a result, in the absence of the Oceanides, Shelley in 'Mont Blanc' is as a lyric poet not immersed in a 'Sea profound, of ever-spreading sound'; he is confronted by a 'loud, lone sound no other sound can tame,' which he further describes as an 'unresting sound' of 'ceaseless motion' (31–3), the chaos of a Heraclitean flux. Indeed, Shelley's 'Power' is in certain essential respects the blind divinity of the 'mechanical philosophy,' Coleridge's '*something-nothing-every-thing, which does all of which we know, and knows nothing of all that itself does*' (*BL* 1:120). 'If to destroy the reality of all, that we actually behold, be idealism,' Coleridge argues, 'what can be more egregiously so, than the system of modern metaphysics, which banishes us to a land of shadows, surrounds us with apparitions, and distinguishes truth from illusion only by the majority of those who dream the same dream? "*I* asserted that the world was mad," exclaimed poor Lee, "and the world said, that I was mad, and confound them, they outvoted me"' (1:262).

As if himself banished by the inaccessible 'Power' as it becomes in the mind Coleridge's 'system of modern metaphysics' (1:262), Shelley finds himself in 'Mont Blanc' 'in the still cave of the witch Poesy, / Seeking among the shadows that pass by / Ghosts of all things that are, some shade of thee, / Some phantom, some faint image' (44–7). That is, Shelley finds himself again in the now familiar realm of 'charnels' and 'coffins,' pursuing 'hopes of high talk with the departed dead,'

even calling 'on poisonous names [God] with which our youth is fed.'
Shelley's Narrator cries, lamenting the death of the Visionary in himself
in *Alastor,*

O, that God,

Profuse of poisons, would concede the chalice
Which but one living man has drained, who now,
Vessel of deathless wrath, a slave that feels
No proud exemption in the blighting curse
He bears, over the world wanders for ever,
Lone as incarnate death! O, that the dream
Of dark magician in his visioned cave,
Raking the cinders of a crucible
For life and power, even when his feeble hand
Shakes in its last decay, were the true law
Of this so lovely world! But thou art fled
Like some frail exhalation.   (675–87)

In 'the still cave of the witch Poesy' in 'Mont Blanc' the 'frail exhalation' of Shelley's brain is, as a projection, returned to its source ('the
breast / From which they fled recalls them'). The result is: 'thou art
there!' (47–8). The mountain that existed in Shelley's brain only as a
'feeble shadow' ('faint image') of itself is suddenly miraculously replaced by the mountain. Viewed in terms of the 'system of modern
metaphysics,' which both Shelley and Coleridge opposed, the 'faint
image' of the mountain constructed by the brain as a result of its
intercourse with the eye is what Coleridge describes as 'the mere quick-
silver plating behind a looking glass [the inverted image of the retina];
and in this alone consists the poor worthless I!' (*BL* 1:119). Shelley calls
this 'worthless I' a 'delusion' when it is not recognized as a 'modification' of the 'one mind.'

'It is the table itself ['thou art there!'], which the man of common
sense believes himself to see,' Coleridge declares, 'not the phantom of a
table, from which he may argumentatively deduce the reality of a table,
which he does not see' (*BL* 1:261–2). In his refutation of the 'mechanical
philosophy,' Coleridge affirms the presence of what he calls 'a mechanism and co-adequate forces in the percipient, which at the more than
magic touch of the impulse from without is to create anew for itself the
correspondent object.' Elaborating on this 'more than magic touch,' he
argues that the 'formation of a copy is not solved by the mere pre-

existence of an original; the copyist of Raphael's Transfiguration must repeat more or less perfectly the process of Raphael. It would be easy to explain a thought from the image on the retina, and that from the geometry of light, if this very light did not present the very same difficulty. ['We see only because the light strikes our eyes etc. – But what then is light? Again an object!,' writes Schelling (1:138n).] (1:137). The necessity of repeating 'more or less perfectly the process of Raphael' brings Coleridge to his notion of the 'primary imagination' as 'the living Power and prime Agent of all human Perception.' The 'primary imagination,' Coleridge concludes, summarizing in a sentence the argument of his unwritten *Logosophia*, is (must be) 'a repetition in the finite mind of the eternal act of creation in the infinite I AM,' which Shelley, avoiding the 'poisonous' name of God, calls the 'one mind.' The 'ghosts of all things,' which fled in the 'still cave of the witch Poesy' (the brain) from the 'breast,' return to their source in order to release the mountain from the limitations of perception understood as projection. This release, Shelley speculates, is the gift of the 'one mind' understood, as Coleridge understood it, as the gift of the primary imagination. Hence, Shelley's final question addressed to the mountain, which is now present to the eye as the gift of the 'one mind.' In this radical respect Shelley in 'Mont Blanc' has exorcised what he describes as a 'trance sublime and strange' in which he 'muse[s] on [his] own separate phantasy' (35–6) as if he were a 'dark magician in his visioned cave, / Raking the cinders of a crucible / For life and power.'

In his own gropingly articulated way, Shelley anticipates not only Jung's work on alchemy, but the entire psychological system that emerged from it. Jung's break with Freud, it may well be argued, had its prototype in Shelley's and Coleridge's break with the 'mechanical philosophy.' Unlike Coleridge, though very like Jung, Shelley lacked the kind of metaphysical system that Coleridge spent most of his life erecting as a system of knowledge (gnosis) that would support his Christian faith by relieving it of its irrationality. Shelley, on the other hand, remained in the absence of Coleridge's God in a position that he described (and yet again with Wordsworth in mind) as 'awful doubt, or faith so mild, / So solemn, so serene, that man may be / But for such faith with nature reconciled' ('Mont Blanc' 77–9). Shelley stops short of any reconciliation with nature because of the way it is bound to Wordsworth's perception of it, that is to say, because it is bound to natural religion and to the moral law that Wordsworth attributes to it. Indeed, for Shelley, freedom resides in the disjunction between man and nature, a disjunction that endows the mountain with precisely what Moses's mountain of God would not allow: a 'voice ... to repeal / Large codes of fraud and woe; not understood / By all, but which the wise, and great, and good / Interpret, or make felt, or deeply feel' (80–3).

Shelley's 'awful doubt' releases the mountain from its containment in Coleridge's logos or 'eternal act of creation in the infinite I AM.' As Derrida explains,

> Crisis or oblivion perhaps is not an accident, but rather the destiny of speaking philosophy – the philosophy which lives only by emprisoning madness, but which would die as thought, and by a still worse violence [dictatorship], if a new speech did not at every instant liberate previous madness while enclosing within itself, in its present existence, the mad-man of the day. It is only by virtue of this oppression of madness that finite-thought, that is to say, history, can reign. Extending this truth to historicity in general, without keeping to a determined historical moment, one could say that the reign of finite thought can be established only on the basis of the more or less disguised internment, humiliation, fettering and mockery of the madman within us, of the madman who can only be the fool of a logos which is father, master, and king. ('Cogito' 61)

For Shelley, as for Derrida after him, freedom resides not in its containment in the logos, but in what Derrida calls 'the *other* light, a black and hardly natural light, the vigil of the "powers of unreason" around the Cogito' (61). Jung calls this '*other* light' the Shadow, which as the transcendent principle, releases the imagination from its imprisonment in the fixed system of the logos. The 'black and hardly natural light' lights the way of what Jung calls the *opus contra naturam*, which, as the '"powers of unreason"' circling the Cogito, forever releases the imagination to construct mythopoeic tales that are forever in danger of becoming either 'forms of worship' or forms of 'madness.' In the name of this freedom, dialectically affirmed in 'Mont Blanc,' Shelley constructed his greatest affirmation of it in *Prometheus Unbound* as what Demogorgon (the 'one mind') allegorically describes as 'the spells by which to reassume / An empire o'er the disentangled Doom' (4.568–9). Realizing in his final fragment that an 'empire' was not that much more preferable than 'a disentangled Doom,' Shelley, like Shakespeare's Mercutio, proclaimed in *The Triumph of Life* a 'plague' on both of them.

The 'Black and Hardly Natural Light'

The freedom that resides in 'awful doubt' is, in the end, a freedom that releases, rather than reinforces or even renews, the bonds connecting the human being to the senses, that is to say, the earth. Freedom, in some ultimate sense (and Shelley was never satisfied with less), is, like Lacan's 'desir,' bound to death. The ultimate act of freedom lies in the choosing of death as the formless form of freedom itself. Confronting Shelley in the shaping of the metaphorical body that is his poetry, a shaping that, 'under the power of the artist,' he compares to 'a child in the mother's womb' (DP 504), is the fear that what is taking shape is the ghostly or phantasmagoric form of the material body, which is suspended, as metaphor is suspended, between matter and spirit, partaking of both and belonging to neither. The strange creature of this fear is what Blake calls, with reference to Satan, 'a mournful form double; hermaphroditic: male & female / In one wonderful body' (M 14[15].37–8). Locke calls it a 'Centaur.' In Frankenstein, Mary Shelley explores the trauma of some such monstrous birth to which she had almost daily access in her negative relationship to Shelley's gothic imagination, in which his writing of poetry appeared to be related to his negotiations with the dead. These negotiations were ultimately connected to his obsessive desire for some sort of intercourse with the 'Mother of this unfathomable world,' which, in Alastor, conducted him, in the projected figure of the Visionary, towards his own death in a futile, nightmarish pursuit, if not of her, at least of 'some lone ghost / [Her] messenger' (27–8), which already had, 'like a dark flood suspended in its course, / Rolled back [her] impulse on his vacant brain' (190–1).

In Alastor, a 'restless impulse' urges the Visionary to board an abandoned and rotting shallop and 'meet lone Death on the drear ocean's waste' (304, 305). His journey – the demonic counterpart of Shelley's recently completed journey to the source of the Thames – takes place along a stream that images the Visionary's life. It is, as Shelley allegorically describes it, a journey through 'the poisonous waters that flow from death through life' (DP 505), the world itself becoming 'the contagion' arising from Death's 'slow stain' (Adonais 356), where 'we decay / Like corpses in a charnel' (348–9). In his account of the Visionary's journey to death as the source of life, Shelley had in mind the nightmare journey of Coleridge's ancient mariner, over which presides the 'Nightmare LIFE-IN-DEATH ... / Who thicks man's blood with cold' (193–4).

'For well [the Visionary] knew,' Shelley explains, 'that mighty Shadow [of his dream] loves / The slimy caverns of the populous deep' (304–5). In these 'slimy caverns' Coleridge's 'thousand thousand slimy things,' like Shelley's Visionary, 'lived on' (*Rime* 238–9) even as, for Shelley, Wordsworth's child awoke in the grave. As if momentarily making his peace with this nightmare by lyrically settling into it (as in his final months he momentarily settled into the lovely lyrics addressed to Jane Williams), Shelley wrote 'A Summer Evening Churchyard, Lechlade, Gloucestershire,' published in the same 1816 volume as *Alastor*. 'The dead are sleeping in their sepulchres,' he peacefully reflects, 'And, mouldering as they sleep, a thrilling sound, / Half sense, half thought, among the darkness stirs, / Breathed from their wormy beds all living things around' (*Complete Poetical Works* 19–22). As he looks forward to his actual journey, the 'contagion' of 'mouldering' corpses in their 'wormy beds' is 'solemnized and softened' (25). 'Death,' for the moment, 'is mild / And terrorless as this serenest night' (25–6). In this rare state of mind, Shelley, like Wordsworth in 'We Are Seven,' could hope, 'like some inquiring child / Sporting on graves, that death did hide from human sight / Sweet secrets, or beside its breathless sleep / That loveliest dreams perpetual watch did keep' (27–30). In another lyric in the same volume, 'Oh! there are spirits in the air,' written according to Mary Shelley with Coleridge in mind, Shelley wrote, mindful of *Christabel* and *The Rime*:

> Thine own soul still is true to thee,
> But changed to a foul fiend through misery
>
> This fiend, whose ghastly presence ever
>   Beside thee like thy shadow hangs,
> Dream not to chase; – the mad endeavour
>   Would scourge thee to severer pangs,
> Be as thou art. Thy settled fate,
> Dark as it is, all change would aggravate.   (*Complete Poetical Works* 29–36)

Shelley's dismissal of the individual mind ('*I, you, they*') as a 'delusion' in 'On Life,' which probably belongs to the period of 1815, culminating in the writing of *Alastor*, is a failed metaphysical attempt to exorcize the 'foul fiend' by dismissing it as a 'delusion.' The material 'marks' made on a white sheet of paper become a 'separate phantasy' which radically distorts the operations of the 'one mind.' As if determined to exorcise this 'separate phantasy' by substituting 'the still cave of the witch Poesy' in 'Mont Blanc' for the dream of the veiled maid in *Alastor*, Shelley struggles actively to process the enchantment of the 'witch Poesy' rather than, as in *Alastor*, passively submitting to it. As a result, 'Mont Blanc yet gleams on high.' It does not assume the hallucinogenic guise the veiled maid in *Alastor* assumes when she appears before the Visionary as a poisonous serpent conducting him to his death.

In 'the still cave of the witch Poesy,' as in his dream of the veiled maid, Shelley knows that he is looking down 'the dark abyss of – how little we know,' an abyss where the mind becomes 'dizzy' and 'words abandon us.' In 'On Life,' Shelley insists that he had no wish to 'look down the dark abyss' (*SPP* 478). 'It is,' he writes, 'a decision against which all our persuasions struggle, and we must be long convicted, before we are convinced that the solid universe of external things is "such stuff as dreams are made of"' (476).

As his own 'separate phantasy' requiring ceaseless exorcism, Shelley's confrontation with the 'dark abyss' was a confrontation with a primordial crime for which, long before he got here, he had been sentenced to death. His life, beginning with conception in the mother's womb, was the carrying out of a death sentence for a crime about which he, like Franz Kafka after him, had never been informed by 'the bungler who brought us into existence at first' (*Letters* 2:954). Struggling against this reading of the 'dark abyss,' in the final months of his life Shelley turned increasingly to Goethe's *Faust*, where the 'charm of despair' lies in 'the scorn of the narrow good we can attain in our present state.' 'Perhaps,' he writes to Gisborne (10 April 1822), 'all discontent with the *less* (to use a Platonic sophism) supposes the sense of a just claim to the *greater*, & that we admirers of Faust are in the right road to Paradise.' And then thinking yet again of Wordsworth, whom by now he fully despised, he adds: 'Such a supposition is not more absurd, and is certainly less demoniacal than that of Wordsworth – where he says – 'This earth, / Which is the world of all of us, & where / *We find our happiness or not at all*' (*Letters* 2:406).

After *Alastor*, Shelley struggled to construct a mythical vision of the operations of the 'one mind' that would allow him imaginatively to perceive a Paradise as well as an Inferno in the 'dark abyss of how little we know.' Here his model was the Catholic Dante rather than the Puritan Milton, whose attempted Paradise was defeated by the binding of his creative power to the same fantasized crime that plagued Shelley.

'Nothing can exceed the energy and magnificence of the character of Satan as expressed in Paradise Lost,' Shelley insists in his *Defence of Poetry*. 'It is a mistake to suppose that he could ever have been intended for the popular personification of evil' (498). 'Mont Blanc' is the poem in which Shelley, confronting his demons, fully explores his struggle with them less in the language of myth than in what would later better be understood as the language of psychology. What he learned about the operations of the creative mind in the act of composition he was able to project onto the myth of Prometheus, there to enact as the unbinding of Prometheus what he had psychologically achieved in 'Mont Blanc.' Henceforth, in Shelley's mind myth became the creative enactment of its powers.

Shelley's confrontation with the 'dark abyss,' particularly from the composition of *Alastor* in 1815 to the composition of 'Mont Blanc' and 'Hymn to Intellectual Beauty' in 1816, covers a period of inner exploration that finds its counterpart in Jung's descent into the 'dark abyss' after his break with Freud in 1912. The account of this descent has already been explored in the first chapter. Its Romantic prototypes are to be found in the various descents of Blake, Wordsworth, Coleridge, Keats, Shelley, and Byron. In Coleridge's case, his exploration of the unconscious, bound in part to the 'foul fiend' of opium which acted as an incentive, was teleologically oriented to the shaping of a metaphysical system partly borrowed from German philosophy and largely determined by his need to find a rational basis for his Christian faith. Like Jung nearly a hundred years later, Shelley was more interested in restoring metaphysics to what he considered its psychological origins than in using those origins either to affirm a metaphysical system or even to construct one. At the same time, however, he realized that without a metaphysics to support his descent into the 'dark abyss' he was entering a realm of hallucination to which he knew himself from early childhood to be vulnerable. Shelley knew that the 'madness' of which he stood 'convicted' was a 'madness' of which, however unwillingly, he had to become 'convinced.' His poetry at its best, like the poetry of Blake, is a celebration of the sanity of madness. Referring to 'the charm of despair' in Goethe's *Faust*, Shelley uses the word in the sense of magic, spell, or incantation, which works on 'despair' either to make it endurable or to transform it into its opposite while still containing it.

In his biography of Shelley, Richard Holmes quotes from a loose collection of Shelley's foolscap notes in the Bodleian MS.Shelley Adds.c4,

Folder 21–3, which, he suggests, are best described by Shelley's own phrase 'the science of mind.' 'But thought can with difficulty visit the intricate and winding chambers which it inhabits,' Shelley writes. 'It is like a river whose rapid and perpetual stream flows outwards – like one in dread who speeds through the recesses of some haunted pile and dare not look behind' (cited in Holmes 292–3). As in *Alastor*, Shelley has in mind Coleridge as Wordsworth's Spectre. Coleridge writes in his *Rime*,

> Like one, that on a lonesome road
> Doth walk in fear and dread,
> And having once turned round walks on,
> And turns no more his head;
> Because he knows, a frightful fiend
> Doth close behind him tread.   (446–50)

As for Wordsworth, Shelley assumed that his settled metaphysics had rid him of any further encounters with 'a frightful fiend.' Thus, while Wordsworth introduces his books on the French Revolution by comparing the movement of his mind to a river turning back towards its place of origin as if fearing 'to shape a way direct, / That would engulph him soon in the ravenous sea' (*P* 9.3–4), he immediately supplants it with another, less threatening image in which the fear of engulphment is carefully amended:

> Or as a traveller, who has gained the brow
> Of some *aerial* Down, while there he halts
> For breathing-time, is tempted to review
> The region left behind him; and, if aught
> *Deserving* notice have escaped regard,
> Or been regarded with too careless eye,
> Strives, *from that height*, with one and yet one more
> Last look, to make the best amends he may ...   (9.10–16; italics added)

'Dream not to chase,' Shelley warned Coleridge. He was always already in the 'haunted pile' that awaited him. He should leave it as it is, embracing it as his fate, as, Shelley would soon realize, Byron had successfully done. Confronted by a psychotic state arising from within after he separated from Freud, 'something whispered within [Jung], "Why open all gates?"' (*MDR* 171).

'"If it were possible to be where we have been, vitally and indeed,"' Shelley continues in his foolscap notes, '"– if, at the moment of our presence there, we could define the results of our experience – if the passage from sensation to reflection – from a state of passive perception to voluntary contemplation were not so dizzying and so tumultuous, this attempt would be less difficult"' (cited in Holmes 293). In the 'dizzy Ravine of Arve,' Shelley found the objective correlative for the 'dizzying' and 'tumultuous' state of 'passive perception' ('My own, my human mind, which passively / Now renders and receives fast influencings' [37–8]), which 'in the still cave of the witch Poesy,' he subjects to 'voluntary contemplation.' Had he not made the difficult transition 'from sensation to reflection,' he might have been overwhelmed by the 'ceaseless motion' and 'unresting sound' of a hallucinatory state.

'An incessant stream of fantasies had been released,' writes Jung of his experience after separating from Freud,

> and I did my best not to lose my head but to find some way to understand these strange things. I stood helpless before an alien world ['a trance sublime and strange,' writes Shelley in *Alastor*]; everything in it seemed difficult and incomprehensible. I was living in a constant state of tension; often I felt as if gigantic blocks of stone were tumbling down upon me. One thunderstorm followed another ... Others have been shattered by them – Nietzsche, and Hölderlin, and many others. But there was a demonic strength in me, and from the beginning there was no doubt in my mind that I must find the meaning of what I was experiencing in these fantasies. ['Be thou, Spirit fierce, / My spirit!' (61–2) declares Shelley to the west wind.] (*MDR* 176–7)

While Winnicott acknowledged that Jung successfully overcame his 'childhood schizophrenia,' at the same time he rejected the mythical form the healing took. Jung's image of the self as a fourfold mandala to which his psychology aspired as the total form of itself was, Winnicott (as already noted) argues, a 'defensive construct, a defence against the spontaneity which has destruction as its next-door neighbour.' 'The mandala,' he insists, 'is a truly frightening thing for me because of its absolute failure to come to terms with destructiveness, and with chaos, disintegration, and the other madnesses. It is an obsessional flight from disintegration ... The centre of the self is a relatively useless concept. What is more important is to reach to the basic forces of individual living, and to me it is certain that if the real basis is creativeness the very next thing is destruction' (491).

This same argument is brought to bear on Shelley by those who find in his notion of 'the One' an 'obsessional flight from disintegration.' However, with reference to Jung, Shelley, and Blake – all of whom were considered mad by their critics – Winnicott's notion that Jung failed to 'come to terms with destructiveness' ignores the fact that his psychology is grounded in his refutation, not only of the limitations of Freud's sexual theory, but of the scientific materialism of the last three centuries, both of which, he argued, have led 'to an annihilating judgment upon culture.' The laws of nature prescribed by the natural sciences have virtually extinguished the life of the soul so that, as Shelley argued, 'man, having enslaved the elements, remains himself a slave' (*DP* 503). Mythically portraying the creative mind of God as a '*complexio oppositorum*' (*MDR* 353), Jung insists not only that 'destruction' is 'the very next thing' to 'creativeness,' in terms of his dialectic, but that it also subsists *sub specie aeternitatis* in the process of its creation. Separated from destruction, creation is fixed and dead.

Jung's first remembered dream, which occurred between the ages of three and four, particularly as interpreted by Marie-Louise von Franz, contains within it the archetypal model of what would become Jung's life work: 'a struggle to free the "new king" from the depths of the collective unconscious' (*MDR* 184). In his dream of the underground phallus 'the royal phallus' is in the grave and the infant Jung fears that it might 'crawl over him like a worm and creep toward [him]' (12). Paralysed with fear, he hears his mother shout, '"Yes, just look at him. That is the man-eater."' Still bound to his mother, from whom he was forcibly separated when she was confined to a mental hospital, Jung in the dream negatively experiences the 'new king' within his mother's uncanny matriarchal frame. Von Franz argues,

> The 'old king,' the Christian outlook or the Christian God-image, is dead and buried; that is, he has fallen into the depths of the collective unconscious, into matter, and into everything that would be attributed to his adversary. There it has to be transformed into the worm-like phallus which raises itself up toward the light. The worm or serpent in alchemical symbolism is the first form taken by the phoenix and by the old king. After his death they are the beginning of his rebirth; it is an initial, primitive archaic life-form, out of which the new image of the king develops. The orientation of the phallus toward the light ['On the very top of the head was a single eye, gazing motionlessly upward' (12)], in Jung's dream, shows that a new content is striving toward the region of consciousness. (183–4)

This dream constellation is repeated over and over again in the poetry of the Romantics. The poet, that is, must descend to the land of the dead. 'The eternal gates terrific porter lifted the northern bar,' writes Blake in *The Book of Thel*: 'Thel enter'd in & saw the secrets of the land unknown; / She saw the couches of the dead, & where the fibrous roots / Of every heart on earth infixes deep its restless twists' (6.1–4). Terrified, like the three-year-old Jung, she 'fled back unhindered' (6.22) to the now forbidden realm of innocence over which presides the enfolding arms of the mother, not yet perceived as Tirzah and therefore all the more sinister. In this realm, Thel sees herself as the 'helpless worm' seated 'upon the Lilys leaf' (3.30). She asks of her unfallen state,

> Art thou a Worm? image of weakness. art thou but a Worm?
> I see thee like an infant wrapped in the Lillys leaf:
> Ah weep not little voice, thou can'st not speak. but thou can'st weep;
> Is this a Worm? I see thee lay helpless & naked: weeping,
> And none to answer, none to cherish thee with mothers smiles.   (4.2–6)

(In *Prometheus Unbound*, Asia in the cave of Demogorgon describes the state of 'earth's primal spirits' as 'the calm joy' of 'semivital worms' [2.4.35–8]).

Blake's Thel is not yet prepared to release, as Ololon will release, the 'new king' from the depths of matter into which the 'old king' has fallen. She is not yet ready to enter her own 'Vegetable Body' and release the 'new king' that stirs within it like Wordsworth's babe lying awake in the grave. Shelley's poet struggling in vain in *Alastor* to unite with the 'Mother of this unfathomable world' by making his bed 'in charnels and on coffins' is, like Thel, unprepared to find in the grave the 'new king' whom Asia will crown in *Prometheus Unbound*, only to retreat into the 'enchanted cave' of poetry as if fearing 'the serpent that would clasp her with his length' (4.567) as it clasps the Visionary in *Alastor*. Shelley's fear of the feminine, like Jung's, robbed him of his object: the throneless throne of the 'new king' arising from the grave of the 'Christian God-image.' Blake's androgynous Christ is Jung's answer to 'the same 2,000-year-old' question: 'How does one get from Three to Four?'

The anima, Jung argues, is the soul's connection to the collective unconscious. As the land of the dead (the chthonic), the task of restoring to life the gods who have fallen into its vast realm of matter is now, he argues, the supreme task of consciousness. In *The Fall of Hyperion*, Keats faced it as his growing recognition of defeat. Moneta, addressing Keats, declares,

> 'My power, which to me is still a curse
> Shall be to thee a wonder; for the scenes
> Still swooning vivid through my globèd brain
> With an electral changing misery
> Thou shalt with those dull mortal eyes behold,
> Free from all pain, if wonder pain thee not.'

'As near as an immortal's spherèd words / Could to a mother's soften, were these last,' declares Keats; he continues,

> But yet I had a terror of her robes,
> And chiefly of her veils, that from her brow
> Hung pale, and curtain'd her in mysteries
> That made my heart too small to hold its blood.
> This saw that Goddess, and with sacred hand
> Parted the veils. Then saw I a wan face,
> Not pin'd by human sorrows, but bright blanch'd
> By an immortal sickness which kills not;
> It works a constant change, which happy death
> Can put no end to; deathwards progressing
> To no death was that visage ...   (1.243–61)

'The gods have become diseases,' writes Jung in *Alchemical Studies*; 'Zeus no longer rules Olympus but rather the solar plexus, and produces curious specimens for the doctor's consulting room, or disorders the brains of politicians and journalists who unwittingly let loose psychic epidemics on the world' (*CW* 13:54). The gods, that is, are now, for Jung, the collective psychosis of materialism. Jung's diagnosis and proposed remedy have their prototype in the Romantic encounter with the 'mechanical philosophy,' whose 'shocking absurdities,' Shelley writes in 'On Life,' allow 'its disciples [as it once allowed him] to talk and dispenses them from thinking' because matter cannot think (*SPP* 476).

Jung's psychology, like the vision of the Romantics that prophetically preceded it, is not a personal psychology concerned with ego development. The sickness of the individual as he explored it in his 'consulting room' was a cultural sickness whose origins he traced to the necessary collapse of religious systems (particularly in his case the Christian religion) as the age-old custodians of the soul. His concern, that is, was with the archetypal proclivities manifest in any particular psychic illness. The discovery of those proclivities on the part of the individual analysand and the recognition of the psychic dynamics governing their operations carried within them a healing process that, far from releasing his analysands from the collectivity to which they were bound, released a consciousness able critically to engage those dynamics towards the potential new life present in them. By locating the individual in a 'collective,' as distinct from a 'personal,' unconscious (though not ignoring the 'personal' as a way into the 'collective'), Jung's psychology is fundamentally a cultural psychology in which the ruling influences upon an individual's early life (mother, father, siblings, etc.) are released into their archetypal perspectives, rather than remaining bound to a personal perspective. 'What was alive and active within [Goethe],' Jung writes, 'was a living substance, a suprapersonal process, the great dream of the *mundus archetypus* (archetypal world)' (*MDR* 206). This great dream was not, for Jung, a literal or personal dream. 'It is,' he writes to Herbert Read, 'the great dream which has always spoken through the artist as a mouthpiece.' 'What is the great Dream?' he then asks. 'It is,' he answers, 'the future and the picture of the new world' (*Letters* 2:591).

This is the way the Romantics as poets perceived their personal lives. Far from shaping an ego structure to protect themselves against the very real dangers of the collective culture, they surrendered it to the renewal of the dynamics at work in the collective unconscious by bringing it to a new consciousness of its operations. (In the concluding lines of *The Prelude*, Wordsworth describes his work with Coleridge as their joint-labours 'in forwarding a day' of a 'deliverance, surely yet to come' [14.442, 445].) In the realm of space and time, where the work of consciousness goes on, the dynamics of the collective unconscious are always already what Keats's Moneta calls a 'curse' that binds her, as the 'Shade of Memory' (*Fall of Hyperion* 1.282), to a dead order. She tells Keats that she is the '"sole priestess of [S]aturn's desolation."' 'I had no words to answer,' declares Keats, 'for my tongue, / Useless, could find about its roofed home / No syllable of a fit majesty / To make rejoinder to Moneta's mourn' (1.226–31). Keats in the presence of Moneta must put on Blake's 'rotten rags of Memory' if his 'tongue' was to find in its 'roofed home' some 'syllable of a fit majesty.' Keats, that is, greets his chosen epic theme with a silence that he struggles in vain to overcome, the subject of his epic becoming its impossibility for a modern poet. 'I have given up Hyperion,' he writes to John Reynolds, ' – there were too many Miltonic inversions in it – Miltonic verse cannot be written but in an artful or rather artist's humour. I wish to give myself up to other sensations' (*KL* 292). Shelley knew this when he recognized as an epic poet that Jupiter's long reign belongs to a 'no more remembered fame' (*PU* 3.4.169). Among the Romantics, only Wordsworth and Byron consciously bound themselves to memory, Wordsworth searching for a blessing in what Byron recognized as a curse.

6

The Sanity of Madness:
Byron and Shelley

Bending over the corpse of Keats, Urania in Shelley's *Adonais* manages for a moment to animate it:

> In the death chamber for a moment Death
> Shamed by the presence of that living Might
> Blushed to annihilation, and the breath
> Revisited those lips, and life's pale light
> Flashed through those limbs, so late her dear delight.   (217–21)

Shelley here could not have failed to have in mind Mary Shelley's waking vision of the animation of a corpse, recounted in her introduction to the 1831 revised third edition of *Frankenstein: The Modern Prometheus*:

> When I placed my head on my pillow, I did not sleep, nor could I be said to think. My imagination, unbidden, possessed and guided me, gifting the successive images that arose in my mind with a vividness far beyond the usual bounds of reverie. I saw – with shut eyes, but acute mental vision, I saw the pale student of unhallowed arts kneeling beside the thing he had put together. I saw the hideous phantasm of a man stretched out, and then, on the working of some powerful engine, show signs of life, and stir with an uneasy, half vital motion. Frightful must it be; for supremely frightful would be the effect of any human endeavour to mock the stupendous mechanism of the Creator of the world. His success would terrify the artist; he would rush away from his odious handywork, horror-stricken. He would hope that, left to itself, the slight spark of life which he had communicated would fade; that this thing, which had received such im-

perfect animation, would subside into dead matter; and he might sleep in the belief that the silence of the grave would quench for ever the transient existence of the hideous corpse which he had looked upon as the cradle of life. (364–5)

The nightmare described by Mary Shelley is one to which Shelley was subject most of his life, particularly during his final months. Shelley was never unaware of the dark side of his vision which, like the Phantasm of Jupiter, he deliberately invoked in a futile attempt finally to exorcise it. Far from subsiding 'into dead matter,' the 'silence of the grave' quenching 'for ever the transient existence of the hideous corpse which he looked upon as the cradle of life,' Shelley continued to pursue it as a pursuit of Death which, either as material decay or an ecstatic union with spirit, must ultimately claim him as a cradling mother claims her child. 'And death,' declares the Mother Earth, 'shall be the last embrace of her / Who takes the life she gave, even as a mother / Folding her child, says "Leave me not again"!' (PU 3.3.105–7). Prometheus is her child who has just bent down and kissed her. 'I hear – I feel –,' she cries,

Thy lips are on me, and their touch runs down
Even to the adamantine central gloom
Along these marble nerves – 'tis life, 'tis joy,
And through my withered, old and icy frame
The warmth of an immortal youth shoots down
Circling.   (PU 3.3.84–90)

Shelley's Visionary in *Alastor* has here finally united with his Great Mother. 'Like an inspired and desperate alchymist / Staking his very life on some dark hope,' he has 'made / Such magic' out of 'strange tears / Uniting with ... breathless kisses' that 'the charmed night' is compelled 'to render up [its] charge' (31–7). The 'pale student of unhallowed arts' in *Alastor* is fully gratified in *Prometheus Unbound*. Such is Shelley's terror of the 'disentangled doom' (4.569) of madness that he must, Mary Shelley suspected, bring an even greater madness to bear upon it in the hope of transcending it. 'It is seldom that the young know what youth is, till they have got beyond its period,' Mary Shelley wrote in the Preface to her 1839 edition of Shelley's poetry; 'and time was not given him to attain this knowledge. It must be remembered that there is the stamp of such inexperience on all he wrote; he had not completed his nine-and-twentieth year when he died. The calm of middle age did not add the seal of the virtues which adorn maturity to those generated by the vehement spirit of youth' (*Complete Poetical Works* xi).

Her hope that the portrayal of Shelley as Victor Frankenstein would persuade him to abandon the charnels and coffins of his diseased imagination went unheeded on one level. On another, it struck home in a way that forced Shelley to consider his poetry an 'unhallowed art' of which he, as the Visionary, was the 'pale student.' 'For know, there are two worlds of life and death,' the Earth explains to her son.

> One that which thou beholdest, but the other
> Is underneath the grave, where do inhabit
> The shadows of all forms that think and live
> Till death unite them, and they part no more;
> Dreams and the light imaginings of men
> And all that faith creates, or love desires,
> Terrible, strange, sublime and beauteous shapes.
> There thou art, and dost hang, a writhing shade
> 'Mid whirlwind-peopled mountains; all the Gods
> Are there, and all the Powers of nameless worlds,
> Vast, sceptred phantoms; heroes, men, and beasts;
> And Demogorgon, a tremendous Gloom;
> And he, the Supreme Tyrant, on his throne
> Of burning Gold.   (*PU* 1.195–209)

The world that is 'underneath the grave' is the vast realm of the collective unconscious, which is, for Shelley, the realm of poetry, though not as it is forever conceived in the 'one mind,' but as it is written in time by the individual poet. What is written, he explains, is 'a feeble shadow of the original conception' of the 'one mind.' What is originally conceived are 'all forms that think and live.' These forms dwell in the 'one great mind' as the author of 'that great [unwritten] poem ... built up since the beginning of the world.' This unwritten poem, like Keats's 'unheard' melodies sounding, though 'not to the sensual ear,' as 'spirit ditties of no tone' ('Ode on a Grecian Urn' 14–15), is the eternal living form of the realm of shadows perceived by the senses. In death, Earth explains to Prometheus, these shadows will be united with their living forms. Whether or not this happens, the sceptical Keats points out, 'will be known / When this warm scribe my hand is in the grave' (*Fall of Hyperion* 17–18). For Coleridge, the uniting of living forms with their

shadows 'is the dread book of judgement, in whose mysterious hieroglyphics every idle word is recorded! Yea, in the very nature of a living
spirit, it may be more possible that heaven and earth should pass away,
than that a single act, a single thought, should be loosened or lost from
that living chain of causes, to all of whose links, conscious or unconscious, the free-will, our only absolute *self*, is co-extensive and co-
present' (*BL* 1:114).

Shelley's lyrical drama, written to be read by no 'more than 5 or 6
persons' (*Letters* 2:388) and taking place in the labyrinthine mind of the
poet, is a vast psychodrama or shadow play that, like Shakespeare's *The
Tempest*, is the product of a 'rough magic' that, lest he and the audience
become its victims, had to be 'abjure[d]' (5.1.50–1). 'As you from crimes
would pardon'd be / Let your indulgence set me free' (5.1.19–20),
Prospero asks the audience in the epilogue. The 'unhallowed' sense of
mocking 'the stupendous mechanism of the Creator of the world' haunts
the poet's creative imagination, most particularly when he insists that
God himself is its product. More than any other Romantic, Shelley left
himself dangerously open to what he calls the 'delusions of an imagination not to be restrained' (*Letters* 2:388). Not without a certain terror of
its obvious implications, he compared himself (in a way that Wordsworth
did not) to 'the knight of the shield of shadow and the lance of
gossamere.' In a very real sense the action of *Prometheus Unbound* takes
place 'underneath the grave,' even as the action of *The Tempest* takes
place on an enchanted island, buried, like Atlantis, 'certain fathoms'
(5.1.55) deep.

'Ye happy dead, whom beams of brightest verse / Are clouds to hide,
not colours to portray,' Demogorgon declares to all who dwell 'beyond
Heaven's constellated wilderness' (*PU* 4.532–5), which is the audience
Shelley sought in vain to reach. By invoking its presence, Shelley, through
the words that declared its absence forced them metaphorically beyond
what, as symbols, they signified. Addressing the 'elemental Genii, who
have homes / From man's high mind even to the central stone / Of
sullen lead,' they, as 'a *confused* VOICE,' reply: 'We hear: thy words
waken Oblivion' (4.539–43). 'Oblivion' or nothingness is what Shelley
was forever seeking 'midst listening echoes' never far removed from
the demons who plagued him. 'Obscurely through my brain like shadows dim / Sweep awful thoughts, rapid and thick,' declares Prometheus,
suspended between Asia and the Phantasm of Jupiter, both of whom
are rising within him. 'I feel / Faint, like one mingled in entwining
love, / Yet 'tis not pleasure' (1.146–9).

Essential to an understanding of the alarming confusion of voices forever arising 'rapid and thick' to consciousness in Shelley's mind is his complex relationship to Byron, a relationship as significant in its own different, yet similar, ways as the relations between Wordsworth and Coleridge. Shelley considered Byron's poetry the only real contemporary challenge to his own. Bringing back to England in the autumn of 1816 the third canto of *Childe Harold's Pilgrimage*, which grew in some ways out of Byron's relations with Shelley during that summer, Shelley knew that, in arranging for its publication, his own stake in it was comparable to Wordsworth's and Coleridge's joint, though anonymous, publication of the *Lyrical Ballads*.

Nowhere in the third canto is this stake more evident than in Byron's account of the broken mirror, which Shelley in 1821 would explore in his very different way as the 'dome of many-coloured glass' trampled to fragments in *Adonais*. This trampling, it would appear, left Byron, as 'Pythian of the age' (250), the sole surviving strong poet among his contemporaries, Keats having died 'on the promise of the fruit' (53). Byron writes,

> Even as a broken Mirror, which the glass
> In every fragment multiplies; and makes
> A thousand images of one that was,
> The same, and still the more, the more it breaks;
> And thus the heart will do which not forsakes,
> Living in shattered guise, and still, and cold,
> And bloodless, with its sleepless sorrow aches,
> Yet withers on till all without is old,
> Showing no visible sign, for such things are untold.   (*Childe* 3.289–97)

Byron's art had become the art of a 'shattered guise,' a posture that Shelley knew all too well and was struggling to overcome, partly by persuading Byron to do the same thing. Nowhere is this more evident than in *Julian and Maddalo*, in which Byron appears to be fully resigned to mortality's tolling bell summoning the soul to confront as matter its awaited return to dust, a vision Shelley himself had articulated in *Alastor*. What most threatened Shelley in Byron's third canto was Byron's ability to multiply in the broken bits of glass a thousand new images as if his imagination thrived upon the shattering that at the same time it appeared to lament.

Byron continues,

There is a very life in our despair,
Vitality of poison, – a quick root
Which feeds these deadly branches; for it were
As nothing did we die; but Life will suit
Itself to Sorrow's most detested fruit,
Like to the apples on the Dead Sea's shore,
All ashes to the taste.   (3.298–304)

Byron's apparent ability to thrive on the 'vitality of poison,' his imagination feeding the 'dead branches' of European civilization when it
should be celebrating its death as the birth of a new one (as Shelley
would enact it in *Prometheus Unbound*), deeply threatened Shelley. He
saw how his apparent opposition to Byron not only fed into Byron's
own powers as a poet, but was necessary to it.

Shelley was forced to confront in Byron the 'vitality' of his own
'poison.' This was particularly the case in Byron's *Cain: a Mystery*.
Shelley considered Byron's *Cain* 'apocalyptic,' a 'revelation not before
communicated to man.' What was the 'revelation not before communicated,' which he would not be happy, however indirectly, to attribute to
himself? In Byron's drama, Cain, like Shelley's Prometheus, rebels against
the Jehovah-Jupiter conception of God. Guided by Lucifer (Shelley's
archetypal hero), he journeys into a pre-Adamite underworld and into
an empyrean beyond the sun and moon, journeys that the Visionary in
Shelley himself had more than once traversed. As the journey unfolds,
Lucifer suggests to Cain, as indeed he regularly suggested to Shelley,
that death may hold the key to the deepest mysteries that perplex man
in his earthly state. Instead of leading Cain to smash the 'dome of
many-coloured glass' to find the 'white radiance of Eternity' as Shelley
had done in *Adonais*, however, Lucifer's suggestion leads him to return
to the world and murder his brother Abel. The murder of Abel ironically dramatizes the rejection of the familiar world identified with Abel
in favour of an ideal world beyond the limits of man's mortality.

The 'apocalypse' revealed to Shelley in Byron's drama, which some
of Byron's friends attributed to Shelley, lay in Shelley's metaphysical
defence of suicide in the final stanzas of *Adonais* ("Tis Adonais calls! oh,
hasten thither, / No more let life divide what Death can join together'
[476–7]), not as the heroic slaying of himself, but as Cain's murder of his
brother. In the seventeenth stanza of his elegy, Shelley invokes 'the
curse of Cain,' commanding it to 'light on [the] head' of the critic who
'pierced [the] innocent breast' (151–2) of Keats with his savage review

of *Endymion*, a poem Shelley himself disliked, sharing his dislike of it with Byron. As if haunted by 'the curse of Cain,' Shelley in the presence of Urania bared 'his branded and ensanguined brow / Which was like Cain's or Christ's.' 'Oh! that it should be so!' (305–6), Shelley cries as if confronting yet again his fantasized primordial guilt, which could not be appeased. Knowing that this primordial guilt was, despite his protests to the contrary, related to the Christian superstition of original sin, he wondered how it may have influenced Byron. 'Amongst other things,' Shelley wrote in his letter to Horace Smith (11 April 1822) concerning two letters from Thomas Moore that Byron had read to him,

> Moore, after giving Lord B. much good advice about public opinion & c. seems to deprecate *my* influence over his mind on the subject of religion, & to attribute the tone assumed in Cain to my suggestions. – Moore cautions him against my influence on this particular with the most friendly zeal, & it is plain that his motive springs from a desire of benefiting Lord B. without degrading me. – I think you know Moore. – Pray assure him that I have not the smallest influence over Lord Byron in this particular; if I had I certainly should employ it to eradicate from his great mind the delusions of Christianity, which in spite of his reason, seem perpetually to recur, & to lay in ambush for the hours of sickness & distress. Cain was *conceived* many years ago, & begun before I saw him last year at Ravenna; how happy should I not be to attribute to myself, however indirectly, any participation in that immortal work. (*Letters* 2:412)

Shelley appears to regret that the sick 'tone' of Byron's drama might be the sign of Shelley's infecting Byron's writing with the kind of religious contagion branded upon his forehead in *Adonais* as 'the curse of Cain,' the mark that he did not esteem his own poetic powers in the face of Byron's success. However, though he insisted that he had no influence on Byron, in the light of the depth of their psychic communication, it was altogether possible that Byron found in his reading of *Adonais* a darker meaning than Shelley thought was there. 'The demon of mistrust & pride lurks between two persons in our situation poisoning the freedom of our intercourse,' Shelley explained to Mary in a long letter from Ravenna, where he was meeting with Byron in August 1821. 'This is a tax and a heavy one which we must pay for being human – I think the fault is not on my side; nor is it likely, I being the weaker' (*Letters* 2:324). Perhaps in surrendering himself to 'the fire for which all thirst' (485) in *Adonais*, in Byron's view he had annihilated the world, returning it to the 'darkness' so vividly described in Byron's poem on the subject:

> The world was void,
> The populous and the powerful – was a lump
> Seasonless, herbless, treeless, manless, lifeless –
> A lump of death – a chaos of hard clay.   ('Darkness' 69–72)

Byron's considerable influence upon Shelley lay in what his poetry and his life constellated in Shelley: the darkness hidden in his apocalyptic vision, a darkness that, far more than Keats's being 'half in love with easeful Death' ('Ode to a Nightingale' 52), was a profound, not to say obsessive, passion in which the sexual and the spiritual were, as in a witch's brew, treacherously intertwined. The result was that the death-like spectacle of Byron in Venice during the carnival week preceding Lent became the final scene of Shelley's brief poetic career in *The Triumph of Life*, in which the broken intercourse between the ghostly figures of Shelley and Rousseau mirror the 'deathwards progressing / To no death' (*Fall of Hyperion* 260–1) intercourse between Byron and Shelley, an intercourse that found its common ground in their shared fascination with the figure of Rousseau.

In his account of the veiled maid in his Preface to *Alastor*, Shelley describes her much as he experienced St Preux's love of Julie in Rousseau's novel. Having absorbed the 'magnificence and beauty of the external world,' he is 'still insatiate,' and continues to thirst for what he cannot find in nature: 'intercourse with an intelligence similar to itself' (*SPP* 69). This 'intelligence' he projects onto a single image that 'embodies his own imaginations' of the poet, philosopher and lover. He then sets out to find her as Rousseau's St Preux found her in Julie. In his dream vision of her, however, his 'strong heart sunk and sickened with excess / Of love' (*Alastor* 181–2), absorbing both the poet and the philosopher into what Byron prophetically described in his third canto as the 'vitality' of its 'poison,' a 'poison' so 'vital' that, as Shelley describes it, 'blackness veiled his dizzy eyes, and night / Involved and swallowed up the vision' (188–9). His insatiable desire became 'a dark flood suspended in its course' which 'rolled back its impulse on his vacant brain' (190–1). 'Alas! alas!' Shelley's Visionary cries.

> Were limbs, and breath, and being intertwined
> Thus treacherously? Lost, lost, for ever lost,

In the wide pathless desart of dim sleep,
That beautiful shape! Does the dark gate of death
Conduct to thy mysterious paradise,
O Sleep? Does the bright arch of rainbow clouds,
And pendent mountains seen in the calm lake,
Lead only to a black and watery depth,
While death's blue vault, with loathliest vapours hung,
Where every shade which the foul grave exhales
Hides its dead eye from the detested day,
Conduct, O Sleep, to thy delightful realms?
This doubt with sudden tide flowed on his heart,
The insatiate hope which it awakened, stung
His brain even like despair.   (207–22)

This stinging of his brain, characteristic of the poisonous brew that
fed Byron's poetic power, becomes in *Alastor* a 'green serpent,' who
wraps the eagle-poet in his folds, so that the poet

                    feels *her* breast
Burn with the poison, and precipitates
Through night and day, tempest, and calm, and cloud,
Frantic with dizzying anguish, her blind flight
O'er the wide aëry wilderness.   (227–32; italics added)

In the rich perversity of their relations, Shelley would experience Byron
on one level as the serpent enfolding the eagle-poet who 'feels *her*
breast / Burn with the [vitality of his] poison.'

In a very real sense, the writing of *Alastor* prepared the inner way
for Shelley's meeting with Byron the following year, his reading of the
third canto of *Childe Harold's Pilgrimage*, and their sailing together to
the sites made immortal by Rousseau's erotic accounts of them. In his
seemingly endless conversations with Byron on the subject of Rousseau
during the summer of 1816, conversations to which he returns in *The
Triumph of Life*, Shelley was better able to grasp the 'vitality of poison'
that inspired the author of *Childe Harold's Pilgrimage* as it inspired
Rousseau in *Nouvelle Heloïse*. In his final fragment, Shelley himself engages its 'vitality' by drinking its 'poison' to the dregs as if
confronting at last the 'monster' of his thought, much as Actaeon
confronts 'Nature's naked loveliness' (275) in *Adonais* as the pursuing

'raging hounds' (279) that in the end, though not in *Adonais,* devour him. In *The Triumph of Life,* Iris, as 'Nature's naked loveliness,' becomes in her 'severe excess' (424) the 'raging hounds' that are, in their final configuration, the Chariot of Life. '"And still her feet,"' writes Shelley,

> 'no less than that sweet tune
> To which they moved, seemed as they moved, to blot
> The thoughts of him who gazed on them, and soon

'All that was seemed as if it had been not,
> As if the gazer's mind was strewn beneath
Her feet like embers, and she, thought by thought,

> 'Trampled its fires into the dust of death.' (382–8)

The pilgrimage Shelley undertook with Byron led in the end to a darker underworld of death than anything Shelley had previously discovered in his own inner pilgrimage.

In *The Triumph of Life,* the mind's 'separate phantasy' upon which he muses in 'Mont Blanc,' 'as in a trance sublime and strange' (35–6), becomes the 'strange trance' of the Narrator that initially spreads a 'shade' that 'was so transparent that the scene came through / As clear as when a veil of light is drawn / O'er evening hills [so that] they glimmer' (31-3). It is in this mental state that the mind lends its inner light to what is perceived. This inner light allows the 'evening hills' to 'glimmer,' even as Mont Blanc 'gleams.' In other words, 'the power is there, / The still and solemn power of many sights, / And many sounds' (127 9) that constitutes the interpenetration between the 'one mind' and the 'human mind.'

Gradually, however, the transparency in which the 'human mind' serves as a veil for the 'one mind' becomes so opaque that the outer scene can no longer be seen through it. The 'glimmer' now becomes so intense that it is blinding. Mont Blanc is no longer there. The operations of Shelley's conscious mind with its conscious will is overwhelmed by the power of the 'one mind,' which now flows from its 'secret springs / The source of human thought' (4–5) as 'a flood of ruin' (107), that is to say, as the 'Chariot of Life' or Iris's 'severe excess.' Shelley describes himself before his mind is overtaken by this 'strange trance' as lying prostrate, his 'faint limbs' stretched

> beneath the hoary stem
>
> Which an old chestnut flung athwart the steep
> Of a green Apennine: before [him] fled
> The night; behind [him] rose the day; the Deep
>
> Was at [his] feet, and Heaven above [his] head.   (*TL* 24–8)

While, under different circumstances, he might have experienced the day rising behind him as a glorious birth, that day is now well behind him. What he sees is the night fleeing before him. As if ignoring entirely his present situation and entering a moment of glory quite other than the moment he is now in, Shelley begins his poem by describing the sun rising 'swift as a spirit hastening to his task / Of glory and of good' as 'the mask / Of darkness fell from the awakened Earth' (1–4). Psychologically, however, his situation is the very antithesis of what he describes, though what it is the poet cannot tell other than to say he had remained all night 'as wakeful as the stars that gem / The cone of night' brooding on 'thoughts which must remain untold' (21–3). That those 'thoughts' had something to do with Rousseau becomes evident when 'the hoary stem' of 'an old chestnut flung athwart the steep' (beneath which in a similar outstretched position lay his own 'faint limbs') becomes the corpse of Rousseau. Shelley, in the figure of Rousseau, is inhabiting his own corpse.

When Shelley and Byron visited the sites made sacred by Rousseau's accounts in his *Nouvelle Heloïse*, they read aloud the appropriate passages at the sites of their occurrence. So powerful became Shelley's identification with Rousseau that, when their boat almost capsized, Shelley, who could not swim, took considerable satisfaction in the realization that the immediate and actual possibility of his drowning took place, as he explained to Peacock, 'precisely in the spot where [Rousseau's] Julie and her lover were nearly upset and where St Preux was tempted to plunge with her into the lake' (*Letters* 2:498). '"If you can't swim / Beware of Providence"' (*Julian and Maddalo* 117–18), Byron in the guise of Maddalo warned Shelley in the guise of Julian.

So far as Shelley was concerned, however, the 'Providence' that would save Byron because, unlike himself, he was an excellent swimmer (both in his life and in his poetry) could by 1822 no longer save Shelley. Byron's 'Providence' was gained at a cost, which Shelley was unprepared to pay. He would rather drown. 'I do not write,' Shelley wrote to Horace Smith in May 1822 while secretly at work, mainly on the boat in which he drowned, on a poem that dealt with 'thoughts that must remain untold.' Shelley stuffed the folded sheets, some of them half-filled with other matters, into his pockets as if wrapping them in his shroud. 'I have lived too long near Lord Byron & the sun has extinguished the glowworm; for I cannot hope with St. John, that "*the light came into the world, & the world knew it not*"' (*Letters* 2:423). Without the presence of Byron, who in the last months of Shelley's life had almost for a time become a daily presence he felt he had to get away from, Shelley might have been able to say of his poetry what St John had said of the light. But Byron's most recent poetry (the fourth canto of *Don Juan*), which Byron read aloud to Shelley even as he was writing it, virtually paralysed Shelley. His own 'light' was almost eclipsed by what he now considered the 'severe excess' of Byron's. What made matters worse, even intolerable, was the world that did not know that Shelley's 'light' rejoiced in Byron's 'severe excess.' Byron's 'sun,' perhaps referred to in the invocation to the sun in the opening lines of *The Triumph of Life,* had extinguished Shelley's 'glow worm,' much as Byron's most recent volume, which included *Cain: a Mystery,* had by its 'severe excess' extinguished *Prometheus Unbound.* Byron's 1821 volume, Shelley told Gisborne, 'contains finer poetry than has appeared in England since the publication of Paradise Regained' (*Letters* 2:388).

The Narrator in *The Triumph of Life* is Shelley's ghost interrogating, as the 'Shade of Memory,' his own corpse, which now inhabits the vast graveyard that has become, for Shelley, what on some fantasized level it has always been: the world. When one thinks of the images of waves, tides, moon, wind, and clouds as they constellated the passions Shelley and Byron shared, particularly their love of Rousseau, one is impressed by the depth of the darkness that in their relationship they explored together. 'The waves were dead,' Byron concludes his powerful 1816 vision of the end of life on earth,

> the tides were in their grave,
> The moon their mistress had expired before;
> The winds were withered in the stagnant air,
> And the clouds perish'd; Darkness had no need
> Of aid from them – She was the universe.   ('Darkness' 78–82)

While in 'Mont Blanc' the 'shadows that pass by' as the 'ghosts of all things that are' are recalled to their source in the poet's 'separate phantasy' so that they are not allowed, as its projection, to overwhelm the external world by reducing it to a hallucination, in *The Triumph of Life* the projected life of the poet's 'separate phantasy' takes over entirely. Herein, as a 'separate phantasy,' lay, for Byron, the power of Venice as a drowning city celebrating during its annual carnival preceding Lent a dance of death, which was in its own demonic way a parody of the crucifixion. As Byron writes to Thomas Moore on 2 February 1818, 'We are in the agonies of the Carnival's last days, and I must be up all night again, as well as to-morrow. I have had some curious masking adventures this Carnival [including gonorrhea]; but, as they are not yet over, I shall not say on. I will work the mine of my youth to the last veins of the ore, and then – good night. I have lived, and am content' (6.10–11).

In the midst of all this, Byron was busy correcting and revising *Beppo*, in which he describes his life in Venice. 'Didst you ever see a gondola?' Byron asks in *Beppo*. 'It glides along the water looking blackly, / Just like a coffin clapt in a canoe, / Where none can make out what you say or do.' Byron then goes on to describe the gondolas as 'a sable throng' waiting in 'their dusk livery of woe,' though, as he explains, 'not to them do woeful things belong, / For sometimes they contain a deal of fun, / Like mourning coaches when the funeral's done' (145–60). Shelley had Byron's account of the gondola in mind in his description of the Chariot of Life in *The Triumph of Life*, in which dwells a 'Janus-visaged Shadow,'

as one whom years deform

Beneath a dusky hood and double cape
  Crouching within the shadow of a tomb
And o'er what seemed the head a cloud like crape

  Was bent, a dun and faint etherial gloom
Tempering the light.   (88–93)

In his description of Rousseau's Shade as 'an old root which grew / To strange distortion out of the [Apennine] hill side' (182–3), Shelley again appears to have Byron in mind. In the fourth canto of *Childe Harold's Pilgrimage*, Byron writes about the 'upas,' the legendary Javanese tree that, as the 'uneradicable taint of sin,' poisoned the surrounding earth:

This boundless upas, this all-blasting tree,
Whose root is earth, whose leaves and branches be
The skies which rain their plagues on men like dew –
Disease, death, bondage – all the woes we see –
And worse, the woes we see not – which throb through
The immedicable soul, with heart-aches ever new.   (4.1128–34)

Particularly as the 'old root which grew / To strange distortion out of
the hill side' becomes the corpse of Rousseau and, by extension, Shelley's
own, do we see just how 'all-blasting' it is. The hanging wide and white
grass around the root is Rousseau's 'thin discoloured hair,' and 'the
holes it vainly sought to hide / Were or had been [his] eyes' (*TL* 186–8).
In *Adonais*, the 'invisible Corruption' must 'wait[ ] to trace / His ex-
treme way' through the corpse of Keats, which is 'her dim dwelling-
place' (67–8), until Shelley has completed his elegy. Only in the surrender
of his poem to the 'fire for which all thirst' can the 'invisible Corruption'
be disposed of, leaving the spirit free if, that is, the spirit had not been
tamed by 'the Conqueror' (*TL* 129). '"And if the spark with which
Heaven lit my spirit / Earth had with purer nutriment supplied,"' the
Shadow of Rousseau explains to Shelley, '"Corruption would not now
thus much inherit / Of what was once Rousseau – nor this disguise /
Stain that within which still disdains to wear It"' (201–5).

Shelley is here suggesting that Rousseau's apparitional form is a
'disguise' staining 'that within' that 'disdains' the 'disguise.' Though he
is physically dead, he is, unlike Keats in *Adonais*, still not fully awake.
He is, rather, suspended between sleep and waking, his soul still hover-
ing about his corpse awaiting the kind of burial Shelley provided Keats
in *Adonais*: a cremation whose fire is his resurrection. 'Peace, peace! he
is not dead, he doth not sleep – ,' declares Shelley of Keats in *Adonais*:

He hath awakened from the dream of life –
'Tis we, who lost in stormy visions, keep
With phantoms an unprofitable strife,
And in mad trance, strike with our spirit's knife
Invulnerable nothings. – *We* decay
Like corpses in a charnel ...   (343–9)

The Triumph of Life as it stands is the 'separate phantasy' that constitutes,
as nightmare, his 'dream of life.' This nightmare had haunted him

throughout his brief poetic career as an 'unprofitable strife' with 'phantoms.' Though he had done his best to exorcise those 'phantoms,' he knew in his rational consciousness that his 'spirit's knife' was striking 'invulnerable nothings.' Yet they continued to plague him, even as they continued to plague Byron. Unlike Shelley, however, Byron could play profitably with them. He knew how to exploit the 'vitality' of their 'poison.' Thus, having confronted the 'all-blasting' upas tree, which poisons the earth in which it grows, Byron deliberately exploits it by planting his poetry in the same poisoned soil. 'Yet let us ponder boldly,' he continues his meditation on the poison tree that constitutes the 'false nature' that is 'our life,'

>   – 'tis a base
> Abandonment of reason to resign
> Our right of thought – our last and only place
> Of refuge; this, at least, shall still be mine:
> Though from our birth the faculty divine
> Is chain'd and tortured – cabin'd, cribb'd, confined,
> And bred in darkness, lest the truth should shine
> Too brightly on the unprepared mind,
> The beam pours in, for time and skill will couch the blind.
>
>   (*Childe* 4.1135–43)

The 'revelation not before communicated to man' in *Cain* is the realization that poetry and the other arts, far from being an imitation of nature, are, as Jung realized, an *opus contra naturam*. Satan is the 'unacknowledged' hero of Milton's *Paradise Lost* because he rebels against Milton's natural religion (creator, creation, and creature) and replaces it with a 'false nature' which, like Byron's Prometheus, is 'triumphant where it dares defy' ('Prometheus' 59). Byron thus goes on to compare the 'mind in creation' to yet another tree, which may be the one Shelley is stretched out on (as): the Swiss tannen, a species of Alpine fir. Without the apparent support of any soil ('Rooted in barrenness' [*Childe* 4.174]), it nevertheless grows taller than any other species of fir in Switzerland as if to 'mock[ ] / The howling tempest' (76–7). Thus, 'the mind may grow the same' (180). In the fourth canto of *Childe Harold's Pilgrimage*, Byron came out from under the veil of Childe Harold, abandoned the very notion of a 'Pilgrimage,' and, as he explained in the 'Dedication' (to Hobhouse), spoke 'in his own person' (*Major Works* 146).

Reading the fourth canto, Shelley was persuaded again that Byron was mocking his idealism. '"You talk Utopia"' (179), Maddalo tells Julian, while at the same time pointing out that Julian '"were ever still / Among Christ's flock a perilous infidel, / A wolf for the meek lambs"' (115–17). Byron was equally persuaded that, if he mocked Shelley's idealism, Shelley, in turn, mocked 'the corse beneath' (*Adonais* 17) in his poetry by adorning it with flowers in order to hide it. 'The spirit in which it is written,' Shelley writes to Peacock of Byron's fourth canto, 'is, if insane, the most wicked & mischievous insanity that ever was given forth. It is a kind of obstinate & self-willed folly in which he hardens himself' (*Letters* 2:58). Shelley then continues (he had just completed the first act of *Prometheus Unbound*, which he had originally recommended to Byron as a project worthy of his powers):

> I remonstrated with him in vain on the tone of mind from which such a view of things alone arises. For its real root is very different from its apparent one, & nothing can be less sublime than the true source of these expressions of contempt & desperation. The fact is, that first, the Italian women with whom he associates are perhaps the most contemptible of all who exist under the moon; the most ignorant the most disgusting, the most bigoted ... Well, L.B. is familiar with the lowest sort of these women, the people his gondoliera pick up in the streets ... He associates with wretches who seem almost to have lost the gait & physiognomy of man, & who do not scruple to avow practices which are not only not named but I believe seldom conceived in England. (2:58)

Over against Byron at one pole, Shelley was tempted to locate the 'sacred few who could not tame / Their spirits to the Conquerors' (128–9). By 1822, however, this polarization no longer worked. When Byron read aloud to him the fourth canto of *Don Juan*, he wrote to Mary telling her it was 'astonishingly fine.' 'It sets him not above but far above all the poets of the day: every word has the stamp of immortality' (*Letters* 2:323). Indeed, the greatness of what Byron read to him, not surprisingly, caused him some despair, among other things having just confronted in himself the delusory nature of his own erotic history as described in *Epipsychidion* ('The Epipsychidion is a mystery – As to real flesh & blood, you know I do not deal in those articles, – you might as well go to a ginshop for a leg of mutton, as expect anything human or earthly from me' [363]). His attempt at another lyrical drama, *Hellas*, perhaps written with Byron's success in mind, was an improvisation 'upon the contest now raging in Greece' (a contest destined to cost Byron his life), which did not satisfy him. 'I try to be what I might have been, but am not very successfull [sic]' (364), he wrote to Gisborne on 22 October 1821. 'I despair of rivalling Lord Byron,' Shelley writes in an earlier letter, 'as well I may: and there is no other with whom it is worth contending. This canto is in the style, but totally, & sustained with incredible ease & power, like the end of the second canto: there is not a word which the most rigid asserter of the dignity of human nature could desire to be cancelled: it fulfils in a certain degree what I have long preached of producing something wholly new & relative to the age and yet surpassingly beautiful. It may be vanity, but I think I see the trace of my earnest exhortations to him to create something wholly new.' (2:323).

Shelley, it would appear, was no longer struggling to rival Byron. In *Adonais*, he had put all such striving behind him. Byron as 'the Pythian of the age' had no need, in *Don Juan*, to slay further dragons or preside over the death of European civilization. He was now a true Apollo, whose stance was Olympian in a 'wholly new' way. He had become a genuine *spectator ab extra*. In the figure of Don Juan he had created for himself a new kind of hero who was essentially disengaged in whatever appeared to engage him, free, therefore, to involve himself in a world from which he remained in the ultimate sense detached. What was 'wholly new' was the absence of the kind of metaphysics that might have bound him, as Shelley was bound, to a reality he would have to expend his intellectual energy deconstructing so as not to be bound by it. He was, in this sense, free even of the traps the mind sets for itself in coming to terms with its own operations. In *Don Juan* Byron had created something 'wholly new' by remaining detached from it, even while engaged in it. In this radical way, he remained in a 'void' or 'intense inane' beyond the circumference of what he was writing. In *Adonais* Shelley had to burn all his bridges to reach this 'void,' while at the same time the 'void' itself lingered in the *mythos* of its becoming. Byron was free of the poem he was endlessly composing in a manner that allowed him to go on composing to no end, like the Adonai of *Adonais*, who remains forever outside the creation even as he creates it. Byron had done what Shelley had set out to do without, in the doing of it, cancelling what he had done. *Don Juan*, which rhymes with ruin, was never in danger of coming to an end because there was no longer an end to come to. 'Thus far our chronicle; and now we pause,' Byron concludes his fifth canto,

    Though not for want of matter; but 'tis time,
    According to the ancient epic laws,
       To slacken sail, and anchor with our rhyme.
    Let this fifth canto meet with due applause,
       The sixth shall have a touch of the sublime;
    Meanwhile, as Homer sometimes sleeps, perhaps
    You'll pardon to my muse a few short naps.   (5.1265–72)

Abandoning metaphors as 'figures ever new' rising on the bubble of consciousness, Shelley turned the discovery of new metaphors over to Byron, who was no longer trapped in them and, by virtue of his freedom, could act in *Don Juan* as if he were always already dead. '[Shelley] was once with me in a Gale of Wind in a small boat right under the rocks between Meillerie & St. Gingo,' Byron wrote to his publisher, John Murray. 'The Sail was mismanaged & the boat was filling fast – he can't swim. – I stripped off my coat – made him strip off his – & took hold of the oar – telling him that I thought (being myself an expert swimmer) I could save him if he would not struggle when I took hold of him ... He answered me with the greatest coolness – "that he had no notion of being saved – & that I would have enough to do to save myself, and begged not to trouble me" (*Letters* 6.126).

The Triumph of Life is a 'separate phantasy' composed in a 'trance sublime and strange,' which deals with 'thoughts that must remain untold.' In the form of a 'dark conceit,' the 'trance' nevertheless reveals (as distinct from tells) its own mystery in something of the same way that the madman (Tasso) in *Julian and Maddalo* reveals himself to Shelley while remaining merely mad to Byron: 'The colours of his mind seemed yet unworn; / For the wild language of his grief was high, / Such as in measure were called poetry' (539–41). In *The Triumph of Life*, the 'colours' of Shelley's mind are not only 'unworn'; they have never been more richly textured. The 'language of his grief' is higher than any poem he ever wrote because it remains, like the language of *Don Juan*, detached from a personal involvement in grief that overshoots its transpersonal target: Shelley, the man, struggling to transcend the language of poetry's limits. In *The Triumph of Life,* the rhetoric is answerable to itself, content to remain within the boundaries of its acknowledged limitations. It does not strain beyond what it is. The highly structured, interlocking *terza rima* in no sense imposes restrictions upon what it contains. On the contrary, it mirrors it in such a way that it becomes identical to it, the content being the form it takes. In this astonishingly conscious way, the poem is artifice entire, Byron's 'false nature,' an *opus contra naturam*, that is to say, culture itself understood as the fundamental human break with nature, not in order to transcend it as if struggling against it, but simply in order to be itself. The poem as it stands enacts the death of the body of nature, which requires no elegy because elegy would only return the imagination to it as a struggle to transcend it. No such dialectic is operative in *The Triumph of Life* as it is in *Adonais*. It inhabits its own madness as the sanity that informs it. The poem breaks off in the unfinished gesture of its folding back upon itself as if to remind the reader where, in fact, the poem does reside and what it means to turn a leaf not looking for something yet to come, but to discover what, as poetry, is always already there.

The poem breaking off with the preposition 'of' is perhaps the lesson about the 'mind in creation' that Shelley learned from listening to Byron read aloud an as yet unpublished canto: the 'mind in creation' inhabits a now that is unending. As Lacan did in his work with his analysands, it is sometimes necessary to get up and leave to recall them to the now they are always already in. Madness, then, is the now of the 'Cogito' that narrative helps us, in the ongoing cause of sanity, to forget. Suddenly to be confronted by a narrative that keeps forgetting that it is a narrative, which, subject to the dancing feet of Iris, keeps extinguishing itself in every step it takes, is to be confronted by a pre-positioning that, standing alone, positions only itself. This pre-positioning, when acknowledged, is the sanity that madness contains awaiting the kind of acknowledgment *The Triumph of Life* supremely provides. Insofar as the dialectic of narrativization (*mythos*) tranquillizes the madness it contains (the now of conception in which 'the Poets Work is Done'), it avoids the truth that propels it. Poetry is the sanity of madness. Jung knew this. For this reason, until he had restored dialectic to the madness that is its unconscious source, the dialectic governing the life of the psyche was devoid of the meaning he sought to release. When Lear cries 'O, let me not be mad, not mad, sweet heaven!' (1.5.49), he does not realize, as Shakespeare does, that he must be mad if he is ever to be sane. Lear's madness, that is, lies in a project that 'exceeds all that is real, factual, and existent,' a project that 'acknowledges madness as its liberty and its very possibility.'

Conclusion

The Dream of Reason Produces Monsters

Goya, *Los Caprichos*

According to Shelley, while the dialectical materialism of modern science has 'enlarged the limits of the empire of man over the external world,' it has also, 'for want of the poetical faculty, proportionally circumscribed those of the internal world,' so that 'man, having enslaved the elements, remains himself a slave' (*DP* 502–3). Blake makes the same point. 'The Great Vintage & Harvest is now upon Earth,' Los declares,

> The whole extent of the Globe is explored: Every scatterd Atom
> Of Human Intellect now is flocking to the sound of the Trumpet
> All the Wisdom which was hidden in caves & dens, from ancient
> Time; is now sought out from Animal & Vegetable & Mineral
> The Awakener is come. outstretchd over Europe! the Vision of God is
>   fulfilled
> The Ancient Man upon the Rock of Albion Awakes.   (*M* 25[27].16–22)

In Blake's apocalyptic vision, the counterpart of Shelley's bound Prometheus is the 'Ancient Man upon the Rock of Albion.' Blake's 'Ancient Man,' Wordsworth's 'first men, earth's first inhabitants' (*P* 3.154), lies asleep in the dreaming realm of the collective unconscious until he is awakened at the Judgment by what he calls in *Europe* 'the enormous blast' of Newton's 'Trump' (13.5). As the immutable law of gravity, Newton's giant intellect gathered together 'every scatterd Atom' of human perception at the limit of its 'Contraction' (*M* 13[14].20). In *Europe*, the soul, physically reduced to 'a portion' of itself 'discernd by the five Senses,' displays its material 'portion' in a wild revelry 'beneath the solemn moon' (14.31) over which Enitharmon presides, much as the dancing feet of Iris in Shelley's *Triumph of Life* trample the fires of the intellect 'into the dust of death.' For Blake, this dance of death is the Orc-Urizen cycle. Orc is the 'Sexual' offspring of Los and Enitharmon who presides over the revolutionary phase of the natural cycle before it is devoured by its own instinctual energy.

> But terrible Orc, when he beheld the morning in the east,
> Shot from the heights of Enitharmon;
> And in the vineyards of red France appear'd the light of his fury.
>
> The sun glow'd fiery red!
> The furious terrors flew around!
> On golden chariots raging, with red wheels dropping with blood;
> The Lions lash their wrathful tails!
> The Tigers couch upon the prey & suck the ruddy tide;
> And Enitharmon groans & cries in anguish and dismay.
>
> Then Los arose his head he reard in snaky thunders clad:
> And with a cry that shook all nature to the utmost pole,
> Call'd all his sons to the strife of blood.   (*Europe* 14.37, 15.1–11)

Shelley deals with the revolutionary 'strife of blood' in his long narrative poem, *The Revolt of Islam*. Here, however, the entire material struggle is viewed within a transcendental framework of the spirit. Returning in *Hellas* to this same 'strife of blood,' Shelley again views it within a transcendental framework. Describing destiny as the 'eyeless charioteer' of *The Triumph of Life*, Shelley in the figure of Ahasuerus, who is raised by thought beyond the reach of power, calls upon the Turkish tyrant Mahmud to 'talk no more / Of thee and me, the future and the past' (*Hellas* 767). They are nothing more than the 'motes of a sick eye, bubbles and dreams' (781). He should look instead 'on that which cannot change – the One, / The unborn and the undying' (768–9). Unlike Shelley's, Blake's poetic vision dialectically confronts, rather than abandons, the psychosis of history.

Throughout this study, the creative role of the imagination in the advancement of consciousness has been examined in terms of its intimate association with madness. Far from viewing the Age of Reason as

the rational triumph of human consciousness over the irrational operations of the mythopoeic imagination, Blake and Shelley identified the
Age of Reason with psychosis and the mythopoeic imagination with the
triumph of sanity. Blake's Urizen and Shelley's Jupiter archetypally
embody the psychosis of history. The psychosis resides in the reduction
of the soul to the condition of matter in which 'every scatterd atom / Of
Human Intellect,' far from 'flocking to the sound of the Trumpet,' falls,
as in *The Triumph of Life*, 'thro' wintry skies seeking their graves; /
Rattling their hollow bones in howling and lamentation' (*Europe* 13:7–
8). Thus, Shelley's bound Prometheus embraces this empire of living
death (Coleridge's 'Nightmare LIFE-IN-DEATH' who 'thicks man's
blood with cold') as superior to Jupiter's 'unenvied throne' (*PU* 1.17)
because Prometheus's 'three thousand years of sleep-unsheltered hours /
And moments' (12–13) constitute his consciousness of Jupiter's delusional reign. Jupiter as a 'Mighty God,' he declares, would become
'Almighty' if, abandoning the sanity of his own pain, he 'deigned to
share the shame / of [Jupiter's] ill tyranny,' rather than remain '[nailed]
to this wall of eagle-baffling mountain, / Black, wintry, dead, unmea-
sured; without herb, / Insect, or beast, or shape or sound of life' (18–22).
The reality of Jupiter's reign is the total absence of life as other than a
psychotic delusion, which, as Satan's empire, Blake describes as the
'Void Outside of Existence.' Psychosis, as explored in this study, is
the soul cut off from its human reality constructing in the void some
delusory form of it over which Shelley's Jupiter, like Blake's Urizen,
presides. As distinct from psychosis, madness, understood as Plato's
'divine madness,' is the creative power of psychosis when it is dialectically processed by the imagination. This processing is best enacted by
Blake as the sanity of madness. In Shelley, it becomes, as the madness of
sanity, the victim of its own dialectical operations.

For Blake and Shelley, Wordsworth's betrayal of the 'poetic faculty'
lay in his failure creatively to absorb into its visionary dialectic the
Terror of the French Revolution. In Wordsworth's case, the terror
demonically mirrored as psychosis the imagination, whose terrors he
found in Coleridge's poetry and sought to exorcize in addressing *The
Prelude* to him. 'Through months, through years, long after the last
beat / Of those atrocities' (*P* 10.398–9), Wordsworth experienced the
nightmare of the Terror in France as, like Blake's *Songs of Experience*,
the demonic parody of 'the innocent authority' of childhood, which
contains within it 'the first / Poetic spirit of our human life' (*P* 2.260–1).
That is, he compares the 'heinous appetites' of the Jacobins to the

'light desires of innocent little ones.' The Jacobins, he writes, 'proudly, eager as a child,' were not content with the gentle motion of a 'toy that mimics with revolving wings / The motion of a wind-mill.' They found their joy in holding their 'plaything at arm's length' and, fronting 'against the blast,' running amain 'that it may whirl the faster' (10.363–73). They forgot, Wordsworth explains, 'that such a sound [a 'gentle motion' rather than mighty 'blast'] was ever heard / As liberty upon earth' (377–8).

Wordsworth's unconscious association, which he identifies with his consciousness of 'some other Being,' is with the 'gentle breeze' invoked as the 'sweet breath of heaven' in the opening lines of The Prelude. Released from 'natural piety' the 'gentle breeze' becomes in Wordsworth's mind 'a tempest, a redundant energy, / Vexing its own creation.' Unconsciously identifying (associating) the Terror in France with this 'redundant energy' that, as a poet of nature, he sought to repress, Wordsworth's 'redundant energy' nightly became in dream 'a voice / Labouring, a brain confounded,' pleading before 'unjust tribunals.' Awakening from the recurring nightmare, he was haunted by 'a sense, / Death-like, of treacherous desertion, felt / In the last place of refuge – [his] own soul.' Instead of, like Coleridge, exploring in the Romantic depths of the unconscious the writhing torments of his own repressed creative energy, Wordsworth consciously clung to what Keats described as the 'egotistical sublime,' Wordsworth imaging himself as 'Adam, yet in Paradise, / Though fallen from bliss' (P 8.659–60). Wordsworth's consciousness assured him that he was as 'far as angels are from guilt.' He rationalized the unconfronted terrors of Orc within himself as 'juvenile errors' (11.54). In this way, he cut himself off from the dialectical, 'Soul-making' life of the imagination. By thus rationalizing the psychotic episode within which the imagination announces itself, Wordsworth made for his imagination 'a well-wrought urn,' described by Paul de Man as 'the endless prosopopoeia by which the dead are made to have a face and a voice which tells the allegory of their demise and allows us to apostrophize them in our turn.' 'Thus having been, that thou shouldst cease to be,' Shelley concluded his sonnet 'To Wordsworth' after reading The Excursion. 'I see in Wordsworth the Natural Man rising up against the Spiritual Man Continually & then he is No Poet but a Heathen Philosopher at Enmity against all true Poetry or Inspiration,' Blake concluded after reading Wordsworth's 'Poems Referring to the Period of Childhood.'

Significantly, in Alastor Shelley enacted in his account of Wordsworth's death as a poet his fear of his own death. This death, as Shelley describes it in his preface to *Alastor*, resides in the failure to find in the operations of external nature what he calls 'an intelligence similiar to' the operations of his own poetic mind upon which the mythopoeic imagination depends. He became, as a result, the victim of his own 'feigning,' possessed by a narcissism that finally enfolded him in its demonic arms. The pursuit of an objective other mirroring his own creativity as the affirmation of it was nothing more than the constellation of a spell by which he perpetually reassumed an empire over the disentangling doom from which it arose and into which it dissolved. What remains in the self-cancelling *mythos* of Shelley's final fragment is 'a Sea profound, of ever-spreading sound' into which, 'like one in slumber bound,' Shelley, as the most musical of Romantic mourners, 'float[ed] down, around' (*PU* 2.5.82–4), the *terza rima* framing an oblivion that could not entirely hide or encompass its psychosis.

This study of madness, as it descends into psychosis in order creatively to shape the inchoate energy psychosis contains as its hidden treasure, found in the archetypal psychology of Jung, a theoretical model within which to explore the complex achievement of the Romantics, which includes rather than excludes their failures. Jung discovered the archetypal unconscious in his experimental work first with schizophrenics at the Burghölzli and then, following his psychotic break with Freud, in his experimental work with what he describes as 'an incessant stream of fantasies' issuing from what he would later call the collective unconscious. Doing his best 'not to lose [his] head,' he sought 'to find some way to understand' them. As it evolved, this understanding led to the recognition of a dialectic at work, arising not out of the operations of the unconscious alone but out of the indissoluble bonding of those operations with the observer of them, neither one of which is independent of the other. In this dialectic, he concluded, lay the gradual expansion of a distinctly human consciousness that, as an *opus contra naturam*, constitutes the making of a ceaselessly unfolding human world as what he called a *complexio oppositorum*, the 'true Friendship' that, for Blake, resides in 'Opposition,' 'Opposition' remaining the condition of a Fourfold consciousness.

In the mythopoeic achievement of the Romantics, bound as it is to its historical limitations, dwells, I suggest, the birth of a modern consciousness that the twenty-first century must finally learn to inhabit if human life is to continue, not without God, but with a conscious understanding of the human, mythopoeic garment that Blake's Enitharmon, as the

Emanation of Los, wove for his androgynous descent. This garment should be distinguished from the metaphysical one woven by Coleridge that, as rotting rags, becomes the garment that Wordsworth adopted. Equally, it must be distinguished from the garment that Shelley knew he could not wear even as he wove it. As for Byron, the mock apparel of a Venetian carnival was a garment that required a display of wit that both set him apart from his contemporaries and, at the same time, painfully exposed as fictions, if not delusions, what many of them were logocentrically persuaded to affirm. As for Keats, whom Shelley considered the youngest and the last of the Romantics, he, perhaps more than any of his contemporaries, positively confronted in the 'Grand march of Intellect' (*KL* 96) the ever-advancing obsolescence of the gods, who had now, as gods, to 'die into [human] life' (*Hyperion* 3.130) if, as psychology ('Soul-making'), they were to survive. The burden of divinity falling upon the human imagination in his two attempts at *Hyperion* enacts, as it does for Blake, what Keats calls 'the struggle at the gate of death' (3.126), which, in *The Fall of Hyperion*, he enacts as his own. The poetic extinction enacted by Keats is very different from the one Shelley imposed upon him in *Adonais*. *Hyperion* breaks off with Apollo shrieking in pain as his 'limbs / Celestial' (135–6) fall away to be replaced with Keats's tubercular ones.

As a transformative power of healing, the 'celestial' at work in a tubercular human body (Shelley's 'contagion of the world's slow stain') is perhaps the image of Romanticism in its nineteenth-century historical setting that best describes what Shelley in his *Defence of Poetry* calls its vision of 'futurity' casting 'gigantic shadows' upon the painful 'present' (508). Certainly, this image is alive and fully operative in Coleridge's account of the 'truths of all others the most awful and mysterious ... [lying] bed-ridden in the dormitory of the soul, side by side, with the most despised and exploded errors' (*BL* 2.82). The transformative power of the imagination resides in waking the sleeping soul upon Blake's 'Couch of Death' by what Coleridge calls 'that freshness of sensation [vital metaphors] which is the constant accompaniment of mental, no less than bodily, convalescence' (2.81). For this convalescence to progress, however, the diagnosis of what Keats describes as the soul's 'immortal sickness ... deathwards progressing / To no death' (*Fall of Hyperion* 1.260–1) had first to be more fully understood in its larger cultural context, perhaps best understood, at least in this study, in terms of Jung's notion of the collective unconscious.

The unconscious as Jung described it in his 'misprisioning' opposition to Freud is an autonomous realm from which consciousness emerges, rather than a realm whose content consists of what consciousness rejects. What, for Jung, is in the unconscious never in itself becomes conscious. As consciousness, the unconscious assumes the appearance or likeness of itself, a likeness that, as other than itself, is the fictional form of itself by which it is represented. The realm of consciousness is a fictional realm, a psychic reality, which remains forever answerable to the larger reality of an unconscious realm that in itself is unknowable.

Like Plato before him, Jung identified this unknowable reality with the archetypes that, as the phenomenal realm of images, assume a likeness of themselves. Also like Plato, Jung was careful to distinguish the images from the archetypes themselves, the distinction becoming the very ground of his psychology of the image understood as the symbol of an unknown archetype. Those who are not trained in the dialectic that conducts to the essential distinction between the noumenal realm of the archetypes and the phenomenal appearance of them (Jung's depth analysis providing a dialectical training) are likely, Jung argued, in this materialistic age to live out their lives in the dark cave of the five senses that they take to be real.

This realm of illusion, empirically embraced as reality, is, for Jung, the materialism that science asserts. Jung broke with Freud because Freud's psychology was in his view not only bound to matter, but dogmatically bound to a point of opaqueness in which the real, in itself unknowable, had no way of making its presence felt as other than a delusion. The violence of Jung's break with Freud (Freud was convinced that Jung was unconsciously determined to kill him), was not an act of conscious volition; it was an act over which he had no conscious control. It was, in his understanding of it, an archetypal event whose source was the collective unconscious compelling Jung to defend human culture against Freud's psychosexual reduction of it to a farce. Jung attributed this archetypal action of the collective unconscious to what he called his 'No. 2 personality,' which, as the 'daemon of creativity,' ruthlessly had its way with him throughout most of his life. Jung quotes Hölderlin, whose insanity, like Nietzsche's, he had reason enough to fear:

'Shamefully
A power wrests away the heart from us,
For the Heavenly Ones each demand sacrifice;
But if it should be withheld,
Never has that led to good.'   (MDR 357)

Driven by his 'daemon of creativity,' Jung was unable or unprepared to trace in Freud's later progress the transformation of what Jung early (prematurely) rejected as 'farce' into the tragedy it became for Freud.

Though, according to Donald Winnicott, Jung in his childhood showed every sign of what Winnicott diagnosed as 'childhood schizophrenia,' it was apparent to Winnicott, after reading *Memories, Dreams, Reflections*, that Jung, though 'at a price,' had managed to heal himself by what he rather dismissively describes as the strength of Jung's personality. On the contrary, the healing lay for Jung in a collective, rather than personal, view of the unconscious as the archetypal ground of human experience, which the scientific spirit of the age had reduced to the physical senses to which Freud remained bound. For Freud, Jung's archetypal notion of the unconscious was grounded, not in science as a source of truth, but in the occult as a still lingering source of superstition. Jung's unconscious eruption when, in conversation with Freud, Freud dismissed 'precognition' and 'parapsychology' as 'nonsensical' (*MDR* 155) was collective rather than personal. It was directed, not at the person of Freud, but at the materialistic spirit of the age, which his theory of the unconscious embodied. In 1900, well before he met Freud or became acquainted with (and briefly converted to) his ideas, Jung wrote his inaugural dissertation for his medical degree at the University of Zurich, 'The Psychology and Pathology of So-Called Occult Phenomena,' which was destined to play a decisive role in the later development of his psychology, particularly with reference to his notion of the collective unconscious. Observing and analysing the mediumistic powers of his cousin, aged fifteen and a half, in a series of seances, he was later psychologically able to describe, particularly in witnessing her later mature development up to the age of twenty-four (she died of tuberculosis at the age of twenty-six, having regressed at the end to the level of a two-year-old) 'how a No. 2 personality is formed, how it enters into a child's consciousness and finally integrates into itself' (*MDR* 107). This process – the shaping of a No. 2 personality – became the hypothetical framework for his experimental work with schizophrenics at the Burghölzli. As Jung understood it in the confirming context of the analysis of his own childhood, the No. 2 archetypal personality first enters a child's mythopoeic consciousness (Wordsworth's six-year-old 'Mighty Prophet! Seer blest!') before it integrates into itself as a separate personality that, as Wordsworth describes it, is 'in most, abated or suppressed.' In some few, however, as what Wordsworth calls 'the first / Poetic spirit of our human life,' it remains 'through every change of growth and of decay, / Pre-eminent till death' (*P* 2.260–5). Jung argues, however, that for this pre-eminence to occur, the ego must be strong enough to surrender to what he calls the 'higher will' of the collective unconscious in its conscious, though secondary, participation in the shaping of the No. 2 personality. The recognition of the essential relationship between ego and archetype if sanity is to be fluidly rather than rigidly sustained lay, for Jung, in coming to grips with the psychotic episode that followed his break with Freud. The Romantic alignment between madness and genius in which 'the No. 2 personality' emerges from the dialectical encounter with madness is writ large in the work of Jung.

For Jung, because schizophrenia results from a radical impairment of the ego, amounting to trauma, it is wrong to diagnose the almost unconscious state of a child whose ego is not yet shaped into an identity as schizophrenic. The essentially egoless infant, as Wordsworth recognized, inhabits as its natural state an archetypal world, rather than a 'common' one. Therefore, when Jung, as the unconsciously triangulated child of his father's false self and of an 'uncanny' mother whose ego was temporarily shattered, is diagnosed as schizophrenic, the Winnicottian diagnosis is erroneously grounded in a Freudian view of the unconscious that is alien to Jung's. For Jung, as for Wordsworth and his fellow Romantics, the child who inhabits an archetypal world not yet abated, suppressed, or shaped by the ego is simply the child of nature understood as 'the first / Poetic spirit of our common life.' The trauma of the natural child in Jung's case lay less in the temporary loss of the mother assigned to a mental hospital than in the unconscious, numinous presence of the archetypal mother, at once 'prodigious and unthinkable,' which was partly constellated by his biological mother's absence. Again, it lay less in the unconscious presence of his father's false self than in the unconscious presence of the archetypal Father who was equally 'prodigious and unthinkable.' It lay, that is, in the unconscious presence of what Jung at the end of his life described as 'a *kosmogonos*, a creator and father-mother of all higher consciousness' (*MDR* 353). This '*kosmogonos*,' the natural birthright of every newborn infant, is the apocalyptic reality that, as the 'Four,' is the archetypal ground of all life that Blake celebrates in *Jerusalem*, his entire dialectic, like that of Jung's 150 years later, acting as the 2,000-year process of its becoming. Therefore, when Winnicott dismisses Jung's symbolic treatment of the fourfold mandala during a crucial stage of Jung's analytical investigation of the dynamics of psychic growth as what Winnicott calls 'a blind alley,' a 'defensive construct,' a 'relatively useless concept' (491), he ignores entirely the dialectic in which it is engaged. Winnicott fails to grasp the essential role of the archetypal unconscious in its opposition to dialectical materialism as the spirit of the age to which Freud, in the name of Thanatos, remained darkly, if tragically, committed.

Jung's unconscious bodily outburst against Freud's dismissal of his 'so-called' occult interests was an archetypal rejection of what Jung considered a set of delusional prejudices that, as the *deus absconditus*, became for Freud the sexual libido. Freud embraced this material hypothesis as what Jung calls 'the new numinous principle' in which the operations of the psyche are reduced to the operations of matter. Releasing himself from Freud's Oedipal theory (matter as Mater) as a biological binding to the physical parents that only Thanatos can resolve by returning the psyche to its originating inorganic state, Jung in his archetypal theory symbolically explored a triangulated childhood in terms of the psyche's inherent struggle to release itself from the materialistic spirit of the age. Milton, according to Blake, mythopoeically announced this spirit of the age in his Newtonian vision of creation in *Paradise Lost*, a vision against which, in the figure of Satan, Milton's 'first / Poetic spirit of our common life' unconsciously rebelled. What Blake saw in his reading of *Paradise Lost* Jung saw in the sexual psychology of Freud: the operations of a dialectical materialism that, as a *'deus absconditus,'* he embraced, in opposition to his 'Poetic spirit,' as 'scientifically irreproachable' (*MDR* 151). The collapse of the Threefold Sexual into a Newtonian nightmare (gravity as the soul's limit of 'Contraction') prophetically announced for Blake the emergence of the Fourfold Human. As Palamabron, Blake in the Preludium to *Milton* calls down 'a Great Solemn Assembly, / That he who will not defend Truth, may be compelled to / Defend a Lie, that he may be snared & caught & taken' (*M* 8.46–8).

The dialectical movement from Three to Four in Blake's vision became, in Jung's work with Pauli, the same dialectical movement now understood in terms of the role of the unconscious psyche as it synchronistically influences the subatomic motions of matter in quantum physics. Writing to Pauli, Jung describes their work together (the unconscious ground of physics that Newton rejected, which had now become the cornerstone of quantum mechanics) as 'the same 2,000– year-old one: How does one get from Three to Four?' Asked in the language of Blake, as it becomes the psychological language of Jung, the question becomes 'How does one get from the "Sexual" to the "Human?"' For Blake, this quaternity, shaping in what Shelley describes as the alchemy of the imagination, is the Fourfold Jerusalem, 'the bound or outward circumference of Energy' within which the dialectic of its becoming is, in Blake's poetry, mythopoeically enacted. Like Blake before them, Jung and Pauli were working towards the self-knowledge that resides in the union of soma and psyche, which is, for Blake, the sexual or married land of Beulah that inspires the poet's song. From this Threefold world, whose recovery is enacted in Blake's *Milton*, dialectically emerges a Fourfold, which is the subject of *Jerusalem*, *Milton* announcing in its final plate the imagination's constellated readiness for it: the 'Wine-presses & Barns stand open; the Ovens are prepar'd / The Waggons ready' (42[49].37–8). 'From this (third) stage of the [alchemical] opus,' Jung writes to Pauli, 'there emerges ... the *Unus Mundus*, the *one* world' as the circumference of psychic energy that Jung describes in terms of Plato's archetypes as 'a Platonic prior or primeval world that is also the future of the *eternal world*' (*Atom* 129). Blake, in *Jerusalem*, images the 'future of the *eternal world*' as Albion stretching his hand 'into Infinitude,' grasping his Fourfold 'Bow,' drawing it back and releasing 'an Arrow flaming from his Quiver,' which, 'loud sounding' flies flaming 'Fourfold' through 'the wide Heavens' (J 97.6–17, 98.1–3). Jung, equally dramatically, announces the Fourfold to Freud, when, his 'diaphragm ... becoming red-hot – a glowing vault,' it fires 'a loud report' into Freud's bookcase. When Freud dismisses it as '"sheer bosh"' (*MDR* 155), Jung's diaphragm fires again. In Pauli's case, he viewed with considerable fear and awe the materialization of his mathematical labours in the explosion of the first atomic bomb.

'The psychic intensities and their graduated differences point to quantitative processes which are inaccessible to direct observation and measurement,' writes Jung in 'On the Nature of the Psyche,' explaining what appeared to Freud to be 'sheer bosh.' 'While psychological data,' he continues, 'are essentially qualitative, they also have a sort of latent physical energy, since psychic phenomena exhibit a certain quantitative aspect ... as having motion in space, something to which the energy formula would be applicable. Therefore since mass and energy are of the same nature, mass and velocity would be adequate concepts for characterizing the psyche so far as it has any observable effects in space: in other words, it must have an aspect under which it would appear as mass in motion' (*CW* 8:441). Physics, that is, is the conscious body; as conscious, it is, for Jung, the Soul-body (or what the alchemists call the 'subtle body'). Milton's journey through the body of Blake, it would thus appear, anticipates the quantum physics Jung and Pauli explored together. Blake's journey from the Threefold (Sexual) to the Fourfold (Human) prefigures in its break with the materialism of his age not only Jung's break with Freud, but, in the larger sense, Jung's journey, shared with Pauli, from Three to Four. The soul, for Blake, is the body imaginatively perceived at 'the outward circumference of [its] Energy' as its 'Eternal Delight' (*MHH* 4).

Like Hegel before him, Jung viewed the vertical ascent from matter to spirit (from sense to the archetypal ground of sense) in terms of a horizontal, historical progression of consciousness that, as in Blake, is biblically treated as progressive revelation culminating in the Second Coming as the descent of the City of God. The question Jung posed to himself may be stated this way: 'How does the timeless and spaceless unconscious psyche in its engagement with the body (both individual and cosmic) achieve a full consciousness of its own operations understood as the fourth?' Jung, as already noted, alchemically describes the fourth as 'the *Unus Mundus*, the *one* world, a Platonic prior or primeval world that is also the future of the *eternal world*' (*Atom* 129). He agreed with Pauli that any actualization of this '*one* world' required the sacrifice of its conceptual perfection to its imperfect wholeness, the fourth paradoxically residing in the consciousness of antithesis. This consciousness of antithesis is what mentally or conceptually unites into one the existing antithesis.

Mapping the dialectic of this process, Jung provided a model of the psyche's engagement with the body in which the body as the other of psyche is the condition of the psyche's consciousness of itself. Metaphysically describing what Jung would psychologically pursue, Coleridge explains that the subject 'becomes a subject by the act of constructing itself objectively to itself; but ... never is an object except for itself, and only so far as by the very same act it becomes a subject. It may be described therefore as a perpetual self-duplication of one and the same power into object and subject, which presuppose each other, and can exist only as antitheses' (*BL* 1:273)

No statement by a Romantic better sums up the perplexing subject of this book, especially when it is recognized that 'antitheses' are essential to sanity. The Romantic poet writes in the shadow of madness understood as a chaotic state of undifferentiated oneness. Shelley's Demogorgon describes this madness as 'the Abysm' where the 'deep truth' cannot 'vomit forth its secrets' because 'a voice / Is wanting' (*PU* 2.4.114–16). The terror of going mad is, for the Romantic, the terror that composition attempts to exorcize, the poet knowing that a fully success-ful exorcism is the death of poetry itself. The sanity of poetry (the 'voice' that in madness is 'wanting') resides in the ceaseless transformations of madness into levels of consciousness that presuppose rather than ne-gate each other. What separates poetry from madness is the affirmation of consciousness itself.

Afterword: Ross Woodman's Romanticism

Joel Faflak, University of Western Ontario

I see a serpent in Canada, who courts me to his love ...

William Blake, America: A Prophecy

... it is on account of this in-between [between nature and the human break from it] that the subject cannot be reduced to the Self as a 'center of narrative gravity.' Where, then, do we find traces of this in-between in philosophy? In the Cartesian *cogito*. For a systematic deployment of this dimension, one has to wait for the advent of German Idealism. The basic insight of Schelling, whereby, prior to its assertion as the medium of the rational Word, the subject is the 'infinite lack of being [*unendliche Mangel an Sein*],' the violent gesture of contraction that negates every being outside itself, also forms the core of Hegel's notion of madness: when Hegel determines madness to be a withdrawal from the actual world, the closing of the soul into itself, its 'contraction,' the cutting-off of its links with external reality, he all too quickly conceives of this withdrawal as a 'regression' to the level of the 'animal soul' still embedded in its natural environs and determined by the rhythm of nature (night and day, etc.). Does this withdrawal, on the contrary, not designate the severing of the links with the *Umwelt*, the end of the subject's immersion into its immediate natural environs, and is it, as such, not the founding gesture of 'humanization'?

... What we must be careful not to miss here, is how Hegel's break with the Enlightenment tradition can be discerned in the reversal of the very metaphor for the subject: the subject is no longer the Light of Reason opposed to the nontransparent, impenetrable Stuff (of Nature, Tradition ...); his very kernel, the gesture that opens up the space for the Light of Logos, is absolute negativity, the 'night of the world,' the point of utter madness in which fantasmatic apparitions of 'partial objects' err around. Consequently, there is no subjectivity without this gesture of withdrawal; which is why Hegel is fully justified in inverting the standard question of how the fall-regression into madness is possible: the true question is rather how the subject is able to climb out of madness and to reach 'normalcy.' That is to say, the withdrawal-into-self, the cutting-off of the links to the environs, is followed by the construction of a symbolic universe that the subject projects onto reality as a kind of substitute-formation, destined to recompense us for the loss of the immediate, pre-symbolic real. However, as Freud himself asserted in his analysis of Daniel Paul Schreber's paranoia, the manufacturing of a substitute-formation that recompenses the subject for the loss of reality, is the most succinct definition of the paranoiac construction as an attempt to cure the subject of the disintegration of his universe. In short, the ontological necessity of 'madness' resides in the fact that it is not possible to pass directly from the purely 'animal soul,' immersed in its natural environs, to 'normal' subjectivity, dwelling in its symbolic virtual environs – the 'vanishing mediator' between the two is the 'mad' gesture of radical withdrawal from reality, which opens up the space for its symbolic (re)constitution.

Slavoj Žižek, 'The Cartesian Subject versus the Cartesian Theater'

I

The statement from the Romantic poet and philosopher Samuel Taylor Coleridge with which Ross Woodman ends this book is predicated on a psychotic withdrawal from the world that is the founding gesture of the subject, of 'man' or the *anthropos*, which Slavoj Žižek reads in Hegel's idealism. We can debate, as Woodman does, how Coleridge himself dealt with this psychosis, but suffice it to say that it is, in Woodman's account of madness in this book, one of the – if not *the* – founding gestures of Romanticism, particularly of Romantic poetry. Žižek's statement testifies to the profoundly human nature of this withdrawal. It expresses, that is, the profound way in which the human brings to consciousness between the antithetical poles of Nature and the symbolic reconstitution of Nature a sanity of the madness of the psychotic break that constitutes the antithesis in the first place. Northrop Frye's critical vision, as Woodman elaborates it, takes this virtual reconstitution of the human from Nature to its Hegelian limits, transforming the madness of this reconstitution into a supremely intellectual symbolism sustained by the operations of its own mind – what Shelley calls the 'One Mind.' What gets missed in Frye's system, however, is the necessary bringing to consciousness of the madness that sustains the system in the initial instance of its constitution as a radical withdrawal from its 'natural environs' into its own 'virtual environs.' For Woodman, this blindness constitutes Frye's own psychotic break, a break that Jung will analyse in himself in his childhood schizophrenia and later in his break with Freud, so that he can transform its terms by accepting madness as the radical nature of his own humanity *as* human. This radical acceptance of the human is what for Jung constitutes the quaternity, what Blake argues is the necessary movement from the Threefold Sexual, blinded by an acceptance of its symbolic reconstitution of Nature *as natural*, to the Fourfold Human, in which the subject recognizes *this* blindness as necessary and thus marks the inevitably mad withdrawal from the world as the establishing of an impossible antithesis ('opposition is True Friendship,' writes Blake) that *is* the virtually human condition.

Why Blake and not simply Jung, however? Why, that is, a book on Romantic poetry rather than simply a book on Jung or Frye? For Woodman, Romantic poetry takes the dilemma of philosophy, specifically of German idealism, that Žižek outlines (and we need to remember that Hegel and the Romantics were historical contemporaries, and that Schelling was a crucial catalyst to Coleridge's thought as it came to characterize Romanticism's vision of itself) and psychoanalyses this dilemma by turning it back out to human experience. Romantic poetry, as it struggles with its own insights from Blake to Keats, is not Frye's verbal universe radically withdrawn from Nature to its own symbolic or virtual environs; rather, it is the radical working-through of the madness of this withdrawal to account for how the human brings this madness to consciousness in order to live within it. Romantic poetry accounts for the psychology of the profoundly Human or Blakean Fourfold that is the fundamental condition of our being in the world. Romantic poetry is its own necessary antithesis to Hegel's philosophy and to philosophy in general. For if philosophy struggles to *think* the dilemma of the human, poetry struggles to make this thinking *feel* itself, not by swerving away from the operations of the mind, but by making these operations answerable to the very human terms they struggle to understand in the first place. That this humanity is also profoundly virtual or symbolic, as Žižek writes, *is* its nature *as* human nature. Yet it is a human nature distinctly messy and heterogeneous – distinctly human – not reducible to the inherently systematic terms of its own functioning to which it would reduce itself but discovers it cannot. That is, the great paradox of this virtual withdrawal from the world is that it functions very much like the body of the *Umwelt* from which it emerged and to which it recurs as the uncanny reflection of its own mad withdrawal. The psychology of this uncanny reflection, as Woodman accounts for it in Romantic poetry, which is for him one of the pre-eminently modern articulations of this reflection's accounting for itself, is the subject of this book.

II

We are so utterly consumed by the transformations of modernity, to which Romanticism marks the entry point, that to stand outside these transformations in order to reflect upon them seems unthinkable. Is it, or was it ever, possible to do so? Is it any longer necessary or even desirable to do so? One of the most telling – and, for some, disturbing – manifestations of post-Romanticism has been the purported demise of disciplines such as literary studies, which have always secured authority from their ability to communicate, via the reading of literary texts, a prescribed set of cultural values. Even now that literary studies has opened itself to the task of interrogating and even dismissing this authority and thus pulling the rug out from underneath its own feet, still the prospect of reinscribing literary studies as the arbiter of its own demise persists. The spectre of this demise is what might be called this book's tutelary spirit – or rather its dark, phantasmal heart. As an afterword to Ross Woodman's *Sanity, Madness, Transformation: The Psyche in Romanticism*, this essay will attempt to evoke the cultural psychology of his particular 'telling' of Romanticism rather than rehearse a critical history of his corpus. This book, and indeed any of Woodman's writings to do with Romanticism (that is to say, all of Woodman's writings, whether they overtly address Romantic literature or not), demonstrate how any point of entry into Romanticism is always a psychic transformation of one's knowledge about Romanticism and about the larger culture that contains it, both then and now. Woodman's Romanticism is read first and foremost through its specific texts; yet this reading is always shaped by the influence of a broader popular culture on the students he taught for over forty years, as well as on the larger academic community within which he continues to publish.[1] That this influence, as we shall see, has grown increasingly profound makes Woodman's exploration of it through the example of Romanticism a potent reflection of how we might, if at all, transform the terms of this influence.

For Woodman, all culture is popular culture within a global arena where, on one hand, we struggle to find ourselves while, on the other, culture attempts to do the finding for us. Within this process 'transformation' suggests a Romantic agency able to transcend material, social, or political contingencies. This Romanticism is typical of Woodman's early education under Northrop Frye. However, how Woodman came to understand and to teach Romanticism offers a more complex and ambivalent reading of psychic transformation. This is not to say that our current critical climate might easily recognize Woodman's idea of a Romantic psychic reality. The psyche is now, if at all, an object of cultural study, the generation of a socio-historical matrix of forces through which the idea of the 'subject' is put aside as the residue of an Enlightenment examination of the human (*'Was ist der Mensch?'* asks Kant) whose time is long past. However, if the subject is only reflected in the endless quotidian surface of the effects of culture, to invoke our current critical paradigm, to what extent are these effects, as well as our interrogation of them, free from Enlightenment imperatives? Put another way, to what extent does Kant's question remain hauntingly all too present?

The current desire to critique culture's surface *at its level*, and thus sometimes to confuse mere description with critique, often produces the hegemonic reflection of 'History' and its 'subject,' whose truth-value we have supposedly come to suspect. Our passion to recover culture's archaic artefacts and voices betrays a post-Enlightenment desire to classify history exhaustively and thus definitively. This desire has produced what Jean Baudrillard calls the 'dance of the fossils,' a 'hypertelic memory which stores all data in a constant state of instant retrievability, excluding any work of mourning' ('Dance' 72–3). In the nineteenth century this desire evoked a reaction to an Enlightenment liberation from the burden of the past that itself was, as those in post-revolutionary France learned soon enough, a feint of Reason. Our current taxonomical imperative, like that of the Victorians before us, for instance, ends up reifying the terms of its archaeology and thus, however unintentionally, ascribing cultural power to this act of naming as a mastery of a past for which we *appear* to care little, but about which we are obviously rather more anxious. Woodman was taught by an earlier school of criticism to respect this mastery's formalism, as in Frye's neo-Hegelianism. But he remained suspicious of it in all its manifestations – as his treatment of Frye in this book makes ferociously apparent. Instead, he would insist upon reading the psyche of culture as a type of phantasmatic locus of articulation beyond the reality of criticism and its histories. In this way his corpus offers an incisive allegory of the critical state of things, past, present, and future, or what Woodman calls in his introduction a 'hybrid,' which itself is a type of psychoanalysis of critical fashion. For Woodman, the psyche is like Demogorgon's Cave in Shelley's *Prometheus Unbound*, a site of blank reserve ('the deep truth is imageless' [2.4.116]) where culture stages the scene of its power in order to legitimate its influence. Woodman in turn critically stages this interiority as if to conjure, as in the same text Mercury conjures for both Prometheus and Jupiter, its multiple phantasms haunting culture as the inaccessible trauma of its ideological sway.

In 1964 Woodman published his path-breaking study, *The Apocalyptic Vision in the Poetry of Shelley*. This book, based on Woodman's doctoral dissertation, which had been supervised by Frye, was shaped less by Frye's critical anatomy of the imagination's self-contained symbolic vision of itself than by a McCluhanesque sense of the apocalypse of globalism, which has ultimately borne the greater burden of proof. Heralding the revolutionary consequences of technology for the new world, however brave, McCluhan emphasized the transformational extensions of globalism as a fluid and therefore inherently unstable process, a process born of improbably Blakean antitheses. The latter point has recently been made more explicit (although not with reference to either McCluhan or Blake) by Michael Hardt and Antonio Negri. They define Empire as 'a new global form of sovereignty,' 'a *decentered* and *deterritorializing* apparatus of rule that progressively incorporates the entire global realm within its open, expanding frontiers' (xii). But Empire is open to the very apocalypse of transformation by which it was first generated. These forces of counter-Empire are played out on the 'imperial terrain itself' in order to 'contest and subvert Empire,' taking advantage of precisely the fact that Empire is 'not unified or univocal' (xv). This apocalyptic *in*stability of Empire suggests a certain political technology of the human imagination, open to its own contestation, that is germane to a construction of the imagination as this project was tendered in the late eighteenth and early nineteenth centuries. Woodman's book maps the fate of this imagination, and its often mythopoeic ambitions, as the site from which to interrogate the fate of the *human* in our own time. As he writes in his conclusion, 'in the mythopoeic achievement of the Romantics ... dwells ... the birth of a modern consciousness which the twenty-first century must finally learn to inhabit if human life is to continue, not without God, but with a conscious understanding of the human.'

Hardt and Negri accept a 'humanism after the death of Man,' who 'stands separate from and above nature' and therefore 'has no place in a philosophy of immanence': 'Once we recognize our posthuman bodies and minds, once we see ourselves for the simians and cyborgs we are, we then need to explore the *vis viva*, the creative powers that animate us as they do all of nature and actualize our potentialities' (91–2). By contrast, Frye offers a rabid humanism, a totalization of Man's powers within a system that manages and masters its own contingencies. Here the 'transcendence of God is simply transferred to Man' (Hardt and Negri 91), so that Frye's critical system offers a kind of totality-cum-globalism that stays the unexpected chaos of its own critical mutations. This is to distinguish Empire or its counter-movement from imperialism, which for Hardt and Negri reflects the 'modern sovereignty' of the nation-state, one that 'constructed a Leviathan that overarched its social domain and imposed hierarchical territorial boundaries, both to police the purity of its own identity and to exclude all that was other' (xii). Frye's universe in *Anatomy of Criticism* mounted its own imperialist technology of imagination, yet without the politics of an attendant self-subversion. Understanding this self-subversion is essential to understanding how the imagination works in Woodman's vision of it.

Woodman's writings thus are framed by the 1960s and their anxious utopianism about a future global technocracy (itself a response to the anxious conservatism of the 1950s) and by our own anxiety about the embodiment of this prophecy as technological truth. For Woodman, Romanticism is characterized by a schizophrenic struggle between utopia and idealism on one hand and skepticism, disillusionment, and resignation on the other. It is to the schizophrenia or psychosis of culture inherent within this Romantic struggle that Woodman most powerfully addresses himself, especially as this confrontation with madness provides a fascinating parallel to our own time, particularly in terms of both periods' embracing of change. In this sense Woodman has always been concerned about the complex nature of transformation as it affects the subject whose identity is enmeshed within his cultural milieu. One can here distinguish change, society's acculturation of the subject to the terms of its own unfolding, from transformation, as the way in which the subject himself responds to change. Judith Butler argues that the subject is formed from his *subjection* to 'regulatory power' by 'producing and exploiting the demand for continuity, visibility, and place' (*Psychic* 29). The subject's psychic life is thus determined by power's 'iterability' as the inbred effects of social regulation. This iterability, paradoxically, constitutes the subject's agency, the way in which power acclimatizes the subject to its arbitrary nature by repeating itself so as to appear *natural* or *given*.

Butler continues, 'nevertheless [this subject is] haunted by an inassimilable remainder, a melancholia that marks the limits of subjectivation.' In this haunting remainder lies the chance for an agency that 'consist[s] in opposing and transforming the social terms by which it was spawned' (29). The repetition of power's effects also offers the *possibility* of transformation, not as transcendence, but as the subject's opportunity productively to alter, recreate, or transgress these effects – as it were, to *de*naturalize them as culture. Woodman, like Butler, would not think to question the *determinism* of this positing power of subjectivity. However, he does recognize its transformational potential. His exploration of Romanticism argues for an overdetermined Romantic agency through which the subject is continually in dialogue with, and frequently against, the given terms of his subjectivity. Specifically addressed to literature as a site of cultural regulation, Woodman's writings explore how the literary text inculcates, on behalf of culture, a form of subjectivity in the reader against which he must struggle on his own terms. In the specific form of Woodman's writing, this struggle against the text, yet within its own terms, evokes a transformation *of* these terms.

It is thus significant that Woodman's writings are not overtly a cultural study of the text as surface or artefact. At this level, despite our apparent resistance to any metaphysical, foundationalist, or essentialist logic, we remain suspended within the illusory warp and woof of culture's ideologies and idealisms. Here, culture's effects may *seem* endlessly novel and worthy of our investigation; but, in fact, here is where we as subjects are most susceptible to the powerful repetition of culture's machine. One of Woodman's central metaphors for this entanglement is the Romantic vision of a liberated Promethean man, 'Sceptreless, free, uncircumscribed – but man' (*PU* 1.4.194), but recognized as a mask for the promise offered by democracy to hide the more Jovian tendencies of life's triumph over idealism. Even more insidious than Jupiter's tyranny itself is how Promethean freedom, the site of man's ascendance over his own anthropology, itself becomes the cause of his imprisonment. One must not forget that in Shelley's text Prometheanism attempts to contain contesting facets of its multiple (cultural) personality within a univocal vision, but that this vision itself is 'pinnacled dim in the intense inane' (*PU* 3.4.204), what Shelley in

Adonais calls the 'void circumference' (420). This paradox necessitated Shelley's addition of a fourth act to his lyrical drama, wherein the text reads itself as 'spells by which to reassume / An empire o'er the disentangled doom' (*PU* 4.568–9). Here Shelley, by performing culture as an arena of conflicting voices, struggles to transform the prison of an illusory freedom from culture into a viable – that is, livable – knowledge of its prescriptions, 'freedom' being, paradoxically, pre-eminent among them; this knowledge Shelley will mirror rather more darkly in *Adonais* and *The Triumph of Life*. As Žižek states, 'radical democracy' is not 'pure, true democracy; its radical character implies, on the contrary, that we can save democracy only by *taking into account its radical impossibility*' (6).

Woodman's writings, then, come to reflect the radical impossibility of culture that is culture's constitutive trauma. Madness embraces this impossibility, the possible being the tranquillization of madness. For Woodman, as for Shelley and Blake, culture reflects a type of regulatory madness from which the reader, through the literary text as one of the constitutive forms of this madness, must perform her own liberation. Paradoxically, this can happen only by entering into the sheer madness of things that culture, in its 'other' madness of cultural prescription, would regulate. In the chaotic apocalypse of culture's madness used against itself lies, for Woodman, a transformation as if from within the terms of this madness, so that, perhaps most radically, culture's traumatic impossibility becomes the site of its madness *as* transformation. Woodman argues that apocalypse in the poetry of Blake and Shelley thus becomes less a celebration of political revolution than an affirmation of revolution's vitally metaphorical nature. I shall return to madness and apocalypse in section V. For now, however, it is enough to note that this study's reflections on various forms of madness comprise a type of ongoing psychoanalysis of its scene of articulation in Romantic texts and in texts and writers, particularly Jung and Frye, profoundly influenced by Romanticism. Woodman's writings thus offer a sustained engagement with psychoanalysis, although less so with its frequently restrictive theoretical terms. Indeed, we need to be reminded that Coleridge coined the term 'psycho-analytical' in 1805, a term symptomatic of a desire to think through the cultural dead-ends offered by metaphysics, philosophy, deconstruction, or politics, among other things.

Thus, it is key that Jungian psychology emerges as one of this book's central concerns. The spectre of Jung all too frequently conjures images of New Age spiritualism or flying saucers. Yet in Woodman's hands the occult nature of Jung's account of psychoanalysis is potent precisely for its transformation of a Freudianism all too frequently reductive in its scientific materialism. Woodman touches upon this epochal break between these two Titanic inventors of the modern science of the psyche.[2] Of central importance to Woodman's conception of Romanticism is Freudianism's abjection of Jung's transgression of Freud, the threat of which radically altered the development of psychoanalysis and psychoanalytic literary studies. Bound via his sense of cultural propriety to ensure the scientific authority of psychoanalysis, Freud immediately departs from the radical encounter of the psyche with its own madness, as in his preliminary studies on hysteria. As Jung experienced it at first hand (the reason he attempted to convince Freud of it in turn), madness comprised the radically transformational undoing of psychoanalysis as a 'discipline,' an undoing that was its defining feature. Hence, the cultural and epistemological significance of Jung's break from Freud becomes a constitutive madness that would resist cultural prescription by transforming its terms, a transformation attempted in the equally epochal encounter between Jung and the Nobel Prize-winning quantum physicist, Wolfgang Pauli. Woodman argues that Jung was exploring 'psychology' as the work of thought in which the mind comes to know itself through a knowledge of its operations. What emerges in this exploration is a sense of how the phantasy of dreams and literature, always under threat by the voices of science, becomes the crucial modus operandi in a psychoanalysis of science's rational ego. In short, what emerges for Jung is a sense of how Romanticism, as it comes to signify the radical terrain of this phantasy, provides a necessarily counter-intuitive ballast to modern science.

As Woodman notes, this book's most counter-intuitive gestures, apart from its attention to Frye's critical heritage, are its attention to Jung and to deconstruction and the connection between them. Certainly, in terms of the language of Romanticism, Woodman found in deconstruction a postmodern way of dealing with the Romantics that extended his understanding of them beyond the limits of modernism as, in one sense, modernism culminates in Jung. In a review of the collected poems and selected essays of Czeslaw Milosz, Adam Kirsch describes the modernism that Milosz exploded in his poetry and prose: 'Modernism inflated poetry like a balloon with vapours of vanished meanings, religious, social, mythic, and produced masterpieces of fragile iridescence' (3). The Jung with whom Woodman deals presided over the death throes of western civilization and, very differently from Yeats, Eliot, or Lawrence, attempted to breathe new life into the 'vapours of vanished meanings' that, as restless Shelleyan ghosts not yet laid to rest, continue to haunt our postmodern world, suspended, as Kirsch suggests, between nihilism and a new humanism. Confronting in recent years the increasing evidence of nihilism in the fast-spreading globalism that is driven by an information revolution that in his view remains ironically mindless, Woodman has allied Jung with the postmodernism that hopefully contains within it a new humanism capable of embracing a world, one that, too often equated with American imperialism, now appears to be increasingly polarized. This study, by gesturing towards Nietzsche's account of the tightrope walker suspended between two towers, rather powerfully evokes this polarization in terms of the terrorist attack on the World Trade Center. This polarization provides startling evidence of the destruction inherent in creation when creation is viewed in the apocalyptic fashion that largely defines the understanding of Romanticism that launched Woodman's academic career.

Woodman's use of Jung also points to a provocative (and as yet relatively unexplored) relationship between Jung and Nietzsche, the spectral presence of which haunts the uncanny relationship between Nietzsche, deconstruction, and Romanticism's metaphorical body. In a series of seminars on *Thus Spake Zarathustra* conducted over a period of five years, Jung explored in minute detail the signs of an imminent psychosis in this work of considerable genius. Nietzsche's influence on the work of Jung is everywhere acknowledged, though what is perhaps of particular interest is the way in which Jung sees in Nietzsche's incipient madness the presence of his own. He thus uses Nietzsche as a way of coming to grips with it by absorbing it into consciousness rather than allowing it to split off. Conducting the seminars in Zurich between 1934 and 1939, Jung makes continual reference to what is happening in Germany on the other side of the Alps as the shaping of a mass psychosis that is mirrored in Nietzsche. In a series of unpublished lectures, Woodman used Jung's reading of Nietzsche's *Thus Spake Zarathustra* to reflect upon our current state of global madness.

In 'Blake's Fourfold Body,' Woodman constructs a dialogue between Jung and Blake as a way of psychoanalysing the scientism of Frye's theoretical vision. In Frye's rescuing Blake from the lunatic fringe of Romantic studies in the 1940s (the world having only recently come face to face with the spectre of the delayed mobilization of its own conscience in the horror of the liberated death camps), Woodman reads Frye's recognition of Romanticism as being at the lunatic fringe of

Frye's own vision. Frye represses this extremity within a vast critical system that remains eerily suspended from the culture that produced it. In Frye's displacement of Jung, then, Woodman in turn reads a figure who would expose Frye to the madness of his vision by resituating it within the psyche of culture. Or rather, whereas Shelley would save culture only by negating the terms of its given experience, Jung, like Byron, would immerse Frye in the psychosis of this experience's chaos. Woodman's use of the 'psycho-analytical' thus comes to signify the psychology of the subject attempting to find her place in a world that would overdetermine her identity. His engagement with Romanticism's madness itself is a psychological process engaging the complex psychological struggle with the self and culture that marks Romanticism's always shifting identity as what Shelley calls 'mirrors of the gigantic shadows which futurity casts upon the present' (*DP* 508).

III

Woodman's readings draw heavily upon the texts they address, but not at the level of these texts' formalism. Rather, his critical stance evokes a textual phenomenology that, via the text's materiality, performs culture's struggles with its own materialism, a key theme of the present study. This phenomenology reflects a type of epistemological anxiety about mastering cultural meaning and making it *useful*, and thus reflects a *Victorianization* of Romanticism and Romantic studies that continues to define Romanticism's fate. That Woodman's writings do not fit any particular critical school suggests within his corpus a more unsettling and provocative subtext that pits Romantic heterodoxy against Victorianizing orthodoxy.[3] When in 1993 the Keats-Shelley Association named Woodman Distinguished Scholar for his contribution to the humanities, Tilottama Rajan introduced him in the following manner:

> I remember in 1984 an older colleague expressing surprise that one would take Shelley as seriously as Wordsworth. It is therefore particularly appropriate that the Keats-Shelley Association should honour the [author of one] of the earliest full-length studies of Shelley: [a study] whose historical importance went unrecognized in the seventies because of [its] Canadian authorship, and which in the eighties it became all too easy to relegate to a bygone critical era. Those who have been Ross Woodman's students or who (like myself) have reaped the pedagogical benefits of his legacy, know the role he has played in keeping Romantic studies alive in a

country confederated in the Victorian period. He could not have done so without an openness to new theoretical developments which was then rare in the Canadian academy, but which informed both his teaching and his published work. And that openness, in turn, had much to do with the nature of his earliest work. For if one's choice of a particular writer as a syncedoche of 'Romanticism' is symptomatic, it is significant that even in the sixties Woodman read Romanticism neither as secular scripture nor as natural supernaturalism, but through a proto-deconstructive Shelley whose very marginality at the time gave him an enunciative position outside Frye's *Anatomy of Criticism*, a position from which he could then revision Blake and Wordsworth in the eighties.[4]

That Shelley himself was once marginalized in Romantic studies seems a quaint notion now that Blake, Wordsworth, Coleridge, Shelley, Byron, and Keats share the canon with, and in many respects have been displaced by, its previously marginalized figures. Apparently against this trend, and its de-privileging of literature amid other cultural forces and disciplines, Woodman has dealt primarily with the canonical male Romantic poets, albeit by neglecting Byron. But as addressed in this study's final chapter, this exclusion is offered by Woodman as the symptom of a critical Romanticism within whose shifting fortunes we remain all too often entangled. That is, Woodman has come to read a Romanticism that resists itself *as* Romanticism.

We might view this study, then, not so much in terms of its particular manifestations but palimpsestically as versions of a Romantic cultural psyche whose contingencies reflect back to succeeding criticisms their own arbitrary nature. Woodman retired from teaching just as the fallout from deconstruction was producing in literary studies a succession of methodological interests informing the terms of post-structuralist debate: gender studies, post-colonialism, queer studies, new historicism, cultural studies, to name only a few. His more recent work does not take particular account of these trends, although the original impact of deconstruction has been profound, both in his work's anticipation of it and in its influence via this work on a subsequent generation of Romantic scholars in Canada. Nonetheless, his writings evoke current ideological concerns about politics, sexuality, gender, and history, if not exactly in the terms of discussion according to which we might currently recognize these issues. At some level, that the form of these terms is beside the point *is* Woodman's point.

A telling symptom of the critical state of things is how recent trends have tended to fall under the rubric of a cultural materialism. However, does attention to culture's materiality only ensure against forgetting literature's responsibility to a larger world of social, political, or economic forces that an earlier criticism would see literature as transcending? Or does it ensure other types of forgetting as well? In reading Woodman's Romanticism against Frye's critical Victorianism, Rajan reminds us how Frye's influence, tied to the fortunes of New Criticism, for so long dominated Romantic studies in Canada.[5] Although a later criticism would unmask the bias of his formalism's ideological imperatives, one could argue that it remains difficult for criticism to resist its own Victorianizing tendencies. Perhaps we are most resistant to seeing these tendencies as still conditioning our idea of Romanticism when, like Matthew Arnold, we miss seeing how this resistance is anticipated in Romanticism itself. Arnold called the Romantics 'premature' (240) because they did not know enough, evoking a period identified, and in need of identification, by Victorian prescriptions. However, Romanticism can be seen as ambivalent about the immanent Victorianization of its desire to master its identity. Framed within 'a country confederated in the Victorian period,' Woodman's Romanticism occupies a productively constitutional *otherness* within the evolution of criticism since Frye. This otherness has offered his students, including the present writer, an enunciative position within criticism's contemporary terms, yet allowing for a transformation of these terms' regulatory effects.

In reading Canada's political unconscious as a surviving member of the Commonwealth, Rajan suggests how Canada, insofar as its psyche remains haunted by its colonial status, would create the necessity for the type of critical transformation offered by Woodman's writings. Indeed, perhaps *because* the empire, as defined by Victoria's reign, has been superseded by other conglomerates, as defined by Hardt and Negri, we remain all the more susceptible to the epistemic pull of power's Victorianizing effects. This susceptibility has continued to be pervasive, in ways we might not at first suspect. In another forum, Rajan, by addressing the recent shift in Romantic studies from 'an overemphasis on the linguistic and philosophical to an equal and opposite stress on the sociopolitical,' evokes the Victorianizing turn of literary studies toward the social sciences: 'This shift of capital ... has coincided with a Victorianization of the period informed by complex demographic pressures and ideological fantasies that have as a byproduct a regionalization of the field as 'British' ... As Romanticism is absorbed into the nineteenth century, its master themes are increasingly set by a later telos, in a colonization of the period that comes from within English studies itself' ('From Restricted' 7). This internal agenda, Rajan implies, reflects social, financial, political, and historical concerns typical of the later nineteenth century and quietly shaping the current academy to reflect cultural values society wants imparted to those it teaches. On one hand, we have opened criticism to a productively overdetermined speculation about culture as an arena of conflicting energies. On the other hand, making criticism answerable to the sociopolitical and thus socially responsible proves its utility and viability in the academic marketplace and in turn justifies the existence of the academy itself, all at a time of increasing pressure from the marketplace at large. We are here, very much against the apparent will of cultural materialism, within Arnold's fantasy of a world where the ideology of culture rests in its ability to effect social unity.[6] How culture was inculcated, ingrained, and/or institutionalized in its subjects satisfied a Victorian need for making sure the centre held. Rajan suggests that our current criticism, despite its claim to displace this centre, is following a similar path.

IV

How, then, does Woodman's Romanticism fit this critical allegory? David L. Clark follows the example of a post-Frygian Blake, who unmasks the Victorianizing tendencies of the culture within which Blake wrote. Clark argues that, for Blake, creation itself is 'the originary Great Confinement, after which all other illegitimate forms of exclusion and imprisonment are patterned' ('Against' 198). Thus, Blake's reconception of the Creation myth became an object lesson in how the Enlightenment desire for taxonomical distinctions that begins with Linnaeus's *Systema Naturae*, the French *Encyclopédie*, or the *Encyclopedia Britannica* fostered the utilitarian dreams of the nineteenth century. The work of systems and classifications commodified the world by turning all forms of culture into capital, the naming of 'culture' itself facilitating the efficiency of this process. Blake's unsettling of Urizenic metaphysics critiques this taxonomical oppression as the promise of the Enlightenment sold to the middle class in the form of a commercial rationalization that is even today dictating the utility of criticism. This utility is increasingly felt by researchers in terms of making their ideas accountable to the larger social structure that funds them and by teachers whose pedagogy, directed to students who are increasingly shouldering the burden of financing this structure, must always be made *relevant*.

It is not that these concerns are negligible to Clark or Woodman. Indeed, they insist upon a resistant consciousness of the terms culture uses to ameliorate the 'regulatory power' of its utility, especially where this utility names for us a less intractable subjectivity. Clark argues that Blake 'pursues what amounts to a nascent philosophy of finitude ... a philosophy which, very simply put, recognizes that knowledge and the knowing subject are always in arrears vis-à-vis the structuring principle of their articulation' (169). Clark reminds us of what Butler might call the 'phantasmatic structure' (*Gender Trouble*)[7] within the formal distinction of things, its articulation as phantasy. To master this 'structuring principle' is to gain purchase on critical and cultural authority. Yet, Clark suggests, we forget at our peril how we are mastered by this articulation (a fact that places sober limitations on Hardt and Negri's 'counter-Empire'). Culture offers the lure of this purchase while masking its dangers. Where Woodman would read Promethean vision for the transformative potential of its negativity, culture's current Prometheanism is rather more positivistic. The peril behind this culture's often 'inane' surface is the intensity with which it masks its benign idealisms. We seem caught, as Blake might argue, within the illusion of a 'lower innocence' that has co-opted the discourse of its 'higher' form, while forgetting the necessary experience of its struggles. (The sentimentality of spiritual regeneration offered by Oprah Winfrey is one of the more compelling examples of this easy cultural fix.) In this dangerous appropriation of the chaos of phantasy, culture offers its subjects a modern version of the Creation myth that would repress its constitutive madness. As this release of chaos or madness from Creation is one of Woodman's central concerns, we need to situate his writings within a cultural imaginary of Romanticism that extends beyond Romantic studies in Canada and beyond the particular spectre of Canada's colonial status, a marginality that is now rather beside the point.

Conflicted between autonomy and compromise, Canadian identity, I have suggested, reflects an uncanny ability to recolonize itself according to the will of the Other. For so long we obeyed a country from whose union of conflicting perspectives within an imperial Victorian vision we derived our own identity as the obedient child of an absent cultural parent.[8] Since the repatriation of our Constitution, this absence has figured less in our national make-up. Now, however, along with the rest of the world, we are governed by capitalism. Its locus appears to our south, in a country that said 'no' to the motherland, as Prometheus said 'no' to Jupiter. As Frederic Jameson reminds us, however, capitalism's 'network of power and control' is a 'decentered global network' that is 'difficult for our minds and imaginations to grasp' (80). This network has now become like Shelley's 'Sea profound of ever-spreading sound' out of whose productive chaos in Shelley's text culture has seized the opportunity to grant us the illusion of a liberated yet orderly identity. Both everywhere and nowhere at once, capitalism replicates strategies of power not entirely dissimilar from those of the empire, a power often as oppressive as that by which Jupiter chains Prometheus to a cliff in the Indian Caucasus for 'Three thousand years of sleep-unsheltered hours' (*PU* 1.12).

The British Commonwealth (a misnomer if ever there was one) functioned by keeping invisible the effects of domination marked on those it colonized – via the spiritual profit of religion or education's indoctrination by the myth of cultural progress – and by silencing those for whom these effects – via poverty, class, incarceration, racism, slavery, the displacement of indigenous peoples – were not so invisible. Insofar as Canada, taught to internalize the marks of its discipline, embraces the utopianism of techno-cultural progress, it is perhaps because the majestic confidence of globalism resembles a form of symbolic power by which we have been called before. But we are not alone in this respect. One of the more insidious forms of this interpellation is its irresistible pull towards a paradigm of efficiency, by which technology and economy tolerate few obstacles to the fluidity of capital in all its forms. This new version of a nineteenth-century utilitarianism suggests that we *buy into* material progress, but only by ignoring its material conditions. This utility tolerates only what conforms to the productive materialism of the machine of culture. I do not mean the materiality of commodities per se, although it is in its fetishized objects that capitalism hides the positing power of its ideologies. Rather, culture would transcend the limitations of the material by, paradoxically, making *visible* culture's autonomous power – that is, by naming, branding, quantifying, and/or classifying this power within an economy of signs that obscures these limitations. For instance, branding its global ambition under the sign of a benign mouse, Disney materializes what Henry Giroux calls a 'politics of innocence' (113–18) through which all social conflicts are resolved and dissipated. The *materialization* of this ideology, that is, *de*materializes other concerns that might affect its economical functioning. Efficiently taxonomical, this economy names all excess that is not surplus as unproductive waste and thus rationalizes any conflicting elements within a larger global process exerting its ever increasing hegemony. As Shelley writes in *A Defence of Poetry*, 'man having enslaved the elements, remains himself a slave.' Man having become 'Man,' that is, forgets how to be 'man,' forgets the difference between 'man' and 'Man.'

Insofar as we have transcended our own primitive nature, we remain indebted to Darwin. To cite another, somewhat longer example, I experienced the effects of our current cultural Darwinism during a recent visit to the American museum of Natural History. All of the Museum's dinosaur skeletons have been remounted to reflect a cutting-edge paleontology. Accordingly, the viewer is brought closer to the Real of history while taught to respect his place *within* rather than *above* our evolutionary descent through this history. Yet, confronting us also with the burden of the Real as 'that which resists symbolization absolutely' (Lacan, *Seminar I* 66), the museum seems all the more compelled to master whatever of the past's capital it has amassed. Scientific and historical revisionism of this type also suggests a forgetting of the past *as* traumatic, a forgetting of our traumatic *inability to* remember.

I read another story in the nameplates of sponsors past and present that accompanied all of the museum's displays (especially those eerie, taxidermic dioramas). I was reminded that, endowed by America's captains of industry old and new, the museum was originally built to showcase dinosaurs as an object lesson in how to *avoid* extinction, or at least to make it an *irrelevant* issue.[9] If culture is dead, pieces of its exquisitely rotting corpse still proliferate everywhere we turn, like the rotting body of the dead poet in *Adonais,* a text to which Woodman recurs many times in his work. *This* story reminded me that, like a type of magic ether (or is it formaldehyde?), capital fuels the machine of culture as smoothly as possible. Like the 'white radiance of Eternity' (*Adonais* 463) in Shelley's poem, it allows the *anthropos* to supersede the filthy materialism of his genesis, even as he is daily confronted by a different body of evidence. Yet we are even now past the 'purer' materialism of commodity capitalism into what Jean Baudrillard refers to as the third-order simulation of the 'code,' 'where capital has finally attained its purest form of discourse' ('Symbolic' 130). According to the 'metaphysics of the code,' the 'burden of utility' disappears, meaning that 'from now on signs will exchange among themselves exclusively, without interacting with the real (and this becomes the condition of their smooth operation)' (125). Baudrillard calls this, of course, the '*hyperreal,*' where the virtual becomes the real.

The hyperreal constitutes a type of primal narcissism wherein, like God before he impregnated the void, we are suspended in a moment of unbroken masturbatory contemplation. The hyperreal avoids the trauma of chaos and instead permits us to be our own divinities, like Wordsworthian children trailing clouds of glory. We are immersed in a world of our own making, any responsibility for this making having been magically removed for us. Such a narcissistic idealism dictates Tom Hanks's and Jodie Foster's narrations of the Space Show at the museum's new Hayden Planetarium. This virtual demonstration, using state-of-the art Hollywood technology, enacts the movement of history back to the Big Bang, but then returns its audience safely (and rather swiftly) to the present. The Hayden show places the museum's dinosaur displays in their proper metaphysical context by rendering them completely obsolete: Bill Gates, Paul Allen, and Michael Eisner meet Andrew Carnegie, Cornelius Vanderbilt, and John D. Rockefeller to divide up the history very much defined by their global vision. Marrying popular culture to science and technology, the planetarium, like Disney or Microsoft, guarantees America's twenty-first-century purchase of the hyperreal as the new signifier of the world's immense store of cultural capital.

That the 'inane' voices of pop culture icons (both double Academy Award winners, no less) are used to describe the inaccessible origin of the universe is not so disturbing as the innocent utility of these voices in covering a rather profound trauma. For Woodman, the hyperreal is the confrontation of Romanticism with its own virtual identity. That is, Romanticism constitutes the psychological struggle of a culture attempting to free itself, not from culture itself, but from its illusory innocence, like the 'flowers' of culture in *Adonais* that 'hid the coming bulk of death' (17–18). There is, for Woodman, a kind of ludicrous reality – a madness – in culture's seemingly endless ability, as Lacan reminds us, to miss the unconscious entirely in the process of naming it. In the name of Forrest Gump and Nell, the Museum of Natural History has appropriated via the language of our supposedly common culture the right to speak with pleasant authority about what most threatens this culture: the now irrefutable cosmic insignificance of humanity's accomplishments. Even to the death drive of its Manifest Destiny, capitalism now claims the inalienable right of ownership. In the hyperreal Hegel's spirit triumphs over Hobbes's body, the consciousness of cultural progress overcoming an unconscious whose pathology would, like Frye's *Anatomy*, derail this progress. In the hyperreal, culture forgets how its body might resist discipline.

This innocent veneer, of course, hides a darker epistemology, which the events of 11 September have now driven home to us with seemingly insurmountable ferocity. A nineteenth-century passion for departmentalization created the museum's privilege, like that of the university, as the inalienable right to examine our anthropological precedence in the destiny of things. But the very culture that built both institutions as symbolizing its sublime wherewithal produced by society's worship of Mammon now finds that Mammon, like the Old Testament god Yahweh, can be a vengeful father indeed. The university's intellectual privilege is now questioned as intellectual isolationism. Higher learning, as if having borrowed too long against the equity of its cultural capital, has now awakened to its lack of profitability. Ironically, the North American academy seems to address this pressure by bending to an economic will that demands the complete consciousness of accountability. The problem is debated at MLA and ACCUTE meetings, which represent departments anxious to refashion the by now paleolithic designation of 'the humanities.' (Again, it is Tom Hanks who cautions us to avoid the anthropocentrism of the merely human, as he states in his narration of the Hayden show; we are no longer earthly 'tourists' but 'cosmic travelers.') The ensuing ideological fragmentation is intended as a form of cultural multi-perspectivalism. But we might be, as Lillian Hellman once told the House Committee on Un-American Activities, cutting our (academic or pedagogical) cloth to fit this year's (critical or cultural) fashion. Literary studies does not need a return to the cultural unity of Frye's vision. Yet as globalism has displaced the Commonwealth – one supposedly a more enlightened pluralism, the other an antiquated and monolithic Victorianism – is our response to the pressures of capitalism, as Rajan suggests, simply producing a late version of the same old thing?

We need to be reminded, finally, that Romanticism emerges at the beginning of the ideological triumph of Mammon in the form of the Industrial Revolution. One could argue that this revolution, like the French Revolution before it, reflected the desire of an oppressed class for citizenship in the world. But the middle class claimed the inalienable right more to material than to political or social progress, especially to the power to exploit and manipulate the myth of this progress. This myth guaranteed the middle class a broader purchase on cultural values earlier controlled exclusively by the ruling elite of an ancestral aristrocracy. Middle-class access to cultural power produced not so much a democritization of high culture, which the regressive idealism of Edmund Burke rails against, than a commodification of culture. Invariably, the Victorians, although at the vanguard of the struggle of Culture against Anarchy, also produced an efficient, homogeneous cultural machine, which profited from Romanticism by appropriating the letter but not the spirit of its resistant heterogeneity.

V

I frame this cultural synopsis because the energy of Woodman's writings on Romanticism has always come from a resistance to any new Victorianism. Like Blake's exposure of Creation to its own constitutive chaos, Woodman would always return Romanticism, and culture at large, to the chaos of its madness. His Romanticism reads beyond the illusion of its own historical specificity, just as we might read beyond the empire or the current zenith of American popular culture, to encounter culture's madness. This madness manifests itself in various forms throughout Woodman's writing. In the penultimate chapter of *The Apocalyptic Vision in the Poetry of Shelley* he argues that *Adonais* is a 'metaphysical defence of self-murder' (172), still one of the most provocative statements about any literary text. While too varied to be reduced to any one enunciative position, Woodman's corpus can be said to unfold from the metaphorical and epistemological possibilities offered by this statement. Woodman offers, via Shelley's example of suicide, the unsettlingly creative phenomenology of the 'mind in creation' (*DP* 503–4)[10] as the locus of a madness whose potential for apocalypse must always be kept immanent.

As it is predicated on the abyss of its own self-destruction, *Adonais* performs the erasure of cultural truths by throwing the entire enterprise of literary writing into a chaos it cannot contain. Apocalypse, then, becomes a type of madness that must in turn overcome the chaos of its own moment – an overturning of the overturning. In turn, apocalypse exposes culture to the chaos or madness of its own making. Madness thus wages a battle *against* madness as part of a struggle – what Blake calls ceaseless 'Mental Fight' – with the forces of cultural dogmatism. *These* forces, Woodman would argue, comprise culture's real madness, from which it would not always release itself. For Shelley, this madness is *poetry*, as a type of ghost within the machine of culture. Or, as Woodman writes of Shelley's 'Mont Blanc,' poetry functions like power to deconstruct rationalism from within, deconstruction itself providing a *theoria* of Romanticism that releases it from the metaphysics that hides its knowledge of itself from itself, even as metaphysics hides Descartes's madness from himself. This poetry within Poetry or Metaphysics or whatever particular form culture takes to express its own regulatory power is a transgressive and unsettling force of re-signification and transformation – the poetry *of* Poetry or Metaphysics.

In *A Defence of Poetry*, Shelley writes:

> We have more moral, political and historical wisdom, than we know how to reduce into practise; we have more scientific and economical knowledge than can be accommodated to the just distribution of the produce which it multiplies. The poetry in these systems of thought, is concealed by the accumulation of facts and calculating processes. There is no want of knowledge respecting what is wisest and best in morals, government, and political economy, or at least, what is wiser and better than what men practise and endure. But ... we want the creative faculty to imagine that which we know; we want the generous impulse to act that which we imagine; we want the poetry of life: our calculations have outrun conception; we have eaten more than we can digest. The cultivation of those sciences which have enlarged the limits of the empire of man over the external world, has, for want of the poetical faculty, proportionally circumscribed those of the internal world; and man, having enslaved the elements, remains himself a slave ... The cultivation of poetry is never more to be desired than at periods when, from an excess of the selfish and calculating principle, the accumulation of the materials of external life exceed the quantity of the power of assimilating them to the internal laws of human nature. The body has then become too unwieldy for that which animates it. (502–3)

Shelley appeals to poetry as the radically chaotic moment founding society through all its cultural discourses. This site of culture's madness is its articulation as phantasy, which it then forgets at its own peril, as its body of historical knowledge becomes the dead weight of a culture threatening to bury its own life. Culture's confrontation with its own constitutive madness thus lies in individuals' bringing to consciousness within culture the delirium of its own relentlessly grinding apparatus, which it must then transform into poetry as its metaphorical body. The Space Show at the American Museum of Natural History seems to enact this radical return by reanimating its own body of cultural knowl-edge from the deadweight of its history. However, that it does so so blithely, *on behalf of* its subjects and in order to make its other ideologies more digestible, would horrify Shelley or Blake. However monumental the struggle against cultural prescription, the idea of not bringing it to consciousness *in the subject*, however unconscious so much of it must necessarily remain, would be for Shelley a type of psychic suicide.

Thus it is that in its seemingly productive breakdowns of madness the Cogito of culture, in the name of progress and enlightenment, seeks to name a new order of things in which subjects are merely entertained spectators of, rather than active agents within, this order's hegemony, as in the Hayden Planetarium's re-visioning of history in order to displace humanity itself. Shelley continues: 'Poetry, and the principle of Self, of which money is the visible incarnation, are the God and the Mammon of the world' (*DP* 503). Shelley would ask his reader to psychoanalyse within the 'principle of Self' offered by capitalism and its cultural machine the pathology of its making and, what is more, to recognize this pathology as an excess that perpetually resists being resolved back into the economy of System – the radical impossibility of culture. In using Shelley as his own particular synecdoche for Romanti-cism, Woodman explores the Self as the corpse-like body of culture always to find the pathology of a life experience – the 'poetry of life' – breeding within this body. This pathology resists hardening into doc-trine by accepting instead its regenerative potential to 'imagine that which we know.' Or, as we might read Shelley *after* Jameson or after Hardt and Negri, to undertake the impossible re-imagining of a world that has become too unwieldy for our conceptions.

Therefore, in *Adonais* the synecdoche for culture *in toto* is the dead body of Keats as the modern Prometheus. The Narrator would at first follow Urania in her attempt to sublimate death as the ethereal pleasure principle of the aesthetic, a cultural arbiter psychotically dissociated from the culture of her own making. The narcissistic purity of culture's immaterialism would transcend the spectral pathology of its consump-tive materialism, figured in Keats's tubercular body. As if at its primal scene, Shelley situates the gothic horror of a necrophilic and cannibalis-tic culture that consumes itself in a frantic bid to outdistance its own rabid materialism. Confronting this horror in Urania, who rises from her own death in order to revive the dead poet by making love to him, the Narrator realizes he has 'With sparkless ashes [been loading] an unlamented urn,' as confronted by his utter irrelevance within the order of things. By constructing the movement from *Adonais* to *The Triumph of Life* as a kind of primal scene of Romantic existentialism, Woodman suggests that literature must be willing with each articulation of itself to sacrifice the dogma of its identity to the pathos of its own self-destruction. This suicide, undertaken by the poet-manque Shelley at the end of the text ('The massy earth and sphered skies are riven! / I am borne darkly, fearfully, afar') is necessary to ensure the self-perpetuation of culture without succumbing to its will towards cultural prerogative. For Woodman this radical self-critique is the locus of a radical analysis always taking place within the psyche of culture as a realization of its 'radical impossibility.' Suicide, that is, is a metaphysical question *in excess* of its own metaphysics.

'I must Create a System, or be enslav'd by another Mans / I will not Reason & Compare: my business is to Create' (10.20–1), cries Los in chapter 1 of Blake's *Jerusalem*, always 'Striving with Systems to deliver Individuals from those Systems' (11.5). In 'Albions Loins,' from which emerges Los's self-making potentiality in the form of Albion's giant body, resides a 'mighty Polypus, vegetating in darkness' (8.40). As Albion exclaims later, on plate 21, all of creation is 'drivn forth by [his] disease / All is Eternal Death unless [one] can weave a chaste / Body over an unchaste Mind!' (10–12). The point, then, is not to dominate chaos but perpetually to recall the psyche to the pathological body of its own imaginative generation in this body's chaos. In this sense Woodman reads Romanticism's giant body as what he calls a metaphorical body, grown from the pathology of its own making.[11] That his vision of Romanticism is essentially mad and apocalyptic means that this body takes shape as a productive aberration within rather than a transcendence of the circumstances that produced it: madness *as* pathology.

Yet even this apparently productive ambivalence produces further questions, both for Shelley and for Woodman. Does apocalypse, however much it is avoided, still signify the potentiality of change, however traumatic? Or is apocalypse, *as* change and madness, merely a buzzword meant to distract us from culture's stultifyingly iterable and interminably normalizing effects, a place where apocalypse is not so much impossible as it is non-existent in an endless deferral meant to prevent the whole system from imploding upon itself? These are questions addressed in startling fashion in the final chapter of this book. Here, Woodman's account of Shelley and Byron offers a fascinating allegory of the currently Byronic culture of things. Their relationship comprises a kind of primal scene of the traumatic inevitability of transformation, which Shelley ultimately recognizes in giving over his vision of Romanticism, via his drowning, to that of Byron. Woodman figures Byron as Rousseau in Shelley's *The Triumph of Life*. Byron/Rousseau would have Shelley submit to Life as the determinism of a cultural materialism in which the machine of culture grinds on autonomously by spewing out a series of cultural icons who vanish as arbitrarily and irrelevantly as they appeared, like 'Figures ever new / Ris[ing] on the bubble' of culture as a 'false and fragile glass' (247–9). Byron/Rousseau seems neither engaged by this 'wretchedness' (306) nor detached from it, neither 'spectator' nor 'Actor or victim.' Whether he perishes in the rubble of the World Trade Center collapse or photographs the suicides of those who are about to die – it's all the same thing.

This thorough disinterestedness marks an epochal shift in Shelley's Romanticism from his apocalyptic engagement with the world in *Adonais, Prometheus Unbound,* or *A Defence of Poetry.* In a world that wants a hero, clamouring for the titillation of Don Juan's interminably serial rendering of the surfaces and artefacts of his culture, Shelley had to rethink radically his metaphysics of radical change. In *The Triumph of Life* he thus allows that perhaps the possibilities of transformation were altogether rather more limited than he had anticipated, suicide seeming more of a real than a virtual alternative. Alluding to Nietzsche's *Thus Spake Zarathustra*, Woodman writes:

> [Nietzsche] images Zarathustra, the creator of language, as a tightrope walker who dances on a thinly stretched rope between two towers beneath which is an abyss. Each step he takes is another metaphor by which the walker 'leaps out of one sphere right into the midst of an entirely different one.' 'Before me fled the night; behind me rose the day,' declares the Shelleyan Narrator in *The Triumph of Life* as the 'strange trance' grows 'over [his] fancy.' '[T]he Deep / Was at my feet, and heaven above my head' (26–9), he continues as if struggling to keep his balance. As Nietzsche's Zarathustra continues along his perilous path, he is unaware of a madman who comes out of the tower behind him and runs after him as if determined to overtake him. The tightrope walker falls into the abyss and the madman, who watches over him, tells him that his soul will be dead before his body.[12]

Having been confronted by a mass grave the size of two city blocks smouldering in Lower Manhattan, as if to mark the primal wound of empire's rabid materialism, we are led in Woodman's account to consider the fate of culture's repression of its own inherent schizophrenia, twinned until recently in the white marble of its own modernist splendour. What (im)materialism is at work in this primal scene, Woodman via Blake, Shelley, Nietzsche, or Jung seems to ask? What hope for humanity after what Mary Shelley in her presciently apocalyptic post-*Frankenstein* account of the end of Man calls *The Last Man*? Byron/Rousseau demonstrates to Shelley that Shelley's metaphorical world of radical transformation was, ultimately, wholly a virtual universe, a 'Life [that], like a dome of many-coloured glass, / Stains the white radiance of Eternity,' one that could all too easily be smashed. The bind, as Woodman demonstrates in following the pathos of transformation from Shelley's Wordsworthian vision of Romanticism to his surrendering of this vision to Byron, must have been excruciating. As Woodman suggests, like Keats's Moneta in *The Fall of Hyperion*, philosophy is 'deathwards progressing / To no death'; or, as Shelley might argue, 'deathwards progressing / To *know* death.' Or as Woodman argues, Blake's Los does not deny God – an impossibility – but instead enacts his pain at becoming human. How this bind plays out in terms of Woodman's own Romanticism, I leave for the reader to decide.

A few years ago a renowed interest in Byron coincided with the advent of New Historicism, focused, among other places, in Jerome McGann's critique of a Romantic ideology. This critique was cathected by McGann's status as a commentator on and editor of Byron, just as Woodman's writing is inflected by his earliest work on Shelley. New Historicism turned deconstruction's textual prosthetics, epitomized by De Man's reading of Shelley, into a multi-perspectival social politics of the text that would stage the primal scene of the text's history. Yet, I would reiterate a final time, the critical fortunes reflected even in this shift might be put aside in the sometimes monumentally difficult task of transforming the terms of critical debate so as not to remain imprisoned by them.[13] Post-structuralism does not liberate Woodman any more than does New Criticism, Deconstruction, New Historicism, or Cultural Studies. But Woodman has come, via psychoanalysis in post-structuralism, to enunciate within literature as the site of cultural regulation its constitutive madness. Where psychoanalysis has often been only a subtext in post-structuralist literary studies, albeit a provocative one, Woodman has mined this subtext by returning repeatedly to the question of the psyche and reading its effects, via culture, post-transcendentally. What appears as the evacuation of the psyche from post-structuralism has allowed Woodman to reintroduce the psyche on his own terms.

Later in her speech introducing Woodman at the 1993 Keats-Shelley Association award ceremony, Rajan states that Woodman's Shelley

> was committed to metaphor rather than metaphysics, to a conception of language which Woodman would later associate with 'a Nietzschean absence of being.'[14] He was to be understood in the way he himself read Dante and Milton, as poets for whom the vocabulary of their age was a mask or mantle hiding an intention that was always already trans-positional. To anticipate what Woodman would say in subsequent work, this meant that Shelley could not be reduced to what he said. For what he said was a metaphorical body for a lightning that had found no conductor, and whose semiotic potential (in Kristeva's terms) was necessarily (mis)represented by any encoding in symbolic form.

One should not reduce Woodman to what he said, in that he is engaged in enunciating a psyche perpetually disarticulated by the body of its own madness. The shape of this body, as Rajan suggests and as Woodman has explored in this book with such startling complexity, is metaphorical; it is formed by the radical and perpetual displacement of the Cartesian Cogito by its own doubt – the madness of its attempt to know itself. Woodman uncovers the madness that Derrida reads in Foucault's attempt to liberate madness from its Enlightenment imprisonment, the underlying subject of all of the papers in this study. In *Resistances of Psychoanalysis*, Derrida revists the scene of madness in his encounter with Foucault in 'Cogito and the History of Madness.'[15] He describes madness as a force constituting yet simultaneously pulling at the weave of Reason's fabric in order to ensure the interminability of the weaving itself. This is an embracing of the process that cannot master it. The death drive towards madness is for Woodman the stuff of life itself, the reason for living, the pleasure of the metaphorical body – a pleasure that, as this book so profoundly demonstrates, is ongoing.

Notes

Introduction

1 Understood as a text that enacts the process of its making, the Romantic poem as I explore it is haunted by the spectre of its death as the thing made. 'The game is done! I've won! I've won!' (197) cries Coleridge's 'Nightmare LIFE-IN-DEATH' in *The Ancient Mariner*. Only by dividing itself as subject from the death that is its object can the Romantic poet in the act of composition contact the psychic life, which otherwise remains hidden in its death. The death in which it is otherwise hidden is, as materialism, nihilism. Viewed in terms of the Romantic opposition to materialism (the 'mechanical philosophy,' as Coleridge calls it), it is soul, the individuated 'I Am that I Am.' For Coleridge, this individuated 'I Am' is the act of perception itself (which he calls the 'primary imagination'), an act that he sought metaphysically to ground in God as the 'infinite I AM.' In my exploration of the Romantic text, it is psychologically grounded in a notion of the unconscious developed by Jung in his opposition to the materialism of Freud. Coleridge, I shall argue, psychoanalytically anticipates Jung's notion. Suspended between metaphysics and psychology, he invented the term 'psycho-analytical' in 1805 to describe his approach to metaphysics. 'So shall thou feed on death, that feeds on men, / And death once dead, there's no more dying then,' Shakespeare writes, addressing the soul. In Romanticism the reality of soul lies in the death of death, psychically enacted as the poet's critical interrogation of the psyche's 'rough magic,' which is, among other things, the Romantic poet's engagement with madness. Rising out of this interrogation has emerged in our time a notion of critical theory as a separate discipline that, in its purest form, sublates poetry by raising it to a condition that Wolfgang Giegerich calls 'the soul's logical life.'

2 Fortunately, this critical situation is beginning to change. Based on a wealth of hitherto unknown archival materials, Sonu Shamdasani in *Jung and the Making of Modern Psychology: The Dream of Science* argues that Freud's influence on Jung, including their parting in 1912, has been greatly exaggerated. Viewed in terms of its nineteenth-century sources, Jung's 'encyclopedic' (18) project, while briefly influenced by Freud, largely developed independently of him. The result is that Jung's psychological project has never been accurately grasped, writings to date about it, particularly by Jungians, being 'hampered by incomplete and unreliable textual sources' (22). Jung's project, as Shamdasani describes it, was to found a science of psychology that would include within itself all science, a metascience, as it were, as the mother or container of science, a science of science itself. While Shamdasani's book appeared too late directly to influence the argument of this book, his understanding of Jung's project supports my own understanding, particularly with reference to Jung's complex relations with Wolfgang Pauli. In his essay 'On the Nature of the Psyche' (1954), Jung, writing under the influence of his work with Pauli, paradoxically argues that 'psychology is doomed to cancel itself out as a science and therein precisely it reaches its scientific goal [as metascience]. Every other science has so to speak an outside; not so psychology, whose object is *the inside subject of all science*' (CW 8:429; italics added). As 'the inside subject of all science,' it may be argued, psychology, for Jung, retains all science under sublation (*Aufhebung*).

Jung's rejection of Hegel in favour of Kant, perhaps in fear of the very thing he most desired (a science of sciences) as empirically ungrounded mental inflation (madness), is crucial to an understanding of the gap between *theoria* and *praxis* evident in Jung's psychology, a gap thoroughly explored by Wolfgang Giegerich in *The Soul's Logical Life*. Jung's fear of madness, I suggest, stood in the way of his hyperbolic project, of what Jacques Derrida calls the 'Cogito.' Interestingly enough, while Jung argues that 'every psychology [including his own] that takes the psyche as "experience" is from the historical point of view both "Romantic" and "alchemystical,"' he nevertheless insists that 'below this experiential level ... [his] psychology is scientific and rationalistic, a fact [that he] would beg the reader not to overlook' (CW 18:1740). By 'scientific and rationalistic,' Jung presumably means the logical life of the psyche as distinct from the experiential, the experiential retained under sublation, a sublation which releases psychology into itself as that which contains all experience, though as the mind's a priori independence from it as mind itself, the 'I Am that I Am.'

We shall see that, under the influence of Pauli, Jung came to think of natural numbers as archetypes, not images of them, which is what numbers become when used as counters. Pauli, a mathematical genius, worked with numbers at an archetypal level, devising equations that were answerable only to their own interior logic. Jung admired Pauli's genius, by 1953 considering Pauli's work in quantum physics far more advanced than his own work in psychology. Jung also feared, as much in himself as in Pauli, the madness that is the raw condition of genius, a condition that, in Jung's experience of it, often manifested itself as schizophrenia. 'Right into old age,' Jung confesses, 'I have had the incorrigible feeling that if, like my schoolmates, I could have accepted without a struggle the proposition that a = b, or that sun – moon, dog – cat, then mathematics might have fooled me endlessly – just *how* much I only began to realize at the age of eighty-four. All my life it remained a puzzle to me why it was that I never managed to get my bearings in mathematics when there was no doubt whatever that I could calculate properly. Least of all did I understand my own *moral* doubts concerning mathematics' (*MDR* 28). Jung realized 'just *how* much' he distrusted mathematics when he himself wrote, rather than dictated to Aniela Jaffé, his account of his school days not from the perspective of the wisdom of old age, but as he actually experienced it as a schoolboy. What presumably surprised him was his realization at the age of eighty-four (when recalling his early years to write his account of them) that, after twenty-six years of working with Pauli (not dealt with in *Memories, Dreams, Reflections*), he still felt the same way about mathematics as he had as a child, not, I suggest, in spite of the notion of the archetypal nature of number, but because of the notion itself. His own personal equation (personal myth) inwardly constructed in *Memories, Dreams, Reflections* was a necessary phenomenological (or Kantian) corrective to the dangerous excess of a purely mathematical (or Hegelian) equation. His '*moral* doubts' about mathematics included, I suggest, his '*moral* doubts' about Hegel. 'Hegel,' Jung writes, 'put me off by his language, as arrogant as it was laborious; I regarded him with downright mistrust. He seemed to me like a man who was caged in the [archetypal] edifice of his own words and was pompously gesticulating in his prison' (69). Protecting himself against the 'prison' of madness as the identification with the archetype, Jung, as he describes it in the final sentence of *Memories, Dreams, Reflections*, concluded that it now seemed to him 'as if that alienation which so long separated [him] from the world has become transferred into [his] own inner world, and has revealed to [him] an unexpected familiarity with [him]self' (359). Jung's insistence upon an empirical method in psychology worked against his visionary conception of it. He remained, as it were, suspended between the 'prison' of madness and what he called the 'prison' of the three-dimensional '"box system"' (?9?). As this book perhaps makes over-abundantly clear, it was a question of 'how does one get from Three to Four' (*Atom* 129).

1: Jung and Romanticism: The Fate of the Mythopoeic Imagination

1 'People who merely believe and don't think always forget that they continually expose themselves to ... doubt,' writes Jung in 'A Psychological Approach to the Dogma of the Trinity' (1948): 'Wherever belief reigns, doubt lurks in the background. But thinking people welcome doubt: it serves them as a valuable stepping-stone to better knowledge. People who can believe should be a little more tolerant with those of their fellows who are only capable of thinking. Belief has already conquered the summit which thinking tries to win by toilsome climbing. The believer ought not to project his habitual enemy, doubt, upon the thinker, thereby suspecting him of destructive designs ... The fact that a dogma is on the one hand believed and on the other hand is an object of thought is proof of its vitality. Therefore let the believer rejoice that others, too, seek to climb the mountain on whose peak he sits' (*CW* 11:170).

2 'My chief object,' Jung writes, '... is to give a detailed exposition of those psychological views which seem to me necessary if we are to understand the dogma as a symbol in the psychological sense. Yet my purpose would be radically misunderstood if it were conceived as an attempt to "psychologize" the dogma. Symbols that have an archetypal foundation can never be reduced to anything else, as must be obvious to anybody who possesses the slightest knowledge of my writings' (*CW* 11:171).

3 Giegerich's 'rigorous notion of psychology' (278) in *The Soul's Logical Life*, as what he calls 'the logical form of consciousness,' sublates (negates, retains, transforms) the unconscious work of the psyche into the soul's knowledge of itself as the 'I Am that I Am.' 'To-day's psychological problem can no longer be dealt with on the level of contents (images, symbols, rituals, myths, Gods, doctrines)' (24), he argues. Psyche is the animating principle in Romanticism that becomes in Jung's psychology the unreliable anima who, as the archetype of life, forges in the name of psychology the precarious connection between the unconscious and consciousness. Giegerich rejects this Romantic or Jungian notion of psychology as pre-psychological and therefore obsolete because it is still bound to a representation of the soul (i.e., psyche), rather than being the soul's reality.

In his 'Ode to Psyche,' Keats comes upon Psyche 'on a sudden, fainting with surprise,' as he wanders 'thoughtlessly' in the licentious 'forest' (7–8) of Apuleius's *The Golden Ass,* which in its literary context is where Jung also first found her. Keats recognizes Eros, 'the winged boy' (21), but not Psyche, who lies as if entranced in his embrace in a manner that suggests to Keats a realm of love that far surpasses the lust crudely portrayed in what he has 'thoughtlessly' been reading. 'You must recollect that Psyche was not embodied as a goddess before the time of Apuleius the Platonist who lived after the Augustan age,' Keats writes to his brother and sister-in-law (14 February – 3 May 1819), 'and consequently the Goddess was never worshiped or sacrificed to with any of the ancient fervour – and perhaps never thought of in the old religion – I am more orthodox than to let a heathen Goddess be so neglected' (*KL* 253). Though in the now 'faded hierarchy' of Olympus, she had 'no shrine, no grove, no oracle, no heat / Of pale-mouth'd prophet dreaming,' and though it is now 'too late for antique vows, / Too, too late for the fond believing lyre' (34–7), he will nevertheless be her 'priest' and 'build a fane / In some untrodden region of [his] mind' (50–1). Keats's building of the 'fane' (his Ode) becomes, as feigning, his fanciful account of 'Soul-making,' which, Giegerich suggests, Jung unreflectingly associated with a pseudo-psychology. Psychology, he suggests, too often, particularly at Bollingen, became for Jung the work of 'a fond believing lyre [liar].'

Keats's 'Ode to Psyche,' it may be argued, provides a parodic model of everything Giegerich rejects as fiction or superstition in Jung's depth psychology. For Giegerich, the entire account of the unconscious as it archetypally propels the psychic process toward a teleological realization of the Self is the fiction of psychology as distinct from its reality or truth. 'The Self, the *genius,* the Gods *as positive images or symbols* are obsolete,' he insists. 'The time of this logical innocence, where truth could still *really* happen [psychic reality] in the *form* of symbols, images, or rituals, has long been passé. In the shows of television and the images of advertising we have the constant reminder and the objective ('material') representation of the psychological or logical obsolescence of the "image" as such' (23–4). Bound to fiction, Jung's 'mythopoeic imagination,' Giegerich contends, seduced him into betraying the truth, Jung, invoking Kant as opposed to Hegel, insisting that the archetypal reality itself was unknowable except as the symbols of it. Opposing Jung, Giegerich invokes Hegel as opposed to Kant and argues that psychology is the discipline of interiority, which contains within itself its non-empirical other by which it is logically (dialectically) known, not as other but as itself. Psychology, that is, is the 'I Am that I Am,' not the fictional, mythopoeic representation of it.

Jung's rejection of the anima's insistence that the fantasies he was inscribing immediately following his break with Freud were art, which, as the substitution of fiction for reality, allowed him to turn away from reality, provides, as we shall see, one confirmation of Giegerich's conviction that despite Jung's betrayal of the true nature of psychology and despite the empiricism upon which he insisted, he nevertheless '*had a real Notion or Concept of "soul"*' (41) that was, as 'Notion or Concept,' true to Giegerich's 'rigorous notion' of psychology. For this reason, and perhaps for this reason alone, Giegerich, rejecting as psychology Jung's making of a personal myth, continues to think of himself as a Jungian analyst.

The Jung whose work is explored in this book on the Romantic psyche is essentially the Jung whom Giegerich rejects, his rejection providing a critique not only of Jung but of the Romanticism for which Jung is here associated as a theoretical spokesman. The transformation that, for Giegerich, comes with sublation (myth retained under sublation as a moment in it) is a transformation that turns over the rejected empiricism of Giegerich's notion of psychology to its implicit enlightenment. My argument in this book, *contra* Giegerich, is that the Giegerichean enlightenment that confronts the empiricism of Jung's psychology must always (as Derrida argues) turn itself over to its own implicit madness in order to remain human. Giegerich rejects the role of madness in the soul's logical life. I embrace it.

4 See Coleridge's Notebooks (2:2670). Kathleen Coburn was the first to point out the neologism in *Experience into Thought* (4), having earlier excerpted the relevant passage from Coleridge's *Notebooks* in *Inquiring Spirit*.

5 'In the strict sense of the word,' writes Coleridge, 'every being capable of understanding, must be mad, who remains as it were, sunk in the ground on which he treads ... who gifted with divine faculties of indefinite hope & fear, born with them, yet fixes his faith upon that in w^{ch} [which] neither hope nor fear, have any proper field to display themselves' (*Collected Works* 5:326).

6 Jung's psychological break with Freud in 1913, it may be argued, found its scientific analogue in Niels Bohr's break with Newtonian physics in the same year. The transformation of the inner world in Jung's psychology has its counterpart in the transformation of the outer world in quantum physics. Writing to Pauli (10 October 1955), Jung deeply regretted that 'psychology at the moment is lagging so far behind that there is not much of value to be expected from it for quite a while yet. I myself have reached

my upper limits and am consequently hardly in a position to make any contribution of note.' To which he adds: 'Your courage in tackling the problem of my psychology is a great source of pleasure to me and fills me with gratitude' (*Atom* 133). Both of them realized that because psychology was lagging so far behind quantum physics, which had technologically reduced the globe to one country, humanity, lacking a psychological consciousness commensurate with the quantum reality of the physical world, was increasingly in danger of extinction.

For Jung and Pauli, the synchronistic connection between the inner and outer worlds in which the psyche can acausally act as matter and matter can acausally act as psyche made it increasingly evident that humanity's future depended upon a consciousness of what Shelley in 'Mont Blanc' described as the human mind's 'unremitting interchange / With the clear universe of things around' (39–40) as 'the everlasting universe of things / Flows through' it (1–2). In his essay, 'The Influence of Archetypal Ideas on the Scientific Theories of Kepler,' Pauli deals with the role of the psyche, particularly alchemy, in the birth of physics. Because Jung had dealt with essentially the same subject from the psychological point of view in his long essay, 'Synchronicity: An Acausal Connecting Principle,' they decided to publish both papers together in a single volume, *The Interpretation of Nature and the Psyche*. Binding the two papers together, beyond the empirical evidence of the acausal connection between psyche and matter, was Jung's notion of the 'psychoid archetype,' in which he argues that it is probable that psyche and matter are two different manifestations of the same power, which at a 'real zero point' (without extension) 'touch and do not touch,' as Jung writes in 'On the Nature of the Psyche' (*CW* 8:418). For Descartes, extension is the realm of matter. The 'real zero point' without extension is mind, upon which extension or matter logically depends.

7 *Adonais*, the title of Shelley's elegy on the death of Keats, fuses Adonis, the perpetually dying and rising vegetation god imminent in the creation, and Adonai, who transcends the creation entirely. Shelley's experience of himself in the writing of the elegy as 'a Power / Girt round with weakness,' so weak that 'it can scarce uplift / The weight of the superincumbent hour [the hour chosen to compose his elegy]' symbolically enacts the dying Adonis. 'It is,' Shelley continues, 'a dying lamp, a falling shower, / A breaking billow; – even whilst we speak / Is it not broken?' (281–6). The inspiration that informs the creative process (Shelley's instantaneous Fourfold intuition of the poem as a whole as distinct from its Threefold process of creation) is symbolically represented by Adonai. The symbolic action of the elegy (its Threefold structure or movement) contains within it

the Fourfold. In his actual drowning, I suggest, Shelley may have literalized the symbolic process of his elegy, the elegy becoming what I have elsewhere called a 'metaphysical defense of self-murder' (*Apocalyptic Vision* 172). Within the elegy itself, Shelley's symbolic drowning ('I am borne darkly, fearfully afar') carries the elegy from the Three to the Four, the Four becoming its containing form.

8 '"A terrifying abyss of all kinds of questions, a wealth of responsibilities stretched out before me,"' writes Wassily Kandinsky in turning from representation to abstraction. '"And most important of all: what is to replace the missing object?"' (cited in Ringbom 131). One answer to Kandinsky's question is the replacement of the object with the psychic process of its making. 'On the floor I am more at ease,' Jackson Pollock explained. 'I feel nearer, more a part of the painting, since this way I can walk around it, *work from the four sides* and literally be in the painting' (cited in Ross 139l; italics added).

9 In *Paris Present*, Louis Aragon, the surrealist poet, employing similar images, enacts the same disintegrative process: 'He who had finally parted company with his thought when far away the first waves had started licking the wounds of the spurned head stirred from his immobility like an inverted question mark ['Then. what is life? I said' (*TL* 544)]. In the pure air, above the charred sierras, at those altitudes where the earth, scraped to the bone [the charred landscape as Rousseau's corpse] bathes in the diamond sun's implacable glare ['that light's severe excess' (*TL* 424)], where each stone seemed marked with the hoofprint of an ironshod stellar horse' (cited in Ashton 91).

10 Shelley's early materialism lay in his commitment to 'Necessity! thou mother of the world!' (*Queen Mab* 6.198). 'Necessity,' he explains in his notes attached to the poem, 'means that, contemplating the events which compose the moral and material universe, he beholds only an immense and uninterrupted chains of causes and effects, no one of which could occupy any other place than it does occupy, or act in any other way than it does act ... The word liberty, as applied to mind, is analogous to the word chance as applied to matter: they spring from the certainty of the conjunction of antecedents and consequents' (*Complete Poetical Works* 809–10).

In his rejection of the 'mechanical philosophy,' Coleridge is more specific in his account of how materialism allows its disciples to talk while dispensing them from thinking in the way 'Necessity' dispenses with thinking. According to the 'mechanical philosophy,' Coleridge explains, it may be as truly said of what he is writing that it was written by Saint

Paul's church; 'for it is,' he explains, 'the mere motion of my muscles and nerves; and these again are set in motion from external causes equally passive, which external causes stand themselves in interdependent connection with every thing that exists or has existed. Thus the whole universe co-operates to produce the minutest stroke of every letter, save only that I myself, and I alone, have nothing to do with it, but merely the causeless and *effectless* beholding of it when it is done. Yet scarcely can it be called a beholding; for it is neither an act nor an effect; but an impossible creation of *something-nothing* out of its very contrary! It is the mere quick-silver plating behind a looking-glass; and in this alone consists the poor worthless I!' (*BL* 1:118–19).

11 'The difficulties [in painting] begin when you understand what it is that the soul will not permit the hand to make,' Philip Guston writes. 'But you begin to feel as you go on working that unless painting proves its right to exist by being critical and self-judging, it has no reason to exist at all – or is not even possible ... Art without a trial disappears at a glance: it is too primitive or hopeful, or mere notions, or simply startling, or just another means to make life bearable ... Frustration is one of the great things in art; satisfaction is nothing ... Certain artists do something and a new emotion [consciousness] is brought into the world; its real meaning lies outside of history and the chains of causality' (93–5). In *Adonais*, the 'real meaning' that 'lies outside of history' is 'Death,' which, Shelley argues, joins together what life divides ('No more let Life divide what Death can join together' [476]). Symbolically understood as the Fourfold, for Jung, as for Shelley, Death is the 'zero point without extension,' the still point around which ceaselessly revolves 'the void circumference.' In the act of composition, the poet's 'panting soul' clasps 'the pendulous earth' as hope kindles hope and lures it 'to the brink' (420–3). For Jung, as for Shelley, Death is the symbol of an unmediated or absolute consciousness, which is the eternal form of soul imaged as the psychic process of its becoming. 'To will a new form is inacceptable, because will builds distortion,' Guston argues. 'Desire, too, is incomplete and arbitrary. These strategies, however intimate they might become, must especially be removed to clear the way for something else – a condition somewhat unclear, but which in retrospect becomes a very precise act. This "thing" is recognized only as it comes into existence' (94). Written 'in retrospect,' *The Triumph of Life* is the 'very precise act' that *Adonais* becomes. The poem folds into the death it cannot become without itself ceasing to be.

12 See n6, above.

2: Frye's Blake: The Site of Opposition

1 The ruthlessness of his 'daemon' lay in the release of his 'No. 2 personality' from the restrictions of what, with reference to the Ten Commandments, Blake described as 'Offering & Atonement in the crue[l]ties of
Moral Law' (M 5.12). In Blake's apocalyptic framework, 'the crue[l]ties of
Moral Law' lay in the sacrifice of Jesus to the 'two-fold Monster' consist-
ing of a 'Dragon red & hidden Harlot [the Whore of Babylon]' described
by John of Patmos in Revelation. As 'Moral Virtue,' this 'two-fold Monster' to which, as the religion of the 'Elect,' Blake's Milton rationally (or
deistically) bound himself in *Paradise Lost* becomes in *Milton* the hermaphroditic form in which Milton enters Blake's body as what Blake describes
as a 'Female hidden in a Male, Religion hidden in War' (M 40[46].20–2). In
his childhood, Jung, like Blake, associated this hermaphroditic form with
priesthood, an association that became the basis of what he described as
his 'first conscious trauma' between the ages of three and four. Playing
alone on the road in front of his house, he saw a man coming down from
the wood wearing what appeared to be women's clothes whom he identified with a notion of Jesus, who, in a song his mother nightly sang to him
before he went to sleep, devoured little children so that Satan could not eat
them. He ran terrified into the house and hid under a beam in the darkest
corner of the attic. At about the same time, Jung had his first remembered
dream of a giant phallus in an underground cave that his mother described as 'the man-eater.' The 'man-eater' became in his imagination
Jesus in the disguise of a Jesuit who contained within himself the power of
life and death, a power he would some fifty years later explore in relation
to 'the motif of cannibalism that underlies the symbolism of the Mass.'
Jung describes the entire 'psychotic' episode as the 'unconscious beginnings' of his 'intellectual life' (*MDR* 10–15). As a memorial to it, he carved
a little mannequin, placed it in his pencil box, and hid it under the beam in
the attic where he had hidden himself. Not until he wrote his long essay
on the psychology of the Mass did he speak of his mannequin buried alive
in his pencil box as a childhood image of death and resurrection. Understood as the conscious shaping of his 'No. 2 personality,' Jung's psychology, I suggest, dialectically illuminates Blake's mythopoeic vision in
'corporeal' ways that (as we shall see) Frye's archetypal criticism rejects.

2 Commenting upon Jung's Fourfold world, which is, like Blake's, the fully
human world, Winnicott writes: 'The mandala is a truly frightening thing
for me because of its absolute failure to come to terms with destructiveness, and with chaos, disintegration, and other madnesses' (491).

Winnicott fails to recognize that the Fourfold, which, as already suggested in the first chapter, Jung identified with quantum physics, grows out of the 'chaos, disintegration, and other madnesses' that emerge from the rejection of the 'single vision' of Newtonian physics in which the psyche as observer is eliminated. ('May God us keep / From Single vision and Newtons sleep' [E 722], writes Blake.) It is the presence of the unconscious operations of the psyche that introduces 'chaos, disintegration, and other madnesses' into classical physics, not because it itself is 'chaos,' but because it reduces the materialism of classical physics to chaos in somewhat the same way that Freud's psychology reduces the psyche to Thanatos, which is to say to the madness of its own extinction. Describing the impact of the poetic imagination on the materialism that constitutes the 'familiar world,' Shelley writes: 'It makes us the inhabitants of a world to which the familiar world is a chaos' (DP 505).

3 In his early childhood, Jung slept in his father's bedroom, which was separate from his mother's. 'At night,' writes Jung, 'Mother was strange and mysterious. One night I saw coming from her door a faintly luminous, indefinite figure whose head detached itself from the neck and floated along in front of it, in the air, like a little moon. Immediately another head was produced and again detached itself. This process was repeated six or seven times' (MDR 18). The repeated splittings, it may be argued, indicate Jung's infantile schizophrenic identification with his mother, Jung describing his father as a substitute for his absent mother.

4 Building Bollingen in the 1920s, Jung on occasion was haunted by the *sälig lüt*, Wotan's army of departed souls. Rejecting hallucination as merely begging the question, he explored the haunting as having some synchronistic connection to an external reality taking shape in the collective unconscious; Bollingen itself became a citadel for it where Jung conducted much of his experimental work. The night before his mother's death, Jung had a frightening dream in which his mother was gathered to the *sälig lüt* by Wotan, the Wild Huntsman. 'It was the Christian missionaries who made Wotan into a devil,' Jung explains. 'In himself he is an important god – a Mercury or Hermes, as the Romans correctly realized, a nature spirit who returned to life again in the Merlin of the Grail legend and became, as the *spiritus Mercurialis*, the sought-after arcanum of the alchemists. Thus the dream says that the soul of my mother was taken into the greater territory of the self which lies beyond the segment of Christian morality, taken into the wholeness of nature and spirit in which conflicts and contradictions are resolved' (MDR 313–14). This 'wholeness' became the fourfold object of Jung's psychology, even as it became the Fourfold

object (Eden) of Blake's mythopoeic vision. The 'psychotic' ground of this 'wholeness' as it is potentially transformed into a new level of conscious-ness constitutes the argument of this book.

5 It was against this Freudian reduction of spirit to matter that Jung's 'No. 2 personality' rebelled in a manner that vividly mirrors Blake's account of Los's struggle at the fiery forge with his recalcitrant Spectre, Jung's dia-phragm, like Blake's Bowlahoola, becoming 'red hot' (*MDR* 155). In the name of Wotan, Jung's 'Vegetable Body' became the site of the paganism that, in the name of the Father artificially creating out of himself without a sexual partner, Christianity had vigorously repressed. Exploring the religious significance of incest, Jung related it to the divine marriage of the Mother of God with her Son, a marriage that, like Blake, he describes in terms of the Fourfold Human, the New Jerusalem descending from heaven as a bride adorned for her husband. The release of energy from its radical repression (which, for Jung, constitutes psychosis) initially as-sumes the form of what Plato in *Ion* describes as divine insanity, an insan-ity to which Frye, in the name of a higher sanity, refers in his account of the gospel of John. This higher sanity (explored by Jung in his work with Pauli), we shall now see, is described by Frye in *The Great Code* as a fourth level of language, which he identifies with the Pentacostal tongues of fire described by Paul (231). Blake himself appears to be anticipating such a language ('unspeakable words' [*arreta rhemata*], 'not lawful for man to utter' [*Great Code* 231]) when he describes the Antichrist as 'a terrible indefinite Hermaphroditic form,' which is the demonic (or psychotic) parody of what is about to issue from the 'Wine-presses' as 'the Great Harvest & Vintage of the Nations' in the concluding plates of *Jerusalem*: 'A Wine-press of Love & Wrath double Hermaph[r]oditic / Twelvefold in Allegoric pomp in selfish holiness / The Pharisaion, the Grammateis, the Presbuterion, / The Archiereus, the Iereus, the Saddusaion, double / Each withoutside of the other, covering eastern heaven' (89.4–8). Blake's view of the fallen relationship between the sexes, which anticipates Nietzsche's, is an issue that Frye largely ignores in his treatment of Blake. The transmis-sion of the creative seed from Los to Blake in the full plate (47) illumina-tion of fellatio in *Milton* needs to be set against the warning of Blake's Spectre in *Jerusalem*: 'The Man who respects Woman shall be despised by Woman / And deadly cunning & mean abjectness only, shall enjoy them / For I will make their places of joy & love, excrementitious[.] / Continually building, continually destroying in Family feuds / While you are under the dominion of a jealous Female / Unpermanent for ever because of love & jealousy (88.37–42).

6 Frye's criticism of my paper on Blake's *Milton* delivered in his first graduate course on Blake was, as we shall see (which, at the time, I could not
see), grounded in my binding of it to the 'Corporeal Understanding' as the
unredeemed feminine, that is to say, the Whore of Babylon. Coming to
grips with the Whore within myself constitutes a subtext within this study
of the Romantic psyche. This coming to grips finally rejects the patriarchal
redemption of the feminine as a false polarization of the masculine and
feminine that Romanticism itself failed to resolve.

7 David L. Clark argues, with reference to Schelling, that the ground of the
arché is not the *Ur-grund* but the *Un-grund* of God's Being. As 'a slag-heap
to capture the waste of becoming' (145n104), the *Un-grund* is always
already in excess of what, as the Logos or Word, God's becoming is. In a
manner that casts considerable light upon Jung's treatment of the 'excrementitious,' Clark writes:

> What is indispensable to God's existence is thereby conserved, albeit it in the
> demonized form of an unnecessary addition whose violent exclusion is the
> means by which God constitutes and recognizes himself as 'all in all.' A sup-
> plementary logic is at work: the impure remainder is maximally real and
> composed of material so resistant that it endures even the fires of the apoca-
> lypse; at the same time, it is sheer rubbish, nothing, or nearly nothing, and,
> as such, it is so insignificant that God can confidently declare his complete
> realization and not contradict himself. It is as if the panoptic eye of God's
> 'luminous consciousness' sees and does not see the gloom into which he has
> chased the remainder. He is blind to this supplement, but unseeing in the
> special way in which seeing is blind to the origin of sight. Out of sight, out of
> mind. '*Blindness to the supplement* is the law,' Derrida writes. ('Necessary
> Heritage' 117–18)

By exploring the *deus absconditus* as God's unconscious side, his blindness
to the supplement, Jung introduces an unabsorbable contradiction into
divine consciousness. He rejects, that is, the Augustinian notion of evil as
the 'privatio boni.'

8 The 'Two Witnesses' (Elijah and Moses) in the Book of Revelation become,
as archetypal figures in *Milton*, Rintrah and Palamabron (9.8). Meeting
Los 'at the Gate of Golgonooza,' they raise up Whitefield and Westley, the
founders of Methodism. 'The generations of men,' Los explains, 'run on in
the tide of Time / But leave their destind lineaments permanent for ever &
ever,' the 'dear Saviour' taking on 'the likeness of men.' 'Were they Prophets / Or were they Idiots or Madmen?' Los rhetorically asks the multitude
who demand 'Miracles.' 'Can you have greater Miracles than these
[Whitefield and Wesley]?' Los replies (22[24].24–62; 23[35].1).

9 The 'silence' of Frye's mother, who, Frye suggests, did not think the thoughts she passed on to her son, became in Frye a 'voluble' silence. In his early childhood, Jung was similarly confronted by the silence of his mother, which, on occasion, became 'voluble,' momentarily releasing Jung from his father's dead religion into a vitally alive pagan reality that he, like his mother, embraced as his 'No. 2 personality.' It was, for example, his mother who recommended he read Goethe's *Faust* at a time when he was struggling in vain to accept his father's religion. The result was that Jung immediately recognized in Mephistopheles Goethe's unacknowledged hero, rejecting the redemption of Faust as the false Christian system his father invited him to embrace.

10 As Christopher Norris argues, Kierkegaard explains in *The Point of View of My Work as an Author* that the ethical stage of his threefold dialectic (aesthetic, ethical, religious) is 'transcended by a recognition of its own insufficiency in the face of authentic religious experience,' the dialectic itself (the aesthetic 'ensnaring' the reader) allowing the reader to 'achieve that inwardness of self-understanding that alone constitutes religious faith' (39). Read retrospectively, Frye's *The Double Vision*, published posthumously, reveals a similar Christian dialectic at work. Explaining Kierkegaard's use of what Kierkegaard calls 'teleological suspension,' Norris argues that 'things being what they are in the present age, the choice must fall between absolute silence and the use of "indirect communication." And, given that choice, a timorous silence is scarcely to be regarded as "a higher form of religiousness"' (40). Applying to Kierkegaard the kind of deconstructive reading that de Man brings to his reading of Rousseau, Norris concludes his essay: 'Kierkegaard's appeal to "Providence" – his trust in an end to the duplicities of language – is thus taken up and applied by his interpreters as a matter of hermeneutic faith. But deconstruction breaks with this providential ethics of reading. It affirms the irreducibility of writing to any preconceived idea of authorial design or truth at the end of enquiry. In Kierkegaard it meets perhaps the strongest, most resourceful, and hard-pressed challenge to its powers of textual demystification' (58). With reference to deconstruction, some defenders of Frye's schematics now argue the same thing.

11 Wolfgang Giegerich argues that psychology proper is the mind's dialectical consciousness of its own operations, which negates the otherness of those operations in order to pass through them to a consciousness of them as the mind itself. In his failure to negate mythology as the form of the mind's otherness, Jung, Giegerich argues, regressed to a pre-psychological stage. In his work with Wolfgang Pauli, it may be argued, Jung remained

suspended between a negation of myth-making and a passing through it to the other side understood as thought conscious of itself, a consciousness implicit, if not explicit, in his notion of the Self. Frye's attempt to release literature from what Giegerich, with reference to Jung's psychology, describes as 'the empirical sphere of experienced or lived life and ... a visual world of existing things,' is, Giegerich argues (with reference to Jung), a failure of 'logical negativity' to truly transgress the visual 'to the abstract sphere of "pre-existence" or "after-life"' (201). Frye's literary theory, like Jung's psychological theory, remains, in this Giegerichean sense, suspended between a mythical affirmation and a negation which constitutes the transcendence of it.

12 See my 'Nietzsche, Blake, Keats and Shelley: The Making of a Metaphorical Body.'

13 Frye used his diaries to record his dreams. See n14, following.

14 This was particularly the case in 1949–50 when he was assembling material for his paper on Blake and Jung. Though the paper was never written in anything like the way it was taking shape in his mind in the midst of the 'jinx' against it, Frye did finally produce at the invitation of the editor of *The Kenyon Review* a vastly abbreviated form, which only indirectly dealt with Jung. The invitation came on 23 June 1950 and Frye mailed the article on 29 July, the actual writing, Robert Denham suggests, taking 'no longer than a couple of days' (*Diaries* 8:xxvi). In the article, 'The Archetypes of Literature,' Frye states (without developing the idea) that 'the fascination which '*The Golden Bough* and Jung's book on libido symbols [*Symbols of Transformation*] have for literary critics is not based on dilettantism, but on the fact that these books are primarily studies in literary criticism, and very important ones' (17). 'I've often wondered *why* we sleep,' Frye writes in his diary (12 February 1950); 'it surely isn't to "rest" our brain, which doesn't rest & doesn't need it ... but to sink it into the domain of creative archetypal imagery & free association, whence it emerges to give directions & basis to the wakened mind' (*Diaries* 8:258). Frye greatly elaborated this point in his diary entry for 4 January 1949 (two days before my fateful *Milton* paper). He is commenting upon his first lecture on Newman in his 'Nineteenth-Century Thought' course in which, having 'nothing to say,' he rehashed what he had said many times about 'the old Verstand [part]-Vernunft [whole] distinction.' In his diary (if not in his lecture), he explores the distinction in terms of 'Jung's counterpoising principle – the unconscious being the realm of the pleasure principle in its upper regions [Freud's personal unconscious] as well as the realm of intuitive apprehension in its deeper ones [Jung's collective

unconscious].' The 'intuitive apprehension in its deeper [Jungian] ones,' Frye argues, 'begins all creative activity.' The 'upper [Freudian] regions,' being regressive, interfere because they seek an ego gratification rather than an archetypal one. In the 'upper regions' of the unconscious, the archetypal imagination hits a snag. The gratification of the desires of the personal unconscious the ego must forgo results in 'anxiety, bewilderment, even suffering.' Avoiding this, the ego deludes itself by falsely claiming the pleasures of the Self grounded in the archetypes of the collective unconscious as its own. The result is an 'emotional vulgarization' of the Self by its confusion with the ego (Frye described my paper on *Milton* as a 'vulgarization' of Blake's archetypal vision). Frye then goes on to explore the struggle between the personal and collective unconscious in the work of Blake's Los at his forge where 'the material from waking consciousness' dramatized in the personal unconscious finds its anagogical meaning in 'the archetypal world of being where everything is a wish-fulfilment comedy.' If this does not happen, as in *In Memoriam*, for example, then dreams will remain 'Freudian sex-dreams or Adlerian power-dreams, concerned solely with an antithesis between reality & desire.' Addressing himself now, at the age of thirty-six, Frye concludes: 'If [from thirty-five on] he is progressing, his individuality, Jung's self, takes form at the centre of the wheel, instead of being one of the foci of an ellipse, the other being a point in the dark' (8:60–1). At the same time, however, Frye wrote in his notebook, 'I don't want *literature* to be turned into a psychological allegory of individuation.' 'On the other hand,' he continues, 'once I move back from literary to existential metaphor I'll come very close to it' (*Notebooks* 5:131), though not as literature, but as life. For Frye, '*Soul-making*' as archetypal criticism, practised by too many Jungians as well as by Jung himself, is 'barbaric' (Cayley 77).

Anagogically analysing his own dreams, Frye, unlike Jung, tended to ignore their '*narrative* sequence' (*Diaries* 8:86), which he had difficulty remembering (as one has difficulty remembering a plot), focusing instead upon their eternal structure, for which the archetypes served as the 'building-blocks.' Out of his own dream world and his anagogical interpretation of it emerged, as its subjective pole, Frye's archetypal theory of literature. 'I think Shakespeare dreamed his plays: I find no evidence that he did anything but hold the nozzle of the hose, so to speak,' Frye writes. 'He just didn't give a damn: all speculation about his personality breaks down on that central point, and his inscrutability is a major source of his eternal fascination. But he leaves the critic absolutely free to do as he likes, & the editor too' (8:59).

15 'At the moment when the question "How to avoid speaking?" arises it is
   already too late,' writes Derrida. 'There is no longer any question of not
   speaking. Language has started without us, in us, and before us. That is
   what theology calls God, and it is necessary, it will have been necessary, to
   speak' ('How to Avoid' 99).

16 In 'The Connivances of Desire with the Figural,' Jean-Francois Lyotard
   explores the ways in which desire in dreamwork as analysed by Freud
   connives with the figural to protect its own illegibility by means of 'disor-
   dered forms and hallucinatory images.' He distinguishes three distinct,
   though interrelated, components: the *'image-figure,'* the *'form-figure,'* and
   the *'matrix-figure.'* The first is 'hallucinations ... set at a distance, a theme';
   the second is 'the perceptible ... [which] may even be visible, but is in
   general not seen: André Lhote calls it "tracé regulateur," the Gestalt of a
   configuration ... in short, the schema'; the third 'is invisible in principle,
   subject to primal repression, immediately intermixed with discourse,
   primal phantasy.' This third, the *matrix-figure*, Lyotard explains, is 'not a
   structure, because it consists in a violation of discursive order from the
   outset, in a violence done to the transformations that this order autho-
   rizes.' In terms of Blake's vision, this 'violence' is the 'Void Outside of
   Existence,' what Lyotard calls 'the "other" of discourse and intelligibility.'
   To enter this 'Void' as the 'Womb' so that it becomes 'intelligibly apprehended' is to break with Freud's notion of the unintelligibility of the
   unconscious itself by imagining it as an archetype, which Lyotard describes as 'a double phantasy' in which, contrary to Jung's notion of the
   archetypal unconscious, 'an hallucinatory *image-figure'* appears as 'the
   object of a primary discourse' located in the 'initial non-locus' or 'primary
   repression.' Blake's notion of the imagination as the 'human form divine,'
   like Jung's archetypal psychology, releases vision from this 'double phantasy' (57–8). The psychological understanding of the creative imagination
   in this book, that is, engages Jung's creative approach to psychosis in
   which Lyotard's notion of 'a double phantasy' is related to Jung's notion
   of the God-image or Self.

3: Blake's Fourfold Body

1 In the fallen creation, writes Blake, there are two limits. The first is the
   creation of Adam as the limit of 'Contraction,' and the other is the limit of
   'Opacity,' which is Satan's 'Void Outside of Existence' (*M* 41[48].37). As
   suggested in the previous chapter, if this 'Void' is 'enterd into,' Blake
   writes, it 'becomes a Womb.' To enter it is to move 'Outside of Existence'

into madness and from this psychotic place to begin again the work of creation. For Blake, as for Coleridge, every creative act of perception ('primary imagination') is to begin again with chaos or psychosis. The 'secret' of madness resides in the apocalyptic perception of its divine nature, the 'divine insanity' of Plato's *Ion* or the 'cloven tongues like as a fire' that 'sat upon' Christ's disciples when 'the day of Pentecost was fully come' (Acts 2.1–3).

2 The opening of the Eighth Eye for Blake takes place, like all acts of God, in 'less than a Pulsation of the Artery.' Describing Messiah's act of creation in *Paradise Lost*, Milton writes, 'Immediate are the Acts of God, more swift / Than time or motion, but to human ears / Cannot without process of speech be told, / So told as earthly notion can receive' (7.176–9). The impasse confronting quantum physics as the Eighth Eye is the immediacy of motion relative to the observer. It is 'more swift / Than time or motion,' which cannot yet be rendered in a way that 'earthly notion can receive.' Jung's depth psychology sought to render as a Fourfold consciousness the immediacy of the collective unconscious, where everything is synchronistically going on.

3   'Behold, I have made thy face strong against their faces, and thy forehead strong against their foreheads.

As an adamant harder than flint have I made thy forehead: fear them not, neither be dismayed at their looks, though they *be* a rebellious house.

Moreover he said unto me, Son of man, all my words that I shall speak unto thee receive in thine heart, and hear with thine ears.

And go, get thee to them of the captivity, unto the children of thy people, and speak unto them, and tell them. Thus saith the Lord God; whether they will hear, or whether they will forbear.

Then the spirit took me up, and I heard behind me a voice of great rushing, *saying*, Blessed *be* the glory of the Lord from his place.

I *heard* also the noise of the wings of the living creatures that touched one another [Blake's larks], and the noise of the wheels over against them, and a noise of a great rushing.

So the spirit lifted me up, and took me away, and I went in bitterness, in the heat of my spirit; but the hand of the Lord was strong upon me.

(Ezekiel 3.8–14)

4 Blake writes:

The Mundane Shell, is a vast Concave Earth: an immense
Hardend shadow of all things upon our Vegetated Earth
Enlarg'd into dimension & deform'd into indefinite space,
In Twenty-seven Heavens and all their Hells; with Chaos
And Ancient Night; & Purgatory. It is a cavernous Earth
Of labyrinthine intricacy, twenty-seven folds of opakeness
And finishes where the lark mounts; here Milton [as Satan] journeyed

In that Region called Midian, among the Rocks of Horeb
For travellers from Eternity. pass outward to Satans seat,
But travellers to Eternity. pass inward to Golgonooza [the city of art].
                                                    (*M* 17[19].21–30)

4: Wordsworth's Crazed Bedouin: *The Prelude* and the Fate of Madness

1 'Adieu! the fancy cannot cheat so well / As she is fam'd to do, deceiving
   elf,' writes Keats in 'Ode to a Nightingale' (73–4).
2 Derrida writes: 'metaphysics has effaced within itself the fabulous scene
   that has produced it, the scene that nevertheless remains active and
   stirring, inscribed in white ink, an invisible design covered over in the
   palimpsest' ('White Mythology' 213).
3 For a somewhat different account of the tension between metaphor and
   allegory in Romanticism, see my 'Metaphor and Allegory in *Prometheus
   Unbound.*'
4 'A man's life of any worth is a continual allegory – and very few eyes can
   see the Mystery of his life – a life like the scriptures, figurative – which
   such [literalist] people can no more make out than they can the hebrew
   Bible' (*KL* 218), Keats writes.
5 Descartes's threefold dream is described in Baillet's *Vie de Descartes* (1691).
   In *New Studies in the Philosophy of Descartes*, Norman Smith translates
   Baillet's account based on a manuscript by Descartes entitled *Olympica*.
   The translation appears in appendix A (33–39).
6 For an interesting reading of Descartes's dreams that bears directly upon
   Wordsworth's withdrawal from the imagination's 'strength / Of usurpation' (*P* 6.599–600), his subjugation of the excesses of metaphor to the
   moral confines of allegory, and his fear of the madness to which the
   'divinity in man' may conduct, see Jacques Maritain, who contrasts the
   Incarnation with 'the anthropotheistic conception which insists that man
   be made god, and which ordinates everything to this conquest of divinity'
   (186). Maritain argues that the Cartesian heritage, which he locates initially in Descartes's three dreams, lies in this anthropotheistic conception.
7 J. Hillis Miller, discussing Wordsworth's epitaphs, suggests that Wordsworth, 'far from always believing that poetry exists primarily as spoken
   language, sometimes felt that a poem only comes into existence in a satis-
   factory form when it has not only been written down but inscribed perma-
   nently on the purdurable substance of a stone' (129). That 'purdurable
   substance' is in the dream of the Arab set against the shell, which is
   identified with voice rather than writing. His desire is to give voice to

the 'purdurable substance' of writing, of a stone. One can, I think, see in this desire the fear that his conversations with Coleridge, now less and less frequent, constituted a dissolution of *The Recluse*, no longer even a voice but the echo of a voice. Coleridge's account in 'To William Words-worth' of 'the last strain [of Wordsworth's voice] dying' as it 'awed the air' (48) powerfully evokes what Wordsworth in the dream heard as he put the shell to his ear. J. Douglas Kneale offers a valuable analysis of what he calls 'the voice-letter alternation' (360) in Wordsworth. Nature's 'speaking face' in which, as Kneale points out, 'natural phenomena tend to the image of voice' (360), is, as metaphor, Coleridge's phantom face, the face of the 'Arab phantom.' Coleridge as subtext (co-author) is the 'welcome stranger,' the 'wind' become a 'tempest,' the voice 'more than all the winds.' He is the metaphor that Wordsworth must eulogize and bury.

8 *Différance* combines the verb *différer* as to differ in space and to defer (put off) in time. Mind and nature cannot inhabit each other as one space, nor can Coleridge and Wordsworth inhabit each other in time. Yet both are demanded by the 'ur-fiat,' both are essential to the writing of *The Recluse*. Against the violence of this 'usurpation' (seen by Derrida as a form of philosophical totalitarianism, a 'metaphysics of presence'), Derrida pre-sents what Alan Bass, in his translator's introduction to *Writing and Difference*, calls 'the counterviolence of *solicitation*' (from the Latin *sollicitare*, 'meaning to shake the totality': sollus, 'all,' and *ciere*, 'to move, to shake'). What is forbidden is the totality, the *archia*. The forbidden appears as an *aporia*, the Greek word for what Bass calls a 'seemingly insoluble logical difficulty ... [It is] *neither* this *nor* that, or both at the same time' (xvi). *The Prelude* is constituted upon an *aporia*, upon the impossibility of metaphor: Wordsworth is not nature, nor is he Coleridge. Both are ghostly forms of himself, the absence of his identity with himself summed up in 'two consciousnesses,' himself and 'some other Being.' Coleridge is the reign-ing metaphor of that 'other Being.' The *aporia* described by Bass with reference to deconstruction and here applied to the notion of 'two con-sciousnesses' in Wordsworth, Coleridge serving as the ghostly metaphor of 'some other Being,' is further explored in my final chapter in terms of the ghostly relations between Shelley and Rousseau/Byron in *The Triumph of Life*. It is also further explored in a very different context in the brief discussion of quantum physics in 'Jung and Romanticism: the Fate of the Mythopoeic Imagination.' The hugely complex subatomic behaviour of matter as particles in one context and as waves in another is psychologi-cally explored by Jung and Pauli in their work together in terms of the acausal or synchronistic presence of the psyche (as observer) as it disrupts the determined behaviour of matter in Newtonian physics.

9 For a discussion of an 'abyss structure' (*mise en abyme*) in *The Prelude*, see James Hulbert's explanation in his translation of Derrida's 'Coming into one's Own': 'the expression "mise en abyme" originally from heraldry where it denotes a smaller escutcheon appearing in the centre of a larger one is [used] to refer to a structure in which the whole is represented in miniature in one of the parts' (147–8). The dream of the Arab is just such a 'smaller escutcheon' in that deeply heraldic poem, *The Prelude*.

10 'There are intelligences of sparks of divinity in millions – but they are not souls till they acquire identities, till each one is personally itself,' Keats writes. The 'two consciousnesses' are a spark of divinity and a soul.

Afterword: Ross Woodman's Romanticism

1 It needs to be stated from the beginning that Woodman's writings on Romanticism form only a small fraction of his overall output, which ranges from books and articles on Canadian and International art and Canadian and British literature to essays on Hurrell's photographs of Joan Crawford, the 1980 Picasso retrospective at the Museum of Modern Art, and Jungian psychology, to name but a few topics.

2 He treats the break at greater length in 'Freud and Jung: The Parting of the Ways.'

3 I do not mean 'Romanticism' and 'Victorianism' as distinct periods, but in terms of a periodizing sway that is the immanent tendency of transgression itself and the various 'periods' that this tendency produces, Romantic, Victorian, or otherwise.

4 This is Rajan's opening paragraph, taken from a transcript of the speech provided by the author. The award was presented at the annual meeting of the Keats-Shelley Association at the 1993 MLA convention, held that year in Toronto.

5 In terms of Frye's status as an 'outsider,' it is ironic to note that, although it acknowledged Frye's work, New Criticism ignored critical voices north of the American academy as strictly as it disregarded contingencies outside the text. I would not agree with an internalized colonialization within Canadian Romantic studies by painting Woodman as Lytton Strachey to Frye's eminent Victorian. I would note, however, how at the beginning of *The Anatomy of Criticism* Frye adopts a Victorian stance: 'My approach is based on Matthew Arnold's precept of letting the mind play freely around a subject in which there has been much endeavour and little attempt at perspective' (3). The resulting perspective of Frye's 'free play' is 'light' and unrestrained in the way that the hand of God 'thoughtlessly' brushes away the life of the fly in Blake's lyric. Frye seems to treat literature as a

type of abject, which he transcends only by thus forgetting or purging it as the radically constitutive power of his critical voice, or literature as the abject larva from which emerges the beautiful form of his critical system. Woodman demonstrates how the type of critical Victorianism demonstrated by Frye's *Anatomy* (Frye's critical corpus is the beautiful completion of a Wordsworthian literary body left in sublime disarray with *The Recluse*) is riddled by the madness of its own making. In this way *The Anatomy of Criticism* is like the Crystal Palace: 'lightly' and 'beautifully,' yet with the brutal ideological force of a hegemonic market economy, it disciplines and contains the heterogeneous mass critical capital, just as the Crystal Palace stood as a kind of doctrinal inculcation in Victorian consumerism. The *Anatomy*, that is, teaches us how to be orderly critical consumers, how to spend our cultural capital wisely.

6 As Terry Eagleton writes, 'culture, in the sense of a common language, inheritance, education system, shared values and the like ... steps in as the principle of social unity' (26) when other forces threaten to tear things apart and thus keeps the 'economy' of culture afloat.

7 Butler argues for the methodological importance of psychoanalysis in uncovering within social constructions of gender a structure of phantasy mobilizing these imperatives – a structure that can be used to transgress gender's essentializing tendencies. A similar analysis, I am arguing, can be used to resist and transform the 'Victorianizing imperatives' of critico-cultural prescriptions.

8 Canada's identity, governed by the metaphor of the multicultural 'mosaic' rather than that of the American 'melting pot' of ethnic differences, is a paradoxically negative image of this imperial vision, in the name of cultural tolerance and inclusivity.

9 I thank Tom Carmichael of the Department of English at the University of Western Ontario for turning my mind to the endless fertility of this idea.

10 The phrase, from Shelley's *Defence of Poetry*, is also the name of a Festschrift of essays presented to Woodman upon his retirement from the University of Western Ontario in 1988. See *The Mind in Creation: Essays on English Literature in Honour of Ross G. Woodman*.

11 Woodman describes this process at greater length in 'Nietzsche, Blake, Keats and Shelley: The Making of a Metaphorical Body.'

12 Personal correspondence, Ross Woodman to Joel Faflak, 13 July 2001.

13 Woodman accomplishes this difficult transition in 'Figuring Disfiguration: Reading Shelley after De Man.'

14 Here Rajan quotes Woodman's 'Nietzsche, Blake, Keats and Shelley; The Making of a Metaphorical Body.'

15 See Derrida, *Resistances of Psychoanalysis*, esp. 70–118.

Bibliography

Arnold, Matthew. 'The Function of Criticism at the Present Time.' *Poetry and Criticism of Matthew Arnold*. Ed. A. Dwight Culler. Boston: Houghton Mifflin, 1961. 237–58.

Ashton, Dore. 'Parallel Worlds: Guston as Reader.' *Philip Guston Retrospective*. London: Thames and Hudson, 2003. 83–92.

Ayre, John. *Northrop Frye: A Biography*. Toronto: Random House, 1989.

Bass, Alan. 'Translator's Introduction.' *Writing and Difference*. By Jacques Derrida. Trans. Alan Bass. Chicago: The U of Chicago P, 1978. ix–xx.

Baudrillard, Jean. 'The Dance of the Fossils.' *The Illusion of the End*. Stanford: Stanford UP. 72–8.

– 'Symbolic Exchange and Death.' *Jean Baudrillard: Selected Writings*. Trans. Mark Poster. Stanford: Stanford UP, 1988. 119–48.

Blake, William. *The Complete Poetry and Prose of William Blake*. Ed. David V. Erdman, with commentary by Harold Bloom. Rev. ed. Berkeley: U of California P, 1988.

Bloom, Harold. *The Anxiety of Influence: A Theory of Poetry*. New York: Oxford UP, 1973.

Butler, Judith. *Gender Trouble: Feminism and the Subversion of Identity*. New York: Routledge, 1990.

– *The Psychic Life of Power: Theories of Subjection*. Stanford: Stanford UP, 1997.

Byron, George Gordon. *Letters and Journals*. Ed. Leslie A. Marchand. 6 Vols. London: John Murray, 1976.

– *Lord Byron: Major Works*. Ed. Jerome J. McGann. New York: Oxford UP, 2000.

Cayley, David. *Northrop Frye in Conversation*. Concord, Ont.: Anansi, 1992.

Chase, Cynthia. 'The Accidents of Disfiguration: Limits to Literal and Rhetorical Reading in Book V of *The Prelude*.' *Studies in Romanticism* 18 (1979): 547–65.

Clark, David L. 'Against Theological Technology: Blake's "Equivocal Worlds."'
    New Romanticisms. Ed. David L. Clark and Donald C. Goellnicht. Toronto:
    U of Toronto P, 1994. 164–224.
– '"The Necessary Heritage of Darkness": Tropics of Negativity in Schelling,
    Derrida, and de Man.' *Intersections: Nineteenth-Century Philosophy and
    Contemporary Theory*. Ed. by Tilottama Rajan and David L. Clark. Albany,
    NY: State U of New York, 1995. 79–148.
Coburn, Kathleen. *Experience into Thought*. Toronto: U of Toronto P, 1979.
– ed. *Inquiring Spirit: A New Presentation of Coleridge from His Published and
    Unpublished Prose Writings*. 1951. Toronto: U of Toronto P, 1979.
Coleridge, Samuel Taylor. *Biographia Literaria*. Ed. James Engell and W. Jack-
    son Bate. Princeton: Princeton UP, 1983.
– *Collected Letters*. 6 Vols. Ed. Earl L. Griggs. Oxford: Clarendon P, 1956–1971.
– *Collected Works of Samuel Taylor Coleridge*. Ed. Kathleen Coburn. London:
    Routledge and K. Paul; Princeton: Princeton UP, c1969–2002.
– *The Notebooks of Samuel Taylor Coleridge*. Ed. Kathleen Coburn. 4 Vols. New
    York: Bollingen Series: Pantheon Books, 1957– .
– *Poetical Works*. Ed. Hartley Coleridge. Oxford: Oxford UP, 1969.
Conrad, Joseph. *Lord Jim*. Ed. Cedric Watts. Peterborough, ON: Broadview P,
    2001.
De Man, Paul. *Allegories of Reading: Figural Language in Rousseau, Nietzsche,
    Rilke, and Proust*. New Haven: Yale UP, 1979.
– *Blindness and Insight: Essays in the Rhetoric of Contemporary Criticism*. 2nd rev.
    ed. Introd. Wlad Godzich. Minneapolis: U of Minnesota P, 1983.
– 'The Rhetoric of Temporality.' *Blindness and Insight: Essays in the Rhetoric of
    Contemporary Criticism*. 187–228.
– 'Shelley Disfigured.' *Deconstruction and Criticism*. New York: Continuum,
    1979. 39–74.
Derrida, Jacques. *Cinders*. Trans. Ned Lukacher. Lincoln: U of Nebraska P,
    1991.
– 'Cogito and the History of Madness.' *Writing and Difference*. Trans. and
    introd. Alan Bass. Chicago: U of Chicago P, 1978. 31–63.
– 'Force and Signification.' *Writing and Difference*. 3–10.
– 'How to Avoid Speaking: Denials.' *Derrida and Negative Theology*. Ed. Harold
    Coward and Toby Foshay. Albany, NY: State U of New York P, 1992.
– *Of Grammatology*. Trans. Gayatri Chakravorty Spivak. Baltimore: The Johns
    Hopkins UP, 1976.
– *Resistances of Psychoanalysis*. Trans. Peggy Kamuf, Pascale-Anne Brault, and
    Michael Naas. Stanford: Stanford UP, 1998.
– 'Structure, Sign, and Play in the Discourse of the Human Sciences.' *Writing
    and Difference*. 278–93.

- 'The Theater of Cruelty and the Closure of Representation.' *Writing and Difference*. 232–250.
- 'White Mythology: Metaphor in the Text of Philosophy. ' *Margins of Philosophy*. Trans. Alan Bass Chicago: U of Chicago P, 1982. 207–72.
- 'Violence and Metaphysics.' *Writing and Difference*. 79–153.
Descartes, Rene. *New Studies in the Philosophy of Descartes*. Ed. Norman Smith. London: Macmillan, 1963.
Eagleton, Terry. *The Idea of Culture*. London: Blackwell Publishers, 2000.
Foucault, Michel. *Madness & Civilization: A History of Insanity in the Age of Reason*. Trans. Richard Howard. New York: Vintage Books, 1973.
Freud, Sigmund. *Beyond the Pleasure Principle* (1920). Trans. and ed. James Strachey. *The Standard Edition of the Complete Psychological Works of Sigmund Freud*. Vol. 18. London: Vintage, Hogarth Press, and Institute of Psycho-Analysis, 2001. 3–64.
Frye, Northrop. *Anatomy of Criticism: Four Essays*. Princeton: Princeton UP, 1957.
- 'The Archetypes of Literature.' *Fables of Identity: Studies in Poetic Mythology*. New York: Harcourt, Brace, and World, 1963. 7–20.
- *The Diaries of Northrop Frye, 1942–1955. Works*. Vol. 8. Ed. Robert D. Denham. Toronto: U of Toronto P, 2001.
- *The Double Vision: Language and Meaning in Religion*. Toronto: U of Toronto P, 1991.
- 'Expanding Eyes.' *Spiritus Mundi: Essays on Literature, Myth, and Society*. Bloomington: Indiana UP, 1976. 99–122.
- *Fearful Symmetry: A Study of William Blake*. Princeton: Princeton UP, 1947.
- *The Great Code. The Bible and Literature*. New York: Harcourt, Brace, Jovanovich, 1983.
- 'Letter to the English Institute, 1965.' *Northrop Frye in Modern Criticism*. Ed. Murray Krieger. New York: Columbia UP, 1966. 27–30.
- *Northrop Frye's Late Notebooks, 1982–1900: Architecture of the Spiritual World*. 2 Vols. *Works*. Vol. 5. Ed. Robert D. Denham. Toronto: U of Toronto P, 2000.
- 'Reflections in a Mirror.' *Northrop Frye in Modern Criticism*. 133–46.
- *The Stubborn Structure: Essays on Criticism and Society*. London: Methuen, 1970.
- *Words with Power*. New York: Viking Penguin, 1990.
- *A World in a Grain of Sand: Twenty-two Interviews with Northrop Frye*. Ed. Robert D. Denham. New York: Peter Lang, 1991.
Gadamer, Hans-Georg. *Truth and Method*. Trans. and ed. by Garret Barden and John Cumming. New York: Continuum, 1975.
Giegerich, Wolfgang. *The Soul's Logical Life: Towards a Rigorous Notion of Psychology*. 2nd rev. ed. Frankfurt: Peter Lang, 1999.

Giroux, Henry A. 'Teaching the Cultural with Disney.' *Impure Acts: The Practical Politics of Cultural Studies*. New York: Routledge, 2000. 107–25.

Guston, Philip. 'Faith, Hope, and Impossibility.' *Philip Guston Retrospective*. London: Thames and Hudson, 2003. 93–6.

Hardt, Michael, and Antonio Negri. *Empire*. Cambridge, MA: Harvard UP, 2000.

Hartman, Geoffrey. 'Words, Wish, Worth: Wordsworth.' *Deconstruction & Criticism*. New York: Continuum, 1979. 177–216.

– *Wordsworth's Poetry 1787–1814*. New Haven: Yale UP, 1971.

Holmes, Richard. *Shelley: The Pursuit*. London: Wiedenfeld and Nicolson, 1974.

Hulbert, James, trans. 'Coming into One's Own.' By Jacques Derrida. *Psychoanalysis and the Question of the Text*. Ed. Geoffrey Hartman. Baltimore: Johns Hopkins UP, 1978. 114-48.

Jameson, Frederic. 'Postmodernism, or the Cultural Logic of Late Capitalism.' *New Left Review* 146 (July/August 1984): 59–92.

Jones, Ernest. *The Life and Work of Sigmund Freud*. Ed. Lionel Trilling and Steven Marcus. Introd. Lionel Trilling. New York: Basic Books, 1961.

Jung, Carl Gustav. *Answer to Job*. 2nd ed. Trans. R.F.C. Hull. Princeton: Princeton UP, 1973.

– *The Archetypes of the Collective Unconscious*. 2nd ed. *The Collected Works of C.G. Jung*. Vol. 9i.

– *The Collected Works of C.G. Jung*. 20 Vols. Ed. Herbert Read, Michael Fordham, Gerhard Adler, and William McGuire. Trans. R.F.C. Hull. Princeton: Princeton UP, 1954–79.

– 'Forword to Von Koenig-Fachsenfeld: "Wandlungen des Traumproblems von der Romantik bis zur Gegenwart."' *The Collected Works of C.G. Jung*. Vol. 18. 773–75.

– *Letters*. 2 Vols. Ed. Gerhard Adler, in collaboration with Aniela Jaffé. Princeton: Princeton UP, 1975.

– *Memories, Dreams, Reflections*. Ed. Aniela Jaffé. Trans. Richard and Clara Winston. Rev. ed. New York: Vintage Books, 1965.

– *Nietzsche's* Zarathustra: *Notes of the Seminar Given in 1934–1939 by C.G. Jung*. 2 Vols. Ed. James L. Jarrett. Princeton: Princeton UP, 1988.

– 'On the Nature of the Psyche.' *The Collected Works of C.G. Jung*. Vol. 8. 159–234.

– 'The Philosophical Tree.' 1954. *Alchemical Studies. The Collected Works of C. G. Jung*. Vol. 13. 251–349.

– 'A Psychological Approach to the Dogma of the Trinity.' 1948. *Psychology and Religions: West and East. The Collected Works of C.G. Jung*. Vol. 11. 107–200.

– 'The Psychology of Transference.' 1946. *The Practice of Psychotherapy: Essays on the Psychology of the Transference and Other Subjects. The Collected Works of C.G. Jung.* Vol. 16. 163–321.

– and Wolfgang Pauli. *Atom and Archetype: The Pauli/Jung Letters 1932–1958.* Ed. C.A. Meier. Introd. Beverley Zabriskie. Princeton: Princeton UP, 2001.

Keats, John. *Letters of John Keats.* Ed. Robert Gittings. Oxford: Oxford UP, 1977.

– *Poems of John Keats.* Ed. Jack Stillinger. Cambridge, MA: The Belknap P of Harvard UP, 1978.

Kirsch, Adam. Rev. of *New and Collected Poems: 1931–2001* by Czeslaw Milosz. *Times Literary Supplement.* 15 February 2002.

Kneale, J. Douglas. 'Wordsworth's Images of Language: Voice and Letter in *The Prelude.*' *PMLA* (May 1986): 351–61.

Kristeva, Julia. 'The Importance of Frye.' *The Legacy of Northrop Frye.* Ed. Alvin A. Lee and Robert D. Denham. Toronto: U of Toronto P, 1994. 335–8.

– *Language: The Unknown.* Trans. Anne M. Menke. New York: Columbia UP, 1989.

– *Revolution in Poetic Language.* Trans. and introd. Leon S. Roudiez. New York: Columbia UP, 1984.

Lacan, Jacques. *Seminar I: Freud's Papers on Technique.* Ed. Jacques-Alain Miller. Trans. John Forrester New York: W.W. Norton, 1991.

Locke, John. *An Essay Concerning Human Understanding.* Ed. Peter H. Nidditch. Oxford: Clarendon P, 1975.

Lyotard, Jean François. 'The Connivances of Desire with the Figural.' *Driftworks.* Ed. Roger McKeon. *Semiotext(e)* (1984): 57–68.

Maritain, Jacques. *The Dream of Descartes.* New York: Hubner, 1944.

McLynn, Frank. *Carl Gustav Jung.* New York: St. Martin's Griffon, 1996.

Miller, J. Hillis. 'The Stone and the Shell: The Problem of Poetic Form in Wordsworth's Dream of the Arab.' *Mouvements premiers: Etudes critiques offertes à George Poulet.* Paris: Cord, 1972. 125–47.

Milton, John. *Complete Poems and Major Prose.* Ed. Merritt Y. Hughes. New York: Macmillan, 1957.

Nietzsche, Friedrich. The Birth of Tragedy *and* On the Genealogy of Morals. Trans. Francis Golffing. Garden City, NJ: Doubleday Anchor, 1956.

– 'On Truth and Lies in a Nonmoral Sense.' *Philosophy and Truth: Selections from Nietzsche's Notebooks of the Early 1870's.* Ed., trans., and introd. Daniel Breazeale. New Jersey: Humanities P International, 1979. 79–100.

– 'On the Uses and Disadvantages of History for Life.' *Untimely Meditations.* Ed. Daniel Breazeale. Trans. R. J. Hollingdale. Cambridge: Cambridge UP, 1997. 57–124.

Norris, Christopher. 'Fictions of Authority: Kierkegaard, de Man, and the Ethics of Reading.' *Intersections: Nineteenth-Century Philosophy and Contemporary Theory.* 39–59.

Plato. 'Letter VII.' *The Collected Dialogues of Plato, Including the Letters*. Ed. Edith Hamilton and Huntington Cairns. Princeton: Princeton UP, 1961. 1574–98.

Rajan, Tilottama. *Dark Interpreter: The Discourse of Romanticism*. Ithaca, NY. Cornell UP, 1980.

– 'From Restricted to General Economy: Romanticism and a Kantianism Without Reserve.' *Literary Research / Recherche Littéraire* 29 (Spring–Summer 1998): 7–14.

– 'Introduction.' *Studies in Romanticism* 28 (1990): 3–8.

Reiman, Donald H., and Sharon B. Powers, eds. *Shelley's Poetry and Prose*. New York: W.W. Norton, 1977.

Ringbom, Sixten. 'Transcending the Visible: The Generation of the Abstract Pioneers.' *The Spiritual in Art: Abstract Painting, 1890–1985*. New York: Abbeville P, 1986. 131–53.

Ross, Clifford, ed. *Abstract Expressionism: Creators and Critics, An Anthology*. New York: Abrams, 1990.

Shakespeare, William. *Anthony and Cleopatra*. Ed. Maynard Mack. New York: Penguin, 1970; rev. ed. 1977.

– *The Tempest*. Ed. Northrop Frye. New York: Penguin, 1959; rev. ed. 1970.

– *The Tragedy of King Lear*. Ed. Alfred Harbage. New York: Penguin, 1958; rpt. 1969.

Shelley, Mary Wollstonecraft. *Frankenstein; or, The Modern Prometheus*. Ed. D.L. Macdonald and Kathleen Scherf. Peterborough, ON: Broadview P, 1996.

Shelley, Percy Bysshe. *The Complete Poetical Works of Percy Bysshe Shelley*. Ed. Thomas Hutchinson. London: Oxford UP, 1960.

– *The Complete Works of Percy Bysshe Shelley*. Ed. Roger Ingpen and Walter E. Peck. Julian Editions. 10 Vols. New York: Charles Scribner's Sons, 1926–30.

– *The Letters of Percy Bysshe Shelley*. Ed. Frederick L. Jones. 2 Vols. Oxford: Clarendon P, 1964.

– *Shelley's Poetry and Prose*. Ed. Donald H. Reiman and Sharon B. Powers. New York: W.W. Norton, 1977.

Shamdasani, Sonu. *Jung and the Making of Modern Psychology: The Dream of Science*. Cambridge: Cambridge UP, 2003.

Smyser, Jane Worthington. 'Wordsworth's Dream of Poetry and Science: *The Prelude* V.' *PMLA* 71 (1956): 269–75.

Spivak, Gayatri. 'Translator's Preface.' *Of Grammatology*. Trans. Gayatri Chakravorty Spivak. Baltimore: Johns Hopkins UP, 1976. ix–lxxxviii.

Tennyson, Alfred. *In Memoriam*. *The Norton Anthology of English Literature*. 4th ed. Ed. M.H. Abrams. New York: W.W. Norton, 1979. 1127–75.

Von Franz, Marie-Louise. *C.G. Jung: His Myth in Our Time*. Trans. William H. Kennedy. London: Hodder and Stoughton, 1975.

Wilson, Milton. *Shelley's Later Poetry: A Study of His Prophetic Imagination*. New York: Columbia UP, 1959.

Wimsatt, W.K. 'Northrop Frye: Criticism as Myth.' *Northrop Frye in Modern Criticism*. 75–108.

Winnicott, Donald. Rev. of *Memories, Dreams, Reflections*, by Carl Gustav Jung. *D.W. Winnicott: Psycho-Analytic Explorations*. Ed. Clare Winnicott, Ray Shepherd, and Madeleine Davis. Cambridge, MA: Harvard UP, 1989. 482–92.

Woodman, Marion. *Bone: Dying into Life*. New York: Viking, 2000.

Woodman, Ross. *The Apocalyptic Vision in the Poetry of Shelley*. Toronto: U of Toronto P, 1964.

– 'Figuring Disfiguration: Reading Shelley after De Man.' *Studies in Romanticism* 40 (Summer 2001): 253–88.

– 'Freud and Jung: The Parting of the Ways.' *Queen's Quarterly* 85 (Spring 1978): 93–108.

– 'Metaphor and Allegory in *Prometheus Unbound*.' *The New Shelley: Later Twentieth-Century Views*. Ed. G. Kim Blank. New York: Macmillan, 1992. 166–83.

– 'Nietzsche, Blake, Keats and Shelley: The Making of a Metaphorical Body.' *Studies in Romanticism* 29 (1990): 115–49.

– '*Prometheus Unbound*: The Case for Jupiter.' *The Mind in Creation: Essays on English Romantic Literature in Honour of Ross G. Woodman*. Ed. J. Douglas Kneale. Kingston, ON: McGill-Queen's UP, 1992.

Woolf, Virginia. *A Reflection of the Other Person: The Letters of Virginia Woolf*. Vol. 4. Ed. Nigel Nicolson. London: Hogarth P, 1978.

Wordsworth, William. *The Fenwick Notes of William Wordsworth*. Ed. Jared Curtis. London: Bristol Classical P, 1993.

– *Poetical Works*. Ed. Thomas Hutchinson. Rev. ed. Ernest de Selincourt. Oxford: Oxford UP, 1988.

– *The Prelude: 1799, 1805, 1850*. Ed. Jonathan Wordsworth, M.H. Abrams, and Stephen Gill. New York: W.W. Norton, 1979.

– *The Prose Works of William Wordsworth*. Ed. W.J.B. Owen and Jane Worthington Smyser. 3 Vols. Oxford: Clarendon, 1974.

Žižek, Slavoj. 'The Cartesian Subject versus the Cartesian Theatre.' *Cogito and the Unconscious*. Ed. Slavoj Žižek. Durham, NC: Duke UP, 1998. 247–74.

– *The Sublime Object of Ideology*. London: Verso, 1989.

Index

Abrams, M.H., 17
ACCUTE, 229
Acts (Book of), 82
addiction, 43
akedah, 135, 136
alchemy, 7, 24, 28, 30, 32, 33, 34, 40,
  89, 160, 165, 207–8
allegory, 55, 56, 92, 105, 121–2, 124,
  126–7, 129, 135–8, 144, 146, 200,
  255n6
Allen, Paul, 228
American Museum of Natural
  History, 227–9, 231–2
analytical psychology, 35, 44. *See also*
  archetypal psychology; psychology
androgyny, 24, 101, 174
anima, 13, 36, 42, 46, 96, 174, 240–2n3
anxiety of influence, 30. *See also*
  Bloom, Harold
apocalypse: and William Blake, 52,
  54, 58–9, 63, 65, 67, 84, 87, 92, 95,
  99–101, 105, 108–9, 112–13, 137,
  141, 162, 197, 205, 208, 218, 233–4,
  246n1, 253–4n1; and George
  Gordon Byron, 183–6, 192; and
  Northrop Frye, 63–5, 137; and

Percy Bysshe Shelley, 11, 151, 162,
  183–6, 192, 197, 218, 230, 233–4;
  and Ross Woodman, 215, 218, 220,
  230, 233–4; and William Wordsworth, 111–13, 127, 133–43, 151,
  197, 200
aporia, 256n8
Aragon, Louis, 244n9
archetypal criticism, 0, 19, 98, 99,
  246n1
archetypal psychology, 48, 58, 67,
  71–6, 201, 253n16
archetypes: and Northrop Frye,
  11–13, 15, 17, 49, 52–6, 70–5, 76–8,
  84–5, 97–9, 104–5, 251–2n14; Carl
  Gustav Jung, 8, 11–15, 17, 24, 26,
  28, 29, 30, 34–5, 40, 45–6, 48–9, 58,
  67–8, 71–5, 90, 93, 104–5, 173,
  176, 201–8, 238–40n2, 240–2n3,
  251–2n14
archia, 256n8
Aristophanes, 77
Arnold, Matthew, 223–4, 257–8n5
arreta rhemata, 65, 88, 248n5
Artaud, Antonin, 80–3
Ashton, Dore, 244n9
atomic bomb, 14, 44–5, 207

Augustine, 106, 249n7
Austen, Jane, 96
Ayre, John, 13, 61–2. *See also* Frye, Northrop

Bacon, Francis, 53, 137
Barbauld, Anna Letitia, 126
Barker, Arthur, 10
Bass, Alan, 79–80, 256n8
Baudrillard, Jean, 214, 227
Beaupuy, Michael, 133
Beckett, Samuel: *Waiting for Godot*, 65; *Endgame*, 75
belief, 240n1
Berkeley, George, 113
Bible, 12, 51, 54, 55, 63, 70–1, 95, 98, 99, 100, 162
Blake William, 3, 4, 5, 7, 8, 10–11, 15–17, 21–2, 24, 26, 43, 45, 50–79, 82–5, 86–109, 110–13, 114, 115–16, 127–9, 132–3, 137–43, 146–7, 154, 155, 160–2, 163, 167, 170, 173, 174, 176, 197–8, 201–2, 205, 206–8, 210, 212, 215, 218, 220, 222, 224–5, 230, 232, 233, 235, 246n1, 246–7n2, 247–8n4, 248n5, 249nn6, 8, 251–2n14, 253n16, 253–4n1, 254n2, 254–5n4, 257–8n5; *America: A Prophecy*, 210; *The Book of Thel*, 54, 69–70, 174; *The [First] Book of Urizen*, 90; 'The Divine Image,' 24; *Europe*, 53, 59, 197–9; *The Four Zoas*, 56, 58–9, 68; 'The Human Abstract,' 86–8, 95; *Jerusalem*, 7, 22, 52, 56–8, 69, 84, 87–8, 91, 95–6, 100–1, 103–6, 113, 205, 207, 233, 248n5; Letter to Butts, 53, 56–7, 83, 95, 99; *The Marriage of Heaven and Hell*, 4, 11, 22, 54, 55, 57, 62, 67, 70, 86–91, 111–12, 142–3, 208; *Milton*, 4, 5, 11,

16, 17, 44, 45, 52–3, 55, 57–9, 62–3, 68–71, 73–4, 78–9, 84, 86–102, 104–9, 110–13, 114, 133, 141, 146, 160, 197–8, 206–7, 246n1, 248n5, 249nn6, 8, 254–5n4, 'A Poison Tree,' 86–8, 95; *Songs of Experience*, 87, 199; 'To Tirzah,' 127–8; 'The Tyger,' 43
Bloom, Harold, 30; *The Anxiety of Influence*, 30. *See also* anxiety of influence
Bohr, Niels, 242–3n6
Burghölzli Clinic, 35, 39, 46, 49, 160, 201, 204
Burke, Edmund, 230
Butler, Judith, 216, 217, 225, 258n7
Butts, Thomas, 53, 56, 57, 99
Byron, George Gordon, 7, 21, 38, 170, 171, 177, 178–96, 202, 221–2, 233–5, 256n8; *Beppo*, 190; *Cain: a Mystery*, 183, 189, 192; *Childe Harold's Pilgrimage*, 21, 182–3, 186, 190–3; 'Darkness,' 185, 189; *Don Juan*, 38, 189, 193–5, 234; *Letters*, 195; 'Prometheus,' 192

Canadian Forum, 56. *See also* Frye, Northrop
Carmichael, Tom, 258n9
Carnegie, Andrew, 228
catatonia, 32
Catholicism, 11
Cayley, Andrew, 251–2n14
Cervantes, Miguel de, 118, 146
Chase, Cynthia, 117
Christian humanism, 9, 10, 17
Christianity, 14, 26, 50–1, 53, 64, 154, 170, 176, 184, 250nn9, 10
Clark, David L., 224–5, 249n7
Coburn, Kathleen, 242n4

Cogito, 10, 17, 35, 60, 64, 79, 102, 108, 130, 144, 159, 166, 196, 210, 238–40n2
Coleridge, Hartley, 119, 131, 138
Coleridge, Samuel Taylor, 4, 6, 8–10, 15, 19–20, 24–6, 28, 37, 40, 42–3, 64, 88, 93, 114, 116–17, 119–20, 126–30, 133–4, 137, 139, 143–6, 152, 157, 160–1, 163–6, 167–8, 170–1, 176, 180–2, 199–200, 202, 208, 211–12, 218, 222, 237n1, 242nn4, 5, 244–5n10, 253–4n1, 255–6n7, 256n8; the psycho-analytical, 25, 28, 43, 146, 212, 218, 237n1; *Biographia Literaria*, 4, 8, 9, 15, 19–20, 24–6, 28, 37, 42–3, 64, 117, 119, 126, 129–30, 139, 157, 160–1, 163–4, 181, 202, 208, 244–5n10; *Christabel*, 168; 'Dejection: an Ode,' 6, 120; 'Frost at Midnight,' 120; 'Kubla Khan,' 144; *Logosophia*, 19, 165; *Lyrical Ballads*, 114, 182; *Rime of the Ancient Mariner*, 126–7, 144, 167–8, 171, 237n1; *Sibylline Leaves*, 42; *Table Talk*, 128
collective psychosis, 49, 175, 220
collective unconscious, 5, 9, 12, 35, 40, 43–6, 48, 52, 97, 99–100, 173, 174, 176, 180, 197, 201–5, 247–8n4, 251–2n14, 254n2
colonialism, 222–6
complexio oppositorum, 173, 201
Conrad, Joseph, 47
Corinthians I, 82
cultural materialism, 223–4, 225, 232, 234–5
cultural studies, 222, 235
culture, 7, 31, 46, 175–6, 196, 203, 213–18, 221, 223–5, 227–35, 258n6

daemon (or genius), 38, 48, 205, 246n1; and poetic genius, 112, 132. *See also* madness
daemon of creativity, 203, 204
Daniells, Roy, 62
Dante, 169
Darwin, Charles, 227
death, 5, 17, 20, 29–30, 46, 50, 63, 76, 88, 100, 103, 128, 159, 173–4, 198, 200–1, 208–9, 235–6, 237n1, 245n11; and George Gordon Byron, 184–5, 189–90; and Paul de Man, 20; and John Keats, 159, 185, 191, 202, 232, 235; and Percy Bysshe Shelley, 20, 29–30, 128, 150–3, 159, 163–4, 167–9, 178–91, 196, 198, 201, 209, 230, 235, 245n11; and William Wordsworth, 117, 152, 154–5, 157, 200–1
deconstruction, 4, 6, 15–18, 60, 70, 76–85, 98–100, 113–32, 194, 218–20, 222, 231, 235, 250n10, 256n8. *See also* post-structuralism
deism, 86. *See also* natural religion
Deleuze, Gilles, 17
delusion, 42–4, 52, 101, 117, 157–8, 160–1, 164, 168, 172, 181, 199, 202–3, 247–8n4, 253n16
De Man, Paul, 3, 4, 6, 17–20, 116–17, 121–2, 136, 144, 152–3, 156, 158, 200, 235, 250n10; *Allegories of Reading*, 136; *Blindness and Insight*, 116–17; 'Rhetoric of Temporality,' 122; 'Shelley Disfigured,' 4, 6, 18, 122, 152–3, 156
Denham, Robert, 251
Derrida, Jacques, 3, 4, 9–10, 14–21, 35, 60, 76, 78–83, 98–9, 102–4, 107–9, 118, 120, 123, 127, 129, 130, 131–2, 134–6, 144, 157–60, 166, 236, 238–40n2, 240–2n3, 255n2, 256n8,

257n9, 258n15; *Cinders*, 9; 'Cogito and the History of Madness,' 4, 10, 14, 16, 19–20, 60, 76, 79, 97, 102–3, 107–8, 120, 129, 166, 129, 131, 160, 166, 236, 253n15; 'Force and Signification,' 80; *Of Grammatology*, 10, 118, 123; *Resistances of Psychoanalysis*, 236; 'Structure, Sign and Play in the Discourse of the Human Sciences,' 98–9; 'The Theatre of Cruelty and the Closure of Representation, 80–3; 'White Mythology,' 118, 127, 255n2

Descartes, René, 15, 35, 102–3, 118, 129, 131–3, 134, 231, 236, 255nn5, 6; *Meditations*, 103, 129

deus absconditus, 67, 88–9, 249n7

dialectic, 3, 10, 22, 38, 44–6, 53, 56, 59, 66, 74, 78, 79, 88, 95, 107, 137, 138, 153, 173, 196, 199, 200, 201, 203, 205–8, 250n10, 250–1n11. *See also* Blake, William; Frye, Northrop; Hegel, G.W.F; Jung, Carl Gustav

dialectical materialism, 197, 203, 205–6

différance, 35, 103–4, 135, 256n8

divine revelation, 10, 55, 63, 85, 86–7, 104, 108–9. See also *kerygma*

dream, 28, 35, 37, 68, 83–5, 176, 251–2n14; and Carl Gustav Jung, 27, 173–4, 247–8n4; and Descartes, 132, 255n6; and the dream of the Arab, 118, 130–1, 133–4, 136–47, 255–6n7, 257n9; and Mary Shelley, 177–8; and Percy Bysshe Shelley, 148; and the Veiled Maid, 169, 247n3. *See also* Descartes, René; Freud, Sigmund; Jung, Carl

Gustav; Shelley, Mary; Shelley, Percy Bysshe

Eagleton, Terry, 258n6

economy, 10, 14, 19, 60, 83, 103, 109, 120, 130, 144

ego, 30, 31, 34, 35, 56, 57, 139, 251–2n14

egotistical sublime, 120, 126, 137, 200. *See also* Keats, John

Eisner, Michael, 228

Eliot, T.S., 219

Emmanuel College, 63, 75–6

empire, 215–16, 223–6, 229–30, 235

Encyclopedia Britannica, 224

Encyclopédie, 224

Enlightenment, 78, 214, 224, 232, 236, 240–2n3

esemplastic power, 160–1. *See also* Coleridge, Samuel Taylor

Eucharist, 80

Euripides, 155

Ezekiel, 111, 254n3

Faflak, Joel, 18–19

fantasy (phantasy), 32, 35–6, 172, 187, 189–90, 191–2, 195, 201

fellatio, 84, 248n5

feminine, the, 13–14, 18, 24, 29, 42, 50, 67–8, 71, 90–1, 97, 100–1, 105, 174

Foster, Jodie, 228

Foucault, Michel, 4, 16–17, 76, 78–9, 81, 103, 129, 131–2, 148, 236; *Madness & Civilization*, 4, 16, 78, 148

Fourfold: in William Blake, 56, 68, 72, 86–109, 174, 201, 205–8, 212; in Northrop Frye, 51, 53–67, 82; in Carl Gustav Jung, 25, 27, 51, 101,

172, 205–8; in John Milton, 51. *See also* Threefold

freedom, 21, 63, 167, 253n16

Freeman, John, 27. *See also* Jung, Carl Gustav

French Revolution, 8, 111, 137–9, 154, 171, 199–200, 214, 229

Freud, Sigmund, 3, 4, 26, 30–2, 33–5, 38, 42, 50, 52, 83, 91–2, 125, 165, 170, 171–3, 201, 203–8, 211, 212, 218–19, 237n1, 238–40n2, 240–2n3, 242–3n6, 246–7n2, 248n5, 251–2n14, 253n16; *Beyond the Pleasure Principle*, 50, 125; *The Interpretation of Dreams*, 31; *Totem and Taboo*, 31, 33–4, 35

Frye, Northrop, 3–4, 8, 10–13, 15–17, 48, 49–85, 86, 96–9, 104–5, 137, 211–12, 214–16, 219, 220–1, 223, 224, 229, 248n5, 250nn9, 10, 250–1n11, 251n13, 251–2n14, 257–8n5; *Anatomy of Criticism*, 11, 12, 67, 78, 97, 216, 257–8n5; *Diaries*, 71–4, 251–2n14; *The Double Vision*, 12, 63–4, 66, 75–6, 250n10; 'Expanding Eyes,' 50–1, 53; *Fearful Symmetry*, 51, 54–5, 57, 67–71, 97, 99; *The Great Code*, 12, 50–1, 52, 55, 60, 65–6, 70–1, 74, 82, 97, 248n5; *Modern Century*, 12; *Notebooks*, 49–52, 73, 76–7, 251–2n14; 'Reflections in the Mirror,' 76–7, 96; *The Secular Scripture*, 11; *The Stubborn Structure*, 50; Whidden Lectures, 11–12; *Words with Power*, 60–1, 73, 75; *A World in a Grain of Sand*, 52, 55, 56. *See also* archetypes

full speech, 118, 123, 127, 134, 136, 157–8, 162

fundamentalism, 52, 63

Gadamer, Hans-Georg, 47

Gates, Bill, 228

gender studies, 222

German idealism, 26, 170, 210, 212

Giegerich, Wolfgang, 25, 237n1, 240–2n3, 250–1n11

Giroux, Henri, 226

Gisborne, John, 161, 169, 189, 194

globalism, 215–16, 220, 226, 229

glossopoeia, 81–2

Godwin, William, 133

Goethe, Johann Wolfgang von, 48–9, 60, 159, 161, 169, 170, 176, 250n9; *Faust*, 48, 60, 159, 161, 169, 170, 250n9

Goya, 197

Gump, Forrest, 228

Guston, Philip, 245n11

hallucination, 46; and schizophrenia, 49, 52

Hanks, Tom, 228, 229

Hardt, Michael, 215–16, 223, 225, 232

Hartman, Geoffrey, 77, 134–5

Hayden Planetarium, 232

Hayley, William, 79, 94, 99

Hegel, G.W.F., 14, 66, 82, 208, 210–12, 214, 228, 238–40n2, 240–2n3; *Phenomenology of Spirit*, 66

Hellman, Lillian, 229

Heraclitean flux, 121, 163

hermaphroditism, 102, 246n1, 248n5

Hermes, 121

hierosgamos, 101–2

history, 8, 12, 63, 198, 199, 245n11

Hobbes, Thomas, 228

Hölderlin, Friedrich, 35, 41, 203

Holmes, Richard, 148, 170–1, 172. *See also* Shelley, Percy Bssyhe

Homer, 66, 70–1; *Ulysses*, 66
Hulbert, James, 257n9
humanism, 10
hybris (demonic hyperbole), 14–15

idealism, 26, 117, 143, 144, 163, 193,
    211, 216, 217, 225, 228, 230. *See also*
    German idealism
imagination, 51, 55, 64, 69, 70, 78, 85,
    87, 90, 104, 105, 119, 130, 139–42,
    149–50, 181, 199, 200, 253n16;
    dialectical imagination, 88, 107,
    138; primary imagination, 25, 26,
    93, 130, 237n1, 253–4n1; secondary
    imagination, 137, 139
incest taboo, 30–4, 35, 134–6
individuation, 31, 252n14
Industrial Revolution, 229
inspiration, 14, 36, 38, 54, 91, 96, 110–
    12, 129, 142, 145, 161, 200, 243–4n7
'intense inane,' 19, 29. *See also*
    Shelley, Percy Bysshe

Jacobins, 199–200
Jaffé, Aniela, 238–40n2
Jameson, Frederic, 226, 232
Jay, Douglas, 64
Jaynes, Julian, 49, 52, 77; *The Origin
    of Consciousness in the Breakdown of
    the Bicameral Mind*, 49, 77
Job (Book of), 88–9
Joyce, James, 12, 17; *Ulysses*, 17
Jung, Carl Gustav, vii, 3–9, 11–15,
    17–20, 23–46, 47–53, 58, 67–9, 71–5,
    88–97, 99–101, 104–5, 129, 156, 160,
    165–6, 170, 171–6, 192, 196, 201,
    202–8, 212, 218–21, 235, 237n1,
    238–40n2, 240–2n3, 242–3n6,
    246n1, 246–7n2, 247n3, 247–8n4,
    248n5, 249n7, 250n9, 250–1n11,

253n16, 254n2, 256n8, 257n1;
    Alchemical Studies, 175; *Answer to
    Job*, 13, 67, 88–9, 100; *Archetypes of
    the Collective Unconscious*, 8, 11, 23;
    Atom and Archetype, 13, 28, 35, 92,
    207–8, 240n2, 242–3n6; *Interpre-
    tation of Nature and the Psyche*, 242–
    3n6; *Memories, Dreams, Reflections*,
    23, 26–7, 31–4, 35, 41–2, 46, 47, 48,
    94, 96, 100–1, 171–3, 176, 203–7,
    238–40n2, 246n1, 247n3, 247–8n4;
    Nietzsche's Zarathustra, 40, 43–5,
    49, 220; 'On the Nature of the
    Psyche,' 207, 238–40n2, 242–3n6;
    'On the Pathology and Psy-
    chology of So-Called Occult
    Phenomena,' 32, 39, 49, 204; 'The
    Philosophical Tree,' 34; 'A Psycho-
    logical Approach to the Dogma of
    the Trinity,' 24, 27, 240nn1, 2; 'The
    Psychology of Transference,' 47;
    Symbols of Transformation, 31;
    'Synchronicity: An Acausal
    Connecting Principle,' 242–3n6.
    See also archetypes; collective
    unconscious; Pauli, Wolfgang;
    unconscious

Kafka, Franz, 169
Kandinsky, Wassily, 244n8
Kant, Immanuel, 23, 214, 238–40n2,
    240–2n3
Keats, John, 4, 12, 19, 29–30, 33, 73,
    116, 120, 126, 127, 139, 144, 145,
    149–50, 158–9, 170, 174–7, 178, 180,
    182–5, 191, 200, 202, 212, 222, 232,
    235, 240–2n3, 243–4n7, 255nn1, 4,
    257n10; *Endymion*, 184; *Fall of
    Hyperion*, 4–5, 30, 73, 139, 158, 174–
    7, 180, 185, 202, 235; *The Jealousies*,

158–9; 'Ode on a Grecian Urn,' 19, 180; 'Ode to a Nightingale,' 33, 185, 255n1; 'Ode to Psyche,' 12, 240–2n3

Keats-Shelley Association, 221, 236, 257n4

Kepler, Johannes, 15

kerygma, 63–4, 65, 66, 75

Kierkegaard, Soren, 65, 250n10

Kirsh, Adam, 219–20

Kneale, J. Douglas, 255–6n7; *The Mind in Creation: Essays on English Literature in Honour of Ross G. Woodman*, 258n10

kosmogonos, 101

Kristeva, Julia, 6, 12, 29, 81, 131; 'The Importance of Frye,' 12

Lacan, Jacques, 76, 127, 136, 167, 196, 227, 228; 'Mirror Stage,' 127, 136; *Seminar*, 227

Lawrence, D.H., 219

Locke, John, 68–9, 104, 113–16, 125, 137, 167; *Essay Concerning Human Understanding*, 114–16, 125

logos (Word), 4, 12, 13, 14, 17, 50, 58, 60, 61, 63, 64, 66–7, 70, 73, 81, 98, 99, 210, 249n7

Lucan, 21, 155

Lyotard, Jean-Francois, 253n16

madness, 3–22, 34–6, 38, 43–6, 78–9, 82, 99, 102, 132, 156, 158, 166, 196, 198–209, 211–13, 216, 218–21, 225, 228, 230–6, 237n1; and William Blake, 15, 17, 45, 58, 69, 78–9, 84, 96, 99, 102–3, 108–9, 110, 173, 198–201; and Jacques Derrida, 4, 10, 14, 15, 18–21, 60, 78–9, 102–3, 108–9, 120, 129, 131–2, 144, 159–60, 166,

236; and René Descartes, 102–3, 129, 131–3, 231; and divine madness, 6, 14, 36, 59, 79, 84, 85, 103, 110, 112, 127, 132, 141, 158, 161, 199, 248n5; and Michel Foucault, 4, 16–17, 78–9, 103, 129, 131–2, 236; and Northrop Frye, 211–12, 221; and genius, 8, 38, 68, 132, 196, 220, 238–40n2; and Carl Gustav Jung, 3–9, 14, 17, 27, 32, 34–6, 38, 43–6, 47–9, 93–4, 100, 166, 171–3, 201, 205, 220; and sanity, 4–6, 15, 19, 21–2, 32, 38, 45, 59, 68, 84, 100, 102, 109, 120, 132, 161, 196, 208; and Friedrich Nietzsche, 43–5, 49, 135–6, 220; and poetry, 196, 209, 230; and the sanity of madness, 5, 21–2, 68, 84, 132, 170, 196, 199, 209, 211; and Percy Bysshe Shelley, 6, 8, 19–21, 38, 156, 158, 160–1, 170, 173, 179, 193, 195–6, 198–9; and William Wordsworth, 8, 10, 110, 112, 118, 124, 129, 132–3, 136–7, 141, 143, 146, 199. *See also* schizophrenia

man, 3, 211, 227

mandala, 42, 72, 101, 172, 205

Manhattan Project, 45

Maritain, Jacques, 255n6

Marx, Karl, 61

masculine, the, 50, 100–1

materialism, 37–8, 44

mathematics (mathematical science), 13–14, 15, 238–40n2

matter, 5, 8, 14, 21, 28, 30, 34, 37, 88, 90, 106, 107, 160, 173–5, 179, 182, 199, 203, 206, 244–5n10, 248n5; and psyche, 6, 23, 26, 28, 30, 39–40, 43–5, 206, 242–3n6, 256n8; and spirit, 34, 167, 208. *See also* Jung,

Carl Gustav; Pauli, Wolfgang;
Shelley, Percy Bysshe
Matthew, Book of, 22
McGann, Jerome, 235
McLuhan, Marshall, 215
McLynn, Frank, 27. *See also* Jung,
Carl Gustav
McMaster University, 11
mechanical philosophy, 25–6, 37, 94,
112, 154, 157, 160, 163–5, 175, 244–
5n10. *See also* Coleridge, Samuel
Taylor
memory, 110, 111, 113, 142
Mercurius, 121
Merlin, 121
metaphor, 6, 55, 60, 64, 66, 75, 77, 93,
116–18, 121–7, 134–41, 144, 145,
255n6, 255–6n7, 256n8
metaphorical body, 69, 104, 167, 220,
231, 236. *See also* subtle body
metaphysics, 28, 37, 98–9, 119, 163–4,
170–1, 194, 237n1, 255n2
metaphysics of presence, 4, 19, 60,
81, 98, 104–5, 122, 127, 144, 159
Methodism, 61, 62, 137, 249n8
metonymy, 60, 66, 116
Miller, J. Hillis, 255–6n7
Milosz, Czeslaw, 219
Milton, John, 5, 10–11, 15, 37, 50,
51, 53, 57–9, 67–71, 82, 84, 86–95,
100–2, 109, 116, 117, 127, 134, 137,
142, 144–5, 157, 159–60, 162–3, 169,
177, 192, 206–8, 246n1, 254n2;
Lycidas, 162–3; *Paradise Lost*, 11,
15, 53, 57–9, 67–8, 70, 84, 86–92,
95, 100, 102, 109, 134, 137, 144,
157, 160, 192, 206, 246n1, 254n2
'mind in creation,' 5, 14, 29, 38, 41,
42, 125–6, 144, 192, 196, 230
mirror stage, 127

mise en abyme, 138, 257n9
misprisioning, 202
MLA (Modern Language Association), 229
Moore, Thomas, 184, 190
Moses, 95
Mozart: *Don Giovanni*, 76
mundus archetypus, 176
Murray, John, 195. *See also* Byron,
George Gordon
myth, 5, 6, 29, 49–50, 70, 73, 92, 94–5,
100–1, 105, 152, 166, 170, 194, 196,
199, 201–2, 204, 206–8, 215; and
William Blake, 5, 55, 69–70, 86, 92,
95, 104–5, 109, 127, 161, 199, 201,
206; and Carl Gustav Jung, 12, 32,
33, 42, 49, 94, 160, 166, 172–3, 240–
2n3, 250–1n11; and Northrop Frye,
49–51, 53, 55, 60, 63–5, 75–7, 82–3,
96–7, 250–1n11; and John Milton,
69, 86, 109, 206
mythopoeic imagination, 23, 42, 50,
94, 149, 201, 240–2n3. *See also*
imagination
mythopoeia, 92, 105

Napoleon, 138
narcissism, 127, 201, 228, 232
National Socialism, 7, 49
natural religion, 86, 90, 165. *See also*
deism
nature, 12, 45, 46, 210, 211
negative capability, 126. *See also*
Keats, John
Negri, Antonio, 215–16, 223, 225,
232
Nell, 228
New Criticism, 235, 257–8n5
New Historicism, 222, 235
new humanism, 220

Newton, Isaac, 28, 39, 53, 86–8, 90, 99, 104, 107, 110–1, 137, 197, 206, 242–3n6, 256n8
Nietzsche, Friederich, vii, 7, 17, 21, 26, 35, 40, 41, 43–5, 49, 98, 135–6, 203, 220, 234–5, 248n5; *The Gay Science*, vii, 17, 40; *On the Genealogy of Morals*, 7; 'On the Uses and Disadvantages of History for Life,' 35, 135; *Thus Spake Zarathustra*, 7, 21, 40, 49, 220, 234
Norris, Christopher, 250n10
noumenal, 36
Numbers (Book of), 95

occultism, 13, 27–8, 32, 34, 39, 42, 204, 206, 218–19
Oedipus, 55
one mind, 19, 156–63, 165, 166, 168, 169, 180, 187, 211
opium (opium addiction), 42, 170
opus contra naturam, 166, 192, 201
Ovid, 70

painting, 244n8, 245n11
parapsychology, 204
Paul, 65, 82, 86, 87, 248n5
Pauli, Wolfgang, 7–8, 13–15, 28, 35, 40, 45, 92, 206–8, 219, 238–40n2, 242–3n6, 250–1n11, 256n8; *Atom and Archetype*, 28, 35, 92, 207–8, 242–3n6; 'The Influence of Archetypal Ideas,' 242–3n6. *See also* Jung, Carl Gustav
Peacock, Thomas Love, 188, 193
phenomenal, 36
phenomenology, 4, 13–14, 17, 221, 230
Pitt, William, 53, 104
Pius XII, 26, 100

Plato, 6, 14, 26, 36, 71, 79–80, 113, 117, 149, 158, 169, 199, 203, 207, 208, 248n5; *Ion*, 6, 14, 36, 158, 248n5; *Phaedrus*, 80; *Seventh Epistle*, 79
poetry, 5, 6, 11, 97, 126, 153, 154, 157, 192, 209, 255–6n7
political unconscious, 223
Pollock, Jackson, 244n8
post-structuralism, 15, 60, 222, 235–6
power, 163–4, 225–6, 230–1
precognition, 204
privatio boni, 249n7
prophesy, 41, 49, 52, 54, 58–9, 87, 89–90, 95, 109, 130, 175, 185, 206, 216
prosopopoeia, 144, 200
Protestantism, 12
psyche, 5, 6, 20, 23–5, 28, 36, 39, 43–5, 49, 116, 139, 207, 208, 238–40n2, 240–2n3, 242–3n6, 246–7n2, 256n8, and soma, 207–8. *See also* Jung, Carl Gustav; matter; Pauli, Wolfgang; *soma psychikon*
psychoanalysis, 8, 19, 25–6, 28, 30–1, 40, 43, 146, 212, 215, 218–19, 220–1, 232, 235, 237n1, 258n7; invention of term, 25–6, 28, 43, 146, 218, 237n1. *See also* Freud, Sigmund; Jung, Carl Gustav
psychology, 5, 27, 34, 35, 43–6, 69, 170, 202, 240–2n3, 242–3n6, 250–1n11; and Carl Gustav Jung, 3–4, 6, 13, 14, 17, 27, 29, 172–3, 175–7, 203, 204; and quantum physics, 14, 39–40, 44–5; and Sigmund Freud, 30, 203
psychosis, 12, 15–16, 31, 32, 36, 40–3, 45, 47–53, 58–62, 65, 69, 73–5, 84–5,

93–4, 96, 99, 110, 112, 137, 171–2,
    198–201, 205, 211–12, 216, 220–1,
    232. *See also* madness
puer aeternus, 136

quantum physics, 7, 13–14, 28, 35,
    39, 43–5, 156, 206–8, 219, 238–40n2,
    256n8
queer studies, 222

Rajan, Tilottama, 17, 221–2, 223, 229,
    236, 257n4, 258n14
Read, Herbert, 176
Reign of Terror, 138–9
repression, 31, 33, 35, 48, 89, 235,
    248n5
Revelation (Book of), 100, 108, 112
Reynolds, John, 177
rhetoric, 115–16, 125, 135, 138
rhetoric of temporality, 121
Richard, Jean-Pierre, 80
Rockefeller, John D., 228
Romantic poetry, 6, 211–13
Romantic poets, 6, 17, 20, 23, 99,
    174–7, 205, 208, 237n1
Romanticism, 3, 4, 5, 7, 10, 12, 38, 88,
    202, 211, 212–15, 216, 217–25, 228,
    229–36, 237n1, 240–2n3, 249n6;
    and Victorianism, 214, 221–2,
    223–4, 230. *See also* Victorianism
Ross, Malcolm, 10–11, 67
Rousseau, Jean-Jacques, 36, 118–19,
    123, 135, 157, 185–6, 188–91, 234,
    235, 244n9, 250n10, 256n8; *Emile*,
    118–19; *Nouvelle Heloïse*, 186, 188
Royal Society, 115–16

Sade (Marquis de), 96
Sandler, Bob, 61. *See also* Frye,
    Northrop
Schelling, F.W.J., 165, 210, 212

schizophrenia, 39, 47–9, 50, 52, 132,
    160, 172, 201, 204–5, 212, 216, 235,
    238–40n2, 247n3
scientific materialism, 27, 38–40, 45,
    95, 160, 173, 203 6, 219
Self, 27, 29, 31, 48, 129, 172, 181, 240–
    2n3, 250–1n11, 251–2n14
semiotic, 6, 29, 81, 131
sexual psychology, 30–1, 34, 35, 38,
    91, 173, 203, 206–7. *See also* Freud,
    Sigmund
sexuality, 222
Shadow, 166
Shakespeare, William, 29, 37–8, 39,
    56, 90, 96, 101, 116–17, 122, 126,
    145, 166, 181, 196, 237n1; *Antony
    and Cleopatra*, 96, 101; *King Lear*,
    90, 196; *Macbeth*, 116–17; *Othello*,
    56; *Romeo and Juliet*, 166; *The
    Tempest*, 29, 38, 39, 117, 122, 181
Shamdasani, Sonu, 238–40n2
Shelley, Mary, 148, 150–1, 154, 158,
    167, 168, 178–80, 184, 193, 235;
    Frankenstein, 167, 178–9, 235; *The
    Last Man*, 235
Shelley, Percy Bysshe, 3, 5, 6, 7, 8, 11,
    14, 17–21, 29–30, 32–3, 36–9, 41, 45,
    57, 105, 116, 118, 120, 122, 125, 127–
    8, 129, 130, 131, 145, 146, 148–77,
    178–96, 197–202, 207, 208, 211, 215,
    217–18, 220–2, 226–7, 230–5, 242–
    3n6, 243–4n7, 244–5n10, 245n11,
    246–7n2, 256n8, 258n10; *Adonais*,
    19, 21, 29–30, 36, 37, 38, 39, 127,
    131, 148–51, 160, 167, 178, 182–7,
    191, 193–4, 196, 202, 218, 227–8,
    230, 232–4, 243–4n7, 245n11;
    Alastor, 19, 21, 45, 116, 118, 125,
    128, 150–3, 155, 156, 159, 164, 167–
    71, 174, 179, 182, 185–6, 200–1;
    Defence of Poetry, 4, 5, 6, 14, 19,

36–9, 41, 57, 149, 153, 155, 157, 160, 162, 167, 170, 173, 197, 202, 221, 227, 230–2, 234, 246–7n2, 258n10; *Epipsychidion*, 8, 30, 193; *Hellas*, 145, 193, 198; 'Hymn to Intellectual Beauty,' 120, 152, 170; *Julian and Maddalo*, 6, 160, 182, 188, 193, 195; *Laon and Cynthia*, 32; *Letters*, 5, 38, 161, 169, 181, 184, 188–9, 193–4; 'Mont Blanc,' 130, 157–8, 162–6, 169, 170, 187, 189–90, 230, 242–3n6; 'Ode to Liberty,' 21; 'Ode to the West Wind,' 151; 'On Life,' 36–7, 153, 156–7, 159, 162, 168, 169, 175; *Prometheus Unbound*, 7, 19–21, 29, 45, 96, 105, 156, 162, 166, 174, 177, 179–81, 183, 189, 193, 197, 199, 201, 208–9, 215, 217–18, 234; *Revolt of Islam*, 32, 198; 'A Summer Evening Churchyard, Lechlade, Gloucestershire,' 168; 'To Wordsworth,' 146, 154; *The Triumph of Life* 7, 18, 20–1, 36, 122, 150, 151–2, 155–6, 158, 166, 185–91, 195–6, 198–9, 218, 232–4, 244n9, 245n11, 256n8. *See also* unconscious

Smith, Horace, 184, 188

Smith, Norman, 255n5

Smyser, Jane Worthington, 132–3

soma pneumatikon, 75. *See also* spirit

soma psychikon, 75, 86, 87. *See also* soul

soul (*psychikos*), 4, 21, 25, 28, 40, 44, 73–5, 101, 105, 107, 144, 160, 199, 237n1, 240–2n3; and Romanticism 22; and spirit (*pneumatikos*) 73–5. *See also* Giegerich, Wolfgang

soul-making, 73, 145, 240–2n3, 251–2n14

Spenser, Edmund, 155

spermatikos, 84

spirit (*pneumatikos*), 34, 73

Spivak, Gayatri, 10

Spurzheim: *Observations on Insanity*, 137

St John, 50, 61

Strachey, Lytton, 257–8n5

structuralism, 80–1

Studies in Romanticism, 17–18

subjection, 216

sublation (*Aufhebung*), 66, 238–40n2

subtle body, 7, 207. *See also* metaphorical body

suicide, 183, 230, 232–4

supplement, 249n7

symbol, 11, 23, 24, 28, 30, 31, 126, 181, 240n2

symbolic, 11, 23–30, 34, 46, 72, 126, 206, 211–12, 215, 226–7

symptom, 222–3

synchronicity, 40, 156, 160, 206, 242–3n6, 247–8n4, 254n2

Tasso, 155

technology, 215–16, 226, 228

telepathy, 43

Tennyson, Alfred: *In Memorium*, 24

Thanatos, 50, 206, 246–7n2

Threefold, 33, 51, 53, 92, 96, 101, 206–7, 208, 212, 243–4n7. *See also* Fourfold

transcendental signified, 60

trauma, 35, 167, 205, 215, 218, 227–8, 233–4

Trinity, 24–5, 27

Trotsky, Leon, 61

uncanny, 205, 213, 220, 225

unconscious, 4–9, 12, 13, 20–1, 24–6, 28, 34, 39–42, 44–6, 49, 51, 54, 69, 70, 78–9, 84, 88–91, 95, 99–101, 103–5, 119, 160, 196, 200–1, 203–9,

228, 232, 237n1; Samuel Taylor
Coleridge, 25, 43, 127, 170, 181,
200; Sigmund Freud, 205; Carl
Gustav Jung, 4–9, 12, 13, 20, 23–4,
26, 28–9, 34, 35, 39, 40–2, 44–6, 49,
51, 88–90, 95, 99–100, 104–5, 160,
176, 201, 202–6, 241–2n3, 246n1,
251–2n14; Percy Bysshe Shelley, 5,
20–1, 157; unconscious and the
work, 4, 6, 12, 196; quantum
physics, 28; religion, 24, 35;
William Wordsworth, 119, 122,
127, 136, 149, 200
University of Manitoba, 10, 67
University of Toronto, 10, 67
University of Toronto Press, 11, 57,
71
unus mundus, 207, 208, 242–3n6

Vanderbilt, Cornelius, 228
vegetable body, 4, 51, 53, 55, 59, 69,
84–5, 87, 92–3, 95, 102–3, 105–7,
143, 174, 248n5
Victoria College, 54
Victorianism, 214, 221–2, 223–4, 229,
230. *See also* Romanticism
Virgil, 70–1
'void circumference,' 19, 30. *See also*
Shelley, Percy Bysshe
von Franz, Marie-Louise, 173

Wagner, Richard, 49
Wasserman, Earl R., 17
Williams, Edward, 148
William, Jane, 148, 168
Wilson, Milton: *Shelley's Later Poetry*,
162
Wimsatt, W.K., 77, 97–8
Winnicott, Donald, 47–8, 51–2, 101,
172–3, 204–6, 246–7n2
Woodhouse, A.S.P. , 10, 11, 67

Woodman, Marion, 20; *Bone: Dying
into Life*, 20
Woodman, Ross, 18, 71, 73, 211–36,
251n12, 255n3, 257n2, 257–8n5,
258nn10, 11, 12, 13, 14; *The Apocalyptic Vision in the Poetry of Shelley*,
215, 230; 'Blake's Fourfold Body,'
220; 'Figuring Disfiguration:
Reading Shelley after De Man,' 18
Woolf, Virginia, 3
Wordsworth, William, 6, 8–10, 21, 23,
37, 96, 110–47, 148–56, 157, 159,
165, 168, 169, 170, 171, 174, 176,
181, 182, 197, 199–202, 204–5, 222,
228, 235, 255n6, 255–6n7, 256n8,
257–8n5; 'Elegiac Stanzas,' 118,
144; *The Excursion*, 113, 128–9,
150–5, 200; Fenwick Note on 'Ode:
Intimations of Immortality,' 117,
132–3, 142–3; 'The Idiot Boy,' 119;
Lyrical Ballads, 114, 182; 'Ode:
Intimations of Immortality,' 113–
14, 117, 127, 131, 138, 142–3 152,
154; *The Prelude*, 6, 8, 9–10, 110–13,
117–47, 149–50, 171, 176, 197, 199–
200, 205, 255n6, 256n8, 257n9;
Prospectus to *The Recluse*, 8, 112–
13, 123–4, 128, 134–5, 137, 139, 145,
150, 255–6n7, 256n8, 257–8n5;
'Songs consecrate to truth and
liberty,' 154; 'Tables Turned,' 120;
'Tintern Abbey,' 113–14, 125, 143;
'To HC, Six Years Old,' 119
World Trade Centre, 220

Yeats, 219

zero point, 14, 34–5, 45, 93, 160, 242–
3n6, 245n11
Žižek, Slavoj, 211–12, 218
Zurich, 13, 31, 45, 49, 204, 220